W9-BBA-741

Eagle's Flight provides training to support
the content of *"In Your Hands: The Behaviors of a World-Class Leader"*.
Entitled Living Leadership™, this training program teaches leaders
how to release the talent and full potential of individuals in the workplace.
It also teaches them how to focus that potential and
reap the benefits to the organization, the stakeholders and those whose
professional lives are influenced daily by those leaders.

Eagle's Flight is an innovative company
that is a world leader in the development and delivery of powerful,
principle-based training programs.

The unique, experiential programs are designed
to improve performance by
stimulating insights and inspiring results-focused action.
As a fast-growing progressive company,
Eagle's Flight is a living model of a highly successful team
that sustains a rich corporate culture,
and a commitment to world-class leadership.

Dedicated to Roz, Sabrina, Sean
and Mom and Dad;
in appreciation of their unwavering
love and support.

"But they that wait upon the Lord shall renew their strength;
they shall mount up with wings as eagles; they shall run, and not be weary;
and they shall walk, and not faint."

Isaiah 40:31

TABLE OF CONTENTS

TABLE OF CONTENTS

CONTENT DETAIL

I. ACCELERATING PERFORMANCE

CONTENT DETAIL

II. BRILLIANT INTERPERSONAL COMMUNICATION

CONTENT DETAIL

III. BEYOND TIME MANAGEMENT

CONTENT DETAIL

IV. EXECUTIONAL EXCELLENCE

CONTENT DETAIL

V. PRODUCING CHAMPIONS

CONTENT DETAIL

VI. SETTING THE PACE

CONTENT DETAIL

VII. CORE PRINCIPLES, CLEAR PRIORITIES, CRUCIAL PRACTICES

CONTENT DETAIL

VII. CORE PRINCIPLES, CLEAR PRIORITIES, CRUCIAL PRACTICES *(continued)*

CONTENT DETAIL

VIII. MASTERING ORGANIZATIONAL COMMUNICATION

CONTENT DETAIL

IX. LEADING IN TRANSITIONAL TIMES

PREFACE

To my readers,

In my early days, under the direction of an extraordinary leader, I was taught how to paddle a canoe, not just so it would stay straight or turn when it should. Instead, he helped me experience a greater vision... to guide a craft that would let me follow a beaver up a river in perfect silence, a way to move through the morning mist in harmony with the quiet peace of a new day, and the soft shimmer of sunlight on the water. I learned how to make the canoe an almost-living extension of myself.

Later in life, I worked for an individual who taught me, by example and instruction, to regard each person as an individual – not as an "employee" or "function head". I then learned to see issues and situations *first* from the perspective of others; and then from *that* vantage point to decide how best to proceed.

More recently, I was guided by another skillful, thoughtful, world-class leader; who supported, challenged and shaped my talents. He taught by example, by inclusion, by availability and most importantly, by holding me accountable for achieving results. Under his leadership I accomplished far greater things than I could have done on my own.

It has been my good fortune to be influenced by extraordinary leaders, such as these, throughout my life. These highly skilled people have been but some of the many influences that have helped me release and harness my own potential. I have written "In Your Hands: The Behaviors of a World-Class Leader" because, as a result of my own experience as both follower and leader, I am passionate about the conviction that within every one of us there is immeasurable worth and unimaginable potential.

"There is within every
human being immeasurable worth,
and unimaginable potential.
Having the privilege of joining
forces with an extraordinary
leader significantly increases
the likelihood of that
potential being released."

PREFACE

Yet, that potential may remain untapped unless it is recognized and nurtured by someone who can guide, teach, and lead. Contributing to the release of that potential is the role and privilege of anyone providing leadership to others.

The content of this book is intended to show how this can be done. It is a document that details practical leadership behaviors, with perhaps less focus on leadership theory. The material was learned, tested and refined over many years in the heat of the battle; and Eagle's Flight was founded, and continues to grow, with this content as a major part of our corporate life blood.

So I offer this as a resource guide, condensing my experience and learning. I believe it provides specific, practical steps for leaders, and emerging leaders, who want to significantly and positively impact the lives of others.

Underlying all the content is my conviction, in fact an absolute, rock solid, unshakable certainty, that leadership behaviors can be learned. And as leadership behaviors are applied, the potential within others will be released. As a result both they, and the organization of which they are a part, will flourish.

I trust this material helps you to make the most valuable contribution you can as a leader; and serves you well as you continue on this challenging, exciting road.

Sincerely,
Phil Geldart
Wildwood Hall
Spring, 1999

"I define 'world-class'
as follows:
'No one, anywhere, does
what you do
better than you do it'."

INTRODUCTORY COMMENT

Leaders are in evidence in many places: supervising others at a snack bar; on the assembly line of a large manufacturing facility; in the Board Room; at Scout Camp; and supervising the fund raising efforts of a local charity.

What all leaders have in common is the responsibility they carry for those for whom they are responsible. The productivity, the sense of accomplishment, the achievement of future aspirations, and the personal satisfaction derived from individual and team efforts are all very heavily influenced by the talent and insight of the leader.

This is a significant responsibility and one which should not be taken lightly. As we recognize this, it increases our understanding about leadership, and the acquisition of those skills which will bring our leadership capability to the world-class level. Behaviors discussed in this book can be yet another tool to help you achieve this objective.

I've often been asked what I mean by "world-class". The definition is important as it sets the stage and the context for your own personal growth. I define "world-class" as follows: "No one, anywhere, does what you do better than you do it". This definition places the world-class performer in with a group of individuals whose performance is such that no one, in any other organization, anywhere in the world, does a better job. They may do the job as well as you do it, but not better. As individual skills and competencies improve, then the "world-class" standard will also rise; and so in order for an individual to retain a world-class ranking their own talent must continue to improve on an ongoing basis.

INTRODUCTORY COMMENT

"The application of this material, and the corresponding impact felt by those you lead, is in your hands!"

INTRODUCTORY COMMENT

I've laid out the material in order to provide a visual summary of each individual behavior on the left hand side, and the corresponding description of that behavior on the right. By viewing the illustration the truth may be self-evident – in which case feel free to move on. On the other hand, if you'd like more elaboration, detail, or clarification then the text on the right will help with that; and the illustration can subsequently serve as a summary of the text.

As you seek to improve your own leadership skills, the Table of Contents and the Content Detail section that follows, can help you navigate through topics of personal relevance. They summarize the content of the book and allow you to go immediately to whatever sections you require. There's no need to read from cover to cover, as each of the sections stands on its own.

The behaviors that follow can help if you aspire to become a world-class leader. The *application* of this material, and the corresponding impact felt by those you lead, is *in your hands*!

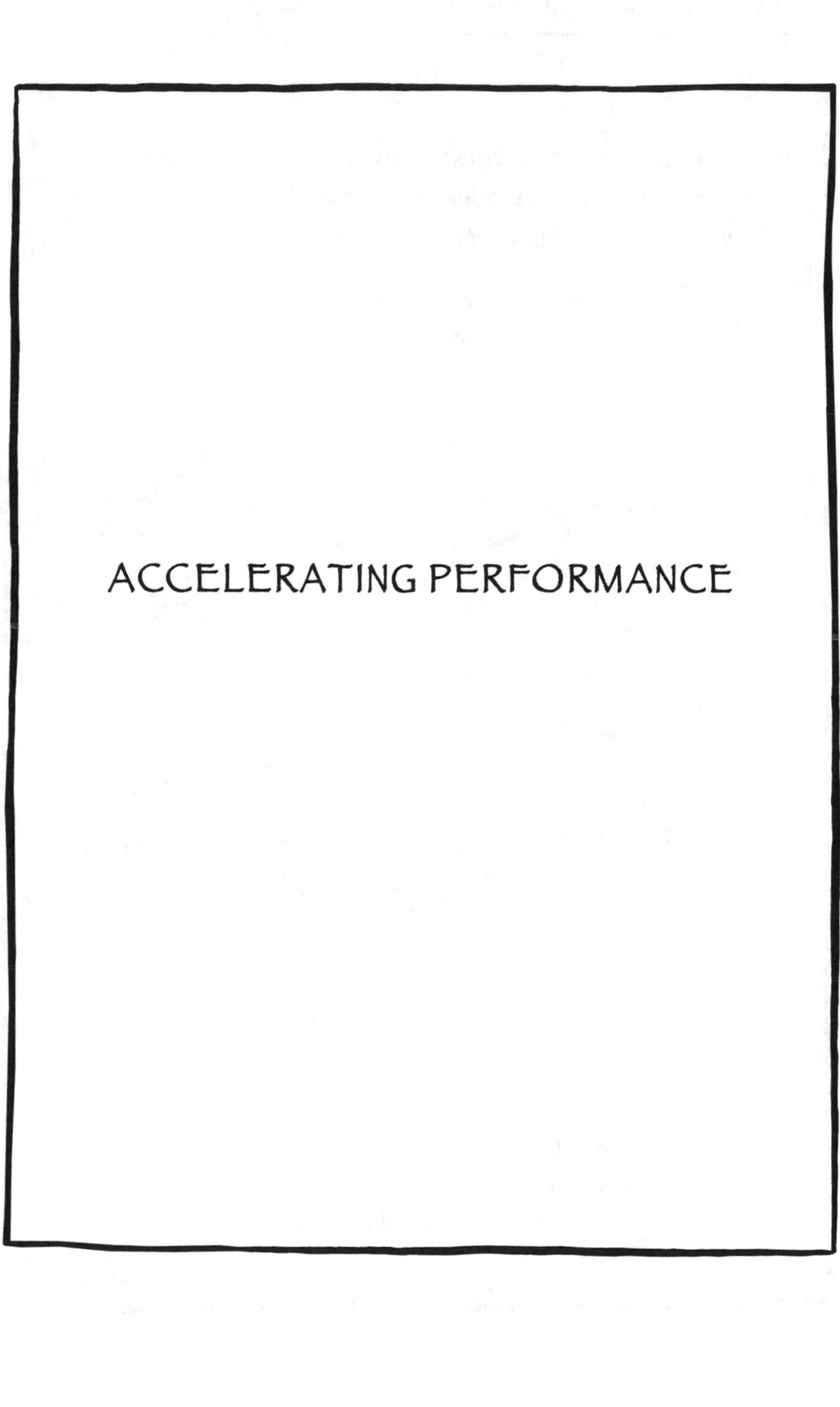

ACCELERATING PERFORMANCE

ESTEEMING OTHERS IS IMPORTANT

Seen in certain circumstances every single person is readily recognized as having the potential for greatness; and many already fulfill that potential in quiet, unseen ways.

Each human being carries within themselves their own thoughts, desires, sacrifices and experiences; and each individual is of great worth.

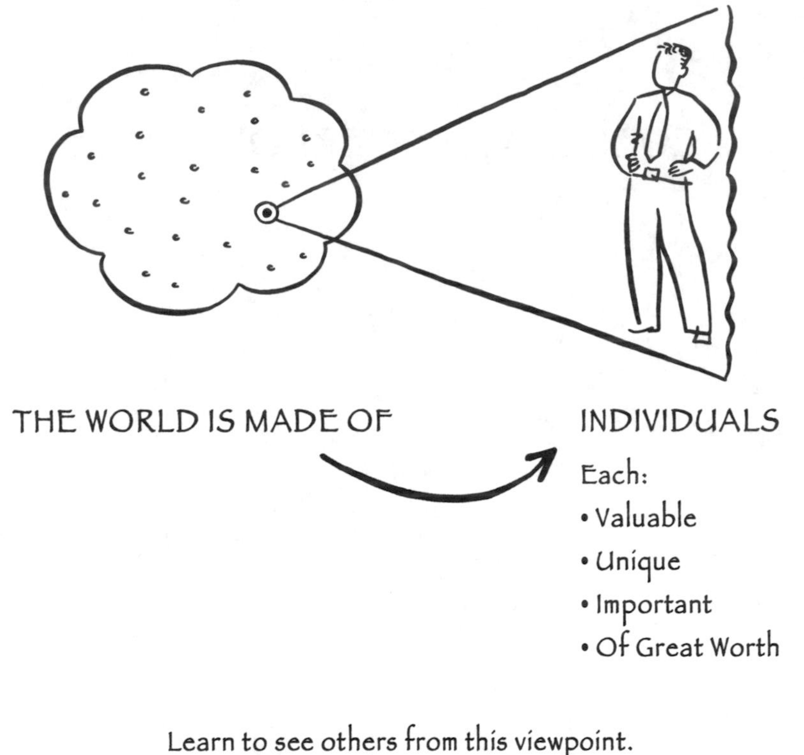

THE WORLD IS MADE OF → INDIVIDUALS

Each:

- Valuable
- Unique
- Important
- Of Great Worth

Learn to see others from this viewpoint.
Then you work hard to bring their value into prominence for others to see.

ESTEEMING OTHERS IS IMPORTANT

The world is made up of individuals: each valuable; each unique; each important; and each of immense worth.

Seen in some circumstances every single person is readily recognized as having potential for greatness, and many already fulfill that potential in quiet unseen ways. Each human being has their own thoughts, desires, sacrifices, and experiences and each individual is of great worth. Learn to see others from that viewpoint. Then work hard to bring their value into prominence for others to see.

Esteeming is valuing people for who they are; valuing people as *people*, not for what they can do for you on the job.

I might walk by someone at work, mutter a quick hello and move on. Perhaps I don't know whether she is married, is a mother, or an outstanding athlete. To someone else this person may be a loving wife, a caring mother, or perhaps she's a marathon runner. She has personality. She has an identity.

It is not that we do not respect this person, but we all tend to see people we don't know well as "two dimensional", when in fact the world is made up of multi-faceted individuals; each of great value. We need to be able to see people as people apart from their title or responsibilities.

When waiting in line at a fast food restaurant I care little for who the person in front of me is. All I am really concerned about is that they hurry up so that I can get my hamburger and fries! The person may be the C.E.O. of the world's largest company, but this probably has little impact on me. I'd still like the lines to move faster!

"Esteeming is
valuing people for
who they are; as people,
not for
what they can do."

But if I work for that company, then I tend to see this person in a different light. In fact I would probably bend over backwards to assist in any way that I can. The person behind *me* does not see the C.E.O. of my company as I do, and they care very little about who he is. They are more concerned that the line go more quickly.

So we tend to be influenced heavily, often too much so, by the "position" the person holds, and their relationship to us. We should be respecting the person *as a human being* rather than in the context of their functional title or role.

It is simple to hold people in esteem who are above us within the organization in rank, prestige, or in some other more tangible ways, such as their earning power or skills. However, it is quite a different thing to hold people in esteem simply because they are human beings. This is especially true if they are below us within the organization, or have not been seen to amass any of the tangible evidence of greatness, as we would judge greatness in a materialistic society.

Esteem for others is based on a recognition that within each human being there is great potential. Not only is the potential there but each person is a living, breathing, human who is capable of great thoughts, outstanding activities, and of awe inspiring behavior.

We tend to focus more readily on the function (what they do). We tend to judge a person's capability on the basis of this alone. But there is much more to a person than the "functional" side of them. There is also the personal side. When focusing only on the functional side we are not judging that person in their totality, we are not esteeming that person *in total*.

"Esteem for others
is based on a recognition
that within each
human being there is
great potential."

ESTEEMING OTHERS IS IMPORTANT

We should hold a person in esteem as a total person even if we are unable to see their "personal side". Once we recognize them as a total person then we can more readily hold them in esteem, and their contribution will emerge.

The other consideration is what *might* be...which is also powerful. Each individual is important to other individuals. For each person you meet there will probably be other people (either alive or dead) who, at one time, saw that particular person in front of you as far more important and valuable than you now see them.

They did not lose that worth: it is simply not being recognized immediately.

We need to hold people in esteem whether their talents are fully developed or not. This means looking beyond what you see and looking at *what might* be. If you see people as human beings with great potential they can then develop and become more capable.

We tend to see the person for what they can do and we then esteem the person based on that. What we need to do is to recognize that the capability also lies in the *potential.* A great leader must see a person for what they could do – recognizing the potential.

Esteeming takes strong powers of observation and faith. It requires effort and seeing beyond the obvious. It grows over time and requires cultivation. A snapshot judgement can be very inaccurate. All individuals are important, any one individual can make a huge difference. We need to base our esteem of others on that perspective.

SHOW ESTEEM FOR OTHERS BY ASKING FOR THEIR OPINION

Even if you feel you have identified all the issues, by asking another (with sincerity!) you demonstrate that you value – place worth on – their opinion. (And so you should!)

Ask another for their opinion!

SHOW ESTEEM FOR OTHERS BY ASKING FOR THEIR OPINION

People greatly enjoy having their opinion asked, and considered. When you ask the opinion of another person you indicate that you do hold them in esteem. You indicate that what they have to say contributes to something you consider meaningful. Simply by asking someone what they think, or how they feel about an issue, is a way in which to demonstrate the respect you have for them.

Even if you feel that you have the answer to a particular question, you still should invite their opinion; by so doing they have an opportunity to contribute, and you reinforce the value in which you hold them. It is also imperative that when asking an individual for their opinion it be done with sincerity. You do not necessarily need to agree with the person but you should listen with respect.

Asking another person for their opinion is a very practical way to show them that you hold them in esteem. You indicate that their opinion is valuable. You indicate that what they have to say contributes to that which you consider to be meaningful.

Every person to whom you speak should be spoken to as if they were:

The repository of great wisdom

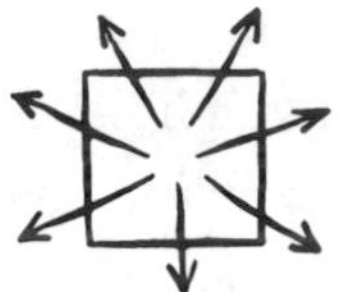

OR

A rich storehouse of experience

OR

A respected superior

By so doing you indicate that you hold that person in high esteem, and in great worth.

ESTEEM FOR OTHERS CAN BE DEMONSTRATED

A specific way to *demonstrate* esteem is to approach another as if that person was someone who was very wise, knowledgeable, or influential. Think of how you would treat a respected boss; you should be treating everyone the same way.

If you hold these approaches in mind when you are speaking to another person, then it will become immediately apparent simply by your attitude, posture, and deference that you hold them in esteem.

Clearly the question arises – what happens if the person is not that wise, does not have more experience than you, or is not your boss?

The answer is that it makes no difference. You should still approach that person from that *perspective*. If you do then you will be demonstrating that you hold them in esteem. It is an attitude, a way of approaching people which is at issue here. This means that treating everyone in the same way is a *how* rather than a *what*. It is an *attitude*. This does not mean that you would say exactly the same thing to someone working for you as you would say to your boss… but the *way* you say it should be the same.

Test this with yourself the next time you are with your boss. Think of how you speak to that person. Think of what you say. Think of how you treat him or her. Then, the next time that you are with someone junior to you, assess whether you followed the same practice as with your boss; e.g. did you allow them to express their opinion before interrupting? Did you truly allow them the opportunity to say what they wanted to say?

This has nothing to do with content – this is recognizing that person as a human being. They have worth, value and you need to treat them accordingly.

"When you are speaking
to another person,
it will become apparent by
your attitude, posture,
and deference that
you hold them in esteem."

ESTEEM FOR OTHERS CAN BE DEMONSTRATED

This is appreciating the value of the individual, treating all others as you would want to be treated. Recognize that others should be entitled to the same degree of respect that you would want. This not only applies to business, it applies to all relationships, whether it be with family, friends, or acquaintances.

Clearly though, if an individual has stepped over the line of social responsibility, we need to deal with these types of circumstances differently (e.g. theft, immorality, assault, etc.) depending on the situation, but these are the exceptions, and should not be the basis for all of our actions.

RECOGNIZING INDIVIDUAL DIFFERENCES DEMONSTRATES ESTEEM FOR OTHERS

EACH PERSON IS UNIQUE –

COMBINE TOGETHER TO YIELD ...

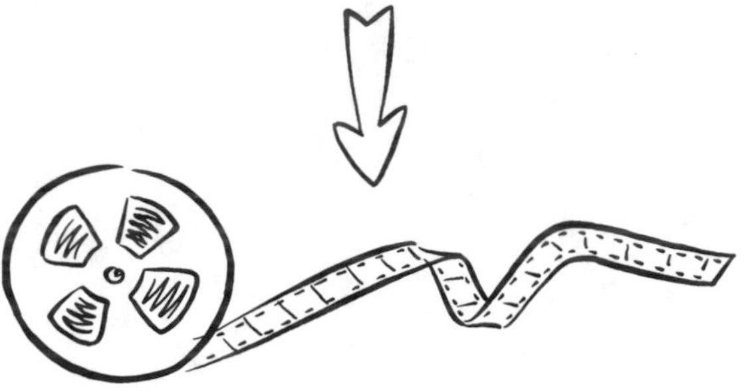

... A GREAT FILM.

Their differences, their strengths, should be used to enhance yours, not wasted, ignored, or spent in opposition to yours.

RECOGNIZING INDIVIDUAL DIFFERENCES DEMONSTRATES ESTEEM FOR OTHERS

When you make a movie you need to have many different people with different attributes. You need people who can act, who can produce and who can direct. These are all necessary for successful completion of the movie, and when you combine their qualities you have a film. There are few people who can do more than one of these jobs really well. There are exceptions, but normally each person has a certain well defined uniqueness.

Once one understands the uniqueness of each individual, one can then recognize the power of that uniqueness, and can use that person's differences, their unique strengths to more effectively benefit the organization. If you truly esteem people then you respect that person's uniqueness.

Unfortunately as leaders we tend to unconsciously force people into doing things a certain way – perhaps a way similar to how we would do it. In doing this we are forcing them into a mold with which they are not necessarily comfortable. Rather than wanting everybody to be the same, rather than having a department where everybody is a clone, the leader must learn to value individual uniqueness and capitalize on it.

It is important to note though that certain boundaries, and order, need to be established, i.e. a sales representative with pink and green hair who wants to call on customers at 2:00 a.m. probably won't fit. These boundaries need to be established, and communicated. Once these boundaries are established, then that uniqueness should be accepted, and utilized!

If you do not tolerate, and use, individual uniqueness you waste talent and potential in individuals.

RECOGNIZING INDIVIDUAL DIFFERENCES DEMONSTRATES ESTEEM FOR OTHERS

"One of the things which truly
tests a leader's skill
is whether they have the
ability to see unique strengths
in other people,
capitalize on them and
work with them."

RECOGNIZING INDIVIDUAL DIFFERENCES DEMONSTRATES ESTEEM FOR OTHERS

A film is the result of producers, actors, directors etc. The better the directors, producers and actors, the better the film. So one should clearly try to get the very best people for each particular category; those whose uniqueness allow them to be outstanding in their own area.

Esteeming others within reasonable boundaries means that you will take an individual's strengths, abilities, and skills and work with them, integrating these into the fabric of the finished product. One of the things which truly tests a leader's skill is whether or not they have the ability to be flexible enough to see unique strengths in other people, capitalize on them and work with them.

ASSESSING OTHERS BY LOOKING AT RESULTS

Trees are identified by their fruit

= APPLE ...THEREFORE: APPLE TREE!!

So:

Learn to assess others by the FRUIT of their life.

Judge by the RESULTS of an individual's actions.

ASSESSING OTHERS BY LOOKING AT RESULTS

Suppose you have a headache and approach a friend with this concern. You are offered a pain reliever – a small colored pill; you say, "Thanks", and take it. If in a few hours the headache is no better, the pill is judged to be of little value. The quality of the medicine has been evaluated, rightly, on the basis of its impact.

You judge something by its impact or by its result. Did the pill work or not? It did not. The results were not there.

In a similar example – some time ago I bought a house and was told that there were apple trees in the backyard. As the seasons changed I waited. In the summer I discovered there were pears on the tree! Clearly they were not apple trees – pears do not grow on apple trees! You judge the trees by the fruit.

Similarly when assessing others, look at the results.

Imagine I leave at my usual time for work and unfortunately encounter a very bad accident on the highway. Cars backed up for miles, ambulances and fire trucks there – truly a terrible accident. As a result of this, I am late for a morning meeting.

A colleague comments, "You are late". I tell him about the bad accident, and he says, "You are late." "No, no, no," I respond, "You don't understand. I intended to be here on time. I'm always on time. These were circumstances simply beyond my control." But no matter how I protest, the circumstances do not alter the facts. All the good intentions in the world, all the legitimate reasons do not take away from the fact that I was late. The facts speak for themselves. If you judge the tree by the fruit – I was late.

When looking at an individual you must look at the *fruit* of their activities; that is, what actually happens. The concept of assessing what *actually happened* is the key (as opposed to considering the intentions).

"Sometimes the fruit of an
individual's action
is not evident immediately,
and only later is the
final result seen. With this
in mind "timing" of your
judgement is very important."

ASSESSING OTHERS BY LOOKING AT RESULTS

Sometimes the fruit is not evident immediately and only later is the final result seen. With this in mind "timing" of your judgement is very important.

Recognize that excuses, reasons, circumstances, events beyond one's own control etc, will all impact the final result; but it is still the final result that is the fruit, hence the thing to be evaluated.

An individual might state that they really care for people, that they really work hard, that they are innovative, that they are productive, or that they are team players. However, when you look at the results of the last three or four months of their behavior on the job, you can then ask yourself questions such as: "Do the people feel good about working for this individual?" "Has the amount of work that has come out of this individual's department been considerable?" "What innovative and creative ideas have we actually seen in the last few months?" "How many new ways have been created for doing things, or how many more productive activities have been generated?" "How many people in the rest of the organization feel that this person is, in fact, building a team and making decisions that are good for the whole?"

If promised or anticipated fruit is to materialize, it will be in evidence during the past six months. If the fruit doesn't match the promise, then, regardless of reasons, there is no confirmation of the original assertion that the person does care for people, does work hard, is innovative, productive, or a team player. There was no fruit.

While this concept of "evident fruit" is a very tough criterion, and one which at times can be very difficult to apply, it none the less is virtually infallible. If a person claims to care for people but just "didn't have time" then you have no indication in the months to come that that person will care for people any more than was demonstrated over the last six months. The results indicate the person does not really care for others, despite what they say.

"Recognize that excuses,
reasons, circumstances,
events beyond one's own control etc.,
will all impact the final result;
but it is still the final result
that is the fruit,
hence the thing to be evaluated.
Leaders must be ruthless in the
application of this principle
if they are to be successful in their
assessments of others."

ASSESSING OTHERS BY LOOKING AT RESULTS

You must judge a tree by its fruit. That is, you must look back in time to see the results of the person's labor and the consequences of the person's behavior, and then make a decision. It cannot be made on the "promise" any more than you can judge a tree by the fact that you dropped a seed in the ground which has the promise of fruit within it.

Recognize that fruit is not always synonymous with measurable activity – it could be the objective of the individual to raise emotions, generate good feelings, provide direction, purpose, etc. These are intangible things but nonetheless real and can still be judged by the fruit.

Other examples of "trees" and "promised fruit":

1. Parents believe it's important to be with their children, but spend no time with them; (no fruit – question the promise).

2. A friend claims to care for others, and during that week does several tasks such as visiting people in the hospital, baking casseroles for sick neighbors, etc.; (very evident fruit – trust the promise).

3. An individual is supposed to be able to come up with new and better ways of doing things, never does so, but always has very good reason for not doing so; (no fruit, great intentions though – question the promise).

Leaders must be ruthless in the application of this principle if they are to be successful in their assessments of others.

GIVE SOME WEIGHT TO INTENTIONS WHEN ASSESSING OTHERS

PLUS

The fruit of an individual's behavior... the results of their actions.

Their motivation, or intention.

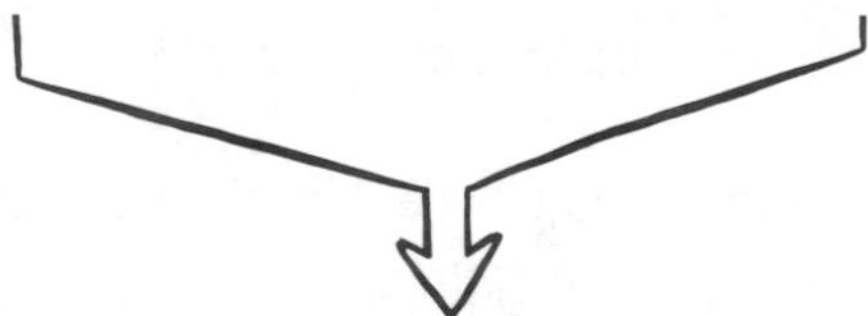

Look at both when evaluating - or assessing the contributions of another.

Sometimes intended results cannot occur.

And so the results themselves do not tell the full story.

In these cases learn to look beyond –

at the motivation, the heart.

GIVE SOME WEIGHT TO INTENTIONS WHEN ASSESSING OTHERS

Intention provides a counterbalance to results. Intention is a nebulous area and tends to soften most decisions made solely on "fruit". However, intentions do not tell the full story and so one must also always consider the fruit.

Think of intention itself as a fruit.

For example, an individual intends to write a letter home but never does. The fruit of that activity is not writing the letter. But the *intention* is to write, and the fruit of that intent could be judged to be a warm heart, a caring spirit, or a love for the person to whom the individual intends to write.

Consequently, you might judge that person as having a caring spirit towards the family but also as having a lack of discipline; or as having a caring spirit but one that doesn't care so much that the person is actually willing to translate that care into something meaningful – other things are always "getting in the way".

In this way, you avoid making the erroneous assumption that because the person didn't write, the person didn't care. If the person didn't care, then there would have been no intention to write. Intention does give you insight into the person but it must be married to fruit in order to provide really meaningful and balanced insight.

Recognize that *intentions do not carry nearly the weight of fruit.* They only help to colour your understanding of the conclusions which you have drawn by looking at the fruit. Even if the intention is consistently "good", it does not override the fact that the fruit is regularly "bad."

Despite the importance of results, the importance of intention should not be entirely overlooked. It should be included, but by degree and only as appropriate, in the overall assessment.

LOOK FOR A WEIGHT OF EVIDENCE

The true measure of an individual – a true test and assessment of their character – occurs after the examination of many instances. Not just one.

MANY SIMILAR RESULTS

PROVIDES A "WEIGHT OF EVIDENCE"

Something Occurring Frequently

Something Occurring Repeatedly

Something Recurring Over an Extended Period of Time

Judge wisely. Judge well. Judge on much evidence.

LOOK FOR A WEIGHT OF EVIDENCE

Always look for something which occurs repeatedly. Look at both the soft side (intention) and the hard side (result). Look for the weight of evidence. Individuals with repeatedly good intentions, but consistently poor results, demonstrate a weight of evidence that their performance is inadequate.

If an individual produces one result out of every six tries, then the weight of evidence would indicate they are successful one in six times. If the individual is talking constantly about what can be done but never produces it, then the weight of evidence is against that person producing it in the future. Even if that individual sometimes manages to succeed, you must still remember that for every six items talked about and promised, ultimately you only get one in return.

Always look for something to occur repeatedly over time. You need to evaluate on the basis of consistent behavior demonstrated over an extended period; for example, if the individual gives you results each time, but each result is inconsistent with the previous one, then you have evidence of inconsistency.

Assessment of this nature is difficult because we usually don't want to be quite so "hard nosed" and realistic about our assessments of people. We tend to more easily accept circumstances and events as justification for poor results, and so place far too much weight on "intention" and not enough on "results". But this is neither accurate, nor fair to the person involved, nor wise.

If an individual promises changed behavior, then you should look back for a weight of evidence that would indicate the ability to change. If what is being promised is modified behavior in the future; look for examples where that person has, on a regular basis, been able to change, or improve, their behavior in the past.

LOOK FOR A WEIGHT OF EVIDENCE

"Judge on the basis
of what has driven
that which
can be observed."

LOOK FOR A WEIGHT OF EVIDENCE

The weight of evidence criterion is very powerful. It says that what you have been getting, you will probably get in the future; but remember not to judge only on the basis of what is observable. Look beyond to judge on the basis of what has *driven* that which can be observed.

For example, if an individual had several promotions – from junior sales rep up to senior manager, and at each point has demonstrated an ability to adapt and learn new skills in a new job, then you have a fair degree of confidence they will adapt well to the next promotion. There is a significant weight of evidence in support of the fruit of teachability and adaptability.

MATCH STRENGTHS TO NEEDS

You must be able to assess in others (not condemn or praise) what is: good and bad, strong and weak, useful and wasteful, contributing and destructive.

From this assessment comes the knowledge of what others can best contribute in any given situation.

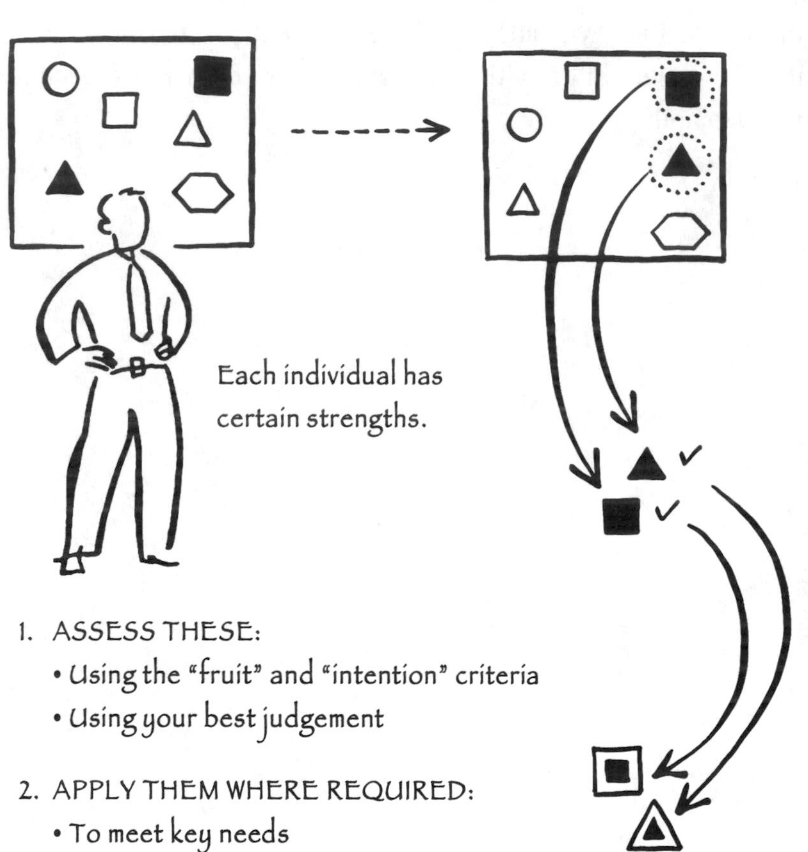
Each individual has
certain strengths.

1. ASSESS THESE:
   - Using the "fruit" and "intention" criteria
   - Using your best judgement
2. APPLY THEM WHERE REQUIRED:
   - To meet key needs
   - To strengthen others

MATCH STRENGTHS TO NEEDS

When assessing other people it is important to objectively identify both the strengths and the weaknesses. Using the criteria of balancing hard results and soft intentions, this assessment should be easier. You also need to learn how to use people's strengths in the best way possible.

Naturally these strengths and weaknesses will be defined in light of the job at hand. A strength for a given job might be a weakness in different circumstances, and vice versa. This is especially true when you consider moving individuals laterally within the organization (i.e. from sales to marketing), or vertically (i.e. a promotion). Moving someone who is competent at one job does not necessarily mean that the person will be able to carry out the responsibilities of the next job, especially if their major skill in their current job is only a minor part of the new job.

When you assess an individual with the intention of capitalizing on their strengths and minimizing their weaknesses, look for behaviors which:

- Are suitable (or unsuitable) for the circumstances you have in mind
- Can either contribute to the overall objective and build the team, or would be destructive, hurtful and wasteful to the team
- Within the organization or environment where that person will be placed, can help (or hinder) depending on what the mission is
- Demonstrate whether or not they are creative, entrepreneurial, people oriented, or technically oriented

"Ask:
in what circumstances
should the individual
be placed to capitalize
on their strengths?"

MATCH STRENGTHS TO NEEDS

The assessment is critical. Once you have made the assessment, then instead of looking at the failures, the weaknesses or the problems, look at the strengths and determine what situation would allow those strengths to contribute most. Ask: where can that individual go, or in what circumstances should the individual be placed, or what people should that person be around, or what systems of procedures should be in place in order to capitalize on their strengths?

In this way your assessment of the individual has been married to the placement of the individual in an environment where their strengths will have an opportunity to flourish. You thereby enhance the impact which that person can have, and the overall effectiveness of the organization.

TO ACHIEVE A VISION REQUIRES CLEAR GOALS

Specific, detailed, actionable goals (i.e. objectives) are essential to ultimately achieving a vision.

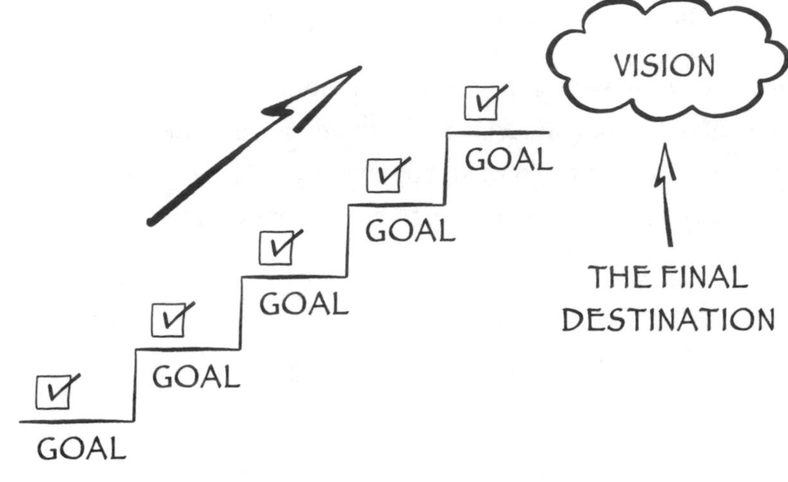

Visions empower:

while goals, or objectives, provide direction.

TO ACHIEVE A VISION REQUIRES CLEAR GOALS

Vision is powerful, especially when it's communicated clearly and with passion. As a result of effective vision people are galvanized into action with the desire to move forward to see that vision realized.

The nature of visions are such that they "point the direction" for action; and if they're effectively communicated they also paint the result which will be tangibly felt once the vision has been realized. By its very nature a vision tends to be broad, sweeping, and encompass great dreams and hopes. This is good because of its motivating force, but also intrinsically dangerous as it provides little in the way of step-by-step direction.

It's the responsibility of goals or objectives, to translate vision into reality.

By taking a series of goals and stringing them together in a logical and coherent form, one is ultimately able to arrive at the achievement of the vision. *The achievement of individual sequential goals is the crucial pathway to achieving a long-term desired outcome or vision.*

Each of these goals has to be very specific, and achievable in a reasonable time frame and within established constraints.

The goals must be actionable, and build upon the previous steps towards the ultimate end. It's exciting to think of reaching the top of a mountain. However, this vision must now be translated into a series of goals such as recruit the team, identify a leader, acquire provisions, plan the route, travel to the foot of the mountain, set up base camp, etc.

The successful leader is one who is able to effectively create a thrilling and exciting vision, but who is also able to translate that into a pragmatic, real, actionable series of measurable steps which, over time, will ultimately see that dream fulfilled.

REALLY GREAT GOALS HAVE SOME VERY SPECIFIC QUALITIES

1. SPECIFIC
   They have a specific deadline; not a fuzzy one, but a deadly accurate one.

2. MEASURABLE
   There's some way to measure the outcome.

3. CRYSTAL CLEAR
   They are expressed so simply and so clearly they are truly "crystal clear" to everyone.

4. ACTION ORIENTED
   They are action oriented, not expressions of intent or desire.

REALLY GREAT GOALS HAVE SOME VERY SPECIFIC QUALITIES

When creating goals as stepping stones towards achievement of a vision, four very specific qualities must be in existence. If the individual specific goals which have been created satisfy each of these four criteria you can then have confidence that achievement of those goals will ultimately lead you to the desired end.

1. ***Goals must have a very specific deadline.*** This deadline has to be precise including a date, and often even a time. A student who says that they will be "studying French today" has created a fuzzy and less effective goal than the student who says, "I will be done with chapter five by 10:00 p.m. tomorrow night." The very act of setting these specific and accurate targets leads to the natural outcome of planning the volume of work that must be accomplished between now and that first target date.

2. ***Outcomes need to be measured.*** At the completion of each goal some tool needs to be in place to determine the degree to which the goal has been met. The student in the example above might measure the completion of chapter five by the ability to conjugate thirteen verbs perfectly, in four tenses, into a tape recorder and then, upon playback, find one hundred percent accuracy in the conjugation.

   The measurement which is created for each goal is not as important as creating measurement which is relevant. The more effective the measurement, the more likely the achievement of the goal. The power of breaking the achievement of some larger vision into step-like goals is that these goals can then be broken into increasingly smaller pieces until each goal is small enough for its own measure.

"At the completion of
each goal
some tool needs to be
in place to determine
the degree to which the
goal has been met."

Even things that are considered "not measurable" can have measurable components attached to each individual goal. For example, the creation of a new game might have a goal somewhere in the process to "design a new way of moving around the board". If this is followed by a measurement such as "individual players must be able to move within thirty seconds of each other without the use of a die", then the definition of that measure provides some structure to help with the achievement of the goal. Clearly the more precise the measure, the more targeted the activity will be toward the goal.

3. ***Goals must be stated simply, and preferably with only a few words in a short sentence or phrase.*** This is a mechanism for ensuring the goal is sufficiently "bite size", and not too large or grandiose an undertaking. Very often individual goals leading to the achievement of a vision are too ambitious, and may in themselves be daunting. It is only when they are broken into smaller, more manageable chunks that they are perceived to be obtainable, and so build a sense of accomplishment as individuals progressively move towards the final vision. A crucial element of keeping these goals from being too large is to ensure that they can be stated simply, with a few words.

   Further, the simple statement of a goal in and of itself provides clarity and tends to avoid the confusion and wasted energy which can easily follow from goals which are too complicated, and not well understood by everyone involved in their achievement.

REALLY GREAT GOALS HAVE SOME VERY SPECIFIC QUALITIES

"The more precise
the measure,
the more targeted the
activity will be
toward the goal."

REALLY GREAT GOALS HAVE SOME VERY SPECIFIC QUALITIES

4. ***Individual goals must be actionable and doable.*** This requires that they be precisely defined in actionable terms and not in terms of intent or desire. Our earlier student who states they'll "work on French today" is far less likely to have the same outcome as the student who says they will be "able to accurately conjugate the verbs in chapter five, without error by 5:00 pm tonight". Simply because the goal is stated in an actionable fashion, ensures that action will be taken!

ONCE UNDERWAY TOWARDS A VISION, FREQUENT REMINDERS OF BOTH THE VISION AND THE GOALS ARE ESSENTIAL

Paths usually start out nice and neat and very straightforward...

BUT LEFT TO THEMSELVES

...They can get fuzzy, obscure, sidetracked, cluttered with all the things that naturally get picked up along the way...

SO

...Keep repeating the vision and the goal. Keep things focused.

ONCE UNDERWAY TOWARDS A VISION, FREQUENT REMINDERS OF BOTH THE VISION AND THE GOALS ARE ESSENTIAL

A clear statement of the vision and subsequent goals to achieve that vision is crucial. These provide clarity and motivation to the listener. However, we humans have a way of easily losing focus when we're assailed by other interests and activities. As a consequence it's important to keep any vision top of mind, and the individual goals clearly front and centre. A periodic refresher of the vision is usually sufficient, but the immediate goal being worked on needs to be referred to repeatedly.

This can be done by charting progress towards the current goal, celebrating successes as they occur, or simply reminding people of this goal on a regular basis, using that opportunity to reinforce why the current objective is so important, and why its place in achieving the overall vision is so vital.

An added benefit in keeping the overall vision, and subsequent goals, top of mind is that it reinforces to people the leader's commitment to this direction, and it's importance.

THE GOAL MUST BE PRECISELY DEFINED

The more clearly and precisely you can IDENTIFY and STATE your goal, objective, or target, the better chance you will have of reaching it.

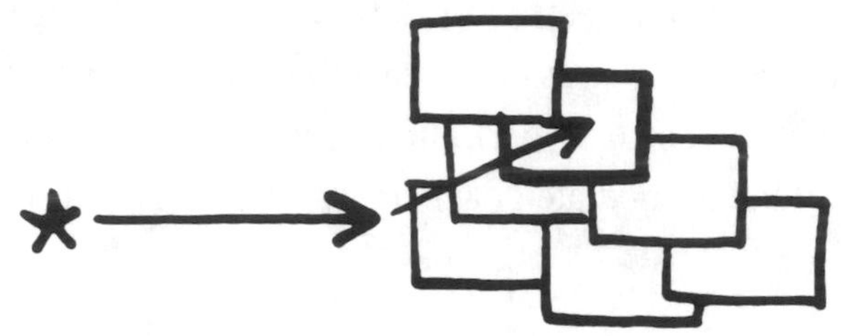

From here, when you start, you must know...

precisely where you are heading.

Not generally	("West")
Not somewhat specific	("California")
Not kind of precise	("Los Angeles")
But – Precisely!	("The front door of the City Hall in Los Angeles, California next Tuesday at 2:00 p.m.")

THIS MAXIMIZES YOUR CHANCE OF ACHIEVING YOUR GOAL.

THE GOAL MUST BE PRECISELY DEFINED

The more clearly and precisely you can identify and then state your goal, objective, or target, the better chance you will have of reaching it.

People function best and most efficiently when they are clear on the goal, mission, standard, philosophy, or approach.

When goals are achieved efficiently a lot of credit will go to the one who executed the task – deservedly so. But a lot of credit should also go to the one who set the goal – for setting it clearly and precisely!

The difference in the level of performance between two people or areas is often directly related to the clarity of instruction, and the specification of responsibilities. It's easier to succeed when you are asked to arrive at the front door of the City Hall in Los Angeles, California next Tuesday at 2 p.m., than when you are simply asked to go "West".

The key is appropriate detail. The more clearly that you are able to state your goal the better chance you will have of achieving it.

TEST EACH GOAL FOR ABSOLUTE CLARITY

A test to determine if, in fact, your goal, objective, or target is as clearly identified as it should be: complete strangers – possessing the same skills as you have – should be able to achieve your goal, without your help, once you have given it to them.

Does yours meet this test?

TEST EACH GOAL FOR ABSOLUTE CLARITY

A test to determine if, in fact, your goal, objective or target is as clearly identified as it should be, is to have it reviewed by someone with the same skill set as the person with whom you originally agreed on the objective. They should be able to achieve it without reference to you. Ask if they feel they can. If so, it's probably clearly expressed.

We often tend to feel that we have stated the goal very clearly, but we rarely test it. It should be tested to ensure that it is clear to all concerned.

While it may seem rather ridiculous to spend so much time on the stating of the goal, it is because it is often easier to achieve goals than it is to state them! As a peripheral comment, other issues often surface in the defining of the goal, such as what we will do if we are hindered, how we will tackle opposition, how we will cope with unforeseen change and so on. These issues should be taken into consideration at this stage, before beginning the activity, since potential hindrances to reaching our objective may have some bearing on the goal itself, and the established timing.

Do not hesitate to test your goals as a way of ensuring that they are specific enough.

ESTABLISH CHECKPOINTS

If you begin without first identifying check points along the way, you have less chance of achieving your goal as efficiently as possible.

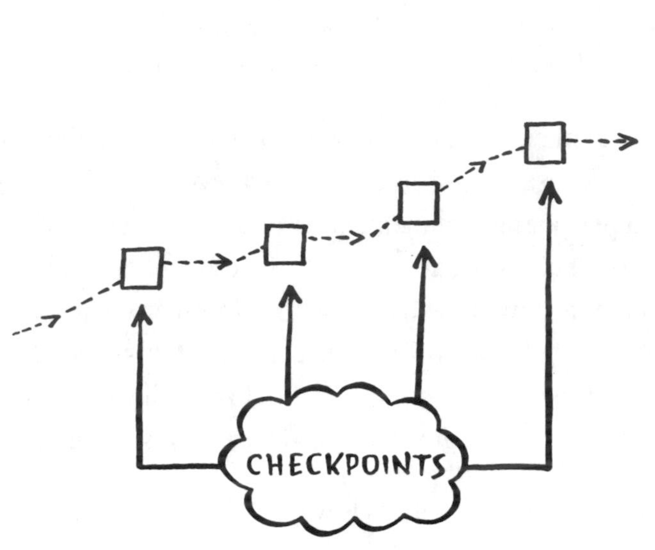

Checking is key!

...and must be done!

Determine how and when you'll do this before you begin.

ESTABLISH CHECKPOINTS

If you leave New York headed for the Los Angeles City Hall, and never check to see where you are during the trip, you'll probably never get there. You must have a way of periodically checking your progress; and then do so.

Once the goals and objectives are set then there must be some way of determining if you are on target. There must be some way to check the pathway you are taking towards these goals. After the goal has been stated, some thought needs to be given to how you will monitor your progress towards the goal. The objective in this case is not to determine whether or not the goal is met, *the objective is to determine whether or not you are on the path correctly headed towards the goal.*

As mentioned earlier, the process of managing toward specific goals is a process whereby guidance is given along the way. There must, however, be some way to determine whether or not the guidance is necessary, and the direction which the guidance should take. Predetermined checkpoints along the way provide this insight.

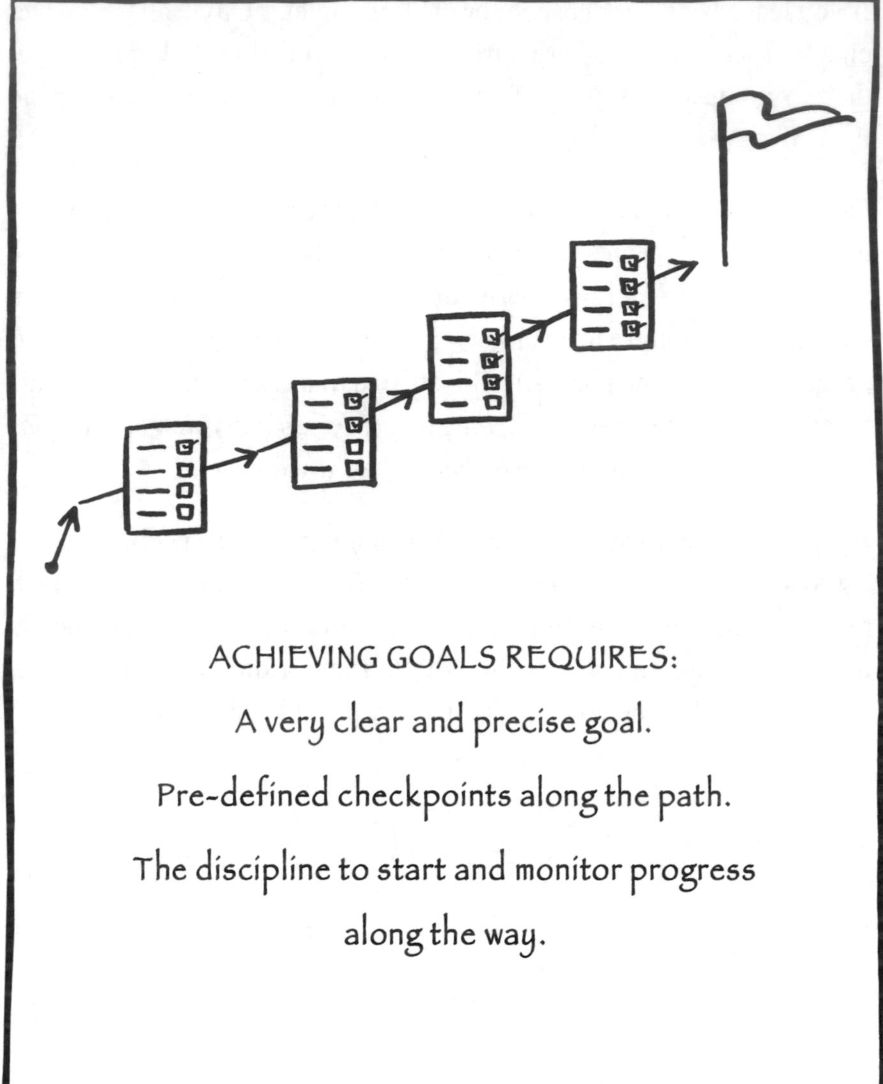
ACHIEVING GOALS REQUIRES:
A very clear and precise goal.
Pre-defined checkpoints along the path.
The discipline to start and monitor progress
along the way.

MONITOR PROGRESS FREQUENTLY

You must monitor progress regularly to ensure your goal is met. This requires committing to checkpoints along the way: mapping out milestones in advance and defining the expectation at each of those points. Checkpoints are critical; and when you get to these checkpoints you need to know what you are looking for.

Imagine a situation where incoming calls at a large switchboard are not being answered effectively, and the phone rings and rings. You could bring the group together and say, "I want each phone call to be answered within ten seconds." The group might become flustered, not knowing what to do, or how to do it.

Therefore, in addition to discussing *how* this could be done, you could provide them with checkpoints where they monitor progress. They might perhaps call the telephone company and ask them to put a device on the phone which would track the time before answering, which could then be monitored twice monthly. After three months they might be able to get response time down to fifteen seconds. Praise them for this, but also reemphasize that you want it down to ten seconds.

Six months later they will most probably have succeeded.

While they undoubtedly ran into a number of obstacles along the way, they were able to overcome these because the goal and methodology were clearly stated, and monitored checkpoints were put in place (twice monthly monitoring of time until answered, and corresponding improvement from the previous checkpoint).

"You must
monitor progress regularly to
ensure your goal is met.
This requires mapping out
milestones in advance and
defining what the expectation
is at each of those points."

Another example: suppose you decide that you will monitor your progress toward some goal a quarter of the way along by checking the impact on the organization; at the half way point by having a meeting with relevant parties that are affected to see whether they are beginning to see a change; and similarly again at the three quarters point. You must then go back to each of these points and provide more detail, as detail is important at each checkpoint.

For example, you might go to the first point and say: "How are we going to measure the impact on the organization?" Specifically this will require pulling the team together and defining the things which are used to measure impact, well in advance of beginning the task. This might include such things as improved customer service levels, faster turn around, less paper, fewer errors, greater sense of morale, etc.

When you are monitoring the impact on the relevant parties at the half way point, you should identify what you expect to hear from them, what they would be saying if in fact you are on track with your goals, what they will say if you are not on track, etc.

Before beginning, you are essentially imagining yourself in the position in which you hope to be at the time of the checkpoint and saying "If we are on track with our goals, and where we want to be, then the people we are using to monitor our progress will say such and such. If they do say this, then we know we are on track."

Once you make this very specific determination of how you will monitor progress at each checkpoint, and it is determined what the expected outcome should be, the next step is to get agreement from the people involved in the initiative. They need to recognize that these are valid checkpoints, and confirm that this is what they would expect to see at each of those points along that path towards the goal.

> "Having solid, measurable checkpoints along the way more than pays for the extra upfront effort required to identify them."

MONITOR PROGRESS FREQUENTLY

If the people for whom the task is being carried out agree that it would be a fair assessment, then you have some degree of confidence that if you arrive at each point, and meet the predetermined criteria, then you will ultimately bc successful.

The added benefits of this particular approach are saving time and energy, and therefore being able to use your resources to the fullest. While initially it may appear to be time consuming to do this level of planning and work at the goal setting stage, in the long run considerable time is saved by staying so closely on track and not deviating. Having solid, measurable checkpoints along the way more than pays for the extra effort up front.

I rely heavily on the checkpoints, and so am far less concerned with the overall process. If checkpoints are properly placed, and measurements there are properly defined, we'll get the results if we're successful at each checkpoint. So I concentrate on successfully passing each checkpoint!

1. Initiate frequent, honest, open communication.

2. Initiate discussion to identify problems, ideas, progress.

3. Provide and reinforce a clear focused vision and direction.

4. Ensure relevant training is applied.

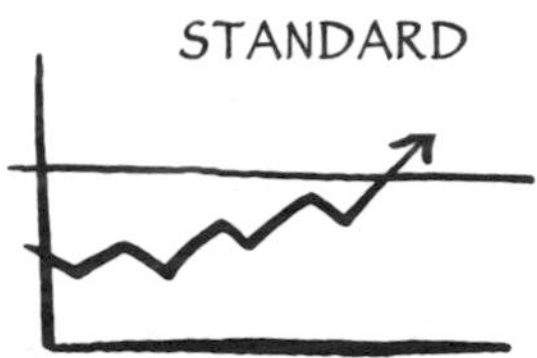

5. Clearly define boundaries, and then allow freedom of action within those boundaries.

MANAGING EMPOWERED EMPLOYEES

The management of empowered employees is discussed throughout this book, and is summarized below in five specific points. It's important to recognize that an empowered employee is one who has defined boundaries within which to act, and defined freedoms.

In the traditional autocratic management style, individuals are not only told what to do, but how to do it. In an empowered environment, they should still be told what to do (the strategy of the organization, department, or team), but they should have the freedom to determine how this task should be done. This allows each individual to use their knowledge and skill to the fullest, by giving them the freedom to participate in the execution of the task to a degree not experienced in the autocratic structure.

One might easily envision an instance where, perhaps during a strike, the engineers go in to operate a factory. At the end of the strike the engineers might make a number of recommendations regarding changes to be made to the lines in order to improve productivity. By working on the lines themselves they had identified many different steps which could be taken to improve productivity or process design.

When these recommendations are put forward, the hourly workers on the floor might note that these were the same recommendations that they had been suggesting for years, but because they did not have the credentials of an engineer they had been ignored! To me, this would be a tragic waste of human talent.

"It is a fallacy to believe that managing empowered employees is easier than managing in an autocratic fashion. It is not. Managing empowered employees is far more difficult because they have been given the freedom to contribute, and as such are initiating change."

Had those employees who have been working with the equipment day in and day out been listened to, then that organization could have gained immensely from productivity improvements as well as employee relations years earlier. The expertise already lay in the hands and minds of those who knew the equipment intimately. It was good that the engineers could identify opportunities for improvement and make changes; but it would have been far better if the organization had been managing from an empowered prospective, which would have allowed the workers to contribute to the "how" of the task for their own area of responsibility.

It is a fallacy to believe that managing empowered employees is easier than managing in an autocratic fashion. It is not. Managing empowered employees is far more difficult because they have been given the freedom to contribute, and as such are initiating change. They have ideas, are innovative, are working together in teams, and have crossed functional boundaries in order to get things done. This requires careful and effective supervision to ensure this initiative is effectively harnessed, and integrated with other groups who may be affected. The supervisor *must* stay in touch at all times with the team and their activities.

Five guidelines for managing empowered employees:

1. ***Communication:*** Communication must be honest between the supervisor and empowered groups. Often suggestions received are not workable, too expensive, or the consequences are not fully appreciated. At other times an individual may have a great idea, but is perhaps going about it in a less than effective fashion. Whatever the circumstances, the supervisor or coach must be honest with the team to ensure the quality of their output is as both parties would anticipate.

"Important in any empowered environment is measuring progress. The objective of the empowerment is to improve the quality or value of the results of the organization. Measurement is key to this, and progress against measurement must be discussed regularly in order to determine whether or not appropriate activity is occurring."

Communication must also be open. Trust must exist between the supervisor and the team, so that both groups feel free to express fully what they are thinking and feeling. Only in this way can they support each other and come to mutual understanding, and subsequent resolution.

2. ***Initiation:*** In the course of any process improvement initiative, or when implementing suggestions on ways to increase productivity, there will be instances when problems surface, ideas are suggested, or progress needs to be reviewed against measurements. The manager must make a point of initiating discussion in each of these areas in order to keep a finger on the pulse of the initiatives going on in the empowered workplace.

   By initiating discussion, then problems are identified early and can be more readily resolved than they might be at a later date. The problem might have to do with the way the team is operating, the way in which an individual feels or is functioning, or with some particular step in a process where the individual or team is unable to overcome a hurdle which has surfaced.

   Help may be needed to keep ideas from being lost or sustained in the process of their review, and in possible subsequent implementation.

   Important in any empowered environment is measuring progress. The objective of empowerment is to improve the quality, or value, of the results of the organization's efforts. Measurement is key to this, and progress against measurement must be discussed regularly in order to determine whether or not appropriate activity is occurring. The leader responsible for empowered employees has the obligation to ensure that discussion is initiated in these areas.

"Empowerment
does not exist in a
vacuum; it exists within
the context of
vision, and direction."

3. ***Direction:*** It is the leader's responsibility to provide very focused vision and direction. Empowerment does not exist in a vacuum; it exists within the context of vision, and direction. Once these are clear, then the individuals responsible for executing the task can do so with the confidence that they are working towards that common vision.

   The leader must ensure that the vision is kept top of mind, and provide focus for the employees who are working to support it and help make it a reality. There are many ways of doing this: referencing it at group meetings, using written materials, sharing victories along the way, using posters or visible reminders, or publishing results of progress.

4. ***Education:*** Crucial to any initiative in the area of empowerment is the provision of relevant training. Individuals are only able to operate to the limit of their knowledge and skill. As an empowered employee continues to operate they will push against the ceiling of their knowledge and skill. They will want to learn more so that they can contribute more. In order to ensure this happens it is crucial that the supervisor determine, with the employee or team, what would be relevant and valuable training in order to accelerate each individual's ability to contribute to their fullest. Once this has been identified, then it is the supervisor's responsibility to ensure that the training is provided.

   Individuals have the capacity to grow and learn. If the organization is willing to give them the freedom to act to improve the way in which they do things, and to eliminate waste, then the investment in that individual's talent will pay back many fold. The more an individual knows, the more they are able to contribute. The more an individual understands, the more wisely they are able to judge appropriate courses of action. Training and education are extraordinarily powerful as they continually increase the potential contribution of each individual employee. Managers must ensure that they provide that relevant training.

"Individuals are
only able to operate
to the limit of their
knowledge and skills."

5. ***Delineation:*** As empowered employees begin to contribute, their boundaries will become more confining. With experience, training, and education, the empowered group can make greater and greater contributions without putting the organization at risk. In this way their boundaries can be expanded slowly and safely, and as a result providing them with a larger and larger degree of autonomy.

   The supervisor is responsible for setting those boundaries. Set them too small, and the employee will feel frustrated and not empowered, despite the words. Set them too large, and the employee will feel lost, insecure, and the organization will be at risk. Supervisors must understand where the boundaries need to be placed to provide the empowered employees with a challenging yet safe degree of autonomy. They must also be sensitive to the need to expand those boundaries as individuals demonstrate experience, track record, and increased knowledge and skill. This is not an easy task, but an important one!

It's easy to make the mistake of assuming that by "empowering" others the role of the supervisor or leader has been eliminated. Nothing is further from the truth. The fact is that the role of the leader has changed dramatically, and new skills are required if the leader is to effectively harness this potential that has now been released in the empowered work force. If these skills are acquired then there is a huge benefit to the organization.

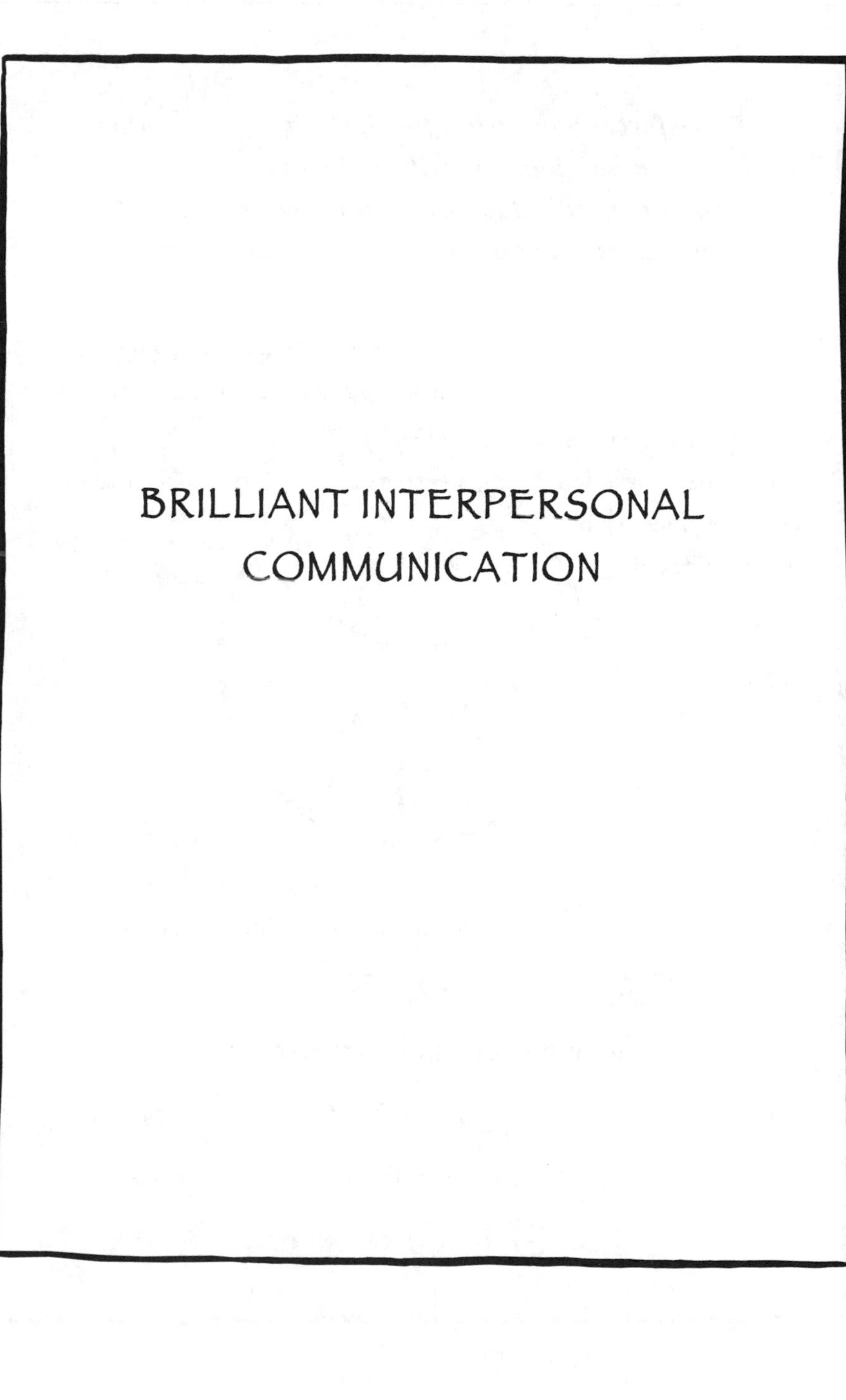

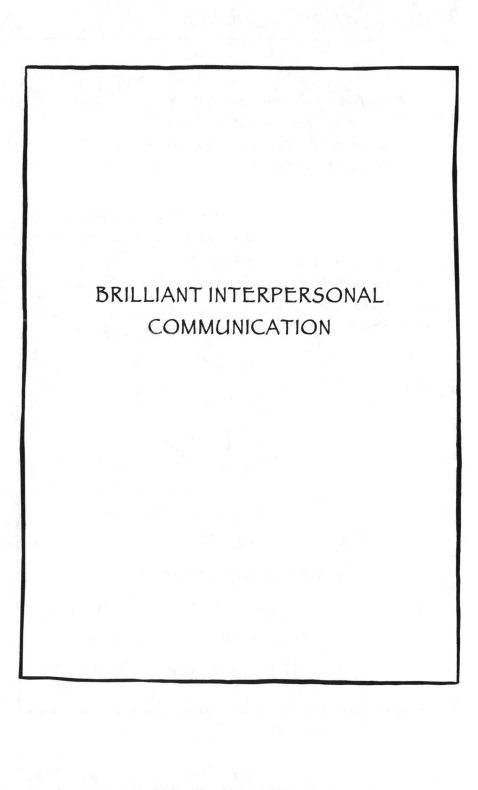

BRILLIANT INTERPERSONAL COMMUNICATION

Three forces have to be effectively brought together in harmony to really make an impact on another individual, assuming you've chosen the right person at the right time for the exchange.

Interpersonal skill, body language, tact, image, appearance, voice control, etc.

Reasoned arguments, replicable knowledge, evidence, unassailable information, etc.

"How you come across to others is too important to be left to chance."

"Logic requires the clear statement of provable truths."

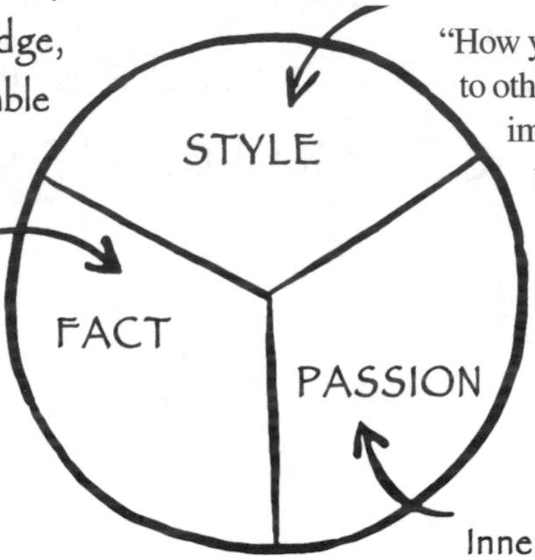

Inner commitment, enthusiasm, motivation, drive, etc.

"Only passion can give birth to passion."

The audience, and circumstances, determine the appropriate proportion – the "balance" for that situation – of these three elements.

ie or or etc.

MAKING A FACE-TO-FACE IMPACT

People often ask for advice on how to make a face-to-face impact. They are more successful in some situations than with others and need guidance on how to be predictably successful, on a consistent basis. There are three forces which have to be effectively brought together in order to make a significant impact when dealing face-to-face.

Your judgement on the degree to which of these should be brought into play is crucial to the final outcome, as is the need to choose the right person and the right time for the exchange! If you're discussing a sales problem with the purchasing manager then perhaps you have not chosen the most appropriate person for the exchange.

Similarly, to suggest to the finance team at year end that they take three weeks off for a team building activity may be less than appropriate, given that at year end book closure is usually an all consuming task.

You must use judgement to ensure that your face-to-face contact is with the right face, with the right subject, at the right time. This is usually not a problem, but is nonetheless the first step to making an impact.

However, assuming – as in most cases – that you are talking to the right person in the right circumstances, then these three forces, if used effectively, will maximize your face-to-face impact.

"How you come across
to others
is too important
to be left to chance."

1. ***Style:*** Since we are all human we all have biases, which may not be logical, but are nonetheless real.

   We take into account the way a person looks, their posture, how they carry themselves and their general deportment. We are influenced by such things as cleanliness, grooming, and attitude. Body language, attentiveness, eye contact, and friendliness are all things which we tend to value and place weight on when determining whether or not we will be receptive in a given situation.

   If you wish to maximize your face-to-face impact you need to ensure your style is one which is conducive to having a positive physical impact.

   "Style" is a difficult topic to define clearly as it is so varied and so unique to each person. Your style is unique and the style of the person with whom you are interacting is equally unique. You need to consider your style, and also consider the style which the other individual values. This will allow you to adopt the appropriate approach, one which will not erect a barrier between you and the person you are attempting to influence.

   Style can include a number of things, such as your approach – laid back or aggressive, introverted or extroverted; your dress – formal or casual, traditional, or local (you dress differently in Dallas than in New York); and your manner – proactive or reactive, leader or follower. These are but a few, and serve only to demonstrate the need to pay attention to style and make decisions regarding what is appropriate in each circumstance.

"Being intimidated
is no
justification for making
a poor impact."

The expression "How you come across to others is too important to be left to chance" was shared with me many years ago by a wise individual who recognized the need to pay close attention to style. "Style" is not something which just happens. If we wish to maximize our impact, "style" is something to which we must give somc thought and then make selections, choices, and decisions.

2. ***Passion:*** Passion is talked about elsewhere, and remains a crucial component when you want to maximize your face-to-face impact.

   Early in my executive career I was asked to make a presentation to one of our very senior executives; and I worked hard to present a buttoned-down, clear, and well thought out presentation. When I was done I could tell that I had been clear, but rather boring. I had failed to really ignite within my listener the same vision and enthusiasm which I felt about initiatives I was currently attempting to bring into the organization.

   My boss at the time took me aside a few days later for some coaching. He pointed out that he felt my strength was my conviction and passion. This passion was rooted in fact, knowledge, and clear logical reasoning; but the success I had been enjoying within the organization, and which was causing others to follow the direction I was charged with leading, was my passion, not only my knowledge.

   He pointed out that I had exhibited none of this passion in the previous meeting with the senior executive, and so had been far less effective than I could have been.

"By itself,
fact is not adequate
for maximizing an impact;
but without it
no impact can be effectively
made that will last."

At the time of the presentation I had been intimidated by the rank of the person to whom I was presenting and so felt I should be entirely analytical. My boss pointed out that being intimidated was no justification for making a poor impact!

It took another two presentations to executives at that level before I was able to overcome my hesitation about being passionate in the presence of senior management, and while I was learning I was clearly less effective in their eyes. However, with continued coaching I was able to master it, until my presentations contained somewhat less data but considerably more passion.

They were then more effective, and had a much bigger impact. Others too became passionate and so could give greater support to what we were doing.

3. ***Fact:*** This is often the element of making an impact to which we turn most readily, as I did in the above example; and it is not to be overlooked. Passion and style without fact are so much fluff and vapor. Facts provide credibility and the root basis for the impact you hope to make.

   Reasoned arguments, reliable knowledge, evidence, and unassailable information are all crucial if you wish to make an impact that is lasting and defensible.

   By itself, fact is not adequate for maximizing an impact; but without it no impact can be effectively made that will last. Do not become over-dependent on fact, but on the other hand do not fail to ensure you have facts which are clear, documented, and effective.

"Use judgement
to ensure that your
face-to-face contact is
with the right face,
with the right subject,
at the right time."

> Imagine the impact: an individual is presenting to a senior manager, with passion about their topic, and demonstrating a winning style. Then when questioned about some of the content of the presentation, they, in response, indicate that the detail is in the binder in front of them. But when asked to show this detail... has to admit it is not there at all. The impact they would make is very different from the one they had intended to make!
>
> Logic requires clear statements of provable truths, and you must provide these logical statements if your impact is to be truly effective.

Of particular note is the need to recognize that these three elements: style, passion, and fact, are unlikely to be required in equal proportions. Different circumstances require a different blend and you must master the ability to select the appropriate blend. Depending on the audience, their experience, their own knowledge and conviction on the topic, and the original motivation for your interaction, you must adjust your approach to provide the appropriate balance of each of these three elements.

There is no formula for the right blend. The first meeting may sometimes require an emphasis on style, sometimes on fact, and sometimes on passion. The last meeting at the end of a series may require a different emphasis on style, fact, or passion. The blend may change over time and you must constantly be evaluating the appropriate mix.

You will need all three and you will need to exercise judgement in selecting each of the three areas to determine the right mix. Experience is a great teacher and with practice these decisions will become easier, and you will become increasingly more effective.

1. PREPARE THE GROUND BEFORE YOU PLANT YOUR CROP
   Your listener lacks the background (past), or vision (future) you have. With it, your message will bear fruit. Without it, it may never take root. But remember... be brief – this is not your message, you are only tilling the soil.

2. SPEAK FROM KNOWLEDGE
   When speaking, what you say must be credible. Your content must be based on accurate, verifiable, and compelling information. The greater the credibility, the greater the effectiveness of the communication.

3. SPEAK FROM CONVICTION, WITH PASSION
   People are informed by information (head), but really moved to action and commitment by emotion (heart). Fire kindles fire. Your communication needs always to motivate, not just inform.

MAXIMIZING YOUR IMPACT

Often in the course of day-to-day life there is the need to be persuasive. Sometimes this is a difficult challenge in that others just don't seem to be willing to be swayed by your point of view and at other times it is less difficult. There are three steps which you can take to be more persuasive with what you say.

1. ***Take a few moments before you get to the heart of your message to prepare the listener for what you have to say.*** In the same way that a farmer prepares the ground before planting the seed, there is great value in preparing the mind of your listener before you plant your ideas.

   In doing this, one of the best ways to approach it is to "back up" in your mind to your own thinking which led you to the conclusion you're about to present. What got you to this point? Why did you begin thinking about this? What were the issues on your mind that led you down this particular route? These and similar questions help you determine what it was you were considering, or what problem you were facing, or what opportunity you foresaw that ultimately led you to the conclusion you will shortly be presenting. Take some time to provide the listener with this early thinking.

   This "early thinking" is not really relevant to the idea you wish to present and hope to have accepted, but it does "set the stage". It gives the listener the rationale for the perspective from which you are coming. Very often it will also serve to create a framework or a reason in the mind of the listener for what you are about to say, and therefore create a similar mindset in them to that within yourself.

"If communication
is to be
effective, it must
be believed."

The more capably you can prepare the mind of your listener, as the farmer does his field, the more effective will be your idea once you present it, and the more persuasive you'll become, as seeds flourish best in prepared ground. A caution: don't overdo it here or it will become the message in itself. Remember, you are only setting the stage.

2. ***Ensure that what you say is credible.*** It's hard to be persuasive when the information you are communicating is not verifiable or accurate. Information is far more compelling when it is clearly based on knowledge, the stringing together of recognized facts that can be seen to be verifiable.

   If communication is to be effective it must be believed. The greater the belief, the greater the effectiveness and hence the persuasion. Use anecdotes, use illustrations, refer to expert authority; all of these work well and will make you more persuasive than simply being perceived to be presenting some unfounded idea.

3. ***Use emotion.*** To summarize the situation expanded on in Section V, Teaching Skills: Frequent Checking is Essential (page 334): if, after you've just sat down to a movie with the family, you're interrupted only to receive a telephone solicitation to buy kitchen cutlery, you will most likely be somewhat irate and so probably not purchase.

   On the other hand, if the phone rings as you're sitting down to a movie and it's a close friend with an immediate personal problem, then the movie is quickly forgotten in your effort to be of assistance.

   In the first case there was no emotion or passion involved. In the second, your emotions were already involved, because it was a close friend, and so you responded quite differently.

"In the same way
that a farmer prepares
the ground
before planting the seed,
there is great value
in preparing the mind
of your listener
before you plant your ideas."

The above truth is valid on a more universal level: people are more engaged when their emotions, or passions, are involved. Consequently, when you speak or present an idea do so with passion, engage your emotions.

Your message not only needs to inform, but to kindle within the listener a sense of conviction, emotion or passion. Fire kindles fire; and if your message carries a motivational component that kindles fire in the mind of the listener then they are far more engaged, and consequently more willing to be involved, and therefore interact, and so hopefully be persuaded.

The three guidelines above are not equally applicable in every situation. However, they should all bc present to some degree. As you seek to be persuasive spend a few moments preparing the ground, ensuring that what you have to say is rooted in verifiable and compelling information, and determining to speak with passion and conviction. You will carry more weight and be more persuasive.

"When" is crucial. Timing makes a big difference.

AVOID

Commenting when the listener is ...

1. Preoccupied
2. Emotionally (positively or negatively) worked up
3. Reliving something in the recent past, or consumed with anticipation for something in the near future

CAPITALIZE

On opportunities when the listener...

1. Has a need
2. Is willing to learn
3. Is mentally "at peace"
4. Is looking for positive, or negative, feedback

Seed sown on prepared soil is
much more fruitful than seed sown on rocky soil.
Watch for the soil to be at its best!

KNOW WHEN TO SPEAK

Selecting the opportunity for your message often contributes significantly to the overall effectiveness of the message. Knowing when to speak can be as important as knowing *what* to say.

When the listener is preoccupied with other things, or emotionally tied up, perhaps dwelling on a recent or upcoming event, it is difficult for them to concentrate on what you have to say.

Developing a sensitivity to the listener, and where they are at, is an important element of being an effective communicator.

Not only is sensitivity required as to when not to speak, but also to be able to seize opportunities when they present themselves. If the listener has a specific need or area where they are seeking help, then clearly they will be receptive to your input at that time. Similarly when an issue surfaces and you are aware that there is a willingness to learn or receive feedback (positive or negative) then again this is an ideal opportunity to present your point of view.

Effective communication requires that the listener be mentally prepared to listen, which not only needs the absence of distracting influences, but also the positive state of being mentally at peace; that is, a calmness that allows them to concentrate on the message at hand. In order to present effectively it may be necessary to help the listener to set aside some current issue before proceeding. Perhaps this could be done with comments such as "We'll come back to this other issue that is on your mind at a later date", or "Although you are currently involved in that problem, let's put it briefly on pause while we consider another perspective."

"Knowing
when to speak can be
as important as
knowing what to say."

KNOW WHEN TO SPEAK

These kinds of comments, which recognize the existence of other concerns, with a promise to return to them, helps to place the listener at ease and allow them to concentrate on the material you have to share.

A few minutes spent preparing the soil – that is preparing the listener's mind to receive what you have to say – is time well spent. Similarly, noticing when the soil is at its best, and seizing those moments to present your thoughts can also enhance their effectiveness.

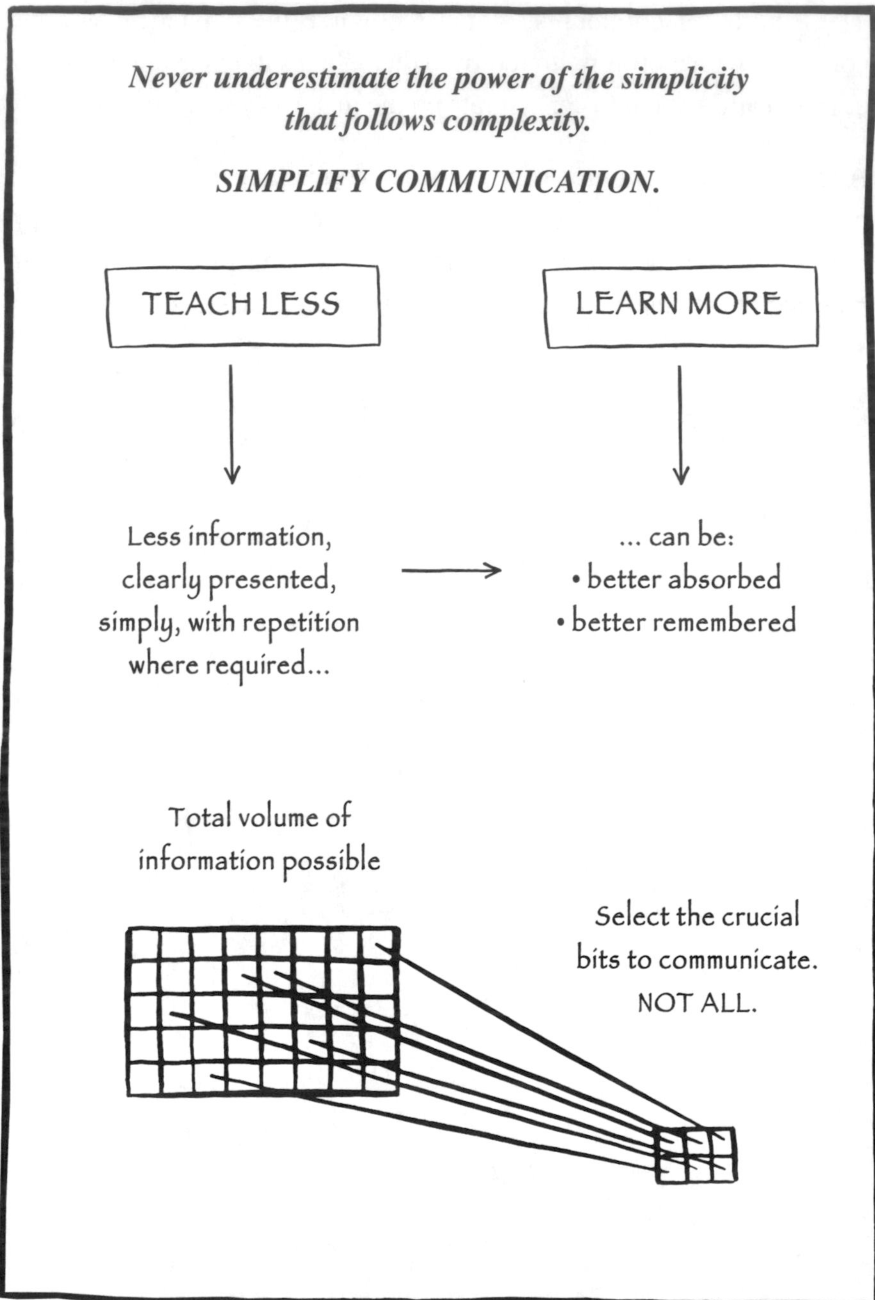
Never underestimate the power of the simplicity
that follows complexity.
SIMPLIFY COMMUNICATION.
TEACH LESS
LEARN MORE
Less information,
clearly presented,
simply, with repetition
where required...
... can be:
• better absorbed
• better remembered
Total volume of
information possible
Select the crucial
bits to communicate.
NOT ALL.

KEEP COMMUNICATION SIMPLE

Many years ago I led a series of Bible studies for a group of counselors at camp, for which I had prepared for months in advance. When I got there I was so enthusiastic to share everything I learned that for forty-five minutes each day for a week I covered passage after passage, and topic after topic. I was so determined to share everything I learned that I successfully pushed six months of study into five, forty-five minute blocks!

At the end of the week an older, and far more experienced leader came to me and asked how the Bible studies had gone during the week. I confessed that I was quite discouraged because the class had not seemed to learn anything despite the abundant wealth of information I had communicated. At that time he gave me some sound advice, which I have followed ever since: "Teach less, learn more."

He pointed out that individuals actually learn more when they have been given less information, but more time to digest it, personalize it, internalize it, ask questions, and ultimately understand it. Where I had failed during that week was that I gave them too much information, at such a pace that they were unable to absorb any of it.

That was a difficult lesson because I felt I would be most successful by telling them everything I knew. Rather, he taught me that I would be more successful by leaving them with some learning that they could carry with them until the end of their lives! This meant that I had to be selective about what I taught, and commit myself to covering it in a more simple and comprehensible fashion.

"Individuals learn more
when they have
been given less information,
but more
time to understand it."

KEEP COMMUNICATION SIMPLE

In practice the speaker needs to select what to say, and what to leave unsaid. This then needs to be followed by a simple presentation of those facts, with illustrations, and then cycling back to the main point, to facilitate learning on the part of the listener.

This does not mean to keep the presentation simple. Rather it means to know the material well, in all its complexity, and then select from that in order that the message will be clearly understood. This is the simplicity that follows complexity and not the simplicity that precedes it.

Teach less, learn more!

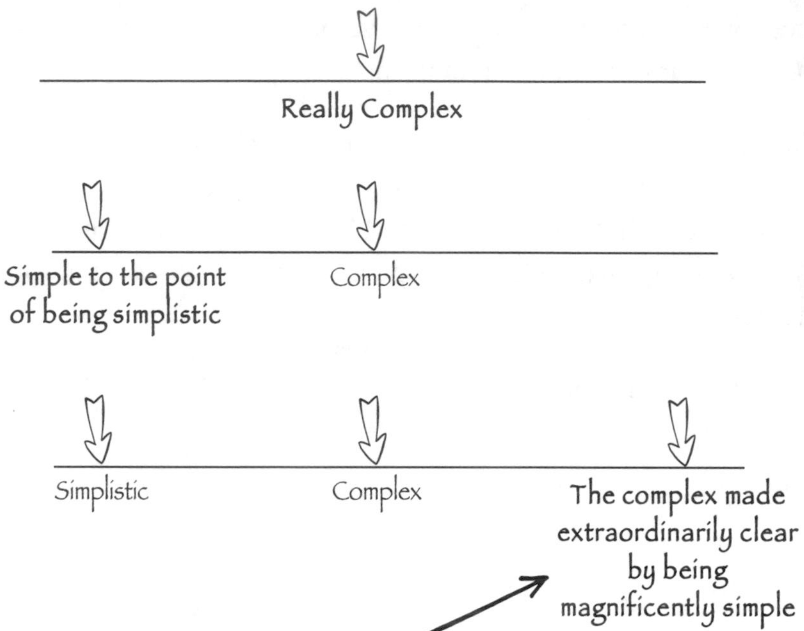

Really Complex

Simple to the point of being simplistic

Complex

Simplistic

Complex

The complex made extraordinarily clear by being magnificently simple

1. Strive always for this

2. Visually, this requires a progression of thought from "left to right": simplistic to complex to magnificently simple.

3. The effort, and perhaps "sacrificial giving up" of some content to move from complex to magnificently simple is often immense, and can often appear to be too much work or effort. It rarely is!

STRIVE FOR MAGNIFICENT SIMPLICITY.

KEEP THINGS MAGNIFICENTLY SIMPLE

Picture yourself sitting in a presentation looking at overheads, and there are many overheads (too many to remember!) each full of figures. One single acetate has perhaps twenty rows and thirty columns each filled with small intricate multi-decimal point numbers. The presentation goes on, and on, and on. This presentation is really complex!

Or imagine sitting in a presentation in which the speaker states all the current business issues could be addressed by simply moving from three operational centers to one; and given adequate authority, the presenter could make it happen. This is really simplistic!

The challenge in management is to keep things magnificently simple, *but on the other side* of complex.

It is simplistic to say that employee problems can be rectified with a few appropriate words. To avoid that simplicity one could move to the far more complex; including charts, graphs, assessments, evaluations, course work, probationary periods, letters, and meetings. Put together, we've moved from the simplistic to the really unnecessarily complex. We need to move one step further on to the magnificently simple *that follows* the complex.

In this third phase – the magnificently simple – the principles espoused in the really complex solution need not be lost, but much of the detail can either be discarded or repackaged to appear at a later date. The employee problem does perhaps need some face-to-face discussion and documentation, followed by appropriate training and monitoring, but it need not include all the complexity that had originally been presented. Some of that complexity may show up as detail or sub-points at a later date, but it certainly need not be included at this point in time.

"We need to think
of moving from the
simplistic through the
complex to the
magnificently simple
at the other end."

KEEP THINGS MAGNIFICENTLY SIMPLE

It is *far more difficult to move to the simple after the complex* because this requires a great knowledge of the subject, a great knowledge of the people who will be dealing with the subject, and a high degree of commitment to ensuring that the material is actually something which will be understood and used on a regular basis by others.

An easy way to grasp this truth shows up in the world of presentations. A superficial treatment of a subject (the simplistic) will be of little use to the listeners; too many points covered in too much detail (the really complex) gets in the way of the listeners' understanding of the key messages and what action is required. Boiling the presentation down to a few key, truly salient points, and then presenting those points with adequate illustrations and examples to ensure clarity moves it to the magnificently simple. The need for the material is still there, the content is still there, the understanding is there, but because of the simple manner in which it is presented everyone listening understands it, and can go away and take action the next day.

We need to think of moving from the simplistic *through* the complex to the magnificently simple. The detail need not be lost, but rather moved to its appropriate position, to show up at the appropriate time.

It was once said "I'm sorry this letter is so long, I didn't have time to write a short one" which sums this principle up beautifully. It takes considerable time and energy to rework all those distribution slides to weed out the unimportant, keep the truly critical and then repackage it in a way that makes it easy to understand and appropriate to the audience; but once done it becomes an effective, meaningful event. The time invested is well worth it, and is a mark of personal excellence.

EXCELLENT COMMUNICATION REQUIRES PATIENCE

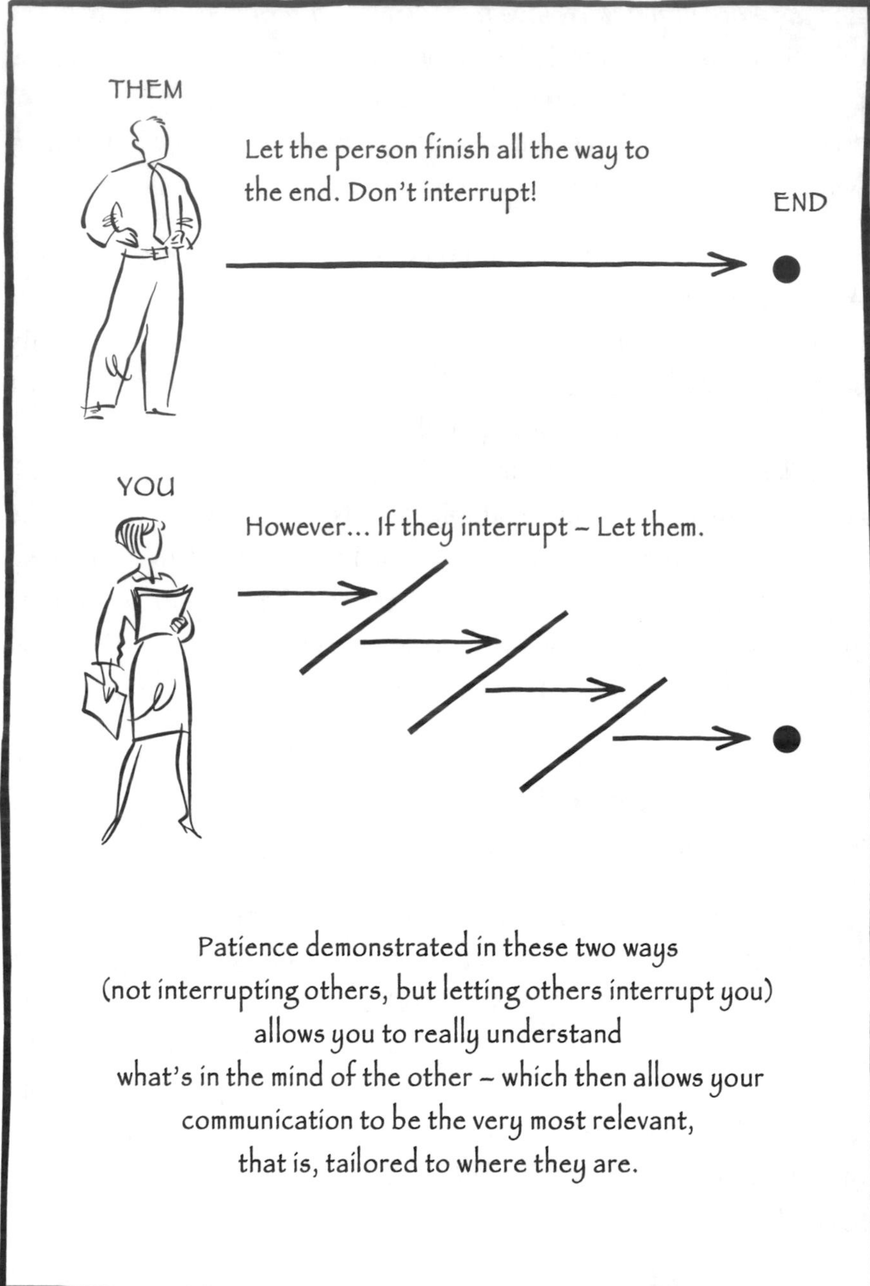

THEM
Let the person finish all the way to the end. Don't interrupt!
END
YOU
However... If they interrupt – Let them.

Patience demonstrated in these two ways
(not interrupting others, but letting others interrupt you)
allows you to really understand
what's in the mind of the other – which then allows your
communication to be the very most relevant,
that is, tailored to where they are.

EXCELLENT COMMUNICATION REQUIRES PATIENCE

To really be a master communicator you need two things:

1. The ability to listen.

2. The ability to send your message right to the person's heart when you speak.

These two skills are very closely linked. If you have the ability to let the person finish speaking through until they are done, without interrupting, then you will be able to understand more clearly what's on their mind and why they feel the way they do.

When you interrupt you cause them to change direction, and then respond to what you said rather then finish what it was they were about to say. The better you understand what they were thinking, the better you are able to respond to them where they are.

Alternatively, when you're speaking and they interrupt, let them! This gives you additional information as to where they are coming from, and what's really important to them. This is difficult when we want to finish what we are saying, but if *effectiveness* is your objective then it is more effective to let them interrupt than to finish what you have to say. What they're really thinking about is what they're going to say when you're done anyway!

As we grow to appreciate the importance of really *effective* communication, rather than simply the sense of relief we feel when we've said what we want to say, even if it's not been heard as well as we would like, then we should be willing to be patient.

This patience when listening, or patience when being interrupted, pays big dividends if you are then able to better understand your listener and tailor your message accordingly.

Always listen for the central theme or pillar.
There will always be one or more.
Everything else either supports that central theme,
rests on it, or is peripheral.

Don't be sidetracked by the periphery.

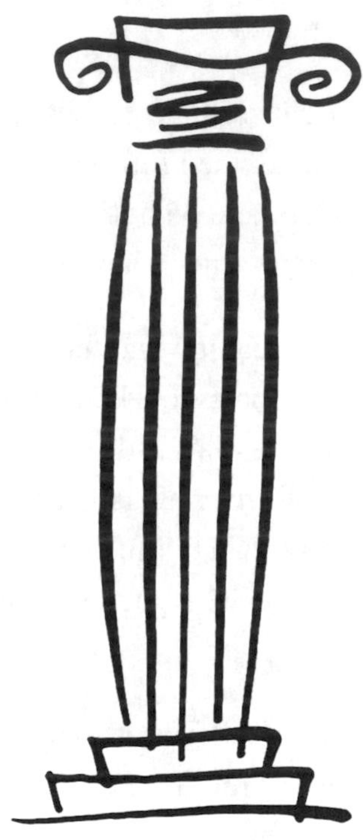

FOCUS YOUR ATTENTION ON THE PILLAR.

LISTENING WELL: LISTEN FOR THE PILLAR

Those who listen attentively when others speak give the impression that they care about the speaker, which is vital since we all want to be treated as important, worthwhile individuals. When you meet someone who really makes an effort to understand what you're saying, and pays close attention while you're talking, you feel good; you make an effort to be complete and thorough in what you say, and you instinctively give, rather than withhold. This makes for great communications.

Those who listen well are clearly held in esteem by others, but they are also more knowledgeable, and appear to have greater insight into issues and situations. They are considered to be successful and approachable.

For many, listening is a very hard thing to do, but the impact of listening well is tremendous. Listening demonstrates respect for others and so earns the good listener the admiration of the speaker. The good listener is perceived to be a great leader, or a fine person, or a sensitive individual, which in turn enhances personal credibility.

Knowledge is power. Since good listeners gain more knowledge, they also end up with a greater ability to influence, or make better decisions, based on more information.

When listening, listen for the main reason the person has for speaking. There is always a central thought, some underlying motivation or theme which the individual is trying to communicate, and everything else rests on that central thought. In order to accomplish this they will use many words, examples or embellishments; but ultimately they are trying to get across one key thought.

A good listener should be able to identify this "pillar", i.e. "What is the person really trying to say?" A person who listens well will try to identify each individual thought, so that they are able to separate the detail from the key thought.

"Knowledge is power.
Since good listeners gain
more knowledge,
they also end up with a greater
ability to influence, or make
better decisions,
based on more information."

LISTENING WELL: LISTEN FOR THE PILLAR

We must identify and then focus on the pillar. If we do this the other things can then be put into perspective. "Many pillars" usually mean many thoughts tied to a central pillar. A change of topic means a new central pillar.

Some pillars are more important than other pillars; i.e. if you were to pull down one of the lesser pillars, the structure would remain. In architecture pillars are often embellished, decorated or disguised. So people will often decorate their "pillar". They will often embellish the central thought. A good listener must be able to distinguish between the embellishment and the pillar even if the degree of decorative work effectively hides the pillar! Remember to look for the pillar, the main thought. The embellishment will then help to better understand the pillar.

There is a church in Salvador, Brazil, that has a great deal of gold inside. It is so overwhelming that when you walk in you are immediately drawn to the gold, so much so that you have to consciously look for pillars, even though they are in plain view.

Similarly, people often decorate their conversation to such a degree that you typically walk away confused, asking, "What did they say?" But the skill of seeing the pillars must be acquired if the benefits of being a great listener are to be realized.

LISTENING WELL:
LISTEN BEYOND THE WORDS, FOR THE MESSAGE

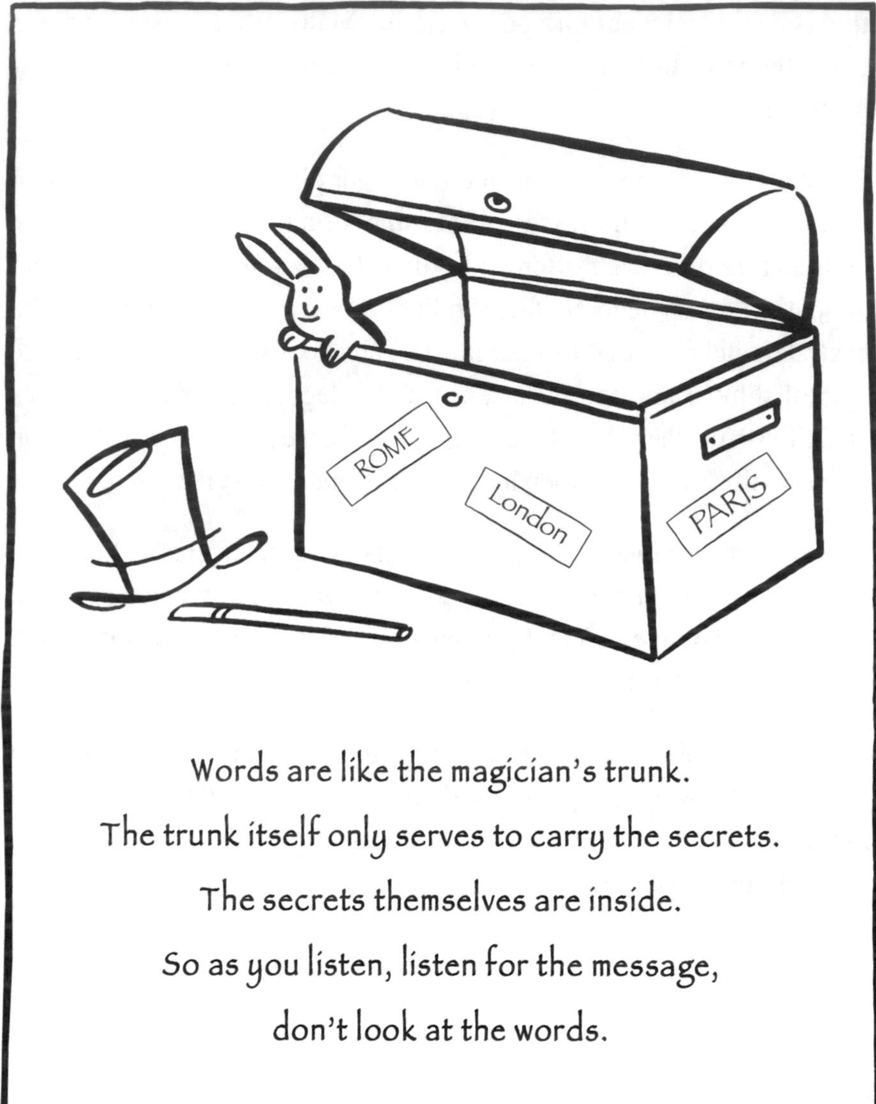

Words are like the magician's trunk.
The trunk itself only serves to carry the secrets.
The secrets themselves are inside.
So as you listen, listen for the message,
don't look at the words.

LISTENING WELL: LISTEN BEYOND THE WORDS, FOR THE MESSAGE

When listening to another person, one often listens only to the words being spoken. This is because the words carry emotion and because they are familiar. The *ideas* which they communicate are often unfamiliar, so that it is sometimes easier to listen first to the words and then think we have the idea.

Further, as we listen to the words, sometimes we make responses based on what we hear in the words. Some words are very emotionally laden and generate strong responses such as "bigot", "unreasonable", and "liar". These words themselves carry so much meaning that it is hard to divorce what is being said from the words themselves.

The words carry a message though, and understanding that message is where the true value comes from. The value comes from the message, not from the words. The need is to fully understand the thinking or motivation *behind* a speaker's words.

In this way words are like a magician's trunk. The trunk carries the secrets. It is true you can see the trunk, analyze it, evaluate it, look at it, and it may generate some emotional response. For example, it might have a label on it from some exotic place which triggers a whole series of ideas. From that you draw a lot of conclusions; but really the secrets, the reason for being, are inside the trunk and are not the trunk itself.

And so when listening, listen not for the "outside" (the words) but for the "inside" (the message).

"Fully understand
the thinking or motivation
behind a
speaker's words."

LISTENING WELL:
LISTEN BEYOND THE WORDS, FOR THE MESSAGE

As an example: my teenage son comes home one day and asks me if he can have a $95 pair of designer jeans. Of course my response to this is, "Absolutely not!" I heard the words and the words told me that my son wants $95 jeans. Like the magic trunk the words carried a message apart from the box. The words though were not the true message; the message was, "Dad, everyone at school has these jeans and if I don't get these jeans then I won't fit in and that would be very difficult, because peer pressure is everything!" The words and the message, were very different!

This can also apply to the work place. Individuals will often come with words, and we deal with the words in and of themselves, because they do have weight. Often though we do not see or understand the true message, which may be totally different from the words. The value is in the message!

LISTENING WELL: LISTEN TO UNDERSTAND, NOT JUST TO BE ABLE TO REPEAT

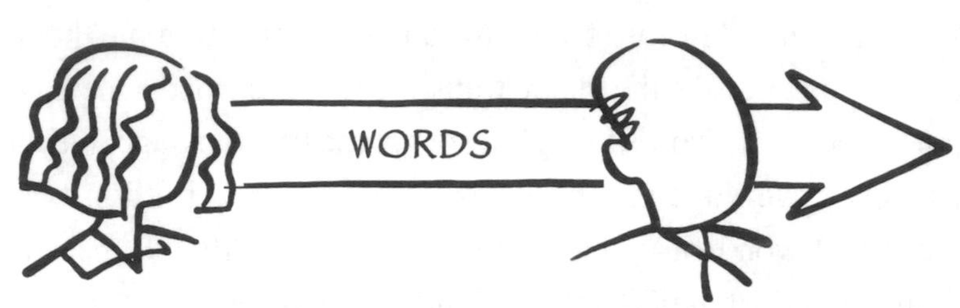

Simply to hear what is said is not to understand what is meant – the words pass right on by.

but ... To understand what is said is truly to have listened.

LISTEN TO UNDERSTAND,

NOT JUST TO HEAR.

LISTENING WELL: LISTEN TO UNDERSTAND, NOT JUST TO BE ABLE TO REPEAT

The Rule of Restatement: Repeat what you just heard *to the speaker's satisfaction*. If you can do that you know you've heard correctly.

Understanding differs from simply hearing and listening; if one truly understands, one could repeat what one just heard, using different words, but conveying the same meaning.

One of the most common comments heard by parents from their children is "You don't understand". What the child is really saying is that their feelings, or their point of view, has not been adopted by the parent. So while the parent has patiently listened to the child speak, perhaps even for 45 minutes, on the issue, the response which the parent then gives leads the child to the conclusion that the parent did not "understand".

Often from the child's point of view understanding can only be demonstrated by agreement. This reinforces the importance of effectively communicating that understanding has occurred, even if, as a result, agreement has not been reached.

Referring to the earlier example of the jeans (on page 109), I may know what the message was that my son was trying to convey, i.e. "If I don't get these jeans I will not be a part of the group." The message may have been clear; but I still may not have understood *why* it was so important for him to have the jeans. I need that understanding as well, to really have mastery of "listening". When listening to another person, one must seek to understand that person's point of view.

LISTENING WELL: LISTEN TO UNDERSTAND, NOT JUST TO BE ABLE TO REPEAT

"If we spend time listening
and we cannot
go away and demonstrate
real understanding,
then we have not
really listened."

LISTENING WELL: LISTEN TO UNDERSTAND, NOT JUST TO BE ABLE TO REPEAT

To best help you understand another person's viewpoint ask yourself "the three whys":

1. Why are they saying this?

2. Why is this important to them?

3. Why do they think I should listen?

To understand is to be able to present the other person's point of view as forcibly as they presented it, but in your own words, even though you may not agree with it. This means divorcing ourselves from hearing the words and concentrating on understanding. If we spend time listening and we cannot go away and demonstrate real understanding, then we have not really listened.

The listener must work hard to really gain understanding by:

1. Probing the speaker for clarification.

2. Asking questions.

3. Making a conscious effort to step inside the speaker's shoes.

4. Playing information back – which is the real test.

Putting our understanding to the test simply means being able to repeat the message back to the individual in our own words (the Rule of Restatement). When we do this often the person will say, "Yes, you have it, but let me just add…" Typically they will then add information to help you better understand, because in their mind you don't understand with the same intensity and the same passion that they do.

A note: Definition of words, alone, without discussion, can often give "instant" understanding. Keep a dictionary handy!

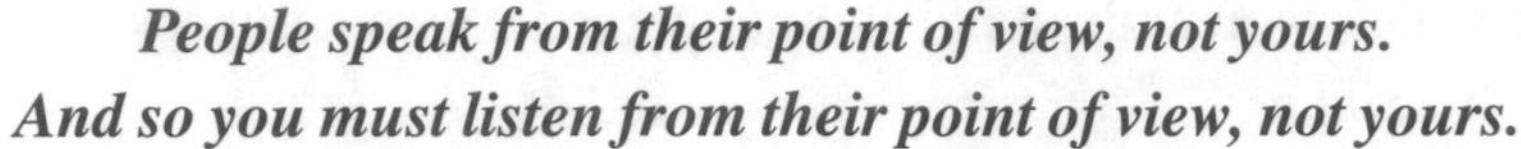

People speak from their point of view, not yours.
And so you must listen from their point of view, not yours.

It is because this is so very hard to do
that most of us feel we are seldom really listened to.

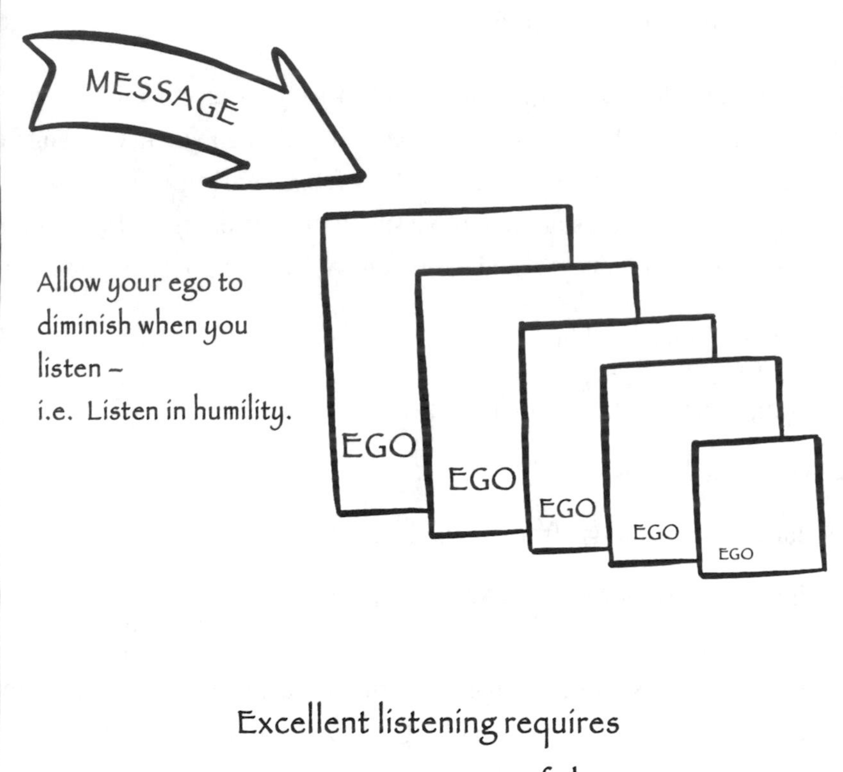

MESSAGE
Allow your ego to diminish when you listen –
i.e. Listen in humility.
EGO
EGO
EGO
EGO
EGO

Excellent listening requires
temporary suppression of the ego!

LISTENING WELL: TEMPORARILY SUPPRESS THE EGO

Listen in humility.

People *speak* from their point of view, not yours, and so you must *listen* from their point of view, not yours. It is because this is so very hard to do that most of us feel we are seldom listencd to.

Think of your mind as a blank blackboard, and imagine yourself saying to the speaker: “I’m here with a blank blackboard for you to write on.” You as the listener must then try not to interrupt, interject bias, or get emotional.

Basically, what you are doing is shutting yourself down in order to let them write whatever they like on this blackboard of your mind. You temporarily suppress your ego, and listen in humility. You listen to the individual whole-heartedly, then when they are done you bring back your ego and form your opinion. In doing this you will be able to speak both from your own experience and the increased knowledge you can now “read” off the blackboard. The hard part is being able to temporarily wipe the blackboard clean at the beginning!

When listening to others, there are a host of things going on within us that inhibit real listening, and make it very difficult to keep from scribbling on the blackboard while the other is talking. (Sometime we scribble so much there’s no room left for the speaker and then we get impatient, periodically tune out, and finally interrupt!)

Some of these forces at work within us are:

1. A little voice within saying, “All my knowledge means I don’t need to listen to this!”

2. Having pre-formed assumptions which are not compatible with an open mind.

"Think of your mind
as a blank blackboard and
imagine yourself
saying to the speaker:
'I'm here with a
blank blackboard for
you to write on.'"

3. We do not like what we hear so we back off and set up a barrier.

4. If we personally do not like the speaker, we tend to mentally run away.

5. Personal prejudice and bias.

6. Our desire to jump in.

7. Our immediate disagreement.

8. Our impatience with the person's presentation skills.

9. Our impatience with the other person's lack of preparation.

10. The "much greater worth" of what we have to say versus their contribution.

11. Our assumed ability to anticipate how they will end up, and therefore jumping ahead in our mind.

12. Lack of respect for others.

We need to recognize these forces and proactively resist them.

Truly good listening requires temporary suppression of the ego, that is – the ability to temporarily withdraw oneself out of the picture. This means being able to hold in abeyance our own pride, our own ego, and our own desires to allow the speaker a clear mind on which they can write whatever they choose. We do not have to agree with what's said, but to be good listeners we should allow them the opportunity to present it fully.

"Those who listen well
are highly esteemed
by those
who do the talking."

Really great listeners do not stop there. When the speaker has finished they probe and ask questions, to see whether there is anything else that could possibly be added to the blackboard.

In short, they allow the person to completely run out of ideas and thoughts before responding, and in this way are absolutely sure they have picked up everything which the speaker has to say on the topic. This is very hard to do because of the discipline we have to exert not to respond just yet. But, as always in life, difficult things are the things which produce the greatest reward. Those who listen well are esteemed most highly by those who do the talking.

Be willing to change, or be changed because of what's heard.

LISTENING WELL: USING INTERRUPTIONS TO MAXIMIZE YOUR COMMUNICATION

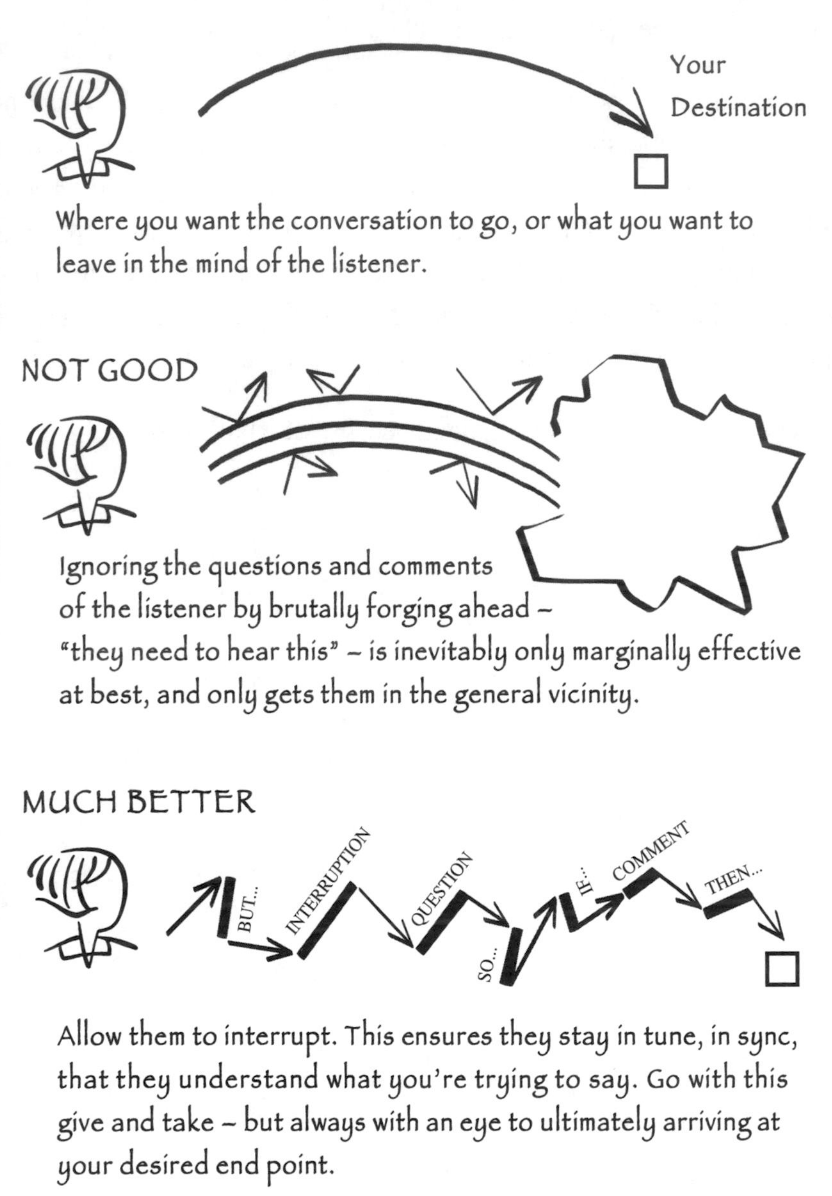

Your Destination
Where you want the conversation to go, or what you want to leave in the mind of the listener.
NOT GOOD
Ignoring the questions and comments of the listener by brutally forging ahead – "they need to hear this" – is inevitably only marginally effective at best, and only gets them in the general vicinity.
MUCH BETTER
BUT...
INTERRUPTION
QUESTION
SO...
IF...
COMMENT
THEN...
Allow them to interrupt. This ensures they stay in tune, in sync, that they understand what you're trying to say. Go with this give and take – but always with an eye to ultimately arriving at your desired end point.

LISTENING WELL: USING INTERRUPTIONS TO MAXIMIZE YOUR COMMUNICATION

As speakers we are often frustrated at being interrupted. We see interruptions as annoying, getting in the way of what we have to say, slowing us down, and generally being unnecessary.

This is not necessarily the case – I'd rather have my listener interrupt me than fall asleep! Someone interrupting is engaged and involved, trying to communicate their point of view.

Consequently, as a speaker I need to learn how to deal with the interruptions. I have two choices:

1. ***Ignore them and forge ahead ruthlessly.*** This is the brute force approach and is probably of little value. It ignores all the input from the listener and assumes that your message is as important to everyone else as it is to you; and that they will lock on and understand what you are saying with the same conviction and passion that you have. In most cases this is an unrealistic perspective.

2. ***Use each interruption to your advantage.*** This is a more effective way. When you begin speaking you must know where you want to end up, that is, have your goal clearly fixed in mind. Then, as you are in conversation, you can always steer from wherever you are to the goal. To do this it is important that your goal is clearly articulated, at least in your own mind, before you begin. In short, you *must* be able to answer the question "When I am done, what do I want this person to know?"

"Someone interrupting
is engaged
and involved."

Once that goal is clearly in your mind you can then be patient as you set off on the journey of communication. With every interruption you gain a little insight as to where your listeners are coming from, and can use their comments as one more stepping stone to your final goal, by linking what they have just said to the path you are forging towards your objective.

By listening carefully to each comment by your listener, and responding to that comment as you move towards your goal, you help the listener walk the path *with* you, rather than forcing the listener to stand aside and watch you run to your objective. *It is far more effective if you can bring the listener step by step along a path you jointly create towards your goal.* This requires that you use each interruption to your advantage, and see them as a way to mentally stay connected with your listener on the journey to your destination.

is like

Fire – it burns hot,
and is often destructive.

is like

A summer day –
warm and inviting.

As you practice thinking and expressing yourself with analogies, they become easier to use.

WORK AT IT.

ANALOGIES: THE ULTIMATE IN COMMUNICATION EFFECTIVENESS

An analogy is a word picture – usually simple – which captures and describes a set of circumstances – usually complex. Its power lies in the fact that it takes the complex and hard to understand, and makes it more easily comprehensible, usually also making it much clearer in the process.

As such, analogies are powerful tools which can be used to help you explain things to others, and also help you better understand what others are trying to tell you (by you putting their thoughts into an analogy and playing it back to them). Analogies are common in everyday life; but mastery of their use is not.

Some examples are: notes are an analogy for music; math symbols are an analogy for ideas; sports is an analogy for corporate business; and temperature is an analogy for emotion (e. g. white hot anger, ice cold hate).

As you practice thinking and expressing yourself in this fashion, analogies become easier to use.

We use analogies all the time and don't really recognize it; for example, "That's like comparing apples to oranges", "dig deep" (referring to personal effort); and "deep waters" (in challenging times), etc. The problem is that we don't use them frequently enough; yet they are a tremendously powerful communication tool.

Analogies act as a bridge to understanding.

"An analogy provides you with understanding, rather than just information."

For example, if my young son comes home and says, "Dad, I want to be a fireman", what does this mean? – "I want to be a fireman." So I ask my son, "How badly do you want to be a fireman? Do you want it as badly as the airplane model that you wanted all last year?" He replies, "No... I want it as badly as I want an ice cream cone now!" I as the father now have a better understanding of what my son means. I now know better how badly he wants to be a fireman. The analogy has helped match my understanding to his.

An analogy is a picture, which makes something clear that otherwise was not clear in the first place. It provides you with *understanding*, rather than just information.

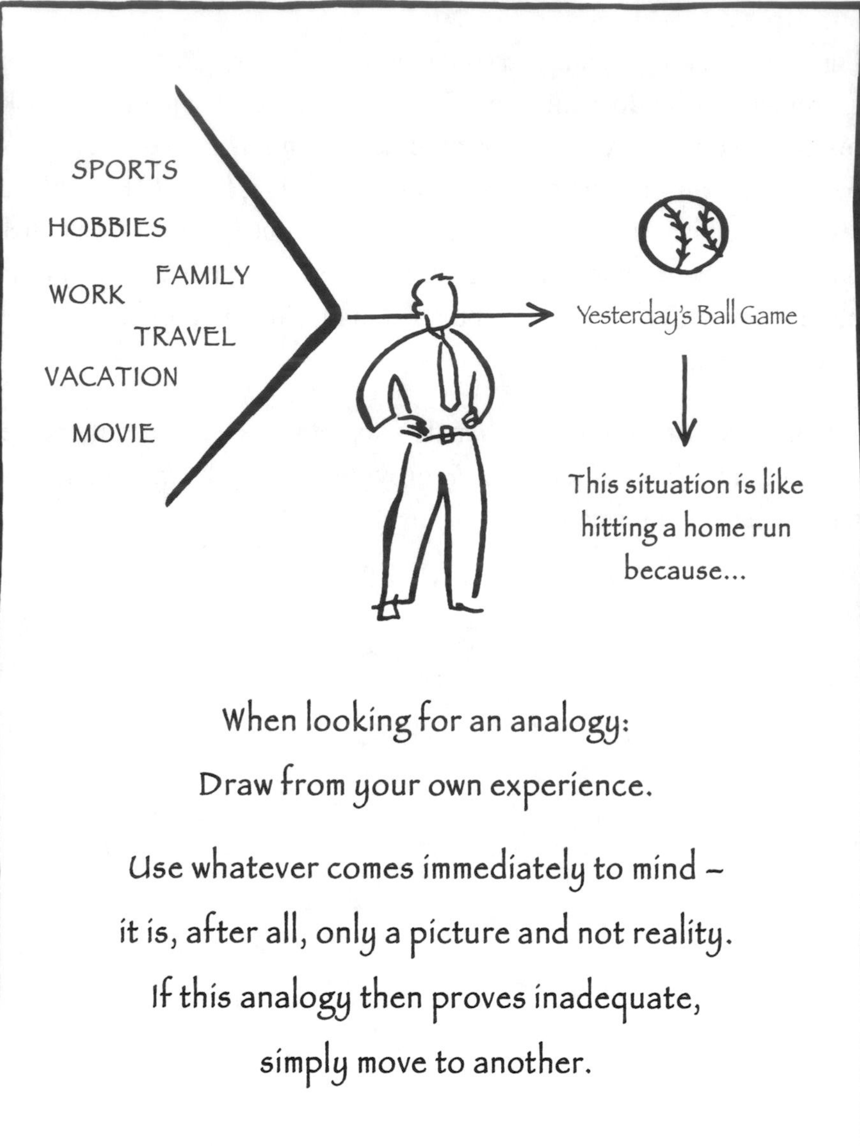
SPORTS
HOBBIES
FAMILY
WORK
TRAVEL
VACATION
MOVIE
Yesterday's Ball Game
This situation is like hitting a home run because...
When looking for an analogy:
Draw from your own experience.
Use whatever comes immediately to mind –
it is, after all, only a picture and not reality.
If this analogy then proves inadequate,
simply move to another.

ANALOGIES: USE WHAT YOU KNOW

When looking for an analogy, draw from your own experience. There is no “right” one to use, so use any subject, hobby, or experience with which you’re familiar.

Where possible, use an analogy with which your listener is also familiar. This avoids having to spend quite so much time on the description of the example or situation you’re using for the analogy.

If you find the analogy you’ve chosen is not providing the understanding you’d hoped for, simply move on to another analogy and try again.

Give the listener the complete analogy, with some detail, before explaining how the analogy ties into the point you wish to make.

IT'S LIKE A ....

A well painted word picture. Rich with full, colored, detail.

BECAUSE...

ANALOGIES: PAINT WORD PICTURES

The objective of using analogies is to provide the listener with a word picture, which has been painted in their mind by describing the picture in your own mind.

Think of the five senses (touch, taste, sight, smell, and hearing) and where suitable use them in your description; this will help to paint a more vivid picture in the listener's mind. *Then* explain how the analogy illustrates the point you wish to make.

It's usually necessary to practice using analogies, as they may not come easily at first; but the effort is worth it!

You need to develop a personal conviction that analogies make your thoughts clearer and more effective.

ILLUSTRATIONS = ANALOGIES

Analogies are POWERFUL

ANALOGIES: THE SKILL INCREASES WITH PRACTICE

It is imperative that a conviction is developed about the importance of analogies, as well as an understanding of how to use them. Analogies do not have to be long or complicated – they can be simply a phrase, or a few words usually beginning with: "It's like…" which carries the message. The degree of detail in the analogy depends upon the amount of time available to communicate the point, and the complexity of the issue being explained.

Understanding is often enhanced by giving three or four short analogies, all of which speak to one aspect of the subject.

Use analogies so that the listener can understand your key points, which are usually more crucial than remembering all the specific details.

When listening to another you can often say something like, "If I understand you correctly, it's like..." which throws an analogy back to the listener on the subject which they just presented to you. In this way you are able to determine whether or not you truly understand what you have heard. If you provide an analogy that the other person agrees reflects what they were trying to say to you, then both of you leave with the conviction that what was heard is what was intended to be heard.

The mind stores best in pictures, not in words. Analogies paint those pictures.

BEYOND TIME MANAGEMENT

SETTING PRIORITIES – KEY CRITERIA

How crucial is it that this task be done soon (immediately, now, etc)?

If very crucial
move up the priority list.

How high a priority is this in opinion of leadership?

The opinions of leadership
(authority) should
carry very significant weight.

How long will it take to complete this task?

Time to completion should be
considered. A short task
can often be moved up the list.
Similarly, a long task may
need to be delayed, or broken into
several smaller tasks, over time;
each of which is now short,
so can more easily move up.

Once this task is done, what will be the impact?
Will it be great, very significant?
Conversely, if the task is not done, or delayed, what will be the consequences?
How severe will they be?

Determine the priority by its
impact once completed.
Work to make a difference.
Items of little consequence should
move down the priority list.

SETTING PRIORITIES – KEY CRITERIA

Setting priorities is one of the most effective ways to manage time and people. The most effective use of one's resources is to ensure that they are focused on the items of the highest priority. This leads to the challenge of knowing what items should be where on the priority list. In order to create an effective priority list four criteria need to be considered:

1. ***Urgency:*** Urgency is distinct from importance in that *urgent* things require an immediate response. *Important* things do not usually carry with them the same need for the immediate response that urgent things do.

   In determining where an item should fit on the priority list consider the degree of urgency for its completion. If there is a critical need for the task to be completed immediately – that is, it is truly urgent – then it should move high on the priority list.

   This raises a second question as to who is determining that the task is urgent. Sometimes one individual or a team's urgent need is considered less so by another group or individual. Before automatically placing urgent requests high on the priority list it is worthwhile to ask, "What will occur once I complete it?" This is a simple way for you to check whether or not it is indeed urgent, and therefore by when it must be completed.

   Frequently asking this question results in some very interesting responses, varying from: "The world will fall apart (metaphorically speaking)", to "I don't really know, someone just said they needed it now". Clearly in the first instance it can remain an urgent priority; but in the second instance some further probing should be done to determine what will happen once it's completed, and therefore the degree of urgency.

"The requests
of a leader
should always be a
high priority."

Do not automatically assume something is urgent simply because you've been told it is; probe to determine the outcome of the completed task and *thereby* determine its urgency.

2. ***Authority:*** The requests of those in authority should carry significant weight, and so be a major consideration when establishing priorities. The requests of a leader should always be a high priority.

   A truly world-class leader is aware that their requests will immediately go high on the priority list, and so *in advance* carefully evaluates the consequences of making that request, asking about the impact on the other priorities that will perhaps then be pushed lower. Leaders who simply use their authority to get their work done without reference to the priorities of others are missing the opportunity to manage productivity for the greatest possible outcome.

   Those in authority often see a larger view of a situation than those responsible for executing instructions; and so leaders will often establish priorities or make requests which, from the recipient's perspective, may not be felt to be important, but which from a leader's perspective are crucial. The reason for the authority which is invested in leaders is in order to enable them to determine what is most important, and ensure that it takes precedence over lesser priorities. It helps greatly when they pass on the rationale for their requests to those charged with executing the tasks, especially when those requests are going to significantly alter the priorities of others.

"Rather than simply focusing
on completing tasks,
or "getting the work done",
an analysis of the impact
once the job is completed
can help:
the greater the impact
the higher the priority."

Individuals receiving instructions from those in authority should not necessarily follow blindly, but rather should provide input and counsel when they believe that their perspective on the situation is of value and may not have been considered by the leader. Their opinion is important if they feel their thoughts might have some bearing on where the task should net out on the priority list (higher or lower).

This idea of authority carrying weight and moving things up the priority list is a difficult one because, from one perspective, it could be followed blindly. Sometimes this is necessary, but much more often the input from those charged with fulfilling a task can be of significant value and should be considered. Sometimes the leader will indicate a request is urgent simply because they know its importance and require it immediately; other times input from followers can be of great value and serve to adjust the level of urgency of the request.

One particular note, leaders do not always add the "due date" to their requests! Those receiving the requests then automatically assume that it has to be "done immediately" and give it a higher priority than may be intended. Simply asking the leader when the work is required may also help to determine where it should sit on the priority list, if the leader does not voluntarily provide that information.

"The most effective use
of one's resources
is to ensure that they are
focused on the items
of the highest priority."

3. ***Time Required:*** Sometimes tasks can be accomplished in very short order with many beneficial side effects: you feel good for getting the job done; others get their requests satisfied more quickly; a long list of "to do's" is eliminated; and a lot of miscellaneous things can be quickly eliminated, saving time, mental energy, or resources for more major work.

   In these cases short tasks can jump up the list to receive a higher priority than they are perhaps entitled to on the basis of their own merit. One danger with this approach is that short tasks are sometimes the fun ones to do, or the easy ones to do, but not really the important ones, so be careful using this criterion – don't follow it without thinking!

   On the other hand there are many instances when a task is going to take a long time to complete, and getting an early start on it is important. In that case it should also move up the priority list, even though it may not be immediately required. One mechanism for dealing with these situations is to attempt to break the larger task into as many smaller pieces as possible. This gives you many more things to prioritize, which may make it easier to set the priorities on any given day, and make it easier to choose which portions of the larger project will be tackled first.

"Leaders who simply use their authority to get their work done, without reference to the priorities of others, are missing the opportunity to manage productivity for the greatest possible outcome."

4. ***Impact or Consequence:*** Rather than simply focusing on completing tasks, or "getting the work done", an analysis of the *impact* once the job is completed can help greatly; the greater the impact the higher the priority. There are times when determining the impact is very difficult, for example when the individual is a part of a much larger process chain. However, even in this case individuals should attempt to gain some understanding of the impact, even if it's only *relative* to other activities.

   When an individual is able to establish the anticipated consequences of each of the activities on their list, and then focus on the ones which are judged to have the greatest possible impact or consequence, then the time will be maximally spent.

Setting priorities is often a difficult task as it requires judgement. However, judgement is easier when one understands the factors which must be weighed up. Urgency, authority, time required and the anticipated impact must all come together in the mind of the individual setting the priorities. Each activity needs to be evaluated with these four criteria in mind to determine the sequence in which the tasks should be ordered, and then the focus given to the most important one first.

MATCHING PRIORITIES TO TIME AVAILABLE

Since there's limited time, all these pressures need to be pushed through the criteria of Setting Priorities on page 136; and then a best judgement applied to sort the requirements such that they fit the time available.

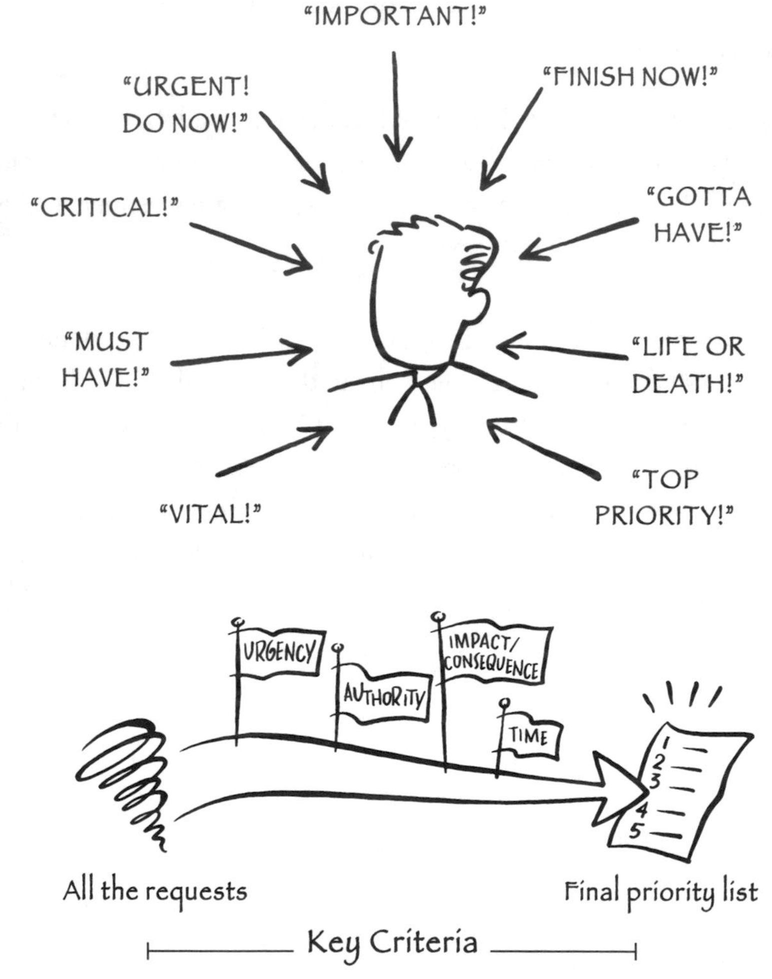

MATCHING PRIORITIES TO TIME AVAILABLE

It's important to acknowledge that there is limited time available for any particular task or activity. It is artificial to assume that you can simply load down yourself, or someone else, with work in the hopes that it will "somehow get done". There are only a limited number of hours in the day and each hour spent working must be appropriately planned to generate the maximum possible output.

At the beginning of each day, or business cycle, or project initiative, depending on how your work is arranged, there needs to be a great deal of thought given to the establishing of the order, or sequence, in which the work will be done, bearing in mind the need to do the most important things first. This is the process of setting priorities and ensures that at the end of the day you've made the greatest possible contribution.

Since we all seem to have work coming to us from various sources – customers, leaders, the priorities of others, our own initiative, etc – then we must have some way of ordering this work. The way to do so is to push each of these requests through the four filters outlined in Section III, Setting Priorities - Key Criteria on page 136.

By reviewing each item against the degree of urgency for the request, the rank of the person making the request, the time it will take to complete it, and the impact or consequence it will have, you have created the best possible set of screens for sorting the requests and putting them into the most appropriate order.

This order becomes the priority list numbered from the most important to the least important, and then serves as the template for action. Start with the most important, and work through to the least important.

"Set aside time
to periodically review
all requests, and to
re-juggle your priorities."

In the real world additional requests are also constantly coming in. The best approach in these circumstances is to set aside time to periodically review all the requests, and re-juggle your priorities. In practice, this means taking your existing ordered list, reviewing the recent requests that weren't considered when you made it, and re-ordering your priorities. The only thing to bear in mind here is that you ensure that you do this re-ordering at the *completion* of a given task, *not in the middle of one*. There are only a very few set of circumstances (e.g. a true crisis) when the time is not available to complete the task that you are currently working on, or at least a reasonable portion of it, before re-ordering your priorities.

The rigorous application of these principles, that is the sorting of priorities against these four criteria, is the best way to ensure that your time is being maximally productive.

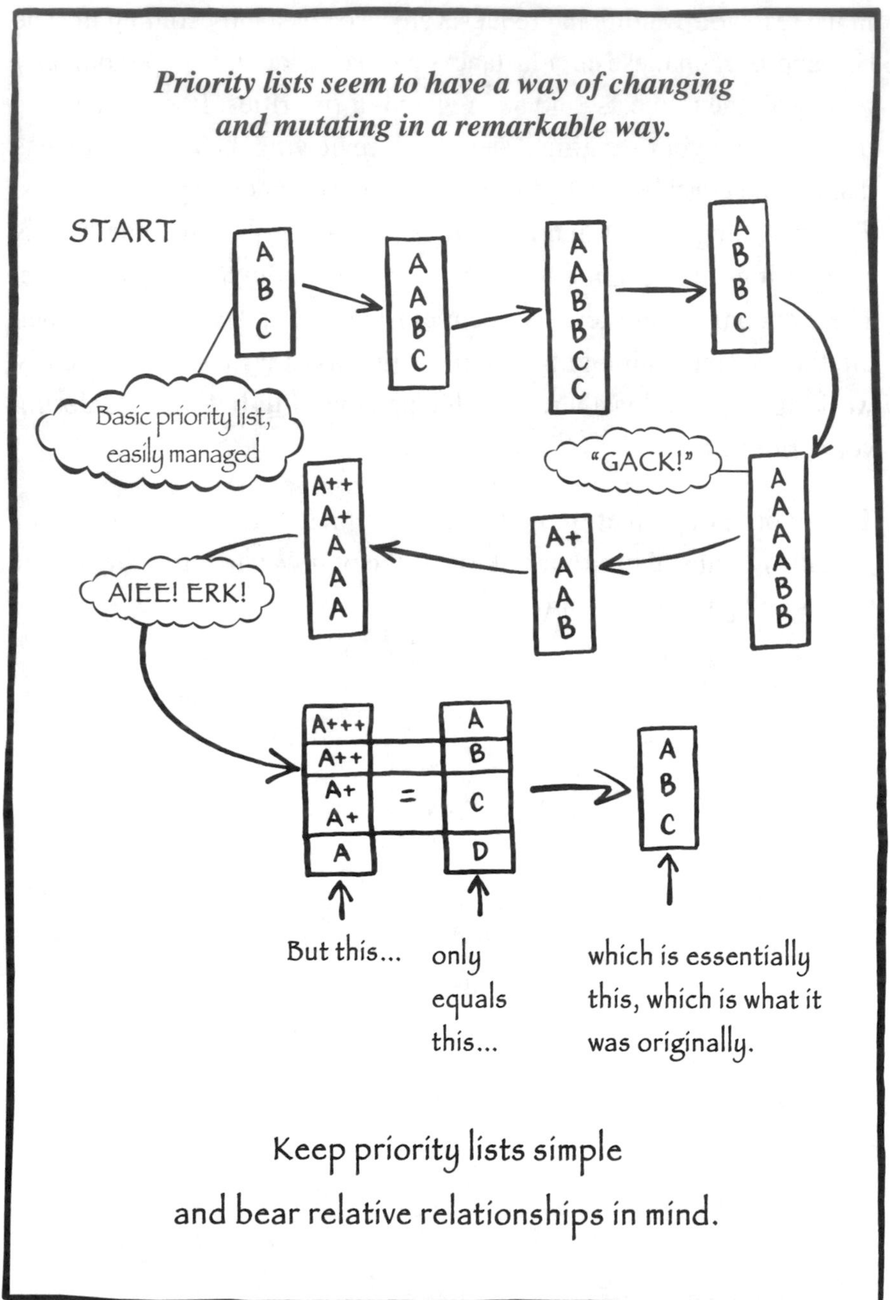

Priority lists seem to have a way of changing and mutating in a remarkable way.
START
A B C
A A B C
A A B B C C
A B B C
Basic priority list, easily managed
"GACK!"
A A A A B B
A+ A A B
A++ A+ A A A
AIEE! ERK!
A+++ A++ A+ A+ A
=
A B C D
A B C
But this...
only equals this...
which is essentially this, which is what it was originally.
Keep priority lists simple and bear relative relationships in mind.

RESPONDING TO CHANGING PRIORITIES

One of the most distressing things about priority lists is they seem to grow and mutate every moment. You no sooner get a nice neat list buttoned down and settle down to do it when the phone rings, some piece of paper is handed to you, the customer calls, your boss comes rushing in, or some other unforeseen event interrupts your day. Inevitably this seems to happen even before you get started on the first item. How often have you lifted up your head after missing lunch realizing that the things you had intended to do that day haven't even been started and you spent all your time on other things!

This is because priorities tend to change constantly, and new work flows in at an alarming rate. How to handle this?

The first thing to do is to realize that priority lists must be in constant flux. The list that you have at any given time is only valid until something new comes on your desk which requires you to reexamine the entire list. If you think of yourself as having three items set into a simple priority of A, B, and C and then something else enters in, you immediately add it to the list. This results in lists that could stretch from A to Z!

In addition, new items may be more important than the ones you already have; and so you have to add to the top of the list as well as the bottom. You now have A +, A++, and A+++ priorities!

Rather than letting this constant addition above and below the existing list be a worry, recognize that all priority lists have A's, B's, and C's. Your original A, B, and C no longer exist. The A+++ has become your "A", the A++ has become your "B", and A+ has become your "C". Everything else is lower than that. While this may be frustrating because you really had your mind set on completing your original list, you need to remain flexible and recognize that your priorities *will* change.

"If you're able to identify
the most important thing
at any given point in time
and focus on that,
persevering through to
completion, then
your efficiency will be at
its maximum."

RESPONDING TO CHANGING PRIORITIES

In order to establish some peace of mind simply keep juggling so that you know what is the most important, what is next, and what follows that. If they stay in place long enough to accomplish them in that order, great. If not then re-juggle and remain focused on the most important priority.

Two particular bits of advice in this area:

1. ***Persevere:*** As much as possible try not to juggle items on the priority list until the item you are currently working on is completed. If it is a large item break it into smaller pieces and at least ensure that you have completed one piece before juggling your priorities and leaving some items unfinished.

2. ***Plan for change:*** One thing which I've done successfully is keep *uncommitted time* as a priority. For example, I leave an hour every morning free with nothing scheduled in it, and no plans for it. If at the beginning of the day, or at the tail end of the previous day, some urgent need requires my immediate attention then I've already got the time set aside for it (that one unplanned hour at the beginning of each day) which I then can allocate to this unforeseen task, without putting at risk all my other priorities.

   If nothing surfaces requiring that unscheduled hour, then I simply use it to get ahead of my priorities and begin with the first priority of the day in that hour.

The real secret in managing priorities is to keep the list simple and clear and not get frustrated with, or flustered by, constant change. If you're able to identify the most important thing at any given point in time and focus on that, persevering through to the completion, then your efficiency will be at its maximum.

THE LINK BETWEEN "PRIORITY SETTING" AND "JUDGEMENT"

There is usually no "right" answer – only alternatives. Consequently for each of these priority setting activities, it's important to realize that: sound effective judgement is a prerequisite.

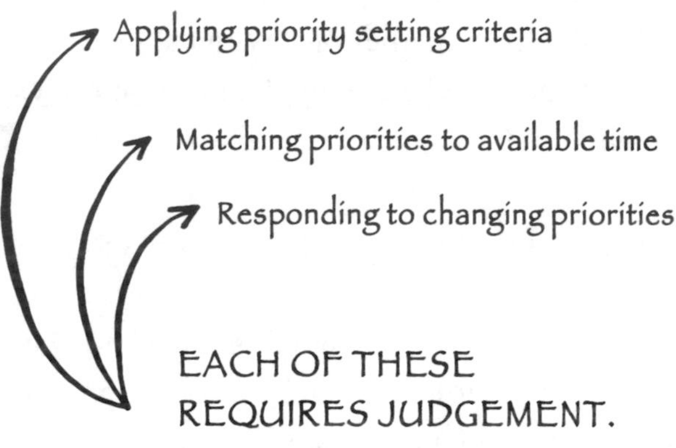

Applying priority setting criteria
Matching priorities to available time
Responding to changing priorities
EACH OF THESE REQUIRES JUDGEMENT.

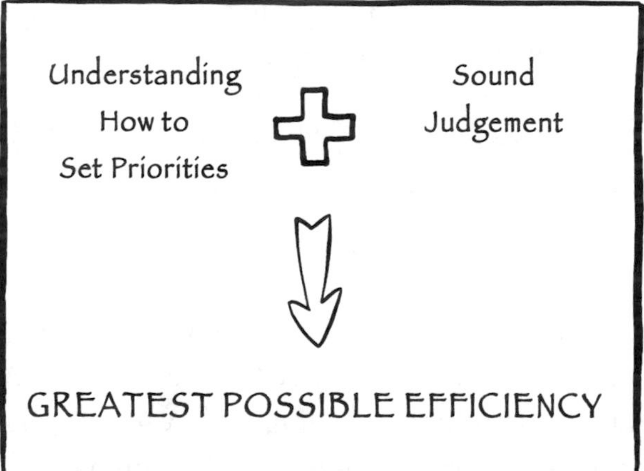

THE LINK BETWEEN "PRIORITY SETTING" AND "JUDGEMENT"

I was once given the point of view that a critical quality in any individual in business is "judgement." This is very interesting, and an insight which I've come to value.

(As an aside, I would personally not place it as the most important quality. Rather, I would place a higher value on personal integrity and the ability to learn. With these two qualities at the core a great deal is possible. But once they are in place the quality of judgement would then certainly be high on my list.)

In the whole task of setting priorities the issue of judgement is constantly surfacing. You are given the priority criteria (Section III, Setting Priorities – Key Criteria, page 136), and the knowledge that you have to match these to the available time (Section III, Matching Priorities to Time Available, page 146). This is further compounded by the need to respond to constantly changing priorities (Section III, Responding to Changing Priorities, page 150).

Each of these three steps requires judgement: judgement to be able to determine the degree to which each criterion affects the outcome; judgement in terms of the ability to match the priorities to the time available; and judgement in terms of reordering the priorities given new input. Your personal judgement clearly plays a very key role in the establishment of priorities!

"Judgement is
the compilation of
experience, wisdom,
insight, and the
counsel of others."

THE LINK BETWEEN "PRIORITY SETTING" AND "JUDGEMENT"

Judgement is an interesting thing in that there is no right answer. Judgement is, by definition, the point of view of the individual making the judgement. It is the compilation of experience, wisdom, insight, and the counsel of others. Over time one's judgement should improve with experience as we learn what works well and what doesn't. There are ways to ensure that one's judgement is the best possible (in the pages following), but initially the most crucial step is to recognize the value and the importance of sound judgement.

In other words do not be guided by "spur of the moment" thinking, the pressure of others' opinions, or simply the desire to "cast caution to the winds and just get on with it". Rather, rigorously discipline yourself to apply judgement. It doesn't take long, but it pays huge dividends as it ensures that you are bringing the greatest capabilities to the forefront in an effort to maximize your personal efficiency and effectiveness. As a result, your time will be as well spent as possible and the consequences of that time spent will be the greatest they can be.

Understanding how to set priorities, combined with sound judgement, gives you the greatest possible efficiency.

Sound judgement is key to overall success, but it is itself the result of several factors:

1. KNOWLEDGE: Knowing about the subject from many different perspectives.
2. EXPERIENCE: Having "lived through" similar or related situations.
3. COST/BENEFIT ANALYSIS: Fully identifying the "pros" and "cons", the costs and the benefits, in any given situation or circumstance.
4. FORESEEN OUTCOME: The greater the ability to anticipate any given outcome, the more sound will be the judgement.
5. COUNSEL: Advice from respected colleagues, who themselves show sound judgement.

The greater the individual contribution of each of these five, the better the judgement, in any given situation.

vs.

THE ELEMENTS OF SOUND JUDGEMENT

"Sound judgement " is a great asset, and a quality which can influence a number of different activities. When individuals are having to set priorities, make value judgements, assess the performance of others, weigh the pros and cons of different situations, etc. they are in each of these situations faced with the need for sound personal judgement.

The better the individual's judgement, the better will be the decisions which they make, and the impact that those decisions will have on far reaching consequences. Therefore it helps to understand the components of sound judgement so that we can do everything possible to improve our own ability to judge wisely, and with skill.

There are five elements which make up sound judgement:

1. ***Knowledge:*** It is true that "knowledge is power", in that the greater the individual's knowledge, the better they are able to bring that knowledge to bear in the most effective fashion. When the individual is truly knowledgeable on any given topic then they are able to see the many different but related perspectives, and so understand clearly the issues from several different points of view.

   When facing an issue where good judgement is required the greater the knowledge of the subject the better the judgement.

   Knowledge can come from many sources: that which we already have, reading about the topic (preferably from various points of view in order to have a well rounded opinion), the analysis of data, statistics, figures, or results, and observation.

"Sound judgement depends on having sound and comprehensive knowledge."

The expression "a little knowledge is a bad thing" is especially true when applying a criterion of knowledge to judgement. If we have a very little bit of knowledge and we base judgement on that, then we could clearly be significantly off the mark. In as much as we are unaware that our knowledge is limited, or we choose to believe that our knowledge is representative of the total universe, then we have a misguided faith in the judgement that follows.

Knowledge is a broad topic and could extend beyond the issues of simply what we have learned to encompass the area of knowledge of our own self. The better we know ourselves and our own biases and strengths, the more effectively, and objectively we will be able to use the information that we receive.

Never underestimate the value of hard, verifiable knowledge. When making decisions, or seeking to have sound judgement, rely heavily on this particular criteria. For example, in the setting of priorities one criteria is to know the degree of urgency of each item. If we guess at the urgency, clearly that is far less effective than meeting with the individual who made the request and having a short dialogue to truly understand what will happen once that item is completed. Armed with this much greater knowledge it is then far easier to place that item in the proper priority sequence.

Another example comes when we assess other individuals. If we see only a few minutes of a person in a presentation, and base our entire opinion of them on the way in which they made a ten minute briefing to a group, then our judgement may be seriously flawed. We may *believe* that our knowledge about this individual is great because of our exceptionally fine ability to judge individuals based on a ten minute presentation.

"As we move to
make sound judgements
we should understand
our own experience base
and place appropriate
weight on it."

In fact, to truly assess that person we need much more knowledge for example, related to their performance in other situations: in one on one environments, with those they lead, when they are "in their own element", etc. Sound judgement depends on having sound and comprehensive knowledge.

2. ***Experience:*** Experience is one of the finest teachers available. A good experience will show us what to replicate; a poor experience tells us what to avoid.

   When we've been in situations where we've had the opportunity to experience something "first hand", for example to be part of large change initiatives, then our judgement with respect to large change initiatives is much sounder than those who have simply read about it. An experienced sailor is one who has spent considerable time on the water and is able to understand the net impact of wind and waves on the vessel. A novice sailor is one who has limited experience on the water. Clearly the more experienced sailor will make better and sounder judgements relative to sailing.

   Experience is one of the few qualities which cannot be rushed or learned at high speed. The learning from experiences can be accelerated if we make a point of seeking out those who have gone before and truly absorbing their learning; but even this lacks the reality of our five senses, and so is limited. It is better than nothing, but really pales in comparison to having "lived through it". As we move to make sound judgements we should understand our own experience base and place appropriate weight on it. We should also place appropriate weight on the opinions of others who have had experience in the areas where we are being asked to pass judgement.

"The ability to foresee the
outcome is perhaps
one of the most effective
criteria when attempting
to make sound judgements."

3. ***Cost Benefit:*** Sound judgement can often be enhanced with the careful review of the pros and cons of any situation. Recently my daughter was faced with a decision regarding how she should spend her summer. It was difficult to make a decision, and even though we brought our best judgement to bear we were still somewhat stumped.

   Knowing the decision had to be made, we sat down together and made a list of the pros and cons of the two options. This allowed us to crystallize the elements we were considering and so facilitated the decision. We were able to determine the cost and the benefits of each of the pros and cons, and from there settle on what we felt was the most appropriate course of action.

   These steps facilitated the decision making process, and allowed us to make a much better decision than we might otherwise have made had we continued to simply discuss our feelings and try to base our actions on that.

   In order to determine the cost/benefit of each of the pros and cons it is also helpful to review relative statistics, or to seek counsel when we feel that our own information in this regard is inadequate.

4. ***Foreseen outcome:*** I personally place a great deal of weight on this particular criterion. While it is true that many of the other criteria can significantly improve one's judgement, the ability to foresee the outcome is perhaps one of the most effective criterion when attempting to make sound decisions.

"Show sound judgement
with regard to
spending time gathering
the information necessary
for sound judgement."

This refers to the ability to predict the outcome of any particular decision which is made. So, for example, if there are four possible decisions which can be made, and each of these four is extrapolated to the most likely outcome, the outcomes can then be assessed and the best one selected. This can then lead back to what decision to make in the present.

Being able to anticipate the future, or at least anticipate the future consequences of an action, is a powerful way of assessing the value of any particular decision.

Time must be spent on this activity as it is not as easily captured as some of the others. Experience, for example, is just sort of "with us"; whereas identifying the foreseen outcome requires some careful thought and analysis before you are able to settle on the most likely outcome. However, once this is done, it adds greatly to the ability to make sound judgements.

5. ***Counsel:*** One should not feel that they are the repository of all wisdom and knowledge in the universe. There are many other sources, ranging from literature in the library, current periodicals, the internet, and television programs, through to respected colleagues or acquaintances in the industry. Each of these sources may provide counsel on a given issue, which will facilitate your own judgement.

   If a manager is faced with a decision as to which of two individuals to promote, that manager could seek out the counsel of the senior Human Resources person who is skilled in the area of the assessment of people. The Human Resources person could provide the manager with their counsel, which provides the manager with yet one more resource as they attempt to make the best possible decision.

"If we choose to
believe that our knowledge
is representative
of the total universe,
then we have a
misguided faith in the
judgement that follows."

> Sound judgement on your part can and should take into account counsel as often as is relevant. Wise counsel can lead to wise judgement.

It may not be possible in any given situation to make full use of each of the above five criteria, however the greater the individual contribution of each of the five the better the judgement will be in any given situation. Wherever possible seek to employ all five to the greatest possible degree.

My father-in-law commended me once for not having "paralysis of the analysis" (when I asked for the hand of his daughter in marriage!). It was an interesting phrase which stuck with me. It is the offset to the comments about weighing options. You don't want to spend so much time gathering information that you never make a decision. That would be great folly.

Rather, understand the value of each criterion, use them to the full, but use them with dispatch, i.e. quickly. Gather what information you need, and talk to those that you need to talk to. Move quickly to determine which of these criteria will be relevant in any given situation, review the data, analyze it, and then apply your best judgement to the decision.

These steps must occur quickly and with expedience; however, not so quickly as to result in poor judgement which can be very costly; and usually results in having to re-visit the entire situation.

Show sound judgement concerning how to spend time gathering the information necessary for sound judgement.

MAXIMIZING ACCOMPLISHMENT: THE GOOD IS THE ENEMY OF THE BEST

Many things clamor for your time and attention. Most are pressing. While all need to be done, some need to be done sooner than others. Which ones are they?

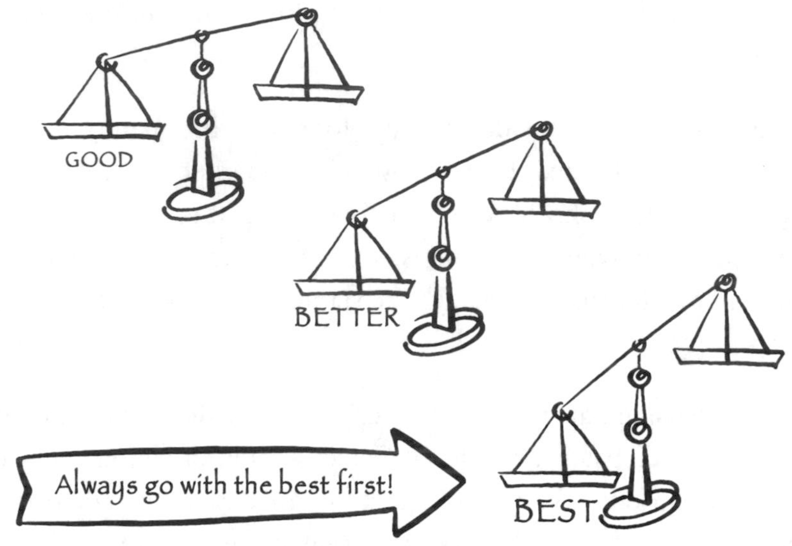
GOOD
BETTER
BEST
Always go with the best first!

THE GOOD IS THE ENEMY OF THE BEST

Avoid spending time on good and worthwhile things,
as long as there are better
(albeit maybe tougher) things to be done.
If the good keeps you from the best –
it is in opposition to you!

MAXIMIZING ACCOMPLISHMENT: THE GOOD IS THE ENEMY OF THE BEST

The objective is to maximize value, not work. That is: although time spent generates work, the *true* objective is the *impact*, or *value*, of that work.

To maximize accomplishment we need to maximize value.

Ask yourself: For the time I spend what is the value? How much do I accomplish? This is important because if you are able to achieve a higher *value* from your work, then you don't always need to spend more time to accomplish more. In other words, if you are able to get more value for the time spent, then you will be more effective.

Always go with the *best*. The good is the enemy of the best. For example: in raising children good behavior may be watching television with them; best behavior may be going out to play baseball and forgetting about television altogether.

Be cautious – simply "adding on" does not necessarily yield "best". *More* is not what's usually required. Rather an *exchange of behavior* (from good to best) is what's needed.

A lot of things often clamor for our time and attention, and as a result we make an evaluation concerning these things, and are then usually clear on the things *not* to do. The problem is that we often don't also rule out good things as things not to do. It is hard to say, "Don't do good things," – they are, after all, good. But often the good is the enemy of the best, as we seek to maximize our accomplishment.

To get as much done as possible concentrate your efforts where they will make the greatest impact in the time allotted – on the best things.

"If you are able to get
more value
for the time spent,
then you will
be more effective."

MAXIMIZING ACCOMPLISHMENT: THE GOOD IS THE ENEMY OF THE BEST

Three Examples:

1. When Raising Children:

GOOD: Telling your child what to do.

BEST: Demonstrating the desired behavior by example.

2. In Staff Management:

GOOD: Giving clear direction.

BEST: Being a coach throughout the task.

3. Use of Time:

GOOD: Responding to every situation.

BEST: Prioritizing by value.

If for some reason you are lured into doing your "C" priorities at the expense of the "A" items, then the "C" things are actually working against you, even though they in themselves are important, and therefore good.

What often happens when you do something that is good is that you stop once it's done. For example, telling your children what to do is clearly not wrong.

In fact, there may be times when you feel that *telling* them what to do is the best thing to do. The problem is that most of the time it is not the best thing to do – *showing* would be better, but having done it ("told") we go no further. We don't even question whether there is in fact a better or best thing to do, because what we are doing is good, and we're getting the job done! But we're not getting it done with maximum value.

"Determining what is best
requires looking at
the total picture.
Best becomes clear when
you look at
the larger view."

MAXIMIZING ACCOMPLISHMENT: THE GOOD IS THE ENEMY OF THE BEST

Unfortunately things that in and of themselves are good, valuable, worthwhile, and meaningful are often also easier, more familiar, can be done with less effort, and have less risk associated with them. In these instances the temptation which these things lay before us is seductive in that we tend to be lured away from doing the other things which are often tougher, more difficult, more time consuming, more challenging and more full of risk; but also often more important, and of higher value.

Any time anything comes between you and an activity which is going to maximize your effort, then it is in fact working against you. It is very difficult to believe that something which may in and of itself be good, can actually be harmful; however it's bad if it keeps you (because of its seductive nature) from doing the most important things first.

The way to increase your effectiveness is to do only the things which are the very best to do at that point in time.

Another example illustrating how the good can be the enemy of the best: imagine you are feeling under tremendous pressure to quickly hire an individual to fill a critical job, and consequently are considering the option of compromising on the qualities of the candidate to get the vacancy filled immediately. The compromise may not be a big one, but it is a compromise.

In the long run, you have decided to go with someone who is good but not the best. In the short term it may fill the vacancy, but in the long term you do not have the benefits of that extra effort, that extra enthusiasm or that extra capability which the best candidate would have brought, had you waited longer and kept looking.

"The way to increase
your effectiveness
is to do only the things
which are the
very best to do at that
point in time."

The good candidate has blocked that vision. How seductive the good can be! It literally will lure us from doing those things that are best.

Determining what is best requires looking at the total picture.

Context clarifies whether a particular thing is the best, or, seen in the total picture, is only good. Best becomes clear when you look at the big picture, as "best" within a narrow context is very hard to define. It is only when you are able to consider the larger view, that is, all the elements, that clarity is achieved.

MAXIMIZING ACCOMPLISHMENT: MAJOR ON THE MAJORS

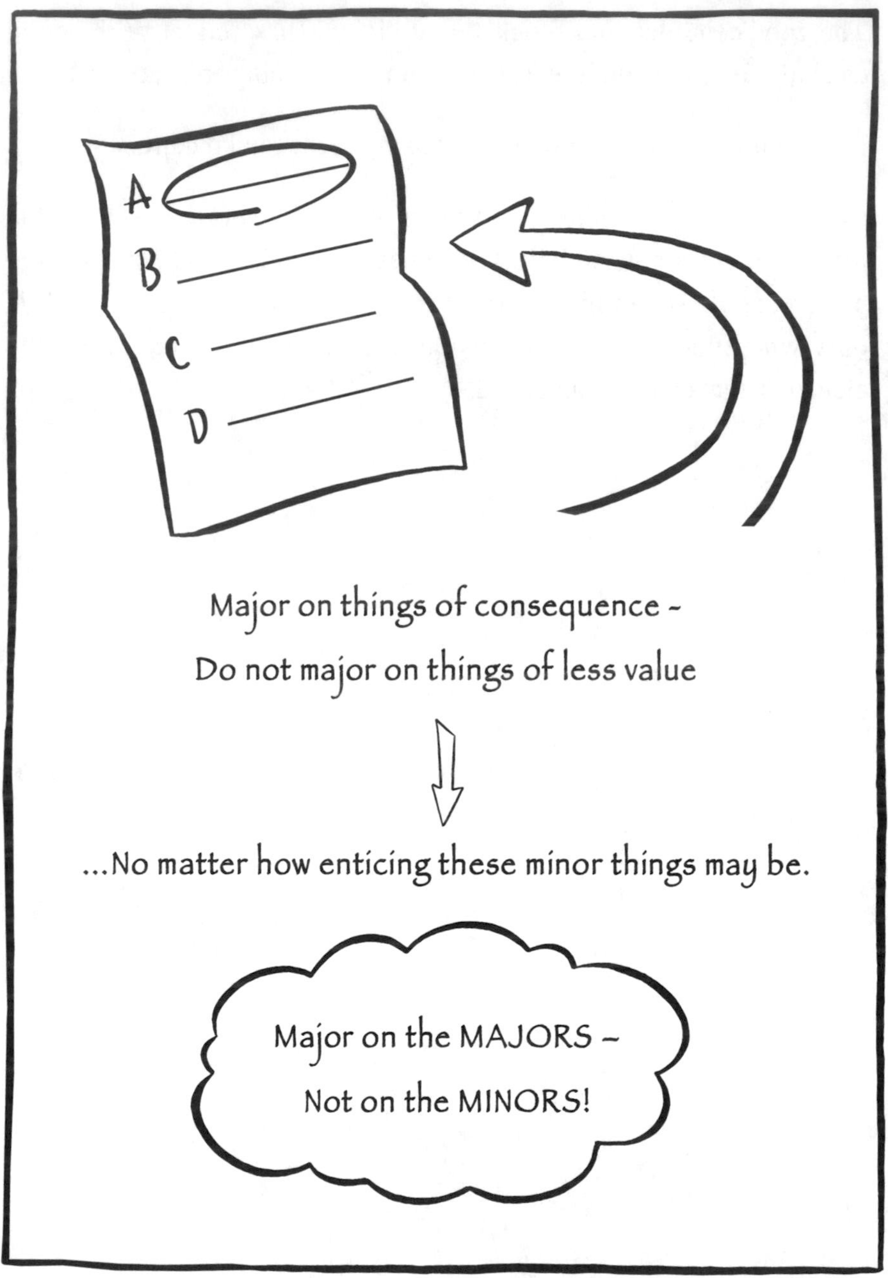

A
B
C
D
Major on things of consequence -
Do not major on things of less value
...No matter how enticing these minor things may be.
Major on the MAJORS -
Not on the MINORS!

MAXIMIZING ACCOMPLISHMENT: MAJOR ON THE MAJORS

The greatest value is to spend your time on those things which are major, ie. have the greatest impact. "Major" is determined by *impact*.

This can be looked at from two points of view:

1. The first point of view is to recognize that if you were able to always classify your activities in the order of the most important – and then you did the most important thing first all the time – you would tend to be majoring on the most important things and so maximizing your impact.

2. A second way to look at this is to think in terms of the *consequences* of the act. Look beyond the activity to see what the results will be. The impact on the long term will indicate the majors – the things of consequence, as opposed to things of minor impact.

Typically we spend more time on the minors. That is to say, we major on the minors as opposed to majoring on the majors. A check of your daily planner will compare how your time is spent in these two areas. We must major on the majors to maximize accomplishment.

Minor things tend to carry with them a real sense of "urgency" and "importance". Consequently, they must be done. However, in doing them it should always be uppermost in your mind to get the time to direct your energies on the major things, those of truly major importance and consequence.

A major is often made up of a number of minors. Therefore it is also important to separate out those minors that contribute to your majors, and those that do not. Focus on the former, and eliminate the latter.

"When we major
on the majors of others,
this becomes a
very efficient use
of time."

MAXIMIZING ACCOMPLISHMENT: MAJOR ON THE MAJORS

Often our own majors are another person's minors; thus when we can also *major on the majors* of others, this becomes a very efficient use of time.

It may also be that your major is another person's minor. In which case, you need to educate that individual on the importance of it also becoming one of their majors.

Minors have their place. The challenge is keeping them in their place to allow you to major on the majors.

***Work at things which will change the future,
as opposed to the present.***

PRESENT:

Some things, once done, will be forgotten.
They will make today better, but not tomorrow.

FUTURE:

Other things, once done, will change tomorrow.
They will eliminate for tomorrow what was urgent today.
Once done they will allow more time in the present.
Concentrate on these things!

MAXIMIZING ACCOMPLISHMENT: CHANGE THE FUTURE

The third major step to be taken in seeking to maximize accomplishment is to work at things which will change the future rather than the present.

Imaginc an individual working away in the garage on a "great idea", and then after three months emerging with the next generation of personal computer – the end result of their effort is that they changed the future!

They invented a new personal computer, rather than "getting a job", which typically we would believe is the right thing to do.

What they did in the present had no meaning to the present.

That individual was working in the present and when they emerged they had the future in their hands! Future based thinking is far more powerful than present based thinking.

For example – consider a junior sales rep. Present based thinking would be choosing not to invest time in training that person. We know a junior sales rep will bring in at least *some* sales, and short term that's good, rather than giving up sales time for training.

Future based thinking would mean investing time and money into training that individual. You realize that there will be a loss of sales in the short term, however you also recognize that the long term payback could be significantly greater.

Effective leaders are those who can guide their employee's behavior in a way that, once followed, results in meaningful change over the long term.

"Addressing the future
is a powerful
use of today's time."

MAXIMIZING ACCOMPLISHMENT: CHANGE THE FUTURE

Things which change the present do exactly that – they change the present. This is important, as we often want the present changed and need to have it changed. We live in the present and are constantly trying to do things to change it. *Things which change the future however are far more powerful.* They look into the future and address it, so that when you arrive at the future, and the future becomes the present, then those things have already been addressed.

Note: Many things which are done today are done, then forgotten; they may often have some impact on the future, but generally they tend to be primarily "today" oriented. Future things tend to change the things which are coming, and consequently give you greater control over "today" when it arrives.

Because the tomorrows that we face will be impacted by the todays, if the work which we do now is done with an eye on tomorrow, when we actually arrive there we will have less urgencies, and fewer things which preoccupy us or force us to attend to the trivial or urgent – we will do less "fire fighting".

Addressing the future is a powerful use of today's time.

Consequently, to really maximize one's accomplishment you have to concentrate on the things that are coming in the future. This is well summed up in the old Chinese proverb: "Give a man a fish – he will eat for a day. Teach a man to fish he will eat for a lifetime". Truly this is a great idea, but inherent in its success is that it takes far longer to *teach* a man to fish then it does to *give* a man a fish. But we must work at finding the time and being committed to taking the time to do the teaching, rather than only doing the giving.

"Things which change
the future
give you greater control
over 'today'
when it arrives."

Further, the more we teach, the less fish we have to give away! While you are future based you may still need to be today based. You will need to be today based until you arrive at the future to reap the benefit. So while we teach this man to fish we must also give him fish to eat, which requires work in the present! The temptation is to stop teaching and to concentrate on feeding him because he's starving and he needs to eat.

So it's key to remember that in order to become future based, it does not mean giving up present based thinking altogether, but rather establishing the right balance between present and future. As an example: future based thinking is building into career advancement; present based thinking means feeling good when you go home tonight. Both are important.

Your level of success is tied to your ability to move to the future. Great thinkers are all working in the future! Greatness occurs in the future.

With present based thinking we may reach our destination, but certainly not in record time, and with the marketplace today this is not good enough. Today we must be able to maximize our accomplishment in order to excel, which requires visualizing the future and so becoming, at least in part, future based in our thinking.

By letting a task sit "on hold" it remains incomplete, and so adds to the list of priorities – thereby making it more and more difficult to know how to tackle that growing list.

Finish what you start, before beginning something else.

FOCUS YOUR EFFORT.

FINISH THE TASK.

PERSEVERE.

MAXIMIZING ACCOMPLISHMENT: FINISH THE TASK

Focusing your effort on a task significantly increases your degree of accomplishment.

To focus one's effort is to discipline oneself to stick to that job until it is completed. There is an exception to this (covered below), but the general principle is: *when in the middle of a job try to persevere and finish it.*

Every time that you fail to finish one of your priorities, you need to add it to a new list, which then makes priority setting for that new list even more difficult. Every time you have a task that isn't completed it adds to the balls you must juggle – you become more focused on juggling than accomplishing! The issue becomes increasingly complex because inevitably there are always more balls in the future waiting for you.

So every time you are able to completely eliminate one ball it gives you increased capacity, and increased capacity allows you to do a better job, in a more stress free situation. In a nutshell: Persevere... finish what you start.

The impact of doing this also results in your not worrying about as many things, and thereby increasing concentration on the issues at hand.

The more things that you have on hold, pending, incomplete, or waiting for more activity the more frustrating life can become, and the more difficult it is to maximize your number of accomplishments.

When you have many balls in the air at once it is harder to make accurate judgements about new issues. Additionally, you have so many things incomplete that it's now difficult to know how long it will take to finish each of them. Whenever a task is put on hold, or not finished, the result is an inaccurate assessment of how much time it will take to complete it. As a consequence you can get in trouble on the planning side. The more tasks that are left undone the harder it is to plan the days that will follow.

"Every time
you have a task that isn't
completed it adds
to the balls you must juggle –
you become more
focused on juggling than
accomplishing!"

MAXIMIZING ACCOMPLISHMENT: FINISH THE TASK

Once you start something, try to finish it. This requires perseverance and a commitment to self-discipline – to doing the job that needs to be done. Often it will also require intense focus of effort on a given task, but that does not take away the power or importance of finishing the job. Wherever possible, discipline yourself to keep the list of "on hold" projects short, by finishing the things that you start before you begin something else. Focus your effort, finish the task, persevere.

The only exception to this is when you have gone as far as you can go on a given task. In this case, clearly you can go no further and you will have to stop and go on to something else, having hit a legitimate roadblock outside of your control.

If you must wait for information or other input before you can go any further, obviously you should start another task. But the key is that when that information or input does become accessible and you are in a position to move forward with the original task you must do just that – move forward.

It is very easy to be lured into a new task and believe that the earlier unfinished one can wait, rather than going back to it and finishing it when the new input or information becomes available. It is not finished; and you must focus your efforts to make sure it is finished as soon as you possibly can.

The way to marry the two principles of finishing a job and putting something on hold when you absolutely can go no further is: try not to start a new task when you do have the information that would let you complete an earlier task that had been put on hold.

In other words, try to keep the number of balls you are juggling at any one time to a minimum. *Focus your effort and finish the task.*

"See the
planning process as
a task in itself."

This is often difficult because, if we can juggle five balls, then we are willing to accept five, knowing that we can handle them. The problem with this particular approach is something may come to us – a sixth or seventh ball that we didn't anticipate or foresee, and now we are running beyond our capacity.

Had we not used up all our capacity, but finished the thing which we had started (tried to keep the balls to a minimum), then perhaps we might instead be juggling only three or four balls and therefore still have the capacity to absorb the unexpected unforeseen – more balls.

A specific step which can be taken to help with this is careful evaluation and planning before beginning a task, to ensure that as much thought as possible has been given to determining how long the task will take, what steps are needed, and so forth. This is the use of sound project management skills. Planning then produces a more efficient use of time, allowing you to maximize your accomplishment by completing the task.

Here are three specific guidelines to help in implementing this principle.

1. ***Remember that a given task does not have to be the entire task, but can be broken down into segments.***

   In other words, in the planning phase you can identify specific segments of the task, which are then treated as separate tasks. The first step, for example, could be planning; the second step collecting of resources; and the third step could be the execution of the project.

   You may not be able to do the complete task in one effort; but you certainly should be able to break it up into various elements each of which you can complete. In this way, you are focusing your effort on segments rather than on the total.

"Keep a list
of things you have
accomplished."

2. ***See the planning process as a task in itself.***

3. ***Accumulate the resources you'll need for the task (time, information, people) as a task in itself. Then perform the task as a separate project.***

Once again, remember that this particular goal of "focus of effort" can be applied to simple areas, and complex ones. For example, if you begin your in-tray, finish it; if an issue arises from a phone call, complete that issue before going on to something else. The principle can thus be applied to small jobs as well as to large areas.

A practical way to reinforce your skill in this area is to keep a list of things you have accomplished. This could be called a "victory list", where you keep running track of the things which you have accomplished over the last two or three weeks. By looking at this list you get positive reinforcement as you see the number of things that you have accomplished mount up. This is far more encouraging than only keeping a list of projects on hold, or pending, or still needing to be done!

Work hard to provide yourself with reinforcement that you are, in fact, doing the right thing, doing it properly, and reaping the benefits.

SEE THE VIEW FROM THE MOUNTAIN TOP!

Pause periodically and consider:

1. Why are things occurring?

?

2. What is really necessary?

✓
✓
X

3. How do single items fit into the whole?

PERIODICALLY LOOK FROM THE MOUNTAIN TOP

When one is caught up in one's own job and the tremendous pressures associated with it, it is very easy to lose sight of the fact that there is a "big picture" – which could be seen from the mountain towering over that valley in which we spend most of our time. This mountain can be climbed, and when we reach the summit we can look at the valley below and take stock. The purpose of seeing the view from the mountain into your valley is to observe, and from those observations to correct or improve.

When you go to the mountain top, go with the intent of answering the question: "How can I make things better?"

It is the activity of looking into the valley from the top of the mountain that restores perspective. The need to see broadly like this is important in order to establish perspective, and so affect judgement.

Judgement is an essential quality. It is crucial to the multitude of decision points to be crossed each day. Your judgement is based on how well you can keep the view from the mountaintop in mind when you are working in the valley!

Going to the top of the mountain can cause a shift in perspective, which in turn can change your judgement, and so ultimately your focus and activity. Looking at the view from the mountaintop tends to reinforce which things are important and so refocus your attention on the true priorities.

There are three key benefits to going up to the mountaintop.

1. ***It allows you to see opportunities for improvement.***

2. ***It allows you to bring that view down to be communicated to the rest of the team.***

3. ***It serves to reinforce the real reason for the activities you do in the valley.***

"The purpose of
seeing the valley from the
top of the mountain
is to observe, and from
those observations
to correct and improve."

PERIODICALLY LOOK FROM THE MOUNTAIN TOP

1. The path as it currently is, as seen from the mountain

2. The path as it should be, reinforced by seeing the view from the mountain.

3. The path as it will then be in reality once you return to the valley and implement your observations; not perfect, but much more direct than what it was.

"Visit the
mountain top frequently,
even if only for a
short period of time,
and review your activities
and direction."

PERIODICALLY LOOK FROM THE MOUNTAIN TOP

One goes about looking at the view from the mountain top by asking these three questions:

a) Why are things occurring as they are?

b) What is really necessary?

c) How do the various single elements with which I'm involved fit into the whole?

This mountain top view also affects how we do things, because looking at issues from the mountain top often shows us that there is a better way to do something, a smoother way, a shorter path.

It may often seem easier to go with the "tried and true", rather than an alternative approach, simply because one is so busy doing things that the tried and true method appears faster at the time. The flaw with this thinking is that, while this method may be faster now, by looking at the total picture from the mountain top you can see that relatively little extra effort might produce a totally new path. This path would be quicker, shorter, or cheaper and could be followed from then on. In the long run it would be preferable.

The impact of seeing the view from the mountain top should be so great that we're motivated to return regularly. Visit the mountain top frequently, even if only for a short period of time, and review your activities and direction.

SEE THE WHOLE MOUNTAIN RANGE.

It is one thing to see your valley from your
own mountain, and so pick out the key landmarks.
But it is another thing to look up and out,
and see clearly the other mountains.

Life is more than job, or family, or
personal well-being, or faith. It is a composite of all.
See the whole mountain range.

CONSIDER THE FULL MOUNTAIN RANGE

If one climbs the mountain from the valley, one can learn to pick out and examine the key points in the valley and so act appropriately. But it is also possible to look up and out to see the entire mountain range. All the other issues which surround us represent the other mountains in that range – family, health, hobbies, etc.

It is important that you don't see the world as only one mountain. As mountains exist in ranges, so very often there are things you can't see from where you're standing, but it does not mean that they are not there. Sometimes your view is obscured, either because of trees or clouds. Sometimes one mountain (e. g. work) is more dominant and obscures others; some are closer and some are far away.

Alternatively, one could consider life as many ranges, each having its own mountains, for example: some of the ranges of life could be: responsibilities, environment, income, family, well being, spirituality, aging, nutrition, and play. Similarly some of the mountains within the mountain range of our job might be: change, rewards, cost, quality, profit, competition, H.R., sales, brands, strategies, and work processes.

At times the mountain that we are on and the accompanying valley we are in are so powerful that we tend to blind ourselves to even the other mountains, let alone the other ranges! The crucial thing is to take the time to take stock of the many ranges that exist.

While it is understandable that at times the "work" portion of your mountain and valley areas seem to dominate everything, it is in reality but one in the total ranges. By looking at the total ranges you are able to see all the areas of your life in perspective. You can see relative height, relative importance, and relative impact.

"Often it is only towards the end of one's life that one actually pauses and looks at all the mountain ranges of life and then perhaps realizes that one's perspective has been wrong. Investment in time and energy may have been focused too heavily in one particular area and not heavily enough in other areas."

CONSIDER THE FULL MOUNTAIN RANGE

Perhaps the work environment is not as important, as high, as big or as major as you tend to think when you are looking only at that range (your organization) and focusing exclusively on that particular mountain (your job).

It is unfortunate, but often it is only towards the end of one's life that one actually pauses and looks at all the ranges and then perhaps realizes that one's perspective has been wrong. Investment in time and energy may have been focused too heavily in one particular area and not heavily enough in other areas.

Balance is key!

We can do a similar exercise at work. One particular mountain might be the delivery of a product or service. But there are other mountains, such as the care of people or the well being of the team. Perhaps these are more important than we realize, or they could have greater impact but are neglected because the focus is so exclusively on one particular mountain, such as the need to prepare a particular report on a regular basis, or to make a sale.

The view of the total mountain range allows us to: give more importance to larger issues and give less importance to smaller issues.

Seeing broadly includes seeing all the mountain ranges, a specific mountain range, and also the big picture from the particular mountain which you are on at that time (be it work, family, jobs, kids, whatever) down into that valley. See all.

You need to be able to understand, and express, both viewpoints.

On any topic, what you feel to be supremely important may not match the viewpoint of others.

MASTER THE ABILITY TO SEE THROUGH THE EYES OF OTHERS

On any topic, what you feel to be supremely important may not match the viewpoint of others. You need to be able to understand and express both viewpoints – yours and theirs.

Seeing broadly does not mean only that you open your mind to relative perspective, but it also means you open your mind to the ideas of others. This reflects the fact that an individual who is able to see broadly can pursue, with an open mind, keenly and aggressively, the thoughts and points of view of other individuals. To understand relative worth means to recognize that your viewpoint is not necessarily that of others. The things which you feel to be very important are not necessarily the same things that another feels to be important.

For example, when purchasing a car, your spouse may value colour, size, and comfort; while you could be considering the power, cost, and fuel consumption. While it is true that we naturally gravitate towards believing that our points of view are the only relevant ones, another individual feels exactly the same way, despite the fact that they hold a totally different point of view.

Seeing broadly means we can accept that different point of view, work within it, understand it, and if need be come to their point of view. You must work at being able to not only be tolerant of another person's point of view and recognize that they have a point of view, but also be able to understand it to such a degree that you can express it clearly.

Mastery of this means being able to take their point of view and defend it as if it were our own, without perhaps their personal conviction. To truly see broadly is to be able to present the other person's point as clearly, succinctly, and effectively as that person could. If we can do so then we clearly do see from their perspective. This gives us the ability to make the best possible judgements – because we can see clearly from both, or all, sides!

GOAL
A
B
C
D
AVOID
a
b
c
d
Never be so caught up in details that
you forget why the activities are necessary.

AVOID UNNECESSARY DETAIL

One of the elements in seeing broadly is avoiding being caught up in a level of detail which prevents you from seeing why the activity is actually occurring.

Detail clouds the essential thought.

One of the ways to avoid falling into this trap is to set a very clear goal, and very specific time parameters, before beginning the task.

A common example where detail has clouded the essential thought is the example of a communication piece, where excessive detail obscures the issue, embellishing it beyond recognition, and resulting in the listener or reader having no real idea what the goal of the communication was in the first place. Being inundated with so much detail, the true objective is completely lost. Remove the detail and the message often becomes much clearer.

EXECUTIONAL EXCELLENCE

WORLD-CLASS LEADERSHIP SKILLS - "THE STERLING SILVER CORD"

This cord is the all important connection between strategy and tactics - knowing what to do, and how to do it, and includes the impact on what to do next as a result of what's just been done. The cord is "two-way".
A strategy is only as good as its execution.
An execution is only as effective as the thinking behind it.
The link between these two must be STERLING!
STRATEGIC SKILLS
The ability to see and articulate "the big picture" - the truly long-term plan or strategy to be followed.
"Thinking Ahead Several Years."
THE STERLING SILVER CORD
The ability to "really get it done", to be fully up on all the necessary detail, doing now what has to be done now.
"Really Showing Mastery of Executional Excellence"
TACTICAL SKILLS

WORLD-CLASS LEADERSHIP SKILLS – "THE STERLING SILVER CORD"

The "Sterling Silver Cord" is the vital connection between the ability to think and operate strategically, and the ability to demonstrate execution at the practical level.

Strategic skills are those which are crucial to formulate policy, establish direction, and determine how resources should be most effectively allocated in order to achieve the larger vision.

It is the strategic thinking skills which are so important when making decisions in the broad context. "Broad" could be in terms of time (5, 10, or even 50 years out); in terms of product (which areas will receive the greatest concentration); in terms of impact (what do we wish to achieve using our time and money), etc. Essentially, strategic skills are crucial in crafting the future.

Tactical skills, on the other hand, are those skills which "put feet to the plan." The importance of clear vision and thinking cannot be underestimated (the strategic skills), but without good tactical skills the benefits of thinking will never be realized, and will slowly dissipate as so many dreams.

Strong tactical skills allow individuals to understand what the objective is and then to break it down into operational pieces. These can then be planned for, have resources allocated, and have clear steps outlined that need to be taken to achieve specific results. Tactical skills look at the immediate details as well as the additional details "around the corner" and "on the horizon". With good tactical skills an individual is able to realize what can and can't be done within a given context, and so utilizes the available talent in the resource pool for the maximum effectiveness.

"Truly world-class, 'sterling', leaders have the ability to travel with ease up and down the silver cord - operating effectively at the top, the bottom, and anywhere along it."

Clearly if an individual is strong in both areas, then there is a huge benefit: the strategic thinking takes into consideration the tactical realities; and the tactical realities are driven by the importance of the strategic plan. This person is able to make decisions along the executional path without endangering the attainment of the final objective. Great leaders who have mastered both these areas of skill can be said to be of sterling quality, with the sterling silver cord joining the strategic and tactical skills consistently strong along its entire length. Their leadership at any point along that cord is maximally effective.

Typically individuals tend to have strength either on the strategic end (knowing what to do) or on the tactical end (knowing how to do it). As we move towards becoming world-class leaders – of sterling quality – our skills need to be developed so that they are equally strong in both areas, and everywhere in between.

In a maximally effective organization, individuals are correctly positioned along the sterling silver cord so that their relative strengths in strategy or tactics are most effectively used on a day-to-day basis.

DIAGNOSING LEADERSHIP TALENT USING THE CONCEPT OF THE STERLING SILVER CORD

Strategic Skills | Tactical Skills

CATEGORY 1

Strong at conceptualizing, but can't execute effectively.

CATEGORY 2

Strong strategically, with some appreciation of the impact of the day-to-day.

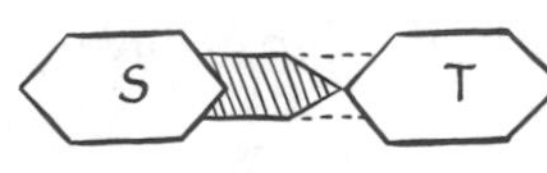

CATEGORY 3

Excellent tactically, and with some ability to ensure that day-to-day activities contribute to the strategic direction.

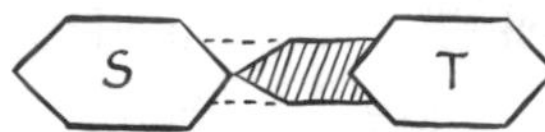

CATEGORY 4

Great at today's priorities, but unable to provide clear motivating vision.

CATEGORY 5

Able to appreciate both strategy and tactics and their relationship, but not yet able to sustain this understanding in turbulent times.

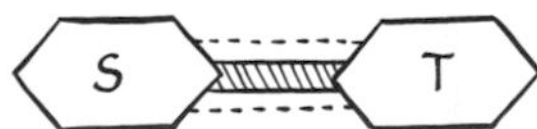

DIAGNOSING LEADERSHIP TALENT USING THE CONCEPT OF THE STERLING SILVER CORD

The first step towards strengthening the silver cord for any given individual – that is ensuring their strength at both the strategic and tactical level, and at points in-between – is to analyze their current position. The analysis can be broken into one of five categories.

1. ***Category One:*** Includes those who are strong at conceptualizing; they are good strategic thinkers, but have trouble executing consistently with predictable results. These individuals could be said to have a well-defined position at the strategic end of the cord but little substance at the other. They require strengthening at the tactical end.

2. ***Category Two:*** These individuals are strong strategically and, while unable to implement effectively, they do have an appreciation for the consequences of the tactical implementation. These people are stronger than those in category one in that they are effective at strategic thinking, and have the added benefit of being able to appreciate the consequences on the execution side. They are therefore able to modify the strategies in order to reflect the realities of the market place, and so bring a more pragmatic approach to the strategic thinking which they provide.

"A 'young lion(ess)' –
one who is able to appreciate
both strategy and tactics,
and their relationship,
but not yet able to
sustain this understanding
in turbulent times."

3. ***Category Three:*** These individuals remain strong at the tactical level, consistently demonstrating that as a strength. In addition, they have an appreciation for the way in which the tactical activities are supporting the implementation of the strategy. Consequently, they are able to proactively modify their behavior at the tactical level, by degree, when it is apparent there is a better way to deliver the strategy than that which was originally intended.

   These are important individuals to have on the team because, practically, they demonstrate a great deal of initiative in making change in thc day-to-day operations to improve efficiency and productivity. They understand clearly what is to be accomplished at the end, and not just at all the points in between.

4. ***Category Four:*** Represents those at the opposite end of the spectrum from category one – they are very strong on the day-to-day tactics and are able to consistently deliver the current priorities. However, these individuals are unable to provide clear and motivating direction to others, as they have little grasp of the strategic framework. They need to develop in the areas of being able to see and shape the broader context.

"The first step towards ensuring strength at both strategic and tactical level, and at points in-between, is to analyze the current position."

5. ***Category Five:*** If a sterling leader is one who has full mastery of both the strategy and tactics, and everything in between, category five is a "Sterling Leader in Development". This is a "young lion or lioness", a high potential individual who has already demonstrated strength both on the conceptual strategy side in knowing what to do; and also the tactical side in having the ability to be involved in the detail and doing what is required to see the strategy implemented. These individuals demonstrate the ability to move up and down the silver cord, effectively modifying tactics as required in line with the strategy, and shaping the strategy as executional pieces are delivered in order to continue making progress towards the ultimate objective. They keep that objective in mind, modifying it when necessary along the way so that the final end result is realized as quickly and efficiently as possible.

   However, these people are in category five because they have yet to develop the strength to retain the clarity of vision between strategy and tactics in turbulent times. When the pressure increases to an intense level, crises loom, or significant unforeseen events occur, then they lose the ability to move smoothly between strategy and tactics, and so fall back to their area of greater strength – either strategy or tactics. At that point they become inappropriately dependent on others whose strength is in their area of greater deficiency.

   These individuals will grow over time, but it needs to be understood that they have yet to develop a thick enough cord to withstand really intense pressures.

Using this diagnostic framework individuals can be effectively assessed. Training or opportunities can then be provided to strengthen their areas of weakness; and they can be positioned appropriately within the organization.

UNDERSTANDING WHAT'S CALLED FOR AT VARIOUS SPOTS ALONG THE STERLING SILVER CORD

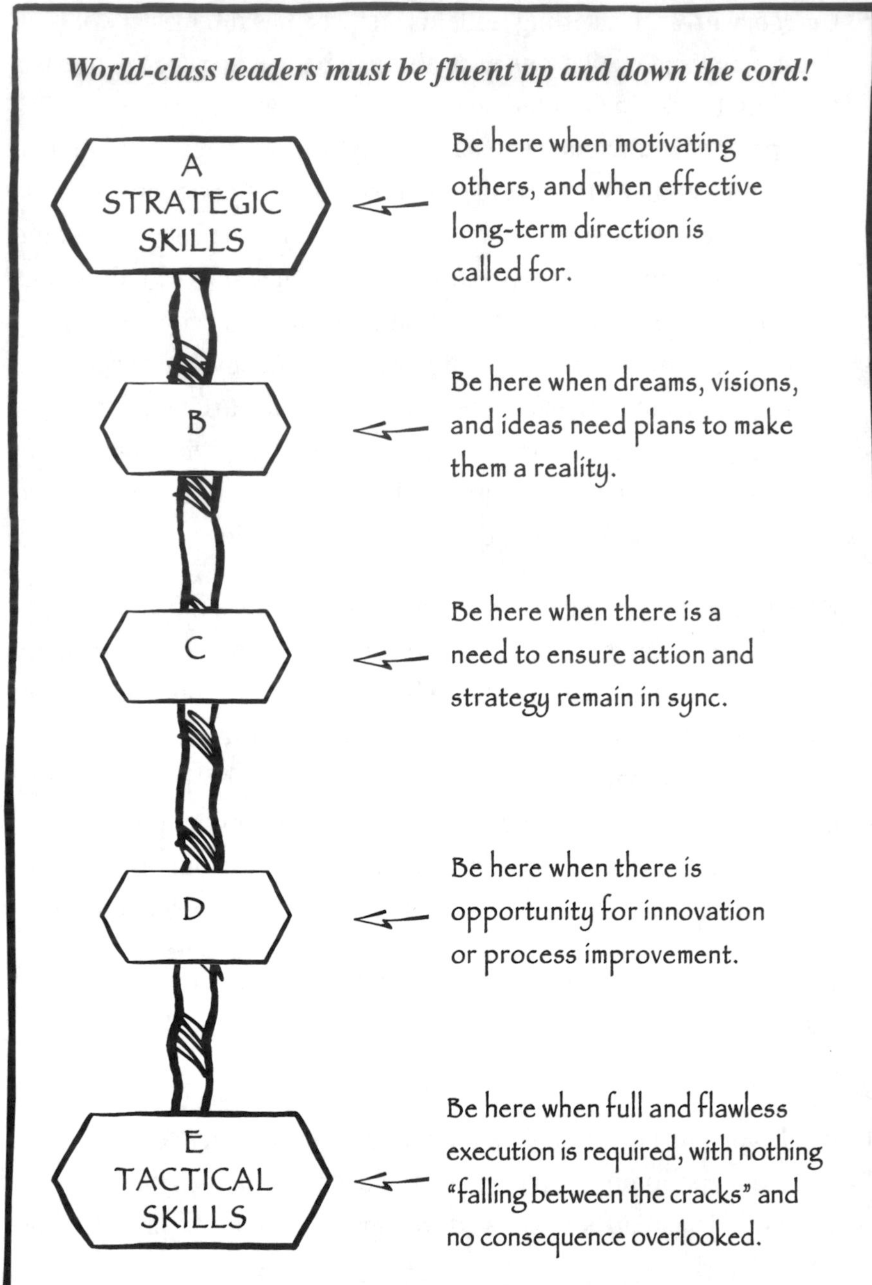

World-class leaders must be fluent up and down the cord!
A
STRATEGIC
SKILLS
Be here when motivating others, and when effective long-term direction is called for.
B
Be here when dreams, visions, and ideas need plans to make them a reality.
C
Be here when there is a need to ensure action and strategy remain in sync.
D
Be here when there is opportunity for innovation or process improvement.
E
TACTICAL
SKILLS
Be here when full and flawless execution is required, with nothing "falling between the cracks" and no consequence overlooked.

UNDERSTANDING WHAT'S CALLED FOR AT VARIOUS SPOTS ALONG THE STERLING SILVER CORD

At any point in time organizations as a whole (not just individuals) are at some particular point on the sterling silver cord between strategy and tactics. If seen from the macro view against the "ten year plan" an organization can seem to be, perhaps, half way up the cord.

On the other hand a micro look at an individual department in the organization could well reveal that they are at a totally different point on the cord, perhaps at the creation of a new strategy, having just delivered a previous objective.

Every activity, department, initiative, or group will be somewhere on that silver cord, and each one could be at a different place. Even in the incredible complexity of a large organization, the view from a hundred thousand feet with regards to where the organization sits relative to strategy or execution can be identified. This will differ from the view at ten feet, when, instead of an average sense of the whole, you are able to see the specific detail of each individual part, and where they each sit.

Within this context it helps to understand what is called for at the various positions along the cord. For the sake of clarity consider looking at five distinct points.

A. At the Top: Strategy is required in its purest form when the organization, department, function, etc., needs vision, and a motivating long term framework for action. At this point individuals want to know what they are trying to achieve, and the context into which they can place the activities and events that make up their day.

B. The Step Below the Top: Plans, dreams, and thinking need to be sketched out in enough detail that a plan can be visualized, and confidence generated that there is a perceived pathway to the achievement of the strategies.

"True tactical brilliance
allows nothing to
'fall between the cracks'.
All eventualities are considered,
charts are made up of
what could possibly go wrong,
and plans put in place
for each of those eventualities."

C. At the Middle: This is the checkpoint where the execution of the strategies, and the strategies themselves meet and must be in sync. It is at this point you look to determine if what's being done is compatible with what needs to be done. Is the way we are going about our tasks truly supporting what we ultimately want to achieve? Similarly, is what we want to achieve coming in view? Do we have confidence that we will arrive there because of the way we are now going about our day-to-day activities, and because of the things which are occurring around us?

D. The Step Above Tactics: At this point tactics predominate, with most of the focus on getting the job done. However, this is an important area as it is where innovation occurs. Once the strategy has clearly been passed to those who must execute, it is at this point on the cord that people initiate change to established ways. It is here that they recognize that doing it differently, using different tools, or applying different methodologies could accelerate the achievement of the strategy. It is clearly a tactical focus but one that bears the strategy in mind, and so is willing to reshape or rework the tactics in order to see the strategy realized more quickly than what would have occurred without the reshaping.

"Every activity,
department, initiative,
or group will be
somewhere on the sterling
silver cord and
each one could be at a
different place."

UNDERSTANDING WHAT'S CALLED FOR AT VARIOUS SPOTS ALONG THE STERLING SILVER CORD

E. Full Tactical Focus: It is at this point where excellence of execution is absolutely crucial. True tactical brilliance allows nothing to "fall between the cracks." All eventualities are considered, charts are made up of all that could possibly go wrong, and plans are put in place for each of those eventualities. Resources are allocated in the most efficient fashion, detailed project plans are in place, experience in world-class benchmarking has been captured, individual strengths have been properly aligned with individual needs, frequent check points have been established, and there is an absolute guarantee that the plan will occur as intended – execution will be seamless, flawless, brilliant, and highly cost effective. Excellence of execution is almost an art form! It is crucial to the success of any outcome.

Having a clear understanding as to what is expected along the silver cord allows leaders to provide that clarity to the organization. Furthermore, it allows them to ensure that the right things are happening at each point on the cord, as well as facilitating their ability to determine where the company, department, group, team or individual should be on the cord at any point in time.

The more effectively the leader is personally skilled at all points on the cord, the more effective is their ability to move the organization to the appropriate point on the cord, and hence the more effective is their overall leadership.

CLOSING DEFICIENCY GAPS ALONG THE STERLING SILVER CORD

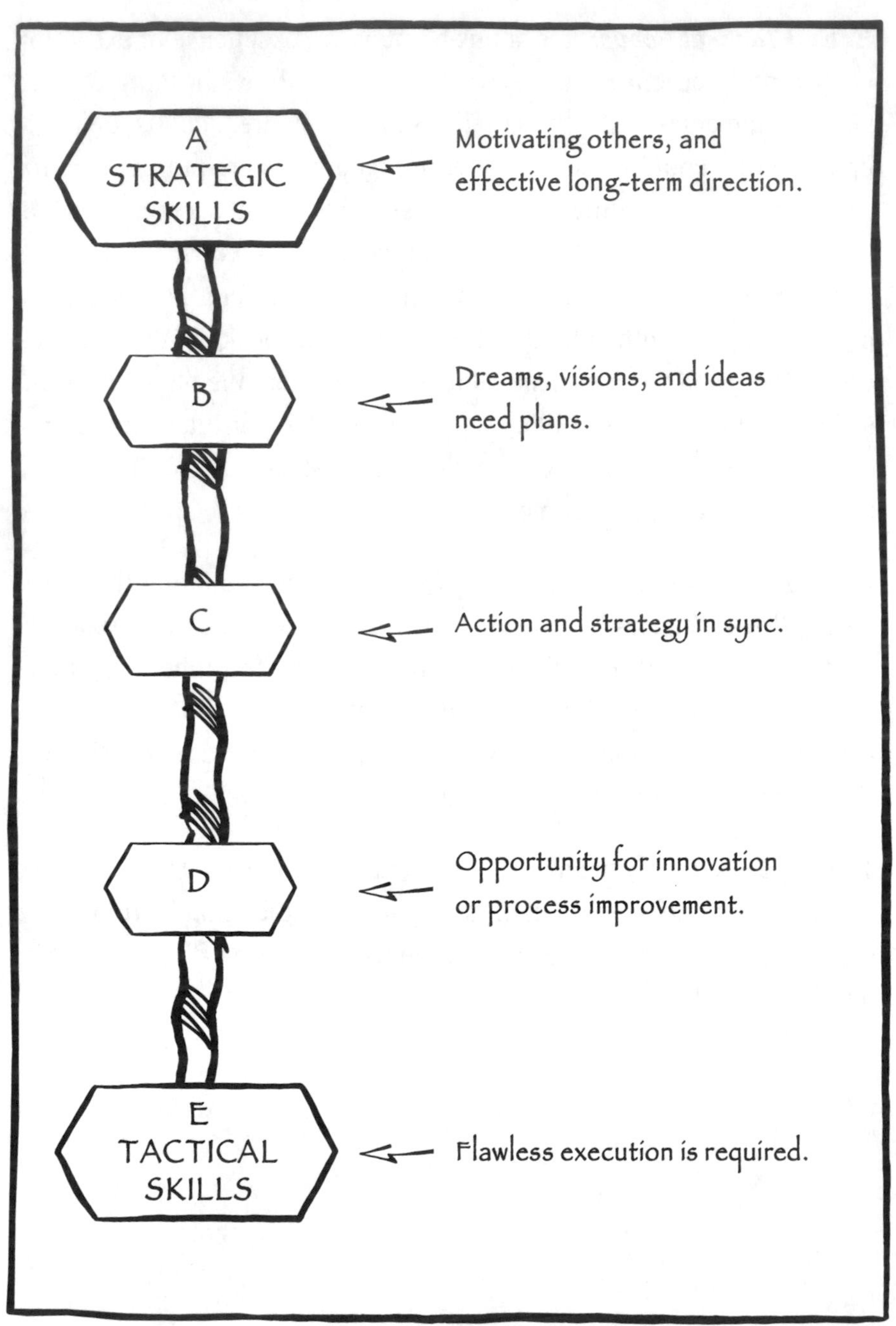
A
STRATEGIC
SKILLS
Motivating others, and effective long-term direction.
B
Dreams, visions, and ideas need plans.
C
Action and strategy in sync.
D
Opportunity for innovation or process improvement.
E
TACTICAL
SKILLS
Flawless execution is required.

CLOSING DEFICIENCY GAPS ALONG THE STERLING SILVER CORD

Once you've identified where an individual or group is along the cord you can then strengthen them as appropriate. To do so requires focused attention. Reference to the appropriate sections in this book will allow you to do so.

PASSION AND CONVICTION WITHOUT SKILL IS NOT LIKELY TO SUCCEED

The practical side of knowing "how to" is key to final success.

If conviction and passion provide the spark, the initiative, it is skill, or talent, that sustains the effort.

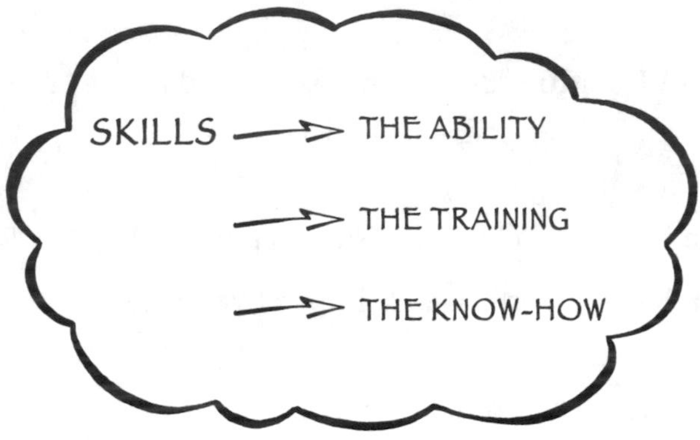

PASSION:

Starts, and rejuvenates whenever necessary

SKILL:

Allows sustained progress.

PASSION AND CONVICTION WITHOUT SKILL IS NOT LIKELY TO SUCCEED

The importance of passion and conviction have just been discussed. But as with the heart and the lungs, passion without skill is not sufficient.

In order to be maximally successful the necessary skills are as important as passion.

By skill is meant the ability to achieve a certain objective; that is, having the training or know how required to effectively implement and achieve the objective. I may wish to beat my partner at the squash club, but until I acquire the necessary skills I will not be successful, not matter how passionate my desire to win.

I do, however, greatly reap the benefit of my passion as it drives me to improve my skills, and so be ultimately victorious. But I do need the skills.

This practical "how to do something" is key to the final success of any initiative, and this is why investment in training, development and education, both of oneself and of those for whom one is responsible, is so important.

Passion ignites, and skills sustain.

SKILLFULNESS WITHOUT KNOWLEDGE CAN EASILY RESULT IN MISDIRECTED (BUT WELL DONE!) EFFORT

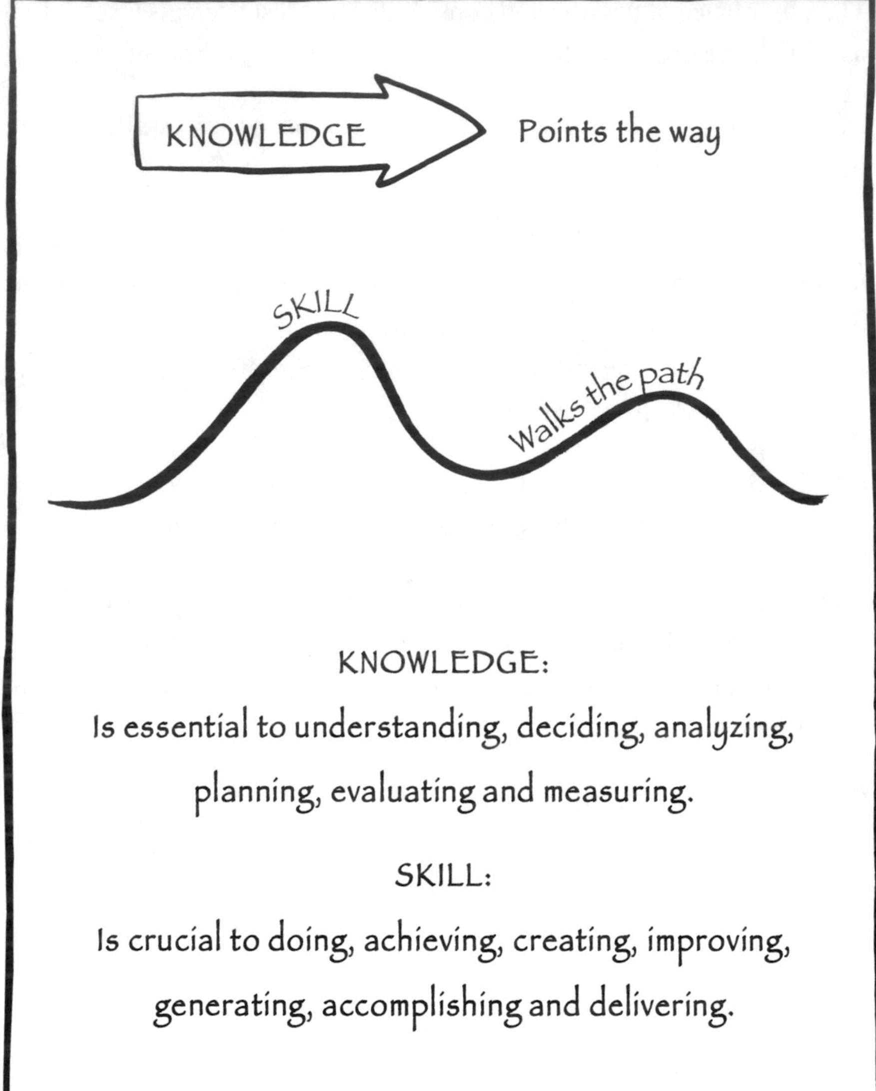

KNOWLEDGE
Points the way
SKILL
Walks the path
KNOWLEDGE:
Is essential to understanding, deciding, analyzing, planning, evaluating and measuring.
SKILL:
Is crucial to doing, achieving, creating, improving, generating, accomplishing and delivering.

SKILLFULNESS WITHOUT KNOWLEDGE CAN EASILY RESULT IN MISDIRECTED (BUT WELL DONE!) EFFORT

Knowledge ensures that skills are applied in the right fashion.

When I'm knowledgeable about a subject, issue, or process then I understand what needs to be done and why. Knowledge gives me the specific intellectual ability required to make the appropriate decisions regarding next steps. It makes me better able to decide on the appropriate approach, and relative worth; and gives me the ability to make go or no go decisions based on information received, cost benefit analyses, etc. When I'm knowledgeable I am able to be focused and targeted, with a clear path to the most appropriate course of action.

Then I bring my skill to bear. The skill is used to enable me to achieve the objective.

If my knowledge is faulty and my skill is high then I will go brilliantly along the wrong path. If my knowledge is high and my skill is weak, then I may go limpingly and haltingly in the correct direction, but never arrive. For maximum effect I need to be both knowledgeable and skillful: I can then move swiftly and effectively along the best course of action.

Knowledge points the way; skill walks the path.

Knowledge allows me to understand, analyze, plan, evaluate and measure. Skill allows me to do what needs to done to achieve, to create, to improve, to generate, to accomplish, and to deliver.

We need to ensure that we are investing both in their knowledge base and their skill base if we are to maximize the potential of each individual for whom we are responsible.

COMPETENCY = KNOWLEDGE + SKILL

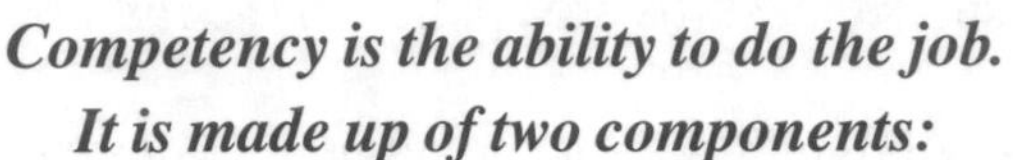

Competency is the ability to do the job. It is made up of two components:

KNOWLEDGE
What the person knows

SKILL
What the person can do

"Head" knowledge
Theory
Theoretical
Rationale, Background,
Specifications
Potential

"Hand" knowledge
Practice
Practical
Action, Results,
Consequence
Talent

Both are equally important.

As they grow, so does individual competency.

COMPETENCY = KNOWLEDGE + SKILL

The combination of knowledge and skill provides competency. When individuals are competent then they are able to do the job the way it is intended to be done.

Take for example a team of firefighters rushing to the scene of a chemical inferno in response to an emergency call. They are judged to be competent if they *know* what to do in this particular situation (chemical fire), and have the *skill* to execute properly. Knowing what to do and how to do it effectively will result in successfully extinguishing the fire – the work of a competent team.

Knowledge is something which we acquire and store intellectually. We might have acquired it from learning or from experience, but it is nonetheless stored away in our mind. It is there to be tapped and as such is a potential resource on which we can draw.

Our knowledge provides the necessary theory, rationale and background to allow us to tackle a task. We can intellectually design a theoretical approach based on our knowledge which will allow us to specify the outcome. The greater our knowledge the more accurate our prediction.

Skill on the other hand is the talent that we have which enables us to execute that which is in our mind. The greater our skill the greater our ability to see the theoretical plan brought flawlessly to fruition. In this way skill is our ability to do; it's practical, it produces results and consequences which can be seen. Skills can be learned, and practiced, and then stored away to be called upon when required.

Both knowledge and skill are equally important. As they grow together so grows the competency of the individual.

TRAINING IMPROVES COMPETENCY

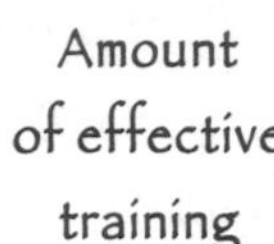

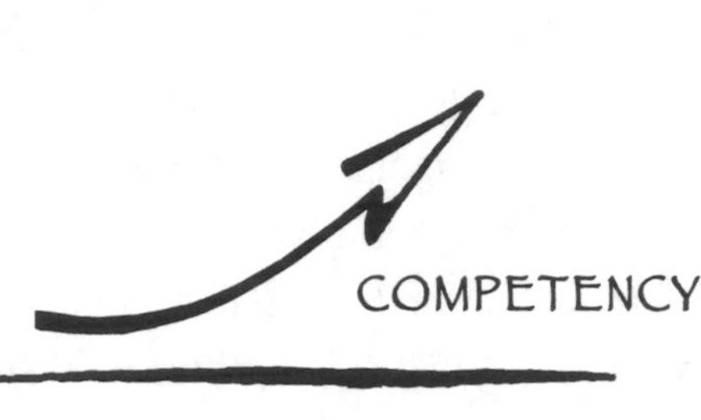

Time

TO DRIVE COMPETENCY REQUIRES
A CONTINUING INVESTMENT IN TRAINING.

Training focused on making people more knowledgeable, with an understanding of how that knowledge applies to the job.

Training focused on making people more skilled – able to do more, faster, better, and at less cost.

TRAINING IMPROVES COMPETENCY

Once a commitment to improving individual competency has been made then training becomes a priority.

By "training" I mean those aspects of personal development which enhance an individual's abilities or knowledge. This could include self-taught courses, attending school, college, university, or other outside programs. Development initiatives sponsored by the organization, perhaps at the corporate university, or from the development department are also included. Similarly traditional training programs and approaches would also fall into this category. "Training" is used as an all-encompassing word to capture the essence of continuing to build into individuals in a *practical way*.

Many times "learning" is really only "exposure to information". No actual learning really occurs, in that the individual does nothing with the material. I think of "training" as a succinct way to indicate that the individual has actually progressed in terms of their understanding, to the degree that they can apply their new-found understanding effectively back on the job, at home, or wherever else the material is relevant.

Training must be effective. Not all training results in individuals being able to act and behave differently. For competency to improve the education source must be an effective one. That is, it must provide the information in comprehensible form, in bite size chunks, with relevance, and interest.

"Because of the
tremendous potential
within each individual
for growth and contribution,
the investment in training
must be a continuous one."

TRAINING IMPROVES COMPETENCY

If an individual is exposed to effective training over time then their competency level will increase. Obviously it is important to ensure that the training provided has relevance to the work required. While it's true that all learning will be of some value, the priority should be to ensure that the training and development provided is directly and visibly aligned to the individual's responsibilities and job requirements.

In an organization committed to using its staff to their fullest capacity the commitment to training must be ongoing. As people learn and apply that learning they grow, and as they grow their ability to influence expands, and with that their ability to make change. As this impact is felt there is a further need for personal development; and so there is a continuing cycle, which is driven by the investment in people through training.

As an organization continues to develop its members those members will continue to provide greater and greater value within their areas of responsibility. Because of the tremendous potential within each individual for growth and contribution, the investment in training must be a continuous one.

Any training and development initiative must fall into two camps:

1. Enhancing an individual's knowledge, so that they are able to act with more understanding.

2. Improving an individual's skills, so that they are able to do things most effectively, that is, faster, better, and at less cost.

TRAINING THAT IS NOT TRULY EFFECTIVE IS OF LITTLE OR NO VALUE

EFFECTIVE:

1. Behavior change occurs, can be seen, and can be sustained.

Sustainable

2. Knowledge acquired can be tested.

A+

3. Competency against predetermined standards improves.

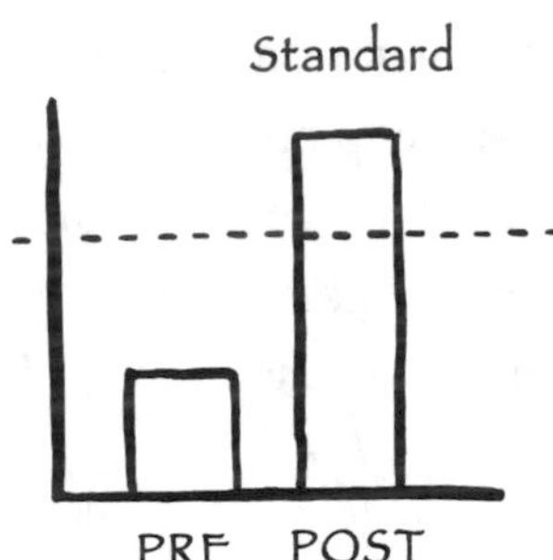

4. Both understanding and conviction are increased.

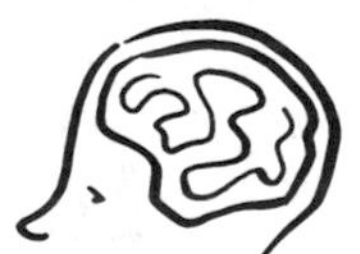

Understanding + Conviction

TRAINING THAT IS NOT TRULY EFFECTIVE IS OF LITTLE OR NO VALUE

Training must be truly effective if it is to have the expected benefit. If the organization is relying on training to improve individual competency, then that training should satisfy four clear criteria in order to be as effective as possible.

1. ***Sustainability:*** The results of the training should occur over time, and be sustainable. That is, the behavioral change which results because of the training should be in evidence in the day-to-day behavior following the training, and *remain so over time*. This is the test of sustainability. If material is forgotten, or quickly falls into disuse, then the training has not been adequately effective.

   Often in order to make this happen the supervisor of the individual who has been trained needs to be involved in the process in some way. If the training department were to provide training that promotes behavior not supported by the culture, or the leadership of the organization, then there is little likelihood of that training actually having any sustainability at all. Behavior taught in a training course must be fully accepted throughout the organization and so supported and modeled by line management.

   Effective training is that which ensures permanently changed behavior.

2. ***Evaluation:*** Typically within organizations, the concept of "testing" or "evaluating" the results of training is not popular. Somehow it seems to remind the participants too much of school. However, the organization has usually assumed the cost of providing this training, both in the opportunity cost by freeing up the individual to attend, and often the delivery cost, as well absorbing the costs related to instructor, materials, classroom, etc.

"Effective training
is that which
ensures permanently
changed behavior."

They have a right to expect an appropriate return for this investment, and to be able to measure that return. Consequently I strongly support the evaluation of competency improvements in individuals.

Training which is focused on enhancing knowledge and understanding can usually be evaluated relatively easily through a traditional form of evaluation (an "exam") occurring immediately or soon after the delivery of that information. Additional tests some months later are often a good idea just to ensure that retention and application have occurred.

Skill tests on the other hand usually cannot occur immediately after the completion of the training, but must occur on the job, and usually several weeks after the training has been completed. This will ensure that there is in fact a permanent change in behavior.

I would also recommend that the evaluation of that acquired skill, the learned behavior, be done by the line manager on the job. Adopting this approach will engage the line manager in the process, and may perhaps require that individual to have some preliminary training in order to perform an effective evaluation!

In some cases the evaluation should not be given for as much as six months after the training (for example: in advanced negotiation courses); in other cases the evaluation may have to be completed three or four times to ensure that the competency has truly been acquired (for example: training on effective presentations).

Whatever the training content the commitment must be made to appropriately evaluate the competency of the individual who received the training. This will both ensure the training is effective, and guarantee its applicability.

"Training that is effective is training which ensures that individual performance meets the expected standard, as defined by line management."

3. ***Standards:*** Effective training is driven by the desire that behavior reach a given standard. Training that is simply done without reference to a previously established standard has no guarantee that it is at a high enough level. Conversely it could be at too high a level.

The organization must work with the training and development provider to establish the appropriate standards for the skills and knowledge which individuals need. Once this standard is established the individual can be assessed against it. If they fall short, then training can be provided to bring them up to standard, or ideally even somewhat higher (given that standards are constantly rising and it might be some time before the individual receives further training in this area).

After the training has been provided, the evaluation can be administered to determine whether or not the individual's behavior has reached the required standard.

In cases where organizations have not yet established standards with regards to knowledge and skill for key aspects of job functions, then this should become a priority.

With reference to the comments above regarding evaluation, there is an obvious marriage between a course evaluation, and a standard. If the individuals setting the standard and the individuals running the course are able to coordinate their efforts then the evaluation of the training should mirror the standard expected.

Training that is effective is training which ensures individual performance meets the expected standard, as defined by line management.

"Training must also generate the conviction that there is value in applying the learning."

4. ***Conviction:*** It's not sufficient for training to simply provide understanding and skill, it must also provide conviction; that is, the importance of the *application* of this knowledge and skill.

   Conviction is something which takes the theoretical and makes it personal. Training which generates conviction is that which allows individuals to personally appreciate the value of learning material and then applying it immediately on the job. They come to develop a personal appreciation for the content and the degree to which it can enhance their own performance.

   Effective training must promote this level of conviction, otherwise the learning will quickly be overshadowed by previously established personal habits.

   Conviction produces action; and since training is intended to shape activity, effective training must generate conviction about the value of the new learning.

A REASON "EMPOWERMENT" CAN FAIL

When the challenge is greater than the competency, the person or team just bangs into a brick wall.

1. Empowerment works as long as the wall (the challenge) is lower than the competency.
2. But these challenges are quickly met – in effect the wall continually gets higher.
3. To maintain the empowerment initiative, competency must improve, or the initiative will stagnate and level off or die.
4. Solution...Training,
   i.e. an increase in competency.

A REASON "EMPOWERMENT" CAN FAIL

The nature of empowerment is such that it has at it heart a commitment to utilizing the competency of each individual in the organization. In an empowered organization everyone is provided with clarity regarding the framework within which they have to operate, and with the encouragement to make changes that will further the organization's objectives.

Over time individuals operate within that framework and make what changes they can. They grow more and more confident, tackling more and more of the issues that they have identified as ones which are opportunities for improvement. Using the analogy of a sandbox, their sandbox has been defined and they are allowed to play within it. Over time they explore it fully, ultimately reaching out to the furthest corners. In due course they outgrow the sandbox.

In a similar fashion a significant limitation to the empowerment initiative is that individuals eventually learn to operate effectively within that framework which they have been given; they make the changes which they can, and then they collide with the framework's walls. They've outgrown their sandbox. At this point there is little additional impact which they can make, and so their initiative to improve the organization's performance falters and the empowerment initiative fails.

In order to rectify this situation, clearly the solution is to move the walls of the sandbox, ie. enlarge their framework. However, with this comes risk to the organization as individuals now have a larger framework and consequently greater opportunity for change, but also greater opportunity for significant error.

"When the challenge
is greater than
the competency,
the individual or team
in effect
'hits a brick wall'."

To address this issue, individual competency needs to be addressed. As investment is made in each individual, by enhancing their knowledge and skills, they are then able to operate as well within a larger framework as they did earlier in the more confined environment. Enhancing competency is a necessary prerequisite to expanding the framework. As a consequence, empowerment will continue and the organization will continue to see benefit.

An organization committed to empowerment must be committed to the ongoing development of each individual employee, enhancing their knowledge and enhancing their skill through training, development, and education. This ensures the benefits realized from empowering the workforce continue without loss of momentum.

Another way to look at this issue is to consider empowerment as the freedom for individuals to make positive change. As they encounter changes of increasing magnitude they will ultimately be blocked and unable to go further, unless their competency has kept pace with the challenge. When the challenge is greater than the competency the individual, or team, in effect "hits a brick wall."

As long as the wall, or the challenge, is lower than the individual's competency they will continue their forward momentum; but inevitably as they move forward they will meet increasingly higher and higher walls. To ensure that they have the capability to continue to move forward, and without being blocked, improvement in individual competency must be a priority.

STAY OPEN TO NEW IDEAS

REMAIN SENSITIVE, OPEN, RECEPTIVE

TO NEW IDEAS.

STAY OPEN TO NEW IDEAS

Having a "willingness to learn new ideas" is different from being sensitive, open and receptive to new ideas.

Consciously seek out new ideas with the possibility of applying them – this gives them the opportunity to make headway in your mind. Be sensitive to new ideas, as they are all around – they come from those you lead, they come from colleagues, they come from other leaders, competitors, books, magazines, articles, movies.

Consider all new input, evaluate new ideas, take advantage of them, and use them to alter your behavior and your way of thinking.

This ability to learn from those around us, the ability to reach out and constantly be searching for new ideas, to make our minds a fertile ground into which worthwhile seeds can fall, is an absolutely crucial skill in any leader.

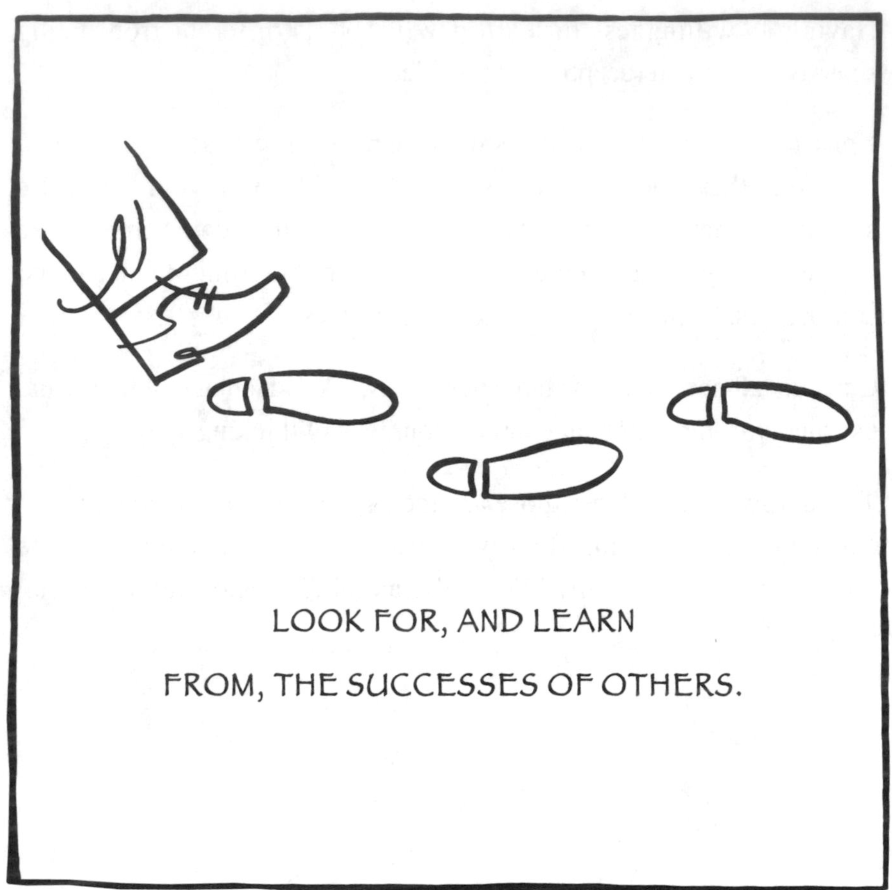
LOOK FOR, AND LEARN
FROM, THE SUCCESSES OF OTHERS.

LEARN FROM EVERY SOURCE

Look for and learn from the success of others. One way to remain open to new ideas is to aggressively and specifically learn from the things that other people have done well. This can be in your own area of expertise, or in areas outside but parallel to your own. Learning the thinking and approaches of these individuals helps a great deal. The more we know, the more competent we become, and the more we are able to effect change. Learning, especially learning from those who have been successful and have a proven track record, can be extremely powerful.

There are people doing jobs comparable to ours in other organizations, in non-competitive areas. Making contact with them, investing time to find out how they do things, exchanging ideas with them and copying their successes, is another excellent way to focus on being receptive.

Look at something, an activity, a result, a process, any observation and ask – "What can I learn from this?" Often people attending seminars walk away with the feeling that they did not learn from the session; i.e. "a different industry was discussed"; "the company discussed was much larger than the company I work for", etc. What they do not realize is that even though the *circumstances* may differ somewhat, the *principles* can still be applied.

Look for principles, and then apply them accordingly. There are also great skills which can be learned by copying from the successes of others such as: public speaking from recognized orators, teamwork from mountain climbers, time management from those successfully managing large projects, etc.

Again, it requires that we remain open and aggressively looking. These things are there if we are willing to invest the time to seek them out and learn from them.

Commit to learning about new things (not more about something you already know about); not necessarily to learn them, but rather to keep the faculty for learning open, effective, and powerful.

To become "set in your ways"
is to close the portals of learning forever.
If they are now shut – pry them open!
They should work on well-oiled hinges.

PRACTICE LEARNING NEW THINGS

Learn new things to become a master of learning.

Hinges that are not oiled ultimately rust and become immovable. The mind is very much like those hinges; and acquiring new information, new skills, new ideas – is the oil.

Unless we commit to keeping the hinges oiled, they will ultimately rust. Similarly, unless we commit to regularly learning things, our minds will grow rusty and insensitive to learning new things.

The constant introduction of new ideas and new thoughts, *as a matter of principle*, is what keeps the mind supple, flexible, and well oiled. Practice it.

When new information is available that is relevant to your needs, it becomes easier to absorb that information if you are in the *habit* of learning.

CONSTANTLY REASSESS CURRENT WAYS OF DOING THINGS

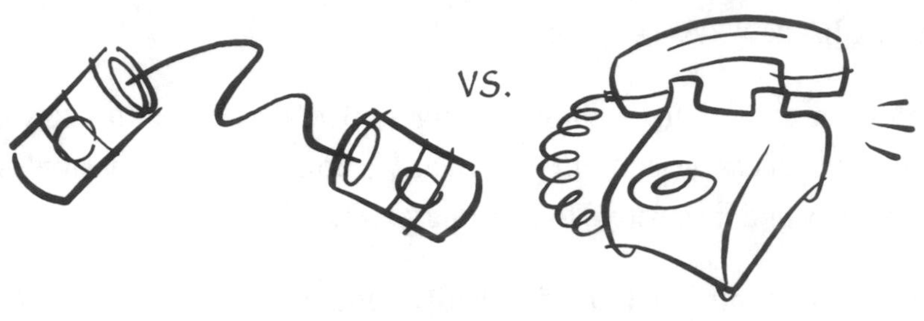

Evaluate your current ways of
doing things in the light of other ways.

Then:
Discard the previous way
or
Reshape the previous way
or
Reaffirm the merits of the previous way.

It is hard to bend a grown tree trunk.
So recognize that it may not be easy to honestly apply
a new template to your existing pattern.

CONSTANTLY REASSESS CURRENT WAYS OF DOING THINGS

It is hard to bend a grown tree trunk. So recognize that it may not be easy to honestly apply a new template to your existing pattern.

One of the specific applications of being receptive is that you will pick up new information which requires action. In fact, the information you pick up may not only require action, but may be disquieting in and of itself. This might be because it indicates that your way of doing things in the past has been wrong, or could be improved. We must overcome complacency, tradition, and pride and move ahead to learn a new way. This can often be extremely tough on the ego!

We may discover that our current way of doing things is completely "off base" – it might have been effective, and had merit at one time; but is now no longer relevant and needs to be replaced with an alternative approach. Often the new approach is "staring us in the face" and it was this that made us realize that the current way is no longer successful!

Alternatively, looking at another approach might indicate that our current approach is fine and with minor reshaping could be even better and more productive.

Perhaps our approach is already at the forefront, setting the pace; in which case this reaffirmation is well worthwhile.

Whatever the reaction to the evaluation of our current way of doing things may be, we need to be willing to respond appropriately.

Being highly receptive is a skill. It takes practice...persevere.

Managing a department or area requires a focus on two things:

PEOPLE

PROCESS

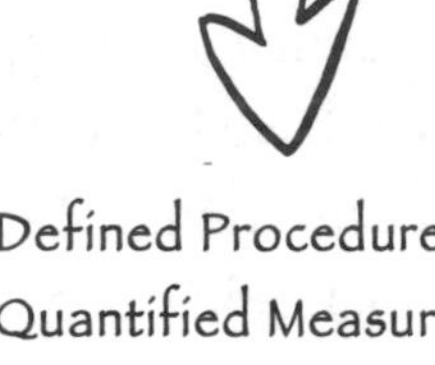

Right Person [1]
Fully Trained [2]
Brilliantly Managed [3]

1. Hire wisely
2. Commit to ongoing training
3. Provide outstanding leadership

Defined Procedures [4]
Quantified Measures [5]
Continuous Process Improvement [6]

4. Have clear steps to be followed
5. Measure everything possible
6. Continuously improve the way things are done until they are best in class (as a result of doing outside comparisons – "benchmarking")

MANAGEMENT OF A FUNCTION

Those responsible for managing or leading a given function must focus on: people and process.

"People" refers to those individuals who look to the manager for leadership and direction.

"Process" refers to several sequential steps which must be followed in order to get a given result.

Sometimes the process under consideration is huge – for example, the supply chain process begins with the procurement of raw materials through their conversion to the finished product, warehousing, distribution invoicing, and ultimately delivery to a customer – a mammoth process. Or the process could actually be quite a short one – for example, opening an email file, reading the email, drafting a response, and sending it to the appropriate party. Both examples though constitute a "process".

The effective leader understands the distinction between people and process and works to maximize both areas. When a problem occurs the question should be "Is it a people issue or a process issue?"

Attempting to resolve a people problem with a process change will be futile; similarly attempting to resolve a process issue by changing a person or disciplining an individual will be counter productive.

"When a problem occurs
the question should be:
'Is it a people issue
or a
process issue?'"

There are three elements to effective people management:

1. ***Have the right person in the job.*** In order to ensure maximum productivity in any environment the right person needs to be in place. Understand clearly what the criteria are for the job, what skills and abilities are necessary, and select wisely. There are times when an individual must be hired from without, and times when an individual can be selected from within the organization, perhaps by promotion into the position. Whatever the circumstances, having the right person in the job is an important first step.

2. ***An individual needs to be fully trained.*** In many cases training can be broken down into several categories, such as functional training (e.g. a finance person that requires a CA designation); skills training (e.g. listening or leadership); and operational training (e.g. how to use the organization's intranet). The proper training and orientation is crucial.

   If you're operating within an empowered environment, the training will be ongoing and continuous. Managing people requires a commitment to this ongoing training, and requires care to ensure that the training time is being spent in the most appropriate fashion, and on the most relevant topics.

"Whom you work for
plays a huge role in determining
your overall productivity,
ability to impact,
degree to which you can make
a difference,
amount of support you get,
and feedback you receive
in order to improve."

3. ***Leadership.*** I believe that *whom* a person works for is often more important to the outcome then *what* a person does, or the culture of the organization. Whom you work for plays a *huge* role in determining your overall productivity, ability to impact, degree to which you can make a difference, amount of support you get, and feedback you receive in order to improve.

   The brilliantly managed individual will eventually become brilliant, assuming they are the right person with access to the necessary training. Consequently you as the leader need to provide outstanding leadership. This creates the necessary environment in which your team can flourish.

When managing a process issue there are three areas which must always be considered.

1. ***The procedures for the process must be clearly defined.*** This is sometimes called a Standard Operating Procedure, or SOP. Unfortunately writing SOP's is a boring, tedious and time-consuming task. Not every process requires clear operating procedures, but most do and certainly all the important ones do.

   The value of a Standard Operating Procedure is that it allows individuals who are executing the process to do it in the most efficient fashion, as has been previously determined and documented in the Standard Operating Procedure. SOP's provide the line manager with the confidence that the task will be done in a particular fashion and allows other processes to link with that one. As processes become linked together, each with its own SOP, there is now predictability of outcome.

"Small incremental changes which accumulate over time can ultimately produce very significant improvements to the final outcomes."

When processes are changed, as they inevitably will be in an organization committed to continuous process improvement, then the procedure needs to be rewritten to reflect that process change. Clear steps to be followed by everyone in a process ensures that minimal errors occur, folklore is not part of the process, and "band-aid work-arounds," which are idiosyncratic in nature, are eliminated. A world-class process has procedures that are well defined, predictable, replicable, and which are known to generate the desired results.

Whether the task is to create a series of gala evenings for opening concerts, or record heart rate readings, there should be a defined procedure in place for doing it in the correct and most efficient fashion.

2. ***Processes need quantified measures.*** Measure everything possible. The more effective you become at measuring, the more effective you will become at predicting outcomes, and changing outcomes where necessary.

   Because processes are intended to produce results they can be measured. These quantified measures allow those responsible for executing various steps of the process to monitor how well they are doing, and adjust as required. Once the target is clear it is much easier to determine how close you are to dead centre.

   Every process needs to have quantified measures. They can be simple (number of customers served per hour) or complex (net deviation from standard per item); but they need to be there.

"The effective leader understands the distinction between people and process, and works to maximize both areas."

3. ***Once a process is defined clearly with measures in place, then steps should be taken to continuously improve that process.*** Small incremental changes which accumulate over time can ultimately produce very significant improvements to the final outcomes.

   Individuals who believe that there is no better way to do what they are doing should invest time in benchmarking their processes with those of other non-competitive organizations.

   By identifying other world-class organizations engaged in a comparable process, and determining how they do what they do, you can bring back what you learned to your own organization. If this benchmarking exercise only serves to reinforce that in fact there is no better way to do it, then that is also of value – it allows you to concentrate on other processes which could be improved.

   If on the other hand new ways of doing things are seen which can be applied, the organization has benefitted and has a target for process improvement in that particular area.

When responsible for managing a function, check to ensure that the right person is fully trained and is being properly managed. Also ensure that each of the individuals know what steps they need to follow and are measuring their outcomes. In this way they will be able to determine whether they are on target, and set new targets for process improvement. This combination of focus on people and process will maximize the output of your function.

Because all management issues are a combination of people and process, this breakdown provides a Leadership Diagnostic to figure out what's wrong, and then how to fix it.

PEOPLE

The individuals involved in the work

Example:
Barb and Jim agree to take Patches, their pet spaniel, for a walk.

+

The steps which the people take to get the job done

THE (9 STEP) "PROCESS"

1. Talk
2. Decide
3. Get Leash
4. Get Dog
5. Put Leash On
6. Go Outside
7. Walk
8. Return
9. Take Leash Off

Why didn't something work?

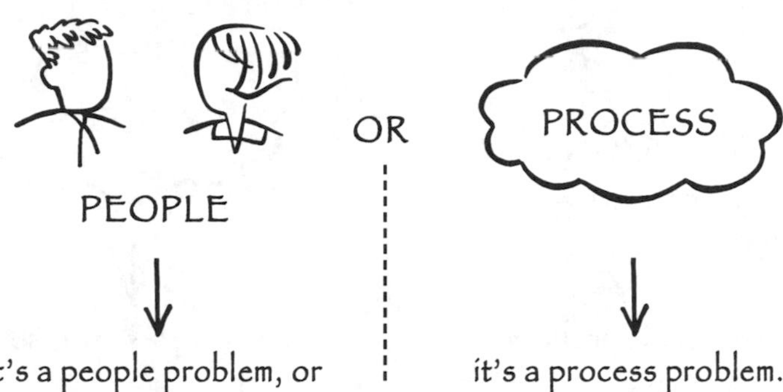
PEOPLE
OR
PROCESS
It's a people problem, or
it's a process problem.

IT WILL BE ONE, OR BOTH - ALWAYS.

Example:
It's 11 PM and the dog still isn't walked.

"PEOPLE"

Barb or Jim didn't do it.

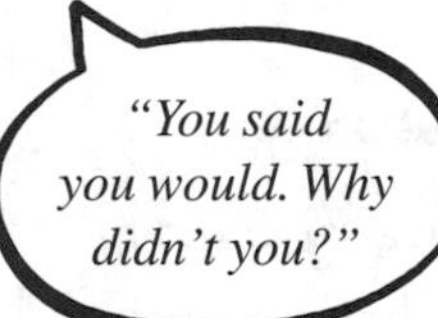
"You said you would. Why didn't you?"

"PROCESS"

The process broke down somewhere:

- They didn't talk
- They didn't agree
- They couldn't find the dog
- Or the leash, etc.

"Hey honey! where's the leash?"

You can't fix a people problem with a process solution; and you can't fix a process problem with a people solution.

PEOPLE AND PROCESS: USING THE CONCEPT

Harry came to work late. Why?

OR

PEOPLE

↓ It's a people problem, or

↓ it's a process problem.

Possible "PEOPLE" causes:

- He forgot to set the alarm
- He decided to stop for breakfast
- He got caught up in a family problem
- He spent too long reading the paper

Solutions:

- Harry could simply behave differently (or learn a different behavior) to resolve the problem

Possible "PROCESS" causes:

- The alarm clock battery gave out
- Traffic lights were out, causing an accident
- His car ran out of gas
- A wrinkled shirt needed pressing

Solutions:

- Harry would have to change the steps he took

eg. Change batteries every 6 months, on schedule

Listen to radio reports of traffic rather than his CD of Mozart. etc.

PEOPLE AND PROCESS: USING THE CONCEPT

Mabel has been coming to work late a great deal recently. Why?

OR

PEOPLE

↓

It's a people problem, or

Possible "PEOPLE" causes:

- She is having stress-related worries because of work pressure
- She is afraid of meeting her boss early in the morning in light of his recent unwelcome advances
- She has recently joined a late night exercise class and is oversleeping
- She hates her job since the department has been downsized

↓

it's a process problem.

Possible "PROCESS" causes:

- The bank repossessed her car and she has an irregular bus schedule
- Her stove is defective, so preparing breakfast sometimes takes much longer
- Construction crews working in her area are causing traffic tangles
- She now has a boyfriend so is often out late. Since the laundry used to be done in the evening, she now has to do it in the morning before work

Finding a solution.

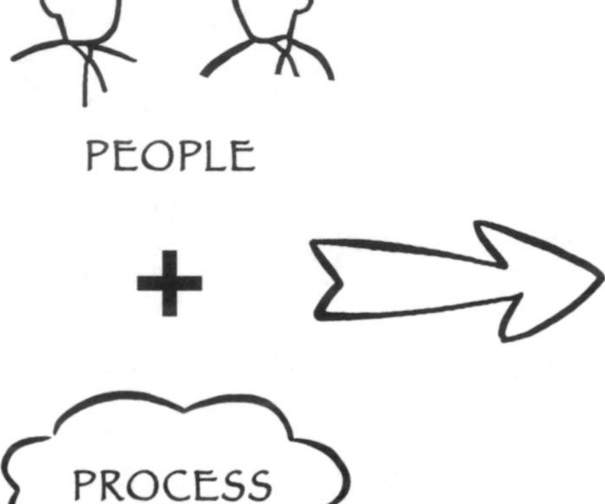

First determine in which area the source of the problem lies.

Then work on developing a solution.

This principle is true whether the issue is reasonably confined (eg. a late employee); or major – such as poor customer service. Is it people providing poor service; or is the process keeping good people from delivering good service?

If a "people" issue:

OR

PEOPLE

3 PRIORITIES

1. RIGHT PERSON
   - Know what the job requires, in detail
   - Recruit accordingly, or train
2. FULLY TRAINED
   - Job requirements
     - Skill
     - Knowledge
   - Close performance gaps with training
3. PROPERLY MANAGED
   - Individual potential can best be fully realized by world-class leadership

Building a training plan:
Whenever possible – recruit with as many of these skills as possible to avoid training costs once the individual is on the job.

- Right person
- Fully trained

PEOPLE

↓

STEPS:

1. Build a grid like this one shown on the right hand side
2. Assess all staff

   eg. ✓ already has it
   ● needs it this year
   ○ needs it next year
3. Build a training plan
4. Reassess annually

	Harry	Sally
Job Related Skills		
eg. Computer literacy	✓	○
Order entry	✓	○
Order fulfillment	●	✓
etc.		
Job Knowledge		
eg. Cost per error	●	✓
Reading inventory reports	○	●
Current items on promotion	✓	○
etc.		
General Skills		
eg. Telephone etiquette	●	✓
Negotiations skill – level 1	○	✓
Listening skill	○	✓
etc.		
Supervisory Skill		
eg. Setting goals	✓	○
Managing performance gaps	✓	○
Annual performance appraisals	✓	●
etc.		

PEOPLE AND PROCESS: USING THE CONCEPT

If a "process" issue:

PEOPLE

OR

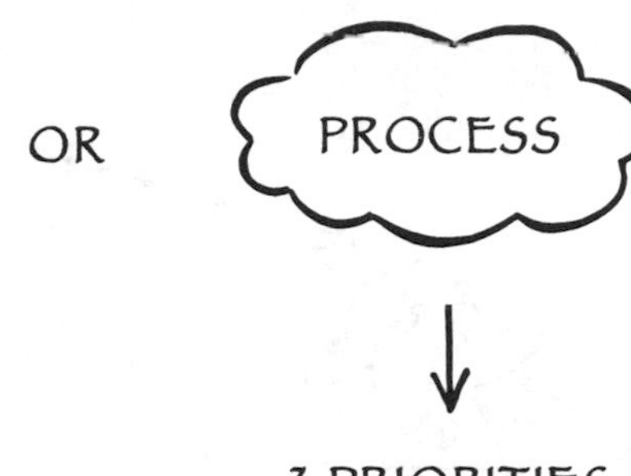

3 PRIORITIES

1. DEFINED PROCEDURES
   The best and proper way to accomplish the individual activities so the process is as fast and error free as possible.

2. QUANTIFIED MEASURES
   What is the process supposed to deliver, by when, at what cost, with what level of quality?

3. BENCHMARKED CONTINUOUS PROCESS IMPROVEMENT

How can your process be changed to give a competitive advantage, reduce or eliminate waste, reduce cost, improve quality, or increase speed?

How do other organizations perform a similar process? Are they more efficient? Why?

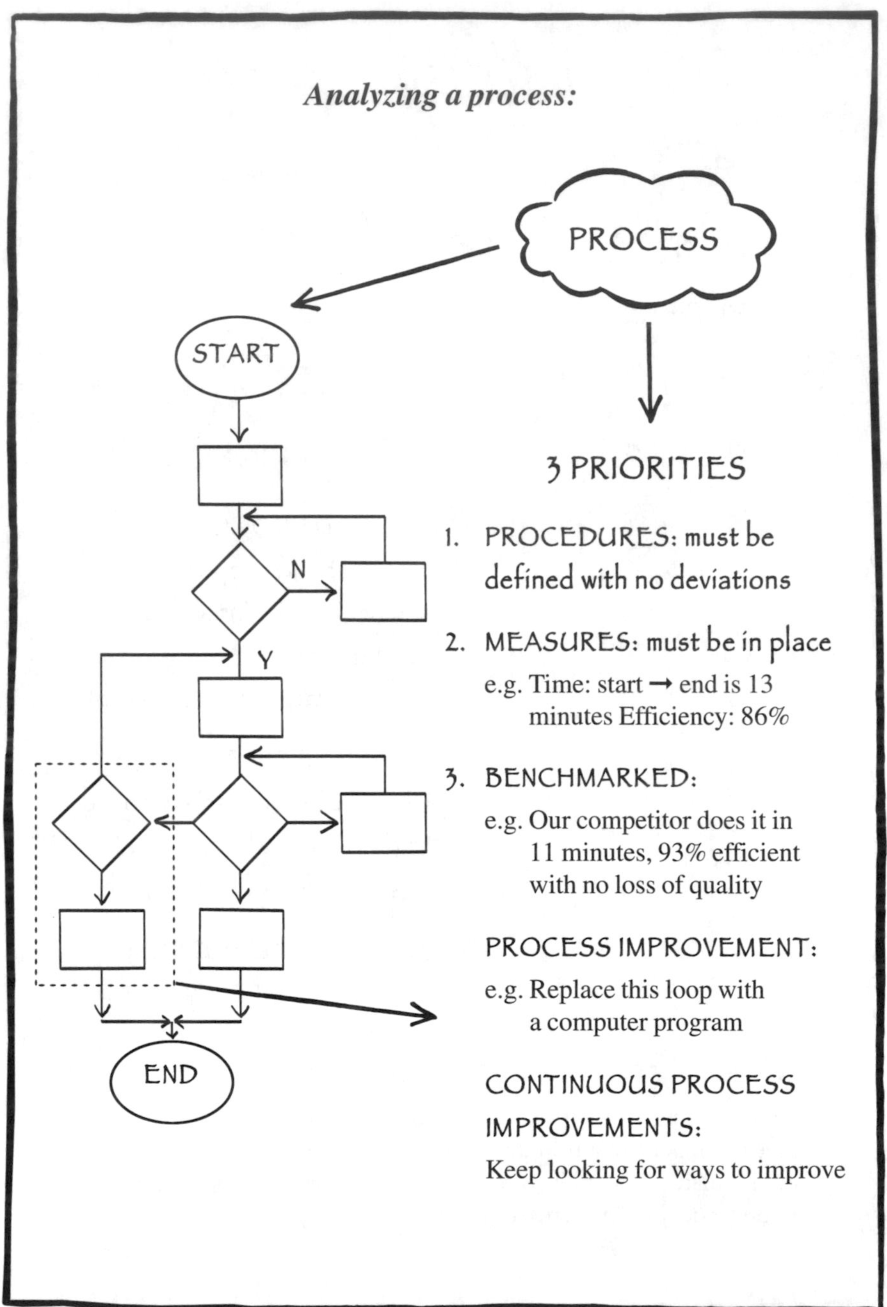
Analyzing a process:
PROCESS
START
N
Y
END
3 PRIORITIES
1. PROCEDURES: must be defined with no deviations
2. MEASURES: must be in place
e.g. Time: start → end is 13 minutes Efficiency: 86%
3. BENCHMARKED:
e.g. Our competitor does it in 11 minutes, 93% efficient with no loss of quality
PROCESS IMPROVEMENT:
e.g. Replace this loop with a computer program
CONTINUOUS PROCESS IMPROVEMENTS:
Keep looking for ways to improve

Peter ordered an all dressed hot dog from "Dave's Dogs".

The result was so bad he vowed never to return – and from then on purchased his "dogs" from another street vendor. Why?

OR

PEOPLE

↓

It's a people problem, or

Possible "PEOPLE" causes:

- Dave was rude
- Dave was sloppy and spilled condiments everywhere
- Dave gave the wrong change, then argued the point

Solutions:

- These could all be solved with training, or by replacing Dave!

↓

it's a process problem.

Possible "PROCESS" causes:

- The buns were stale
- The dogs were cold
- The condiments were dried up

Solutions:

- These all require a change in the steps taken to get dogs to customers

eg. • Buy buns daily
• Start stove earlier
• Purchase and install sealable storage units for buns and condiments

MEETINGS CAN BE MAXIMALLY PRODUCTIVE

1. Know WHAT is to be covered:
   • "What's the reason we're together?"
   ↓
   = The Objective, The Agenda

2. Get INPUT:
   • Ask for Opinions

3. Use KNOWLEDGE:
   • Reference Facts

4. Make DECISIONS:
   • To act, or
   • To get more info, or
   • To do nothing until ______ (your date)

5. ASSIGN Tasks:
   • Who will do what, by when

6. Commit to FOLLOW UP:
   • Did it get done?
   • Consequence = ?

MEETINGS CAN BE MAXIMALLY PRODUCTIVE

Meetings are often accused of being one of the great time wasters of modern civilization. And this is often true!

However, it need not be so. A well-run meeting can not only save time, but can serve to get everyone focused, put information on the table, and allow for rapid progress toward an end result.

Because these benefits are so valuable we often put up with all the waste that also accompanies the benefit! There are six steps that can be followed to make meetings maximally productive, and so eliminate the waste.

1. ***Everyone needs to understand what the objective is.*** An opening question like, "What are we here to achieve?" often serves to focus people's attention.

   Similarly, putting out an agenda in advance helps keep the meeting focused and helps to provide clarity on the tasks to be accomplished (assuming, of course, you have the discipline to stick to the agenda!).

2. ***Be careful not to bring people together when a memo, or video would accomplish the same thing.*** When information is one-way out to others, then often there are more effective vehicles than meetings.

   Therefore meetings should be used when you wish to solicit the opinions of others, or get their feedback on the information which has already been sent out.

3. ***Make sure that the information discussed is based on fact.*** To spend time on issues only to subsequently discover that the original data were faulty is extremely frustrating. Ensuring that items are fact-based tends to eliminate the need to go back and reconsider information at another meeting later on.

"A well-run meeting
can not only save time,
but can serve to
get everybody focused,
put information on the table,
and allow for rapid progress
towards an end result."

4. ***Productive meetings are ones which result in decisions.*** Not all decisions have to be to do something; sometimes the decision can simply be to gather more data, or to wait until some other event occurs, etc. However clarity about decisions that have been arrived at during the course of the meeting significantly enhances their productiveness. Keeping track of the decisions should be done in the minutes of the meeting.

5. ***Any work that follows as a result of the meeting should be assigned to the appropriate individuals.***

   This work assignment should be clearly stated in terms of what is to be expected, what resources will be used, and when the work should be accomplished. Providing this degree of clarity "on the spot" when everyone is clear on the issues discussed is one of the powerful benefits of discussing issues at meetings in the first place.

6. ***Commit to follow-up on the commitments made at the meeting.***

   Individuals need to know that they will be held accountable for the work assigned to them, or that they've agreed to do. Others will now be dependent on the consequences of the discussions made, or action agreed to, so following up to ensure it gets done is crucial.

   Committing to action, and demonstrating the accompanying follow-up, is motivating to those attending as they see progress being made as a result of meeting together.

ONE-ON-ONE MEETINGS REQUIRE SKILL AND CARE

1. CLEAR FOCUS
   A mutually understood objective

2. MUTUAL LISTENING

3. CHECK AND RECHECK
   "If I understood you correctly you said ..."

4. CLEARLY AGREED NEXT STEPS

Remain Patient, Respectful, and Focused.

ONE-ON-ONE MEETINGS REQUIRE SKILL AND CARE

When meetings occur between individuals (rather than in larger groups) different skills are required. There are four clear steps that significantly improve one-on-one interaction.

1. ***Have a clear focus.*** The reason that two people are together needs to be clear to both parties. Consequently a few moments up front making absolutely clear what is looked for as an outcome, is both crucial and key to an effective one-on-one interchange.

2. ***Commit to effective mutual listening.*** Often two people together find themselves with one dominating as the speaker, and the other more passive as the listener. The "speaker" appears to be there to tell the "listener" what they want them to hear. Inevitably, the individual intended to be the listener will also have a point of view and something to contribute.

   Consequently, it's vital that *both* parties enter into a one-on-one meeting with the intent to listen clearly to the other as the meeting progresses, in order to maximize the value of the time together.

3. ***Check and recheck.*** We often assume that, because there are only two of us talking in a meeting, there can be no possible misunderstanding. Often though, misunderstandings are more likely between two people when there are no others in the room to check, validate, or probe another's comments.

   As a result, one of the keys to successful one-on-one meetings is to frequently check and then recheck to ensure that what was heard was what was said. An excellent way of doing this is simply by using the phrase, "If I understood you correctly you said...". This allows the listener to politely check to ensure that the message they received was the one that was intended.

"One of the keys
to successful one-on-one
meetings is to
frequently check and ensure
that what was heard
was what was said."

4. ***Agree on next steps.*** At the end of the discussion something will have occurred. Sometimes it's an action plan, sometimes it's simply an understanding to move forward. Whatever the case both parties need to agree on what steps were committed to, and what will occur as a result of having met together.

COORDINATING INPUT FROM OTHERS: KEEP IT FOCUSED

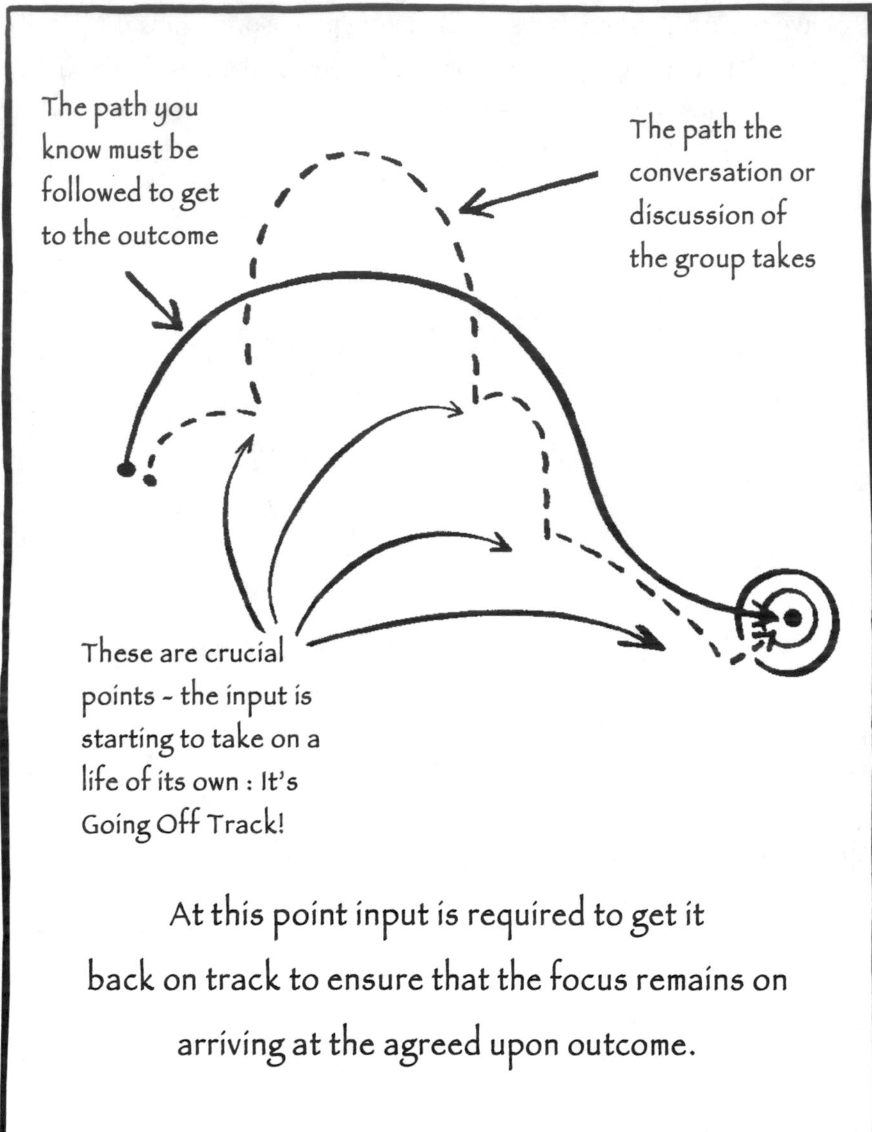

The path you know must be followed to get to the outcome
The path the conversation or discussion of the group takes
These are crucial points - the input is starting to take on a life of its own : It's Going Off Track!
At this point input is required to get it back on track to ensure that the focus remains on arriving at the agreed upon outcome.

COORDINATING INPUT FROM OTHERS: KEEP IT FOCUSED

It often falls to the leader to be responsible for managing input in group meetings or team meetings. This input needs to be managed and coordinated in order to ensure the most desirable outcome.

I recall sitting on a board of volunteers where everyone had a willing and enthusiastic spirit, was keen to contribute, and keen to be heard. The Chair's job was to coordinate all that input and ensure that time and resources were used in the most efficient fashion. We all share this challenge when responsible for coordinating input from others!

A primary objective is to keep the input focused. As the leader you will have some feel for the task or the steps to be followed in order to ensure that the outcome is achieved as required. Clearly it is inappropriate for you to dictatorially drive the group in that direction – this inhibits involvement, and blocks the opportunity to reap the benefit of the experience and viewpoints of the others in the group. But as the discussion progresses, you do need to be able to get from the starting point to the end.

Allow the discussion to flow, and when you feel it's deviating too far from the path then *nudge* it back on track. As long as you feel the general direction is aligned with the path you feel is appropriate, then let the discussion go on. However, once you believe it's taking on a life of its own, or veering *away* from that which you feel to be the most effective path, a nudge is then appropriate.

Clearly this is the longer approach. It would be much faster to simply force the discussion to an end; but then you lose all the benefits which come from effectively coordinating the inputs of others; and have failed to provide the quality of leadership that is expected by the group.

COORDINATING INPUT FROM OTHERS: WATCH RELATIVE VALUE

When value starts to go down (relative to the earlier discussions) it's time to limit further discussion.

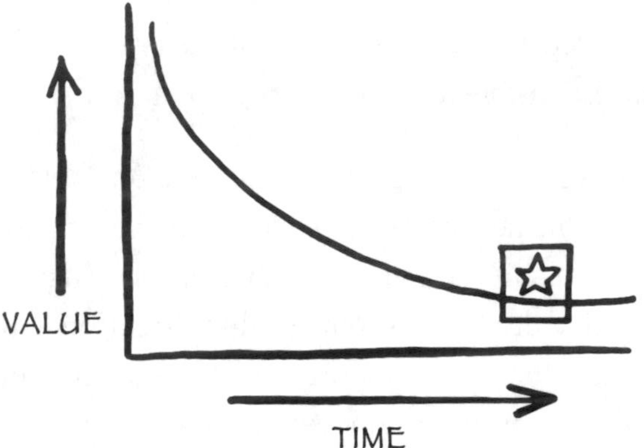

At this point time is being less well spent, arguments are being repeated, and it's time to bring closure to this portion of the discussion.

COORDINATING INPUT FROM OTHERS: WATCH RELATIVE VALUE

In meetings or teams where several individuals are giving points of view, discussion tends to flow around a given topic or series of subjects. You as the leader need to manage the flow. Typically in the early stages of a discussion the input received is of considerable value; however, as the discussion progresses it can become repetitive, ultimately spiraling down into a waste of time for all concerned.

This can be difficult to handle if individuals in the group do not realize that they are perpetuating the spiral, or feel that they are adding new information when in your judgement, they are not.

The challenge as a leader is to know how far to let this kind of discussion go before tactfully moving on with a statement such as: "Allow me to summarize what we've discussed so far; and then I suggest we move on to the next point, after Sally has finished with her current thoughts."

In order to identify when to move a conversation forward think in terms of a graph with "time" on the "X" axis and "value" on the "Y" axis. In the early stages of the discussion there is high value, but as it degenerates into repetitive comments the value is low. As you see this point approaching move the group off the subject.

Relative value is a key guide to knowing how to coordinate the input from others. There is always value in everything anyone says, but *relatively* there can be significant less value once the subject has been examined and discussed thoroughly. At that point there will be greater value in moving on to the next topic, and you as a leader need to be sensitive to this truth and manage the process accordingly.

COORDINATING INPUT FROM OTHERS: RECAP PERIODICALLY

Periodically provide a short recap. This accelerates progress, and avoids unnecessary duplication or loss of group focus.

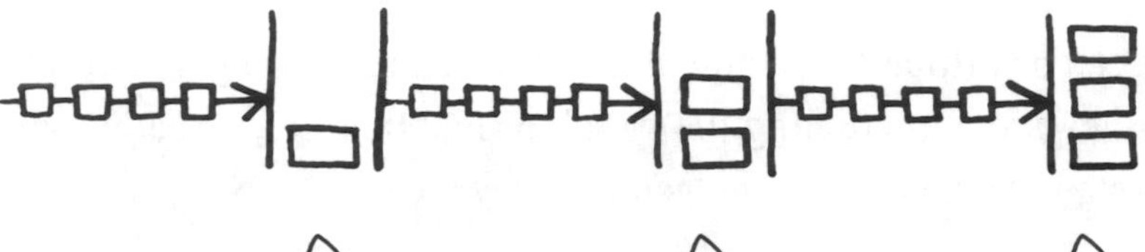

Pause to review and recap what was said

Again, pause and recap – keeping the work accomplished, or issues discussed top of mind

Etc.

COORDINATING INPUT FROM OTHERS: RECAP PERIODICALLY

One of the most effective ways to coordinate input from others is to periodically exercise your authority as leader and recap what has been said. This has several benefits.

It keeps people on track so that their comments and input do not meander and stray from the topic at hand. It also serves to reinforce progress made to date and conclusions already arrived at.

Frequent recapping tends to inhibit repetitive comments as people realize, from your recap, that perhaps what they were about to say has already been said in another way. Lastly, recapping is a powerful way to move from the theoretical to the practical – it allows you to summarize what has been said, what has been agreed to, and what action will be taken. This provides people with a sense of accomplishment, and also clarifies the decisions and thoughts that have been articulated clearly and on which people have agreed.

As you pause periodically to recap what has been said do not neglect to recap your own earlier recaps! You need to provide the group with your summary relative to the most recent discussions, and also keep them apprised of earlier discussions that you previously recapped. This builds a sense of growing achievement and ensures that the group remains focused on the topic at hand.

Group focus is crucial in these kinds of discussions, and recapping is a key tool in making that happen.

COORDINATING INPUT FROM OTHERS: ASK FOR ADDITIONAL INPUT

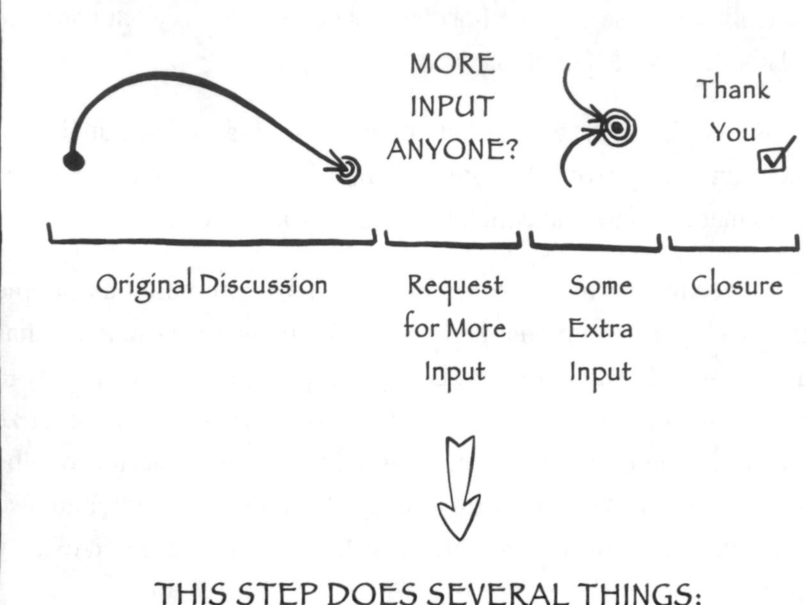

THIS STEP DOES SEVERAL THINGS:

1. Ensures less outgoing individuals do have a chance to contribute

2. Avoids any appearance of "railroading" a conclusion by anyone

3. Often brings out excellent input that was slow in germinating

4. Shows courtesy to all – and therefore strong leadership

COORDINATING INPUT FROM OTHERS: ASK FOR ADDITIONAL INPUT

Once the group has come to resolution the last thing you as leader want to do is ask for more input!

In part, asking for more input may appear to be opening the gate for further discussion; and it may seem to be unnecessary and time consuming. Personally, you may simply be glad that the discussion has finally come to an end and that you can now move on!

However, there are many times when asking for additional input would be of great value. Once you believe the discussion has wound down, and you have made your "final" summary for the group, then pause and say something like, "Before we move on, perhaps we should just take a *moment* to see whether there is any additional input from anyone." This does several things:

1. It provides those less outgoing individuals with a chance to provide their input, if they had not been able to do so to their satisfaction earlier. Sometimes the more extroverted members of the group carry the discussion, and it comes to closure before the quieter ones have had a chance to really express their points as they wish. Often their input is very valuable and worth hearing. Asking for additional input after the more vocal ones have been heard and summarized provides an opportunity for those who are somewhat more shy to contribute, if they still have something to say.

"The mark of a leader
is their ability to draw out
the best from all those
who are
part of the group."

2. It avoids any appearance that the conclusion was railroaded by some members of the group. If there is still strong opposition, or a dissenting voice, then this is an opportunity for them to speak and to allow you as a leader to hear those concerns if they have not been effectively expressed before this point.

   Individuals who disagree, but have had their say, may perhaps speak up with a comment like: "Well I don't agree, but you know how I feel," in which case you are already aware of that point of view and have taken it into account.

   Going forward it is of great value for people to feel that they have had a chance to truly express their points of view, and not feel they are being driven into something which they don't fully support without first having had a chance to voice their concerns.

3. Very often individuals will have a germ of an idea that will take a while to come to fruition. They're thinking something through, preparing their thoughts, maybe even mentally organizing some information to present. While they are doing this the discussion is of course continuing, and may even be drawing to a conclusion. If you as the leader move on without asking for any further comment you may miss that idea which has now crystallized and is ready to be presented.

   This may not happen often, but it does happen periodically and it would be a shame to lose these gems, as they are often of considerable value. The individual putting them forward has, after all, given quite a bit of thought to the matter before speaking.

"Very often individuals
will have a germ of an idea
that will take a
while to come to fruition."

4. It allows you to demonstrate courtesy to the group, and sensitivity to each individual around the table. This is respected and seen as a mark of leadership. Being courteous is clearly key in any leader, and sensitivity to others needs to be top of mind when you have a group of people in discussion, especially when your objective is to coordinate their input, or lead it through to a viable conclusion.

There are times when asking for addition input is inappropriate or unnecessary; but not always. You need to be sensitive to this and act in accordance with your own best judgement. Once any additional input is called for and heard, then include it with your final wrap-up and bring closure to the topic.

The mark of a leader is their ability to draw the best out from all those who are part of the team or group. Being sensitive in this fashion will allow you to do so.

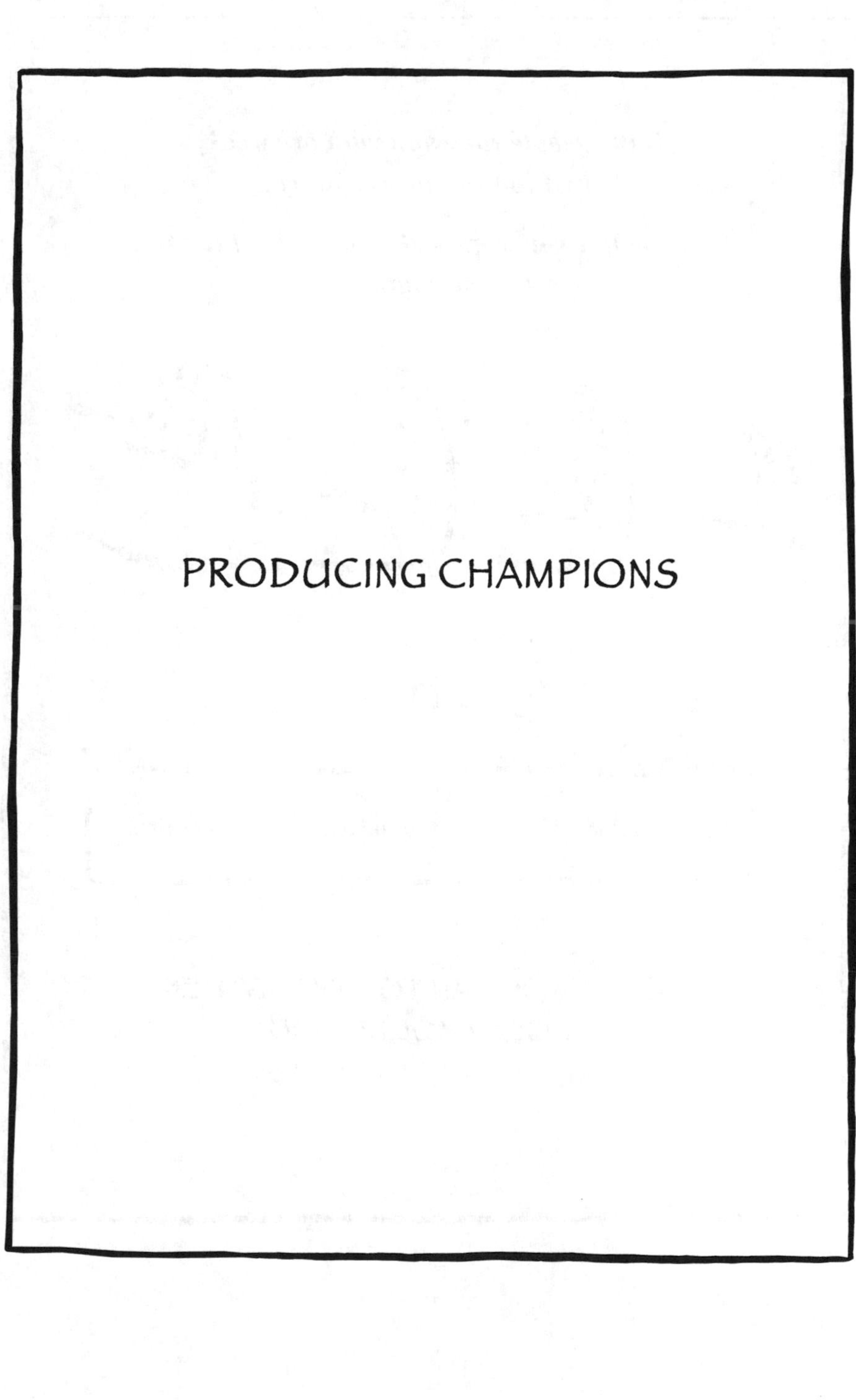

PRODUCING CHAMPIONS

If the people you work with are weak, then you will be weakened.

If the people you work with are strong, then you will be strengthened.

Your regular, consistent input into another, over time

DO ALL YOU CAN TO STRENGTHEN THOSE AROUND YOU.

STRENGTHENING OTHERS

The effort made to strengthen others pays back many times over, as it not only builds confidence and skill on the job, but also results in improvement to overall, long term capability. Further, strong people strengthen those around them, as well as the teams of which they are a part.

There are some things which might be seen as hindrances to investing time in strengthening others: feeling too busy; being threatened that your job may be taken by the one you strengthened; personal ego – the person is unwilling to learn; and, your own fear of failure. However, in each case, this hurdle needs to be addressed head on, and dealt with, and not allowed to block the initiative, given its importance.

Employees need to be competent in each area of their jobs. So identification of the key job components establishes a job profile which then serves as a base against which to assess relative strengths and weaknesses. In areas of weakness a supervisor's responsibility is to close the gaps, which is called "gap management." As it is critical to the success of the organization to have each person competent in all their key areas this requires a fundamental commitment to training and development.

Strengthening others, however, goes beyond gap management and takes an individual beyond their required competence level; the object is to unleash their potential.

Each person has the potential to be better than they currently are, and leaders are responsible for developing this. This then sets two ongoing priorities for leaders:

1. Close gaps – develop the required skills.

2. Release human potential by building in abilities even greater than what is immediately required – build for the future.

"Each person has the potential to be better than they currently are, and leaders are responsible for helping to develop this."

The six steps required to make this happen are:

1. A commitment from both parties to make it happen.
2. The identification of what could be strengthened.
3. The subsequent identification of a suitable strength to be passed on to another.
4. Frequent and ongoing communication.
5. A recognition and appreciation that different people will learn at a different pace, and in different ways.
6. An appreciation by both parties of the importance of this effort and how it fits into the bigger picture.

Success will be achieved if the leader is committed to strengthening others. This initiative though must be done "along the way," i.e. as circumstances allow during the course of day-to-day activities, "teaching by inclusion."

If the commitment is there, and the effort is made as opportunities present themselves, i.e., it's kept "top of mind", then successes will follow and individuals will grow stronger.

Determine the one thing that is your greatest strength,

Then commit yourself to building this strength into others.

PASS ON YOUR GREATEST STRENGTH

Imagine an individual beginning as a mailroom clerk, and bringing a number of skills to this job. As they rise through the organization additional skills are acquired. This is natural as one progresses through a career.

Suppose now this mail clerk has a supervisor who, for example, is very strong at reading a Profit and Loss Statement. The supervisor recognizes that the clerk will not probably need this skill in the mailroom, however identifies this as their own personal strength and decides to pass it on to the mailroom clerk anyway, and does so, *in addition* to providing the necessary help to close any knowledge or skill gaps required for the job (gap management). As a result of this additional strengthening the mailroom clerk now has the ability to read a Profit and Loss Statement; and they have it for life!

Assume the clerk later gets promoted and has a new supervisor. This new boss is very strong at negotiation skills and *in addition* to closing any gaps, passes this negotiation strength on to the clerk...and so on throughout the clerk's career.

Over time this individual advances, now carrying each of these additional strengths as personal competencies. When given their own team of people to lead, they are then able to pass the acquired additional strengths on to this team!

"Leaders who
consistently pass on their
strengths are meaningfully
increasing the
overall intellectual capital
of the organization."

PASS ON YOUR GREATEST STRENGTH

If an organization has 1,500 employees, all of whom are closing gaps *and* strengthening others in this way, then over an extended period of time:

1. Lower levels will have the skills that in the past were only at the senior level.

2. An incredibly strong organization results.

Your greatest strengths may be technical, and related to day-to-day activities on the job; they may be in the area of leadership or supervision; they may be in the area of personal skills, such as getting along well with people. They may be simple, insightful, attitude based or philosophical. Whatever your strengths, *pass them on, in addition* to providing the necessary gap management.

People are always striving either to be better, or to be perceived as better.

If you are seen as someone who accelerates this process in others, then you yourself will be considered as extremely valuable.

Be the force that is instrumental

in causing this to happen!

Work hard to make others look good!

HELP OTHERS LOOK GOOD

Most people are always striving to either be better, or be perceived as better. We should try to accelerate this process by working hard to make others look good.

Setting aside those who are complacent and lack real ambition, there remain two different types of individuals:

1. Those who are good, yet who may believe that they are not being perceived as good. They don't believe they have the visibility or the exposure to be properly appreciated. (They know they are good and it's the perception and visibility that they are after.)

2. Those who feel they have potential to be better. They would say, "Give me the opportunity and I'll really be able to perform!" They want to be stronger.

When told, "I believe in you and will help you get the appropriate visibility and exposure," people's performance will generally rise to meet that degree of confidence expressed in them.

Making the effort to show the true value of others and providing encouragement instills confidence. They are being given the opportunity to develop in areas which they feel are their strengths.

As a person's self-confidence and self-image improves then they are willing to take greater risks, speak with more conviction, and often express themselves more fully. They will contribute many of the things which usually remain hidden inside for fear of ridicule, or lack of confidence.

"Making the effort
to make others look good,
and providing
encouragement,
instills confidence."

By addressing this – by working hard to make apparent the true worth of others -you allow them the opportunity to really demonstrate that they do have worth. You are providing the framework that allows them to rise to high expectations. There are three distinct things leaders can do to instill this degree of confidence.

Give Credit

This is a process whereby if an individual does a good job they receive appropriate credit and, when possible, in front of others.

Note: This is *not* giving credit *away*. Be sure you "keep" appropriate credit for your own contribution. This enhances your overall credibility and reduces the risk of appearing insincere.

Give Way (Listen)

Allow individuals the opportunity to press forward with their point of view, their opinion or their idea. This is analogous to a powerful motor boat meeting up with a small sail boat and the motor boat "giving way" to the smaller boat: allowing it to continue on course, at the "expense" of the motor boat having to adjust its own course somewhat.

There are other circumstances where that same sailboat may find itself in a situation where it must give way, for example, to a canoe. So there are times when you need to give way to others, and there are times when others will need to give way to you. But the way to make others look good is to allow them passage, when it is clear that their approach has some merit.

"By working hard
to make others look good
you allow others
the opportunity to really
demonstrate that
they do have worth.
You are providing the
framework that allows them to
rise to high expectations."

This "allowing of passage" is fundamental to allowing other people to have an opportunity to present their ideas, concepts, beliefs, and convictions. The one in authority must be willing to be swayed if the suggestions are valid.

This at times can be difficult: for example, when an employee has a "great new idea" – but it is an idea that has previously been tried and subsequently been found wanting. The problem with rejecting the idea outright is that the individual may feel as though they have little worth and may be hesitant to bring forward any ideas again, and their next idea may be priceless!

In these circumstances listen completely, ask why it is felt this idea will work (perhaps they're suggesting a new twist to the idea not tried before), and if appropriate collaborate more fully – now or later. Sometimes after the individual has thought things through they will conclude the idea will not work after all. But they were heard! And by so doing:

1. They are stronger as a result.

2. Confidence, trust and respect have been instilled in them.

3. This individual recognizes that you are open and approachable, and so they will be willing to bring forward their next idea.

"As a person's
self-confidence improves
they will contribute
many of the things which
usually remain
hidden inside for lack
of confidence."

Give Support

Giving support is another way in which others can be made to look good. This is a process whereby an individual is supported in an activity. Everything reasonable is done to make them successful, which can include your own experience; providing them with access to resources; and your time as coach or mentor.

Note:

Giving credit is strengthening in the *past tense*... you are giving credit for something already done.

Giving way is *future tense*... you are allowing them to pursue an idea or approach, something they would like to do in the future.

Giving support is *present based*... you are providing them with a "safety net," support for a current activity. This support could be advice, encouragement, money, coaching, etc.

People are strengthened, and significant things are built into their lives, only over an extended period of time.

Recognize this, be patient, and understand it to be a long term process.

SHORT TERM EFFORTS  SHALLOW RESULTS

LONG TERM, SUSTAINED EFFORT AND COMMITMENT 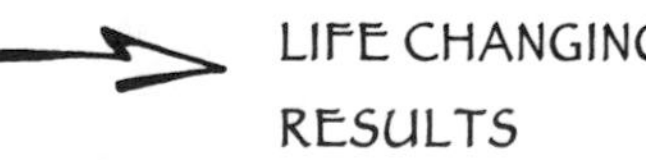 LIFE CHANGING RESULTS

BE PATIENT WHEN HELPING OTHERS TO GROW

Once you embark upon the journey of strengthening others, then patience must always remain top of mind.

People take a long time to learn, new ideas are not readily accepted, old patterns and old ways are not immediately discarded in favor of new ones. Consequently, one must be patient as a builder into people, and must expect that life changing learning will not occur quickly. Continue to be patient, and supportive; and persevere.

Rome was not built in a day. If you plan to build Rome into the life of an individual expect it to take longer than a day!

If a cup of water is poured on the carpet today it will be soaked up, dry out, and tomorrow there will be no evidence that water had been poured onto it. Pouring water on the carpet will darken it temporarily, but will not change it permanently.

India ink, on the other hand, if poured onto the carpet will never come out. It becomes a part of the fabric. Literally, to get it out requires a knife. The portion of the carpet with the stain would have to be cut away from the rest of the carpet.

People are the same way.

The really significant things – like India ink – reach down into the heart and latch on to the inner commitment and values – those areas which drive an individual. These things inevitably take a long time to sink that deep.

Superficial things – like the water – can be taught and learned quite quickly but make little impact.

"The really significant
things reach down into
the heart and latch on to
inner commitment
and values. These things
inevitably take a long time
to sink that deep."

Some examples:

1. Amateur musicians can be born overnight with the acquisition of a small electronic organ. However, world-class musicians who are able to enthrall vast audiences require years of training.

2. It's easy to walk into the grocery store, buy a frozen entrée, and pop it in the oven; but to become a world-class chef takes years and years of training and practice. It takes a long time to develop someone who can prepare a product that tastes that good so consistently. Chefs take a long time to develop.

3. A phrase book is easily purchased allowing one to speak a word or two in a foreign language. But to master a language with its inflections and pronunciations, colloquial jargon, grammar and vocabulary requires a long period of time. Only at the end of that time will one have complete mastery of the language.

Life changing results and meaningful things are accomplished only in the long term with sustained and patient effort.

There will always be the need to "teach" others. Perhaps not in the traditional "education" or "training" sense – but certainly in the "passing of information" sense.

These skills are usually weak, yet the information being passed is important. Hence the need to improve your teaching skill.

Teachers are architects building concepts and ideas into the minds of their listeners. Don't just talk – build; constantly checking your progress against the blueprint in your own mind.

TEACHING SKILLS: BUILD INTO THE MINDS OF OTHERS

Teachers are architects building concepts into the minds of their listeners. They don't just talk, they build constantly checking progress against the blueprint in their mind.

To understand why learning to "teach" is important for any leader in an organizational setting requires a better understanding of the differences between communication, teaching and training. They form a continuum, and the approach depends on what you are trying to achieve.

If you are simply passing on information: *Communication*.

If you are trying to achieve behavioral change: *Teaching*.

If you want to ensure that the behavior is learned: *Training*.

Consider an example that demonstrates that what is traditionally considered "communication" is really "teaching". Your supervisor is supposed to attend a very important conference and something has now occurred which makes it impossible for him to attend. He asks you to attend in his place. The supervisor communicates what he hopes to share and learn from the conference, so you can go and represent him. You listen to what has been communicated and you go to the conference.

"To understand why learning to 'teach' is important for any leader in an organizational setting requires a better understanding of the differences between communication, teaching and training.
They form a continuum, and the appropriate approach to be used depends on what you are trying to achieve."

The supervisor considers this to be communication and has in fact been very effective at it – he has provided you with the key points. The supervisor believes that because he has communicated, you will demonstrate a behavioral change as a result, and act as he would while you're there. He communicates, hands over the flight tickets, and says, "Okay, do it."

By communicating in this way you will be only partially effective. You might know *what* to say and do, but will not be as skilled at *implementing* it as you could be. If the supervisor had said, "I want to communicate *and* teach you," then you would have been very much more effective. In this second situation the supervisor would have had to see this not as a communication exercise, but rather as a teaching exercise, and so ensured the desired behavior occurs by *using different skills* (those of a "teacher" rather than a "communicator") to prepare you.

Since we are usually looking for behavior change most "communication" sessions should really be treated as if they were teaching situations.

Another example –

I once moved to a new home that had a pool, something I had never had before. I needed to close the pool for the winter so I called an expert to see how much it would cost. He informed me that it would cost approximately $250, which I was not willing to spend. I asked him if he could just provide me the equipment and then explain the process to me. As he began to talk I ferociously tried to take notes. At this point the pool expert informed me that it was simply common sense and notes really were not required.

"We often believe
that we should communicate,
when in fact it is
teaching that is required.
Communication is
simply passing on information,
but since we often
want to change behavior,
we should be teaching."

The key observation in this example is that the pool expert saw this process as communication, whereas I saw it as a teaching exercise. If he had his own way he would have communicated the information, and I would not have benefitted to the degree that I needed.

He should have recognized that it wasn't communication that was needed, rather it was teaching. He had no concept in his mind about the difference between communication and teaching. He just thought that he needed to pass on the information and in doing this, the job would be done. I, though, needed to learn new behaviors and this could not be effectively achieved by *communication* skills only. It also needed *teaching* skills.

We often believe that we should communicate when in fact it is teaching that is required. Communication is simply passing on information, and since we often want to change behavior, we should be teaching.

Communication: "You are going to learn to fly."

Teaching: "I will teach you to fly and to understand the principles. We'll work together to learn how it's done and how it works."

Training: "I will not let you fly until you sit in a simulator and fly it successfully."

The CEO wants "to communicate" that we need to achieve a 10% profit increase. In this case teaching is required, not communication, because we want people to generate a conviction so strong that behavior then changes, resulting in 10% improvement to profit.

"You do not need
great communication skills
to be an
effective teacher."

TEACHING SKILLS: BUILD INTO THE MINDS OF OTHERS

If you apply great communication skills to your teaching you would certainly be more impactful, but you do not need great communication skills to be an effective teacher. Those being taught will still learn without your applying great communication skills.

Some may be able to teach quickly and with greater ease because of their communication ability. The real objective though is to ensure that whatever words are used during the teaching, the learning occurs. That simply requires acquiring the specific, mechanical skills of teaching.

Understand that teachers are architects building concepts and ideas into the minds of the listener. Do not just leave the listener with a feeling, but rather a mental blueprint of what the finished behavior will be. When you teach, have a blueprint in your own mind and teach according to this blueprint. Don't just talk – build – constantly checking your progress against the blueprint in your mind.

To create this blueprint ask yourself the following:

1. What is the goal?

2. How will the finished product look?

3. What is the reason for the task? (Provide an understanding of the big picture.)

TEACHING SKILLS: TEACH ONLY ONE THING AT A TIME

#1 – DONE
#2
#3
Focus your effort. Cover only one thing at a time,
until it is "built" and secure.
Avoid trying to teach even two things at once,
or starting a second
before the first is completely finished.

TEACHING SKILLS:
TEACH ONLY ONE THING AT A TIME

Cover only one thing at a time, until it is "built" and "secure". Avoid trying to teach even two things at once, or beginning a second before the first is completely finished.

Take one thing at a time and go through it.

Do not move to the next point until you have taught one thing and you are convinced that the individual has learned that point. *Then* move on to the next point.

To prepare yourself for teaching another person the following questions should be asked:

1. Which point will you teach first?

2. When will this point be completed?

3. How will you know when this point has been learned?

TEACHING SKILLS: BUILD A FOUNDATION FIRST

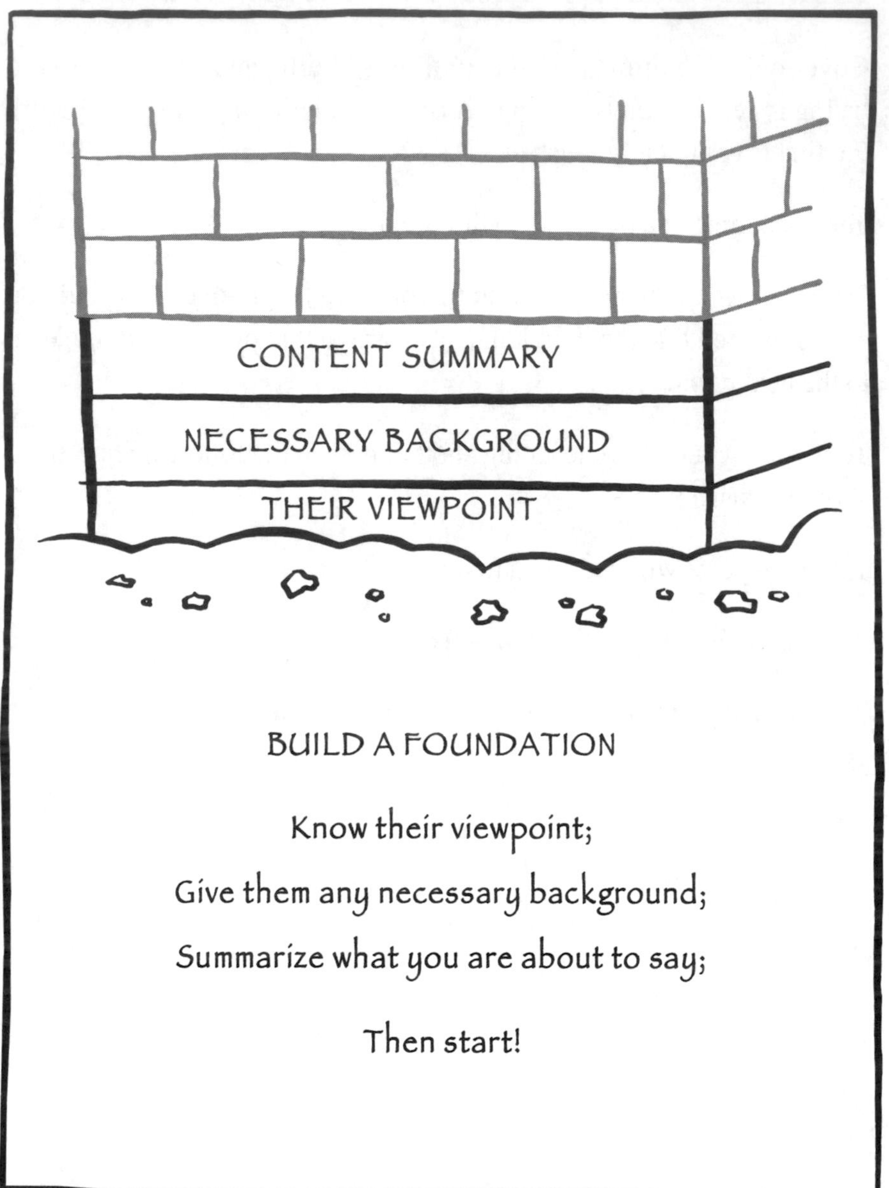
CONTENT SUMMARY
NECESSARY BACKGROUND
THEIR VIEWPOINT
BUILD A FOUNDATION
Know their viewpoint;
Give them any necessary background;
Summarize what you are about to say;
Then start!

TEACHING SKILLS: BUILD A FOUNDATION FIRST

Build a foundation:

1. Know their viewpoint.

2. Give them any necessary background information.

3. Summarize what you are about to say, then start!

Before beginning the teacher must understand what the learner's current level of knowledge and understanding is relative to the topic.

Doing this requires you:

1. Listen to the learner, make notes and understand – what are their key thoughts?

2. Determine what is the background information that they need to know before beginning the task.

3. Summarize for them the key steps in the process that they will shortly learn, without the detail.

TEACHING SKILLS: FREQUENT CHECKING IS ESSENTIAL

Pause frequently and check your progress.
The ideas, biases, creativity, experiences, and
prejudices already in each person's mind
can cause the "learner" to use your building blocks
to put in walls and windows where you
never intended, and where you may not see them.

CHECK YOUR PROGRESS CONSTANTLY.

TEACHING SKILLS: FREQUENT CHECKING IS ESSENTIAL

Pause frequently and check your progress. The ideas, biases, creativity, experiences and prejudices already in each person's mind can cause the "learner" to use your building blocks to put in walls and windows where you never intended, and where you may not see them.

Check your progress constantly.

The architect building a lighthouse must check the blueprint to ensure they are on track. You have to check your progress along the way when you are teaching (building into the mind of another) since this will allow you to identify any gaps, and the areas requiring further reinforcement to ensure the learning occurs. *Ask yourself how you plan to check progress regularly?*

Teaching Skills Summary

1. As an architect:

   a) What is the goal?

   b) Describe the finished product. How will it look?

   c) What is the reason for the task? Provide them with understanding of the big picture.

2. Teach only one thing at a time:

   a) Which point will you teach first?

   b) When will this point be completed?

"Ask yourself
how you plan to
regularly check progress."

3. Foundation:

   a) Listen to them, make notes and understand. What are their key thoughts?

   b) What is the background information that they need to know before you begin the task?

   c) Summarize, without any detail, the key steps in the process that they will learn shortly.

4. Check your progress:

   a) How do you plan to check progress regularly?

A team need not be driven only by the leader's vision – although that may be the predominant one.

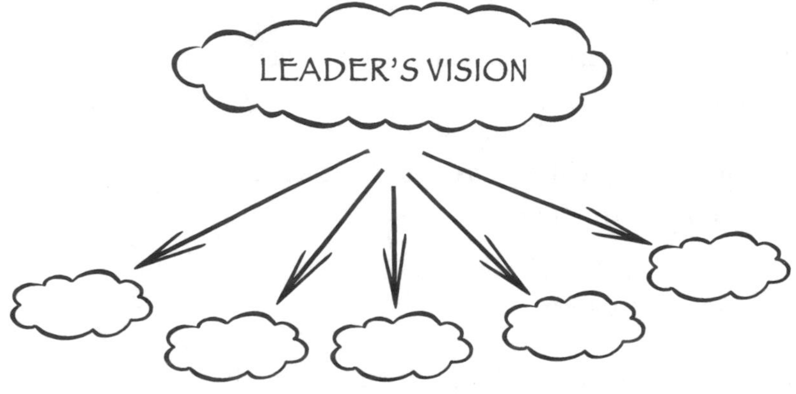

...BUILT INTO OTHERS

...EMPOWERS THE ENTIRE TEAM!

If you see what could be,
or have a vision of a completed project,
you need to build this vision into others.
As they share your vision,
they will become part of the team.

PRODUCING CHAMPIONS: SHARE VISION

To any group of people, the leader *is* the organization. For this group to truly become "champions," the leader is key. Leadership is extraordinarily important to releasing and harnessing the talent, energy, and potential stored up in people.

If you see what could be, or have a vision of a completed project, you need to build this vision into others. If they share your vision, they become a part of the team. A team need not be driven only by the leader's vision, although that will probably be the predominant one.

Assume you are with a group of people at the bottom of the mountain, and the goal is to get to the top. You are half way there and the leader punctures a lung and has to be airlifted away. What will happen to the group? What type of discussion will take place?

Probably something like: "What do we do now? Do we continue?" Some may feel that it would be too risky to continue. Some may want to continue. Others may not be too sure what they want to do. The reason behind this lack of focus is that the group was leader dependent and goal oriented. The situation is now confusing with many new goals proposed (quit, go on, wait, etc.). Very often when you *only* have a goal that goal is very easy to change, especially when you lose the leader.

The alternative is for the leader to share the goal and the vision prior to climbing the mountain. The *goal* is perhaps to get to the top of the mountain (versus learn to work as a team, etc.), but the *vision* is quite different. The leader might express the vision as, "When you get there you will see further than you have ever seen before! You will breathe air like you have never breathed before."

"The difference
between vision and goal
is that a goal is something
towards which you are
all working, whereas a vision
is something which
fires the imagination."

The experience of reaching the mountain top is going to be worth the effort, but more importantly, once you get to the top of the mountain you will look down and will realize what it took to get there. You will realize that despite hurdles, the cold, and possibly despite injuries you will have achieved something that no person can ever take away from you.

"This sense of accomplishment will be with you the rest of your life. From that point on whenever you have a major hurdle to overcome you will be able to say to yourself 'I climbed that mountain. Therefore I can overcome this obstacle also.'"

The leader in this example has given the group a vision, which is a *motivation*, a *reason*, for the goal. So now when the leader punctures a lung and has to be airlifted away, the discussion amongst the team will be very different. The reason for this is that vision empowers. It provides the rationale and the motivation, whereas the goal simply provides direction… there is no passion in a goal.

Champions are those who "take initiative," "pick up the ball and run with it," "excel at getting it done," "can be sent on a mission and then fulfill it," "drive towards and ultimately achieve a given objective," etc. Each of these phrases has as its common thread the fact that they describe someone who is clearly able to articulate the end product. Having articulated it, these kinds of people are also motivated towards achieving the goal, and as such drive towards it.

The skilled leader produces champions. They do this by taking their own vision, the enthusiasm which they feel for that vision, the excitement and drive which they feel, and build that into other people. If the people with whom they are working are able to articulate that vision, which includes more than simply the goal, then those people will themselves become champions.

"Vision is caught,
not taught."

PRODUCING CHAMPIONS: SHARE VISION

The only limits are those of vision!

When you go to the altar to get married, you can have a goal or you can have a vision. If your *goal* is to come together, have a house and two cars, and so live your lives together in this way, your relationship may suffer later on. There may be a career change, you mature, or you realize that you disagree on how to raise your children, and may ultimately part ways.

On the other hand as you go to the altar you may have a *vision* that says you will commit to live together sharing the joys, but knowing also that there will be hurdles and disagreements along the way. The vision is to live and share your lives together for life; with this in mind when you encounter obstacles you do not respond with "We do not agree and therefore we need to rethink the relationship." Rather you respond by acknowledging that the vision is to live your lives together regardless of circumstances, and therefore you must address how you are going to overcome these obstacles together.

The difference between vision and goal is that a goal is something towards which you are all working, whereas a vision is something which fires the imagination. A vision is something which carries with it a component not only of what needs to be done, but also the impact of what will be accomplished once the task is done. A goal will produce "robots", and align behavior. A vision will produce champions, by providing motivation for the goal. Individuals are better able to act independently when given a long-term vision.

"Vision is the

Why.

Goal is the What."

PRODUCING CHAMPIONS: SHARE VISION

Vision is the *Why*. Goal is the *What*.

Vision is something which goes far beyond mission, mandate, or objective. Rather, it is something which helps you persevere when the going gets tough, because you are fired by the impact of the task's completion. To produce champions you must share vision.

As a group becomes stronger, the people within that group will have their own visions, perhaps for an ultimate objective, but more likely for steps along the way. They will have visions as to how those steps can contribute to the overall vision. These are also powerful, exciting and important; don't neglect them.

Vision – empowers; Goal – directs. Both are important, but very different.

It is also important to note that the vision must be: explained, believed, lived, and modeled. Vision is caught, not taught. Vision is marketing the goal. Vision must be shared. Vision sets the tone for everything else.

Plant flags to mark success on the journey toward the goals. Share progress. Spend time on victories; or successes; or the reaching of milestones towards goals. While there is nothing wrong with looking at problems and issues, there is everything wrong with not dwelling extensively on positive achievements.

TRACKING SUCCESS BUILDS A WINNING SPIRIT!

PRODUCING CHAMPIONS: PLANT FLAGS

While there is nothing wrong with looking at problems and issues, there is everything wrong with not dwelling extensively on positive achievements as this builds a winning spirit.

Unfortunately, most of the time leaders must spend time addressing things that are not going as planned. They do, however, need to keep the vision in focus, and along the path recognize that it is important to discuss the progress not only in light of failures, hurdles and obstacles, but also in light of victories.

People gain greatly by looking back and seeing what they have accomplished. Looking ahead, the task may seem very difficult and almost overwhelming; but to look back and see how far one has come along that overwhelming path is motivating, rewarding, and gives one a sense of accomplishment. The leader who produces champions spends time discussing the progress made to date, why the progress has been made, and what can be done to replicate those successes and carry them into the future.

Victories, successes, and milestones toward the ultimate goal or objective contribute toward fulfilling the vision. So – "plant flags" at each milestone.

One of the great untapped resources of motivation is the individual who has had an unrecognized success. That success can go relatively unnoticed, and so the overall team or group doesn't have the opportunity to recognize and appreciate the victories which are occurring, and so may become discouraged by apparent lack of progress. This could be changed simply by checking regularly, looking for victories, and then sharing them with all the others.

"A winning spirit
is something that is built
over time by the
sharing of many successes
and victories.
It is what contributes to a
team of champions."

When discouragement hits it must be *already* prepared for – have been already counteracted – by having shared the previous successes, by having built into people an awareness of the victories which have led them to the point they are now at; and so provide motivation and encouragement to persevere.

It is naive to think that in stretching towards a vision, especially one that is difficult to obtain, there will not be discouragements, set-backs, problems, and hindrances for any number of reasons. These discouragements can tend to loom large and become overwhelming. Planting flags helps prepare for these setbacks.

Recognition is a powerful motivator, and is one way to plant flags. Recognition is something which we give to people who have achieved or done well, or worked hard. They may not as yet have worked all the way to the goal, or to the successful completion, but they are effectively working *towards* that goal. The recognition of both individual effort, and team, occur during the sharing of victories and the sharing of successes along the way.

Celebrate victories – not only within yourself, but also in your own group, in your own organization, and as far out as makes sense. This celebration contributes to a winning spirit and shows that the entire organization is working toward the same ultimate goal. It is important to note that a "celebration" does not necessarily need to be a "party." It could simply be a handshake, written note, or a pat on the back.

A winning spirit is something that is built over time by the sharing of many successes and victories. It is what contributes to making a team of champions.

Positive attitude is key. At all times. In all circumstances.

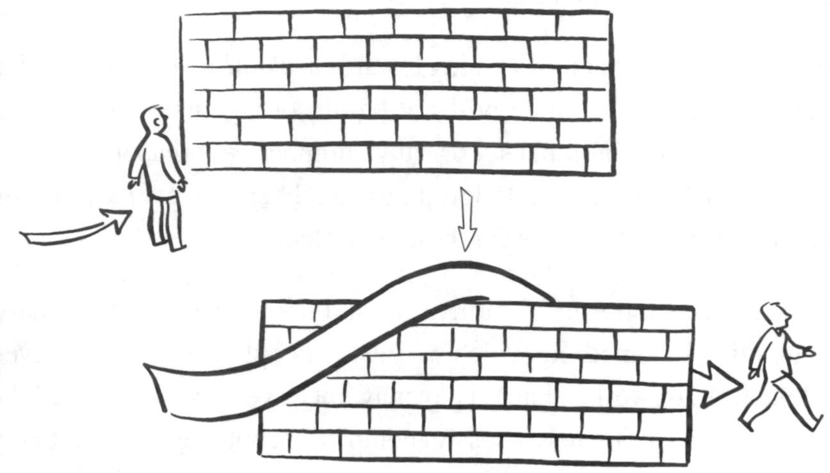

BELIEVE YOU CAN OVERCOME OBSTACLES

Emotions may be at a low ebb.
Intellectual evaluation may judge circumstances to be tough. But the way you react to this, the way you tackle this, is a reflection of your attitude.
Believe and persevere
and encourage others to do likewise.

PRODUCING CHAMPIONS: CREATE BELIEF

Believe you can overcome obstacles.

Positive attitude is key. At all times. In all circumstances. Emotions may be at a low ebb, intellectual evaluation may judge circumstances to be tough, but the way you react to this, the way you tackle this, is a reflection of your attitude.

Believe and persevere, and encourage others to do likewise. In the course of your attempt to get from your starting point to your vision you are going to hit hurdles. The important thing is what you believe when you encounter these hurdles.

This may appear to be "the power of the positive attitude" but in reality is quite different. The difference is that you can create this sense of confidence *by sharing how*. If you believe you know how to overcome the problem, out of that skill and confidence you will build conviction in others, which will then lead to action.

The concept of sharing victories is a tool towards achieving vision. However faith is also a tool. There must be a conviction on the part of every member that obstacles can be overcome. Every hurdle seems insurmountable until it has been overcome. Fatigue, emotional drain, concern, worry, anger, frustration, an argumentative spirit, lack of faith, lack of experience, lack of hope, lack of insight – all these things can contribute to making hurdles or obstacles appear to be insurmountable.

However, confidence, strength, strong leadership, a string of successes, a tremendous inner resource or energy, successful path finding – these things demonstrate that hurdles can be overcome. It is important in the producing of champions that you as leader focus on providing the things which can overcome hurdles.

"If you believe you know
how to overcome
the problem, out of that
skill and confidence you will
build conviction in others,
which will then lead
them to action."

Obstacles must not be seen as roadblocks, but rather as things to be hurdled, as things to be conquered. In pursuing a vision, champions must have an indestructible spirit. They must have built within them a sense that nothing can stand in their way, that all things can be overcome. It is this faith rooted in knowledge that is so critical.

Generate conviction that leads to action in the hearts of the individuals you are leading.

Hurdles are not as big to the leaders - your ability to achieve the vision by clearing this hurdle must be seen by the team, be credible and include how it will be done.

Life is made up of hurdles and obstacles. There are many different ways to overcome them other than simply running at them full force and banging into them until you have knocked them down. Sometimes these obstacles must be climbed over, walked around, or dug under. Sometimes alternate pathways have to be found, sometimes a guide is necessary, sometimes patience or different timing is required. In order to take all these different paths, to try all these different ways, a positive attitude is essential. There must be continuity of attitude. There must be consistent faith and regular belief. It is this constant, consistent, regular faith *in the tools being applied* which helps one overcome hurdles.

There are many other things which can contribute to this positive approach, such as: being in sound physical condition, having a sound marriage, feeling comfortable in the job, and not having undue pressure because of family or personal finances. Each of these can significantly influence our personal attitude.

"Generate conviction
that leads to
action in the hearts
of the individuals you
are leading."

PRODUCING CHAMPIONS: CREATE BELIEF

Despite circumstances, despite emotion, despite the fact that the task intellectually seems gigantic, or that circumstances seem to be against you, it is how you respond that determines attitude. Each of these things in and of itself is an obstacle and a hurdle. It is the *way* in which they are tackled which is important. If you believe your approach is correct, trust the process.

Producing champions requires instilling within others a sense that they should believe and persevere, and that they should encourage their team to do the same.

Seeds abound. Many seeds within each individual: some productive, and some wasted. How they grow and the fruit they yield has much to do with pruning, fertilizing and nurturing.

Tend your own garden and, where possible, help those around you.

Within each unique and potent individual lies the potential for great impact.

Foster the desire for this in yourself; and contribute to its fulfillment in others.

PRODUCING CHAMPIONS: NURTURE AND PRUNE

Every individual carries within themselves the potential for great good, or great evil. You see great good in circumstances where people are called upon to help others in times of famine, plague, or civil strife. You also see great evil when people are misled by evil, wicked individuals, where power is given ruthlessly, or where people sink to an abhorrent level of inhumanity that then goes unchecked.

However, the same individuals who sink to great depths of evil can also move in the opposite direction given the right example, the right leadership, the right cultivation, the right checks and balances at the right times in their lives.

As a leader you have people working for you that have seeds within them that will grow to be either great, ineffective, or disruptive. What develops – in a work context – is a function of how the leader prunes and nurtures along the way. Within each individual is the ability to do many different things. Each can learn, and grow; what comes out of our mind is generated by what went in. A talented musician who is not taught discipline will never be a great musician.

In the producing of champions you must believe and understand that within every individual are many, many different seeds. Some seeds will lead to destruction, discouragement, despair, lack of faith, lack of commitment, lack of contribution to the whole team, lack of personal development, backbiting, condemnation of others, and a critical spirit. Other seeds can lead to support, to help, to encouragement, to motivation, to commitment, to innovation, to constructive behavior, to guidance, and to great leadership.

"'Nudging' is
gently helping the person
understand
which behaviors to
keep and strengthen, and
which to eliminate."

These seeds do exist. They can be groomed one way or another. The good can be encouraged to flourish and the bad eliminated, or the bad can be allowed to grow and spread; left unchecked they will choke out the good.

Your challenge as a leader is to make others into champions, to cultivate in others the specific seeds which you want to see nurtured. Cultivation is not easy, it requires hard work, it requires faithful watering, faithful pruning, faithful weeding, faithful fertilizing, and faithful nurturing.

To produce champions, you must guard the small seedlings, caring for them in the right direction. You must nurture them, providing them with encouragement, direction, and reinforcement, and you must discourage the things of which you disapprove.

You, in producing champions, must constantly encourage the things that you value. This clearly has the corollary that you know what you value, and that you are committed to fostering these things.

Great people do not simply appear. Circumstances, individuals, and events shape our lives to turn them into greatness. Mediocre people have been given only mediocre leadership. Average people receive average leadership.

In short, you must see within each individual tremendous potential. You must see within each individual a number of seeds which can all develop and you must be committed to enhancing that potential by creating a suitable climate, through everything you say, and everything you do. You must also be committed to growing the seeds that you value, and to plucking out the seeds that you don't.

"In shaping others,
do not neglect to
shape yourself."

PRODUCING CHAMPIONS: NURTURE AND PRUNE

In shaping others, do not neglect to shape yourself. Tend your own garden. Develop the things within yourself that are important and which you value. Care for yourself as you care for others, for by so doing you will "set the pace" which they can then follow.

How to prune and how to nurture is summed up in the term "nudging." You are trying to produce a champion. "Nudging" is gently helping the person understand which behavior to keep and strengthen, and which to eliminate, by providing thoughtful feedback as suitable opportunities present themselves. "Nudging" is making this individual a champion in the direction of your vision: bit by bit, helping them grow strong, with careful, appropriate pruning, done over the long term.

CREATING CHAMPIONS IN AN ORGANIZATION: THE DETAIL

Consider having a number of "champions" in your organization as a way of maximizing your results.

A. QUALITIES OF CHAMPIONS

1. High performer
2. Well qualified
3. Shows good judgement
4. Demonstrates sensitivity to people
5. Makes it happen
6. Successful
7. Always learning
8. Innovator
9. Visionary
10. Brilliant leader (if responsible for others)

B. DEFINITION OF A CHAMPION

1. A champion is one who's behavior and results are a role model for others.
2. The above is a progressive list of attributes, i.e. you must have 1 first, then 2, etc.
3. A champion must possess all these attributes; not necessarily in equal amounts, but they must all be there at an operationally effective level.

CREATING CHAMPIONS IN AN ORGANIZATION: THE DETAIL

	ATTRIBUTE	WHAT IT MEANS	HOW WE RECOGNIZE IT
1.	**High Performer**	• Exceeds expectations with respect to personal accountabilities • Does the entire job well	• Consistently high ratings on performance reviews
2.	**Well Qualified**	• Has all the skills necessary to do the job • Includes technical, people, and experience skills	• Completion of the skill set identified for that job
3.	**Shows Good Judgement**	• Consistently doing the right thing at the right time • Effectively listens and evaluates	• Best possible consequences are consistently experienced
4.	**Demonstrates Sensitivity to People**	• Inspires trust and confidence in others • Demonstrates a true care for the opinions of others	• Reputation within the company • Degree to which others feel their opinions are considered
5.	**Makes it Happen**	• Commitments occur on time, on budget every time	• Track record
6.	**Successful**	• Effective at making it happen • Makes it happen well	• Comparatively better results - track record
7.	**Always Learning**	• Not making the same mistake twice • Pride does not inhibit learning new competencies	• You can clearly point to the things they've learned (fruit)
8.	**Innovator**	• Initiates new ways of doing things • Initiates new things to do	• Track record
9.	**Visionary**	• Able to see, feel, share what could be	• Others articulate it, and commit to it
10.	**Brilliant Leader**	• Provides outstanding leadership which maximizes the potential contribution of each team member	• Results of team members

CREATING CHAMPIONS IN AN ORGANIZATION: THE DETAIL

C. THE ENVIRONMENT REQUIRED FOR CHAMPIONS TO EXCEL

1. Managed by a champion
2. Empowered to act
3. Information rich
4. Clear objectives
5. Visible recognition
6. Meaningful rewards
7. Competent colleagues

D. THE ENVIRONMENT DEFINED

1. All elements of the environment must be in place.
2. This is a progressive list of elements of which being managed by a champion is both the most important, and the most challenging to put in place.

CREATING CHAMPIONS IN AN ORGANIZATION: THE DETAIL

	ELEMENT	DEFINITION
1.	**Managed by a Champion**	• One who has successfully demonstrated world-class leadership • One who builds strong teams • One who puts the "right people in the right job"
2.	**Empowered to Act**	• "Define the Framework"-the extent of their authority and decision making is clearly defined; within that framework they are free to act • Note that the limits of the framework must be large enough to challenge the champion, yet constraining enough to avoid disruption to the corporate entity • Risk taking within the framework must be encouraged • More involvement by all employees in decision-making at their level through explanation of clear operational priorities • Enhanced personal accountability
3.	**Information Rich**	• An organization in step with corporate priorities and visions • Meetings management program to allow employees to stay current • Understanding of the long-term corporate plan: strategy, expectations, priorities • Rationale for direction and decisions • Corporate progress report: in terms relevant to them • Opportunities to: make comments, give suggestions, and raise questions, actively encouraging input • Divisional and departmental "fit" into the organizational whole • Personal fit in the overall plan • Communication about this plan • The impact of the Champion's objective on the company • The Champion's future within the organization
4.	**Clear Objectives**	• The results required must be clearly articulated and, where appropriate, quantified
5.	**Visible Recognition**	• Visible recognition of Champions • Visible recognition of employees who excel • Public recognition of a commitment to the impact that can be made by individuals and teams
6.	**Meaningful Rewards**	• Champion's individual worth to be recognized by the organization, frequently in ways beyond only salary considerations (eg. access to advanced training, key strategy meetings, etc.). Champions to have some input on the shaping of their package
7.	**Competent Colleagues**	• Poor performance not tolerated within the organization • A commitment to improve individual competence (knowledge and skill)

SETTING THE PACE

Let the quality of your work and decisions
be the gold standard against which
the performance of others comes to be measured.

BECOME THE GOLD STANDARD

The "gold standard" should be something towards which we strive. There are two aspects to be considered in this regard.

1. ***Your work*** – That is, the activities you perform, the things which you do.

2. ***Your decisions*** – That is, the judgement which you exercise, and the consequences of that judgement.

It is important to distinguish between these two and address each as you strive for mastery.

Mastery is being the best that can be – personally striving to achieve the "gold standard" in your work and decisions. It is important to recognize that striving to have the quality of your work be at the gold standard does not have as its objective to "set you apart" i.e., encourage inappropriate pride or an immodest sense of self-centeredness. Rather, it is an encouragement to behave in such a way that others see your performance, respect it, and come to be measured by it *because of it's innate quality.*

Your performance must be of such a quality that other people, on their own initiative, want to replicate your behavior for themselves. The focus is not on being so good that others are measured against you. Rather, the focus is on you – your determination to work hard *to be the best that can be.*

You should see yourself as a person on a desert island thinking only of how you can be the best that can be, as opposed to trying to be "great" solely in order to be emulated by others. By thinking in this fashion we keep our ego in check, which is critical to our overall success as a leader.

"If in every case
we outperform on an
individual basis, then
our organization will
become a world leader
on a combined basis."

BECOME THE GOLD STANDARD

To achieve mastery we must often reach beyond our immediate sight. If I want to be strong at controlling budgets, then typically I will turn to the person within my organization who is strong in that area. However, by doing this I am confining myself to that particular level of expertise, when in fact a much higher level of expertise *may* be found elsewhere. I should not limit my standards only to those around me. Today we are all competing globally, and hence skills and competencies must be compared to the best in the world in a similar function.

If in every case we outperform on an individual basis, then our organization will become a world leader on a combined basis.

Spend considerable time thinking before acting.

By so doing you avoid numerous pitfalls, and improve the quality of the finished product.

THINKING ...

... BEFORE ACTING

THINK A LOT BEFORE DOING

The brain works far more quickly than the hands. Thus we need to sit down and work through any process mentally first, and *then* execute it.

There are two things we all do: we think; and we act. We need to blend these two and to *think* about our work *before* we act, and *then* act. This allows for numerous "wrong turns," "omissions," "errors," and "Oops, I forgot..." *mentally*, hence there is no loss of materials or wasted effort. Further, the finished result is much better because of the thinking and the ideas which went into the project before it was ever begun.

In order to really achieve mastery, to be as effective as possible in the shortest period of time, the critical component is sitting down well before the activity begins and thinking it through in as much detail, and as thoroughly as possible: anticipate!

While this may seem like a heavy use of time, it is negligible compared to the time which would be required to correct mistakes or address problems. To really achieve mastery one must be absolutely committed to the power behind thinking before acting; be as thorough as possible, not "winging it", that is, giving something only a cursory thought. Every pitfall or dead-end which is identified mentally represents a huge saving in time and resources on the execution side, and is a move towards personal mastery.

STRIVE FOR EXCELLENCE; AND ALSO STRIVE FOR MASTERY

YOUR BEST
YOU
STRIVE FOR EXCELLENCE
Comparing your performance to the best you have to offer, and not to the performance of others
BUT ALSO
1st
THE BEST
YOUR BEST
STRIVE FOR MASTERY
Comparing your performance against the best that could be, and not against the normal standard

STRIVE FOR EXCELLENCE; AND ALSO STRIVE FOR MASTERY

Assume you have hired a sales representative who is fresh out of college. She says that she is going to be the best sales representative that you have ever had. She then does an outstanding job. At the end of the year the results of her effort are tremendous. There was a dramatic increase in sales and this rookie has in fact outperformed any first year sales representative that you have ever had.

The above scenario is an example of an individual who has demonstrated *excellence* – not mastery. Mastery is not just being the best rookie sales representative in the company. It is being among the best of the best in the world.

You may have a rookie sales person who has done an exceptional job, but that does not demonstrate mastery. She still has a lot to learn. This junior sales representative must *initially* work at demonstrating excellence – being the best that she can be. She must *then* work hard at looking at how the best of the best – those with years of experience – do the same job, and then work towards that to achieve mastery.

We should strive to be excellent, but not be content with that. We must strive for mastery of our chosen profession. This is true in every job in every area. Absolute mastery indicates that you could "write the book" on the topic or profession in which you are engaged.

Striving for mastery means searching out guidance wherever you can and committing to learn from that.

STRIVE FOR EXCELLENCE; AND ALSO STRIVE FOR MASTERY

"We should strive
to be excellent, but not
be content with that.
We must strive for
mastery of our chosen
profession."

To use the sales representative example, if you make heavy use of referrals in your sales function then you should be looking in the library, meeting other sales people, and chatting with clients. You should be doing everything you can, and as much as you can, to learn about referrals until there is virtually nothing left to know. You then bring this knowledge into your life. To do so would be striving for mastery in the area of referrals.

Three things impact mastery, and each is explained below:

1. The impact of being a "natural".

2. Context (versus the absolute). Mastery can be relative.

3. Balance of life.

Being a "Natural"

Once you reach a certain level of world-class performance there can be "built in" differences. Each of us has natural human limitations in terms of skills, resources and experience. Our ability to achieve mastery must be within these built in limitations.

Context

I learned to play squash from a person who was in the world rankings. Given my circumstances I could not come close to beating him. But there are other factors involved when you assess my degree of "mastery".

"Striving for mastery means searching out guidance wherever you can and committing to learn from that."

Look at the context. He plays squash all day. I have a 9 -5 job. His job is teaching squash all day long. I have family responsibilities that take up a considerable amount of time, he does not. I have household responsibilities, he does not. There is a significant difference between what I do in my waking hours and what he does in his. It is important that we take these factors into consideration when assessing mastery. Mastery is relative.

Balance

Imagine yourself seeking a serious corporate position and deciding to model yourself on a successful corporate executive. Before stopping there, there is more to consider!

If the person has achieved this level but at a cost – i. e. divorced three times, children are delinquent, and physically this "model" executive is very unhealthy – this then paints a very different picture. Perhaps a more complete one. This life is not in balance. All aspects of life are not in harmony. The other areas of life must also be taken into consideration in addition to business performance, leading perhaps to another model being sought.

So when we think in terms of mastery it is important that we take these three elements into consideration: natural gifts, total context, and balance of life. Within this framework it is possible to achieve relative mastery.

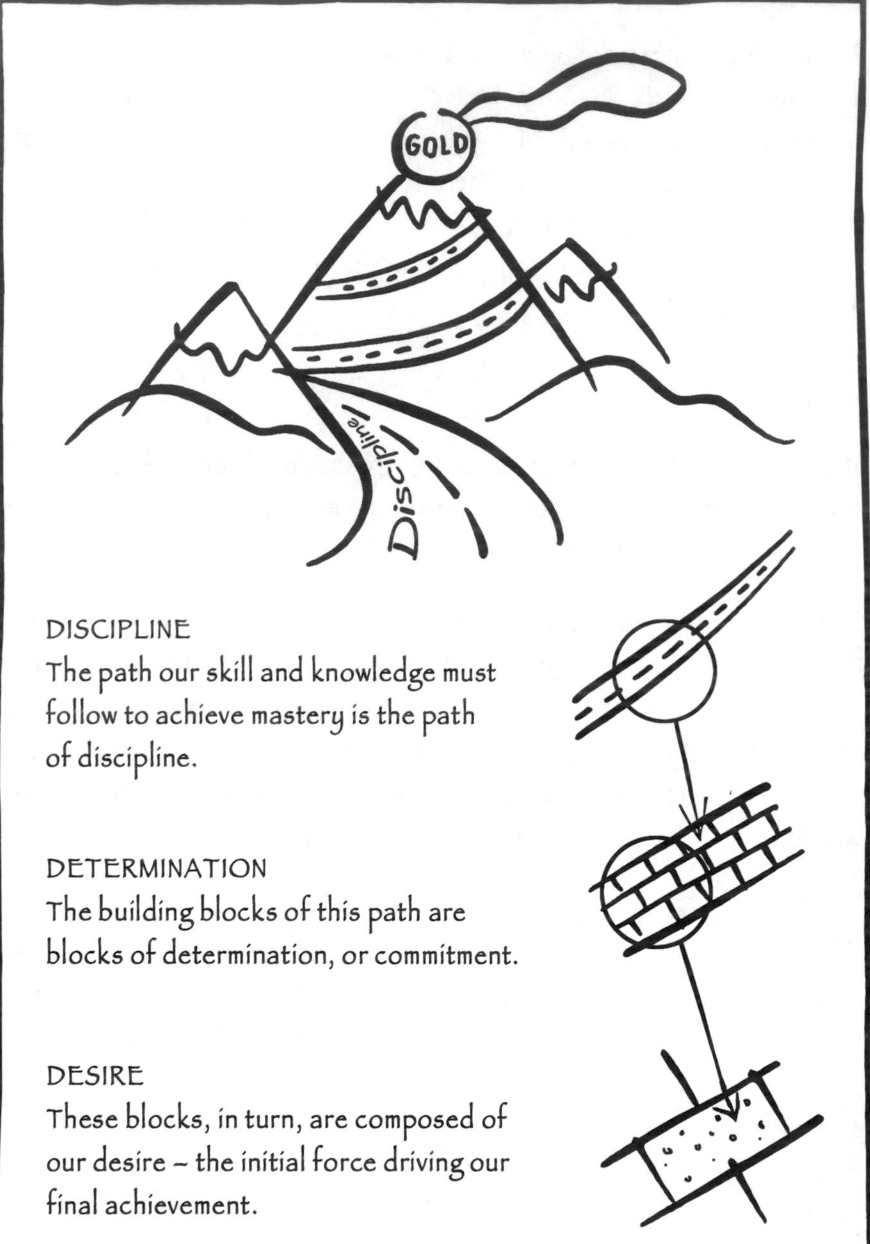
GOLD
Discipline
Discipline
DISCIPLINE
The path our skill and knowledge must follow to achieve mastery is the path of discipline.
DETERMINATION
The building blocks of this path are blocks of determination, or commitment.
DESIRE
These blocks, in turn, are composed of our desire – the initial force driving our final achievement.

BRING PERSONAL DISCIPLINE TO BEAR

Mastery, while made up of a determination to perform at the gold standard, to think before acting, and to constantly strive for personal excellence, also carries with it one further component which influences all of these.

The importance of discipline.

> Action is driven by *discipline*.
>
> The will is driven by *determination*.
>
> The emotion is driven by *desire*.

These three things are necessary to become masters of any given area.

Imagine you wake up in the morning, look at yourself in the mirror, and you say to yourself "I really need to lose weight". You go to work and at the end of the day you stop to talk to a co-worker. You tell her that you really want to lose weight and are beginning to exercise tonight. The next day you see this co-worker again and she asks, "How did you do with your weight program last night?" If your response is that yesterday was a long day and your favorite TV show was on last night, so therefore you spent the evening watching TV, then when you said you wanted to lose weight what you were in fact saying was "I want to lose weight, but I want to watch TV *more.*" The dominant desire wins. Always.

Desire

Imagine you wake up one morning and remember that you have a heavy schedule today. You quickly get ready in order to get to work early and get a good start on the day. When you arrive at work you plan your day and discover that your schedule is going to take you until approximately 6:00 p.m. While working through your plan you also notice a little note at the bottom, right-hand corner of your time planner – "spouse's birthday."

"Determination

is an

act of the will."

BRING PERSONAL DISCIPLINE TO BEAR

You have forgotten your spouse's birthday! You have no card, present or plan for the evening. To top it all you are not going to get home until 7:00 p.m., and this would be disastrous! You don't want this disaster, so you determine to leave work at 4:00 in order to buy a card, a present, and to have some time together that evening.

You have identified that you really want to do this – you have now instituted *desire*. Nothing has happened yet, but desire has been harnessed, and this desire is an emotion which can bear fruit – determination.

Determination

The next step is determination. Determination is an act of the will; and so you look at your daytimer and you reschedule according to your desire, i.e. recognizing your spouse's birthday. Juggling your schedule is an act of the will based on determination. You have now done something which causes the desire to have the potential to be fulfilled. Now your rescheduled day has begun and you must discipline yourself to follow that which desire has initiated (the new schedule).

Discipline

Discipline is the fruit of commitment. If you are truly committed to something and really want to see it happen, that is if your one desire is to see some particular activity achieved, then you will enter into a mental pact with yourself to be highly disciplined in order to achieve that particular goal.

"Discipline
is the fruit of
commitment."

BRING PERSONAL DISCIPLINE TO BEAR

Discipline is not that difficult in that we do discipline ourselves to do some things whether we want to or not – for example, going to work every day. In many ways that discipline is motivated by the need for the consequences (money and self-fulfillment) but it is also motivated by the commitment which we have made to our organization.

On any other day you would have not been able to get away from the office early enough to pick up a present. When you know however that you must have a birthday present, somehow you make the time. This is simply another form of discipline. You have determined that you will do something and then you do it.

This example gives us considerable insight into the nature of discipline. We can be disciplined, and we do discipline ourselves.

Discipline is a part of life already. It is not something new; it is not something which we have to embrace as a particularly large hurdle; nor is it something at which we should look and then groan because it carries with it unreasonable self-sacrifice.

Once we understand the nature of discipline and the fact that it is tied very heavily to commitment – the fact that we want to achieve something – then we can focus our energies in new directions. To achieve anything, we must be disciplined. To achieve any particular goal, discipline must accompany it.

Discipline is an interesting quality. It rightly carries the connotation of not doing something else. If I discipline myself to do one thing, then I am not doing another thing.

"Desire feeds
determination (commitment)
which in turn drives
discipline.
Desire is at the heart
of discipline."

Inevitably when the thing that I have disciplined myself to do is completed, I feel good. I feel strong because of it; and I am glad that I did not fall into the temptation of doing the other things which I might possibly have done.

Discipline is not a mean, nasty thing, which in some way is keeping us from doing the things which we want to do. Rather, it is a friend, an ally, something on which we can draw which helps us to do the things we really want to do, rather than falling into doing things which would be nice to do but which are not as close to our hearts.

The more highly committed we are to one particular goal, the more we will be disciplined towards achieving that goal. In order to maximize your discipline you need to maximize your commitment.

If we understand that commitment leads to discipline – then we could use another word for this concept of commitment: determination. That is, I am "determined" to achieve something – I am determined to get this birthday present – I am determined to be the best that I can be – I am determined to think this thing through. So discipline really flows from determination.

But where does this determination come from? It comes from wishing or wanting something to occur. You want to have a present so you are determined to get one – you are committed to getting it. An individual athlete desperately wants to win a gold medal and so determines to train day after day. Out of that determination, discipline follows, and so when we trace back the real root of discipline through determination we arrive at desire – what you want – what you really want – the thing which you really, really want.

"The more highly committed we are to one particular goal, the more we will be disciplined towards achieving that goal. In order to maximize your discipline you need to maximize your commitment."

In fact, we always get what we want. If you think about brushing your teeth, but you do not want to do that as much as something else you'd rather do at the same time (e. g. going to bed *now*) you don't do it. If you want to brush your teeth, you do. In other words we never do things we don't want to do – we often do things we would rather not do – but we do them because we want the result or the consequence, or in some way we desire what the activity is going to give us – clean teeth, good breath – whatever it might be. So we do it. Again, it is important to understand that we strive for the things that we want.

We may say that we want to be fit, but tonight we are just a little tired. So even though we "Don't really want to," we watch TV; in fact we want to watch TV more than we want to exercise. There may be a good reason for that – we may, for example, be too tired to exercise; but for whatever reason, and these reasons may change, we end up watching TV and not exercising.

That is why we often feel frustrated, because we don't do things that we wish to do. Because in fact what we want are things that take a lot of work, a lot of effort, and the results are seen only in the long term. We want the long-term results but at any given point in time – today, tomorrow – what we really want is a life of ease or something which is less stressful. Consequently we surrender and go for the thing which is immediately gratifying – for example, watching the TV, rather than the thing which is immediately taxing, but in the long term far more satisfying – to be fit.

Desire feeds determination (commitment) which in turn drives discipline. Desire is at the heart of discipline.

1. INFLUENCE
The influence that the example set by the leadership has on the organization should always be top of mind.

2. KNOWLEDGE
One of the most effective ways to lead is to operate from strength – and that strength is in the effective use of what you know. So seek information and knowledge.

3. FOCUS
Focus your learning on those aspects of the business where you know that additional knowledge would make a big difference.

4. COMMUNICATE
Share what you know. This allows others to also operate from strength – the strength you provide. Stronger people mean better results.

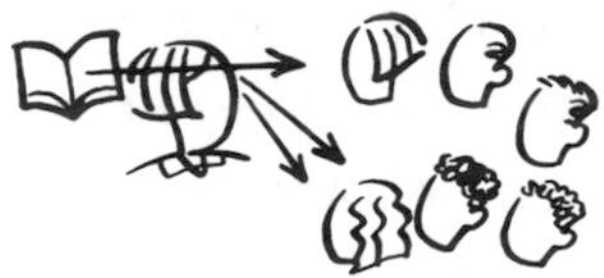

5. MASTERY
Develop a personal action plan, personal measurements, and personal accountabilities in this area of leadership – otherwise this understanding you now have will not translate into daily world-class leadership.

THE LEADER AS PACESETTER

The concept of the leader as pacesetter is an intriguing one. The pacesetter is usually seen as an individual who runs beside an athlete in training – "setting the pace" for the athlete. As the athlete works to grow more fit and skilled, there's a pacesetter always beside them moving them to higher and higher levels of accomplishment by setting a pace which is both challenging yet attainable.

I once worked for a leader who was the consummate pacesetter. He never asked anything of me or any of his other direct reports that he was not willing to do himself. In fact he went beyond simply asking, to personally modeling the behaviors which he expected of us. He truly "set the pace." In many ways this defines the ultimate in leadership.

If, for example, you decide to implement a set of behaviors around bottom-up feedback, where individuals give their managers feedback on the manager's behavior, the leader must be the first to initiate the process – not just do it, but do it first! The leader must then be the first to respond to the feedback, proactively, by asking for ways in which to improve the scores that were weaker, and by asking for suggestions on how their behavior could be improved. The leader can then ask their own team to do the same with their people. The leader sets the example, sets the pace, and demonstrates behaviors such that others can grow and learn by being beside that calibre of role model, and having that kind of coaching always at hand.

The pacesetter not only leads by example, but leads by being beside, and by coaching. There are five specific components to being a leader who pacesets.

"Ensure that the areas
in which you are pacesetting
are areas which
you are confident will build
long-term strength,
and the expected results,
into the organization."

1. ***Influence:*** A company is influenced far more by the behavior of the leadership than is often realized. Leadership which recognizes that their own behaviors are setting the pace for the rest of the company watch carefully how they go, what they say, and what they do.

   This is true whether the leader is a CEO, or the supervisor of a regional distribution centre. Every leader – whether at the most senior level, or at the most junior level – sets the pace for those who watch and are seeking to learn, copy, and grow.

   Influence is that subtle quality which results in outcomes being closely aligned with desires and expectations. When the influence is strong, effective, and in support of the desired outcomes, then the rest of the organization follows that pace and the desired outcomes follow.

2. ***Knowledge:*** Effective pacesetters operate from strength. It's difficult to set the pace in an area where you are weak. Even as you coach others in your area of strength they will grow stronger as they learn from you, and comparatively you will weaken. Consequently, you must continue to operate from strength and strength has its roots in knowledge.

   Consequently, as a pacesetter be committed to seeking information and knowledge, translating it into action in your own life so that you remain strong, able to pass your strengths on, and coach others.

"A leader who pacesets
has at their heart
a determination to develop,
to the full,
the potential of those with
whom they come in contact."

3. ***Focus:*** There are many options available to leaders as they seek to increase in their understanding, grow in their knowledge, and gather relevant information. The priority must be to focus your learning on aspects of the enterprise where additional knowledge, or skill, would make a big difference. Remember that you are pacesetting for others and they will learn and grow from you. Consequently, ensure that the areas in which you are pacesetting are areas which you are confident will build long-term strength, and the expected results, into the organization.

   In the earlier example, if the leader was convinced that highly effective leadership would result in improvements to the bottom line, this conviction might have led to the support of a bottom-up feedback process, allowed the organization to aggressively learn from it, grow from it, and improve. The leader would have made the decision to paceset in an area that was felt to significantly impact on the commitment made to shareholders. As a result of this focus the scores on these evaluations should also be consistently among the highest in the company, another example of pacesetting.

4. ***Communicate:*** Pacesetters must do more than just live by example, they must share what they know. Lighthouses have both a light and a foghorn. At times the light is sufficient, but at many other times the light is ineffective and the lighthouse must rely on its foghorn, because the environment is so turbulent that the light cannot be seen clearly.

   Similarly pacesetting leaders communicate what they know. They take the time to help those who are running beside them to understand and to grow, and so themselves become strong.

   A leader who pacesets has at heart a determination to develop, to the full, the potential of those with whom they come in contact.

"Pacesetters must
do more than just live
by example,
they must share what
they know."

5. ***Mastery:*** Elsewhere in this book mastery is discussed in some detail. However, it's important to understand here that being an effective pacesetter is not something which necessarily comes naturally. Rather it comes as a result of constant self-evaluation, regular feedback, and a personal determination to excel at it; in short, to achieve mastery.

   To facilitate this, develop a personal action plan in this area with measurements and accountabilities. Recognize the need to influence others and determine the degree to which your influence is consistent with what you want to achieve.

   Commit to learning, growing and applying what you learn, being fully aware that what you learn and where you lay your strokes must have significant impact on the organization's overall objectives.

   Commit to communicating what you know so that others can learn from you; be available, be sensitive and be patient.

   Achieving mastery in anything is not easy. You are pacesetting one way or another within your organization if you are in a leadership position. The question is whether your pacesetting is as impactful as possible. To do so requires mastery, it requires a commitment on your part to work at being world-class in this area. This is a commitment you should make.

No matter what the task, there's no reason not to add enjoyment to it.

- People like to play.
- Play enhances creativity.
- Communication flows freely during play.

Surround the task, and the people performing the task, with a climate of fun.

This climate promotes teamwork, encourages commitment, and more fully engages the whole person.

HAVE FUN!

Imagine yourself running a department in a building where a hallway connects your department to another nearby, managed by Mortimer. You both work in the same company, but manage different departments.

Because you believe everyone likes to have fun, and that fun and work are not incompatible, individuals in your department are encouraged to laugh, and integrate the enjoyment that can come from social interaction with the work that needs to be done.

If one day Mortimer comes storming into your office, furious because: "Your people are having too much fun over here and are disturbing my people!" you'd be amazed! Further, chances are you'd find your group to be *more* productive than Mortimer's, because part of the reason people are productive is because fun is included as an element of the job.

The point of the above illustration is simply to reinforce the absurdity of not having fun on the job. Fun is not incompatible with productivity, and there's no reason for it not to be part of the normal workplace. In fact, given the incredible stress and pressure in today's economy, and society, the freedom to release this stress through humour, good-natured banter, and creative activities is a tremendous boon. People can "decompress" more readily through fun, and more frequently, and so enjoy coming to work.

As an example, something simple I once did was to have a white board prominently displayed in the centre of our department on which people were encouraged to write whatever they wished. It was usually erased at the end of each day and so became a central spot for notices of parties, jokes, welcome to new employees, reminders of key company dates, interesting graffiti, etc. Items which appeared there tended to spawn other comparable activity elsewhere in the department (posters, more cartoons, etc.).

"The results of our
activity are
always best when we
love what we do,
and it's easier to love
something that's fun."

HAVE FUN!

Clearly those who enjoy their work, have the freedom to be themselves, and the opportunity to integrate enjoyment into the job will be more productive than those who are forced, straightjacket-like, to stay heads down, bottled up, and to totally separate their after work life (which usually includes fun!) from their at work life.

In addition to being an effective way to manage people, encouraging fun in the workplace serves to promote interaction among individuals working together, which then facilitates communication, expression, and teamwork. The creativity which is an automatic element of any fun environment – because people are thinking of creative ways to have fun – spills over into the work being done and additional creativity flows from that.

The challenge to the leader is to create the appropriate *environment*. This is not an issue of balance. The objective is not to balance work and fun; rather the objective is to focus on the work, but create a *climate* in which individuals are allowed to have appropriate fun. It is the "appropriate" which requires the management skill so the overall climate is maximally productive – including work *and* fun.

Clearly nothing will be accomplished if people come to work to party. This is not the intent. People should come to work to work and furthermore the work they do should be at the highest possible standard (world-class) in the shortest possible time, error free and with absolute quality and service. Individuals need to perform their tasks competently, interact effectively with others, and continually improve those processes with which they are involved in order to reduce cost and eliminate waste.

"The challenge
to the leader is to
create the appropriate
environment."

But there's no reason why this cannot be done in a climate where people are allowed to laugh, joke amongst themselves, not take themselves or their work more seriously than they should, and have about them the same kind of enjoyment of life that they demonstrate after work hours in their leisure time. This is the climate that needs to be created.

The results of our activity are always best when we love what we do, and it's easier to love something that's fun.

MOTIVATING OTHERS REQUIRES THAT THEY BE PERSONALLY ENGAGED, I.E. "LOCKED IN"

For others to be truly engaged, this requires that they…

Understand in what way they can make a personal difference to the outcome.

Understand the things in place that give confidence that the objective is truly attainable.

Understand the importance, or significance, of achieving the objective.

People cannot fully commit themselves to something they don't fully understand.

MOTIVATING OTHERS REQUIRES THAT THEY BE PERSONALLY ENGAGED, I.E. "LOCKED IN"

For people to be fully supportive of a task or an initiative they must be emotionally engaged, or "locked in", to what is to be accomplished and the approach being taken. It is the leader's responsibility to provide the team with this motivation which comes from ensuring that they are truly engaged in this fashion. It is very difficult to be motivated when one does not feel personally committed to the overall task and objective.

To get this form of motivation requires that each member of the team understand three specific things:

1. ***People will be committed to an outcome if they can personally make a difference.*** They need to believe that their contribution, talents, and skills are such that, once applied, the outcome is more assured; and so is dependent on their contribution.

   The outcome is in fact clearly dependent on their contribution, to varying degrees depending on their experience, skills, etc. However, often little time is taken to explain to people the *way* in which their contribution is so crucial to the outcome. Rarely is a team brought together with members who are unnecessary! Rather, every member is important and this thinking needs to be communicated to each individual with respect to their own contribution.

2. ***People need to understand that the objective is obtainable.*** Very often an objective that to many might seem out of reach or beyond achievement to others is in fact attainable, given the approach the leader has in mind, the resources that the leader knows to be available, and the leader's experience.

MOTIVATING OTHERS REQUIRES THAT THEY BE PERSONALLY ENGAGED, I.E. "LOCKED IN"

"'Understanding' is a powerful motivator in that it allows individuals to personalize for themselves the value and importance of their activities."

MOTIVATING OTHERS REQUIRES THAT THEY BE PERSONALLY ENGAGED, I.E. "LOCKED IN"

It's crucial to ensure that each individual is fully aware that the objective is indeed attainable, and so the effort about to be expended will bear fruit. This eliminates the sense of futility which can often overwhelm a team when individuals believe that it can't be done in the first place. Usually the initiator has a good reason for the conviction that the goal is attainable, often based on a wealth of experience and sound judgement. This needs to be clearly explained, and fully understood by those involved in fulfilling the assignment.

3. ***Each individual needs to understand the importance of achieving the objective.*** Within any given context the task, objective, mission, or vision has some inherent value and relevance within a larger context. The importance of successfully arriving at the conclusion may be seen by a few, but not by the many; yet the many are being depended on to deliver the outcome. Consequently, it is crucial that those who understand the importance of a task communicate clearly why it is important, and the difference it will make, to all concerned.

"Understanding" is a powerful motivator in that it allows individuals to personalize for themselves the value and importance of their activities. It can also be a powerful demotivator when it is lacking.

It is very difficult for individuals to fully commit themselves to something which they do not fully and clearly understand.

MOTIVATING OTHERS IS EASIER IF THE LEADER HAS CHARISMA

A LEARNABLE SKILL

10 TECHNIQUES:

1. Smile a lot, be friendly.
2. Be decisive. Decide, then let "yes" be yes, and "no" be no.
3. Be knowledgeable. Do your homework.
4. Listen, listen, listen. Let others fully express themselves, always, before responding.
5. Have ideas. Come prepared.
6. Speak clearly, and with conviction.
7. Encourage others.
8. Create an atmosphere of fun. People enjoy being happy.
9. Speak truth always.
10. Have and share enthusiasm.

MOTIVATING OTHERS IS EASIER IF THE LEADER HAS CHARISMA

Individuals would prefer to follow someone who has "leadership qualities." Many things are often considered to define "leadership," such as the ability to articulate a vision, or create an exciting objective really worth working towards. In addition to these qualities, one which is often sought after is the elusive "charisma". This is more difficult to define; and yet those who have it are often called "natural leaders" and tend to be more readily followed.

In it's simplest terms, charisma in a leader is that quality which attracts others and creates within them the desire to follow, or be part of, the visions or plans of that leader. Although charisma is often considered to be something with which people are born, it can be broken down into component pieces, each of which can individually be learned, making it possible for each of us to project this level of leadership and magnetism.

There are ten specific behaviors which together combine to create a charismatic personality; and while each taken individually will have a significant influence, taken together they create this overall leadership quality which draws others to be part of your team.

1. ***Smiling frequently*** in a friendly manner, and being quick to show happiness is important. It projects a sense of personal confidence and well being, and tends to make others feel positive about the environment in which they find themselves at the moment.

2. ***Being decisive*** is key, in that others feel confident that action is being taken, and being taken without undue deliberation.

3. ***Being knowledgeable*** as a result of being well-prepared breeds confidence. It allows the decisions that are being made to be done so decisively, and on the basis of relevant facts; decisions can then be readily and effectively defended if necessary.

MOTIVATING OTHERS IS EASIER IF THE LEADER HAS CHARISMA

"Charisma in a leader
is that quality
which attracts others and
creates within them the
desire to follow,
or be part of, the visions
or plans of that leader."

4. ***Being skilled at listening*** is important since each of us appreciates being heard, and being listened to. If we know that our thoughts are being considered, we feel more free to express our ideas, opinions and perspective.

5. ***Being prepared with ideas, alternatives, and perhaps innovative solutions*** that others have not considered, naturally allows people to turn to the one with the ideas for suggestions and direction. Be prepared by thinking in advance of possible ideas which are creative or innovative, and certainly different from those which are usually put forward.

6. ***Speak with conviction and clarity.*** Acquiring the ability to communicate in a fashion that can be understood by others is important if you wish to be understood! Further, having the personal conviction which often comes from doing effective prework is an effective tool for harnessing the still unformed convictions of others.

7. ***The ability to encourage*** is a little used quality but one which is greatly appreciated by those being encouraged. Encouraging others is demonstrating the ability to spot something positive in the midst of a task, or at its completion, and then speaking an encouraging word or comment at the appropriate moment. This has the effect of providing an outside, objective, view of the person's activity, and so providing encouragement to the individual to continue.

8. ***Create an atmosphere of fun*** around you in the task and activities with which you are involved. People enjoy working in a fun filled environment, and often a little bit of creative thought and energy focused on creating this environment can result in ideas or activities which make the environment a pleasant one in which to work, and a fun one.

MOTIVATING OTHERS IS EASIER IF THE LEADER HAS CHARISMA

"Although charisma is often
considered to be something with
which people are born,
it can be broken down into
component pieces,
each of which can individually
be learned, making it
possible for each of us to project
this level of leadership
and magnetism."

9. ***Always speak the truth.*** We may believe at times that people would rather not be told the truth, but rarely is this truly the case. In most instances people appreciate the truth if it's spoken with tact and in completeness. Half-truths are often worse than no truth; but if the truth is spoken clearly and kindly it is appreciated. People are then able to rely on you, and know that what you say is something on which they can depend.

10. ***Be personally enthusiastic*** and allow this to overflow to others. Remaining positive, outgoing and excited about the things in which you are involved, and which lie ahead, tends to be contagious, and causes others to want to be a part of that excitement.

These ten areas will require continuous attention to your personal behavior, but their demonstration will provide you with the balanced set of competencies of an effective charismatic leader.

MOTIVATION MUST BE SUSTAINED, IT CANNOT BE DONE INFREQUENTLY AND STILL HAVE ANY IMPACT

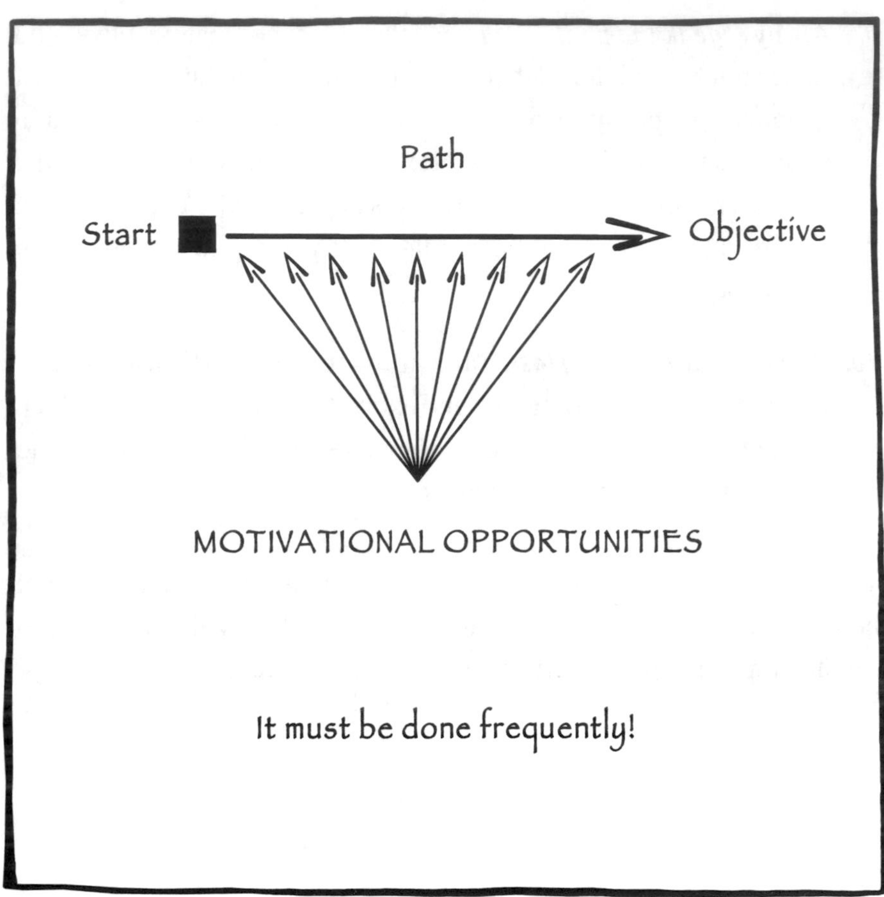

MOTIVATION MUST BE SUSTAINED, IT CANNOT BE DONE INFREQUENTLY AND STILL HAVE ANY IMPACT

Clearly leadership includes the responsibility to motivate others. However, the leader often assumes that this is something which need only be done "when needed," or at previously determined times. Not so. People require frequent motivation as they move along the path towards the objective.

Motivation not only serves the obvious function of providing recognition of progress, but also serves to reinforce the belief that the chosen path is the correct one, and that the current behavior will ultimately lead to the desired results. This is an important consideration, and takes motivation beyond simply a "pat on the back".

Individuals striving for excellence need regular feedback to know whether or not the path they are on will lead to the excellence they desire. As leaders provide words of encouragement, motivational coaching, or positive guidance, the individual is able to remain focused and clear about the value of their contribution, and so stay motivated.

When implementing this approach, one might wonder what the term "frequently" actually means. Simply put, if you see the need to motivate then you've left it too late. The nature of motivation is such that it sustains momentum; consequently when you *anticipate* that momentum could be lagging then it's a clear sign that some motivation is in order.

As you become more skilled at reading these signs then you will be more conscious of, and skilled at, the timing of the motivation in order to ensure that it is not so frequent as to be meaningless, and not so far apart as to be less effective then required. Given that it must be done frequently, several different approaches are required to avoid excessive repetition of the same approach, which would then soon become ineffective. These are discussed in Section VI, Actions That Can be Done Along the Path to the Objective to Motivate those Involved, on page 416.

ACTIONS THAT CAN BE DONE ALONG THE PATH TO THE OBJECTIVE TO MOTIVATE THOSE INVOLVED

1. REPEAT
   Reiterate the rationale for the objective, enhancing understanding.

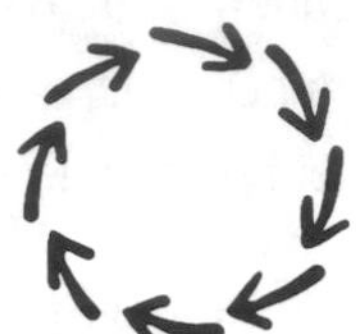

2. CELEBRATE
   Celebrate successes along the path.

3. COMPARE
   Pause to consider how other organizations are tackling similar challenges – identify what can be learned from, or shared with them.

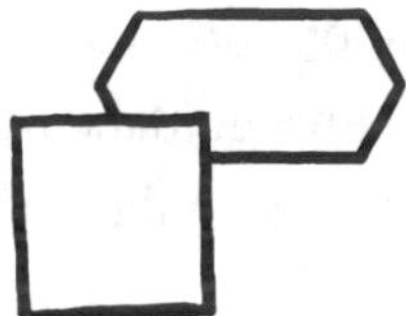

4. MEASURE
   Have measurements, which can be reviewed frequently – even poor results can be motivating when something meaningful has been learned.

5. COMPLIMENT
   Have an outside person come in and compliment progress to date.

ACTIONS THAT CAN BE DONE ALONG THE PATH TO THE OBJECTIVE TO MOTIVATE THOSE INVOLVED

As a leader committed to motivating frequently along the path towards the objective, there are five specific approaches which you can take to provide this motivation.

1. ***Repetition:*** One way of providing powerful motivation is to remind the individual of the original objective, and the important part which they play in it.

   This understanding is itself a motivator as well as a very effective way of keeping the team focused, while still acknowledging the value of individual contributions.

2. ***Celebration:*** Along the path successes can be celebrated. These can be individual successes, or group or team successes. The celebration need not be elaborate, it could be as simple as bringing in a box of donuts, ordering a pizza, or attending a training course together.

   At Eagle's Flight celebration is a large part of our culture. We celebrated our first million-dollar month by taking everybody out to a jazz pub for dinner and time to chat. We've celebrated the team every year with a day dedicated simply in their honor. We celebrate birthdays, special events, large sales, exceptional service, and anything else that's relevant to our people.

   Celebration at Eagle's Flight includes not only the things important to the business (e.g. a million-dollar month) but also things of importance to the people (e.g. birthdays). This is because we see the people and the business as synonymous.

"The nature of celebration
is such that it can
break the normal routine
and give people
pause to reflect and
then refocus."

However, we also celebrate project achievements: for example when individuals successfully completed training on recently purchased software there was a special awards ceremony. Any excuse to celebrate will do! I appreciate that at Eagle's Flight fun is a large part of what we believe is important, and so celebration may take a larger place in our culture than in others. Nonetheless the *principle* of celebration is valid. It is an effective and fun way to recognize milestones along the path and to motivate our teams.

The celebration itself is motivating, *and* serves to reinforce the importance of whatever it is that is being celebrated.

The nature of celebration is such that it can break the normal routine and give people pause to reflect and then refocus. As such it can be a card signed by everyone, a large cookie which everyone shares, a day when everyone wears something purple, or it can be more elaborate such as trips, guest speakers brought in, or training done at a particularly nice location. Celebration need not always be expensive to be effective. As with most things in life, it's the thought that counts.

3. ***Compare:*** One way to motivate individuals is to pause and consider how we are doing compared to others. This increases the awareness of competitors in the marketplace; and also of how other organizations, perhaps non-competitive, are doing similar types of activities and from whom you can learn.

"Motivating others
requires speaking
passionately
and truthfully."

When the comparison is made there will be an opportunity to learn and grow, and see new ways of doing things: as a result the task being reviewed can perhaps be done more simply or more effectively. This is motivating in that it allows individuals to take a quantum leap forward, with less personal slogging. Also, the very act of looking outside the organization, or making a visit to another facility, reminds individuals to keep the broader perspective in mind and stay alert to the learning which is all around us. Since learning is generally a powerful motivator, this form of motivation is particularly effective.

When other organizations are doing something not as well as we are, then that too is motivating as it allows us to realize we are truly world-class at what we do. It reinforces that continuing on in that direction, or even improving it further, allows us to maintain our competitive edge and therefore a prominent place in the eyes of those who use our product or service.

4. ***Measurement:*** Measurement is a practical and realistic motivator. It provides tracking of progress, and preferably tracking against a predefined standard. As individuals are able to track their progress, and see it measured, the results can be highly motivating when success is constantly being reflected by these measures.

   In those instances where the measurements show a shortfall, or performance is below expectation, a skillful manager can draw lessons from this so that improvements can be made. This can also be a powerful motivator. Individuals are able to learn from their mistakes and then subsequently see the measurements reflecting improved performance.

"Measurement is a practical and realistic motivator."

ACTIONS THAT CAN BE DONE ALONG THE PATH TO THE OBJECTIVE TO MOTIVATE THOSE INVOLVED

5. ***Validation:*** When an individual from outside your team or group comes in to compliment or comment on progress to date, that can be extremely motivating. The use of an outside "expert," or individual in authority, to provide an external point of view is often seen to be of significant value.

   Where you can make others aware of the progress of your team, or individuals on your team, and then have them demonstrate an appreciation for that work, you have not only served to motivate your team, but also to educate those around you who depend on the team's results for their own progress.

Motivating others requires speaking the truth and speaking with compassion. It involves speaking passionately. And it involves creativity, sometimes a word, or a hand shake is sufficient, sometimes a card or a note, sometimes simply providing an opportunity for an individual to present their results to date is very effective, or sometimes a more elaborate event should be planned. Whatever you feel is appropriate, and how you feel you should handle it, is at your discretion. The important thing is to remember the power of motivation and act accordingly, and frequently.

PERIODIC SELF-ASSESSMENT OF PERSONAL PRIORITIES PROMOTES EXCELLENCE

STEPS

1. Identify areas for self assessment

   Area A: Personal mastery within your field(s) of endeavor

   Area B: Effectiveness of those who rely on your leadership

   Area C: Overall success of your activities vs. expectations. These areas can be as many or as few as you wish. They can be broad in nature, or very specific

2. Determine the relative importance of each area from step 1 in terms of the short term ("must be done now, or soon") and the long term ("must be sure to be done by ________") (fill in the blank that fits your definition of "long term")

   Remember these are priorities relative to each other, not in the absolute. This is a personal guide to ensure personal effort is appropriately balanced

   e.g.

	Priority		
	high	med	low
Short Term	B	C	A
Long Term	A,B		C

   (entries from those listed in step 1)

3. Sketch out a quick chart – pictures help convey information

   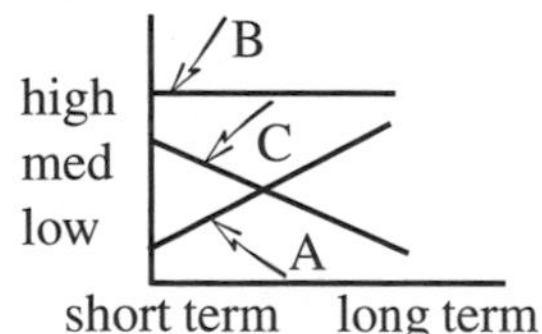

4. Assess; take whatever action you deem appropriate to ensure your present actions are consistent with achieving your intentions

PERIODIC SELF-ASSESSMENT OF PERSONAL PRIORITIES PROMOTES EXCELLENCE

Benjamin Franklin identified a few key qualities which he believed were crucial to his own personal character. He jotted these down on a list, and then made a point of evaluating himself against these on a regular and frequent basis. He was doing a self-assessment to ensure that he was personally developing, and demonstrating the qualities which he believed to be those which promote personal excellence. We need to do the same.

There are four specific steps to be taken in doing this.

Step 1 – Identification: Clearly the first thing is to identify those areas where you are seeking self-improvement. These areas could be in any aspect of your life, such as home, family, spiritual, emotional, personal interests, or behavior at work. The important thing is to identify where you wish to see improvement, and then identify what that improvement should be.

On the accompanying illustration, I've outlined three very broad categories you may wish to consider, and I'll use these as examples as I work through the steps.

Area A: Those aspects where you seek personal mastery in your chosen discipline or profession. For example, the teacher might choose speaking skills, writing skills, or interpersonal skills.

Area B: Leaders might identify the need to ensure those whom they are leading are as effective as possible: for example, do they achieve a great deal in a little time? Are they good at project management, and are their team skills outstanding?

"Benjamin Franklin identified
a few key qualities
which he believed were crucial
to his own personal character,
and made a point of
evaluating himself against these
on a regular and frequent basis.
We need to do the same."

Area C: Your own personal ability to deliver against expectation. For example, are you meeting the commitments you made to deadlines? Are the results as promised? If innovation is expected, is it occurring?

I appreciate that these are very broad categories (as opposed to something specific like losing weight, or writing a book), but they merely serve to illustrate that your personal priorities, and the corresponding assessment, may be either broad or narrow.

The key thing is to identify them, and to do so in a way that makes sense to you (broad or specific); also, be sure you identify them all. There may be as many or as few as you wish.

Step 2 – Relative Importance: In this step you need to take the items of Step 1 and put them in a relative order of importance. Remember this is your own personal list and as such you will not be accountable to anyone for it, so you can easily identify the relative importance of each item in your own judgement.

Of note: If you use the same list for an extended period of time you may find the relative priorities change. For example, in my illustrations above, if at present you lead only a few people, your impact on their effectiveness may not be as important as your own functional skill; however later if you've mastered your functional area and are now responsible for leading a larger number of people, then that element (the effectiveness of those you lead) will perhaps move up to a higher priority.

"The important thing is to identify where you wish to see personal improvement, and then identify what that improvement should be."

When assessing relative priorities you need to also take into account how important it is that you improve in the short term (near future) as opposed to the long term (distant future). This will allow you to blend relative priority (importance) with degree of immediacy (urgency).

Remember that these are priorities *relative to each other, not in the absolute sense*. This is simply your own guide to ensure that the effort you spend is spent appropriately in order to achieve what *you* want. This is illustrated under Step 2.

Step 3 – Chart the Results: By making a chart of the result with "short to long term" on the "X" axis, and "low to high" on the "Y" axis you can then determine how much effort you should spend on these priorities. For example in the chart shown on the illustration it's clear that Area A is a low priority in the short term growing to a high priority in the long term. This means it can be left for the moment, but attention will have to be directed toward it relatively soon in order to ensure that in the long term you have the required skills.

Similarly, Area B is high now and remains high, and so must be a continuing focus.

Area C is relatively important now, although not as much so as B, but still important. In the long term this priority drops and so whatever development you need to do on it needs to be done soon, because over the long term it will get less attention.

"Over time this regular assessment will become an effective and habitual tool to promote personal excellence."

This kind of a chart allows you to determine how to spend your time now, and how you should plan to spend your time in the weeks to come. It allows for a periodic self-assessment to determine whether or not you are investing your time appropriately in the key priorities, and whether or not you'll arrive at the future with the necessary development.

Step 4 – Assessment and Action: Once you have this data you need to determine if your *current* personal development priorities are aligned as they should be. Is the time and effort you are spending being done so appropriately? Will you get the desired results that you require in the future? Are you maximizing the results of the time you are investing, as measured against what you believe should occur?

Once you've done this assessment for the first time then I recommend you review it every couple of months, to see whether anything has changed, and more importantly to see whether or not you are making progress as you intended. Over time this regular assessment will become an effective and habitual tool to promote personal excellence.

A POSSIBLE ORGANIZATIONAL OBJECTIVE AT THE OPERATIONAL LEVEL

The Operational Level is the "how" of our business, not the "what".

"IMITATED"

So good at all you do that others are trying to do it your way.

And therefore you stay in the lead.

"GLOBAL"

You consider yourself a player, or potential player, on a global field.

And therefore will not be taken by surprise.

"COMPETITOR"

Your results are constantly being assessed against the competition.

And therefore you will always know how high the bar is.

Striving to be an imitated global competitor eliminates complacency!!

A POSSIBLE ORGANIZATIONAL OBJECTIVE AT THE OPERATIONAL LEVEL

Organizations can be very skilled at writing mission statements, or establishing a relevant strategy. This is an important skill and one which serves both the organization and the individuals that make up that organization in good stead.

However, there is also significant value in having a corporate objective at the *operational* level. That is, as a mission statement provides strategic direction, a corporate objective at the operational level can provide tactical direction which is equally powerful. This addresses *how we go about* doing our business, not the business that we are in.

If the organization strives for world-class excellence then a very powerful corporate objective is to become an *"imitated global competitor."* This has relevance even if your organization is not operating at the global level... as of yet. These three words are powerful because of what they signify, and the consequence which they bring to the organization.

> ***"Imitated":*** An organization that is imitated is one that is so good at what it does that others wish to do it equally well. An imitated organization is the model, the one which others strive to be like.
>
> You will not be imitated if a portion of your operational performance is stellar but another portion is very weak; for example your delivery systems are perfect but your costs are higher than the industry average. To be imitated you must do what you're doing so well, from a whole system point of view, that others seek to emulate it. When this is the case then you have the confidence that your organization or department is performing at a level which will be seen to achieve the lowest cost and highest quality, in the shortest time frame. Achieving this position would give you an outstanding competitive advantage; and so striving to be imitated in your marketplace is a powerful operational objective.

A POSSIBLE ORGANIZATIONAL OBJECTIVE AT THE OPERATIONAL LEVEL

"Striving to be an imitated
global competitor at the
operational level
sets before the organization
the challenge of being
world-class in everything done,
with world-class results."

"Global": There are two reasons for the word global, the first is that you want to ensure that you do not mislead yourself in terms of your quality of performance. In your home town you might be imitated, but on a global level there might be others who are significantly better. Because you have not looked far enough afield with regard to the content of "imitated" you've lured yourself into a false sense of security. The second reason for the global thinking is that it forces you to evaluate the real marketplace in which you compete – that is, the global marketplace.

By striving to be effective, either in practice or in theory, on a global basis, you avoid being taken by surprise, and ensure that you have done all within your power to be a maximally effective competitor or service provider.

A POSSIBLE ORGANIZATIONAL OBJECTIVE AT THE OPERATIONAL LEVEL

"Striving to be an
imitated global competitor
serves to drive out
complacency."

A POSSIBLE ORGANIZATIONAL OBJECTIVE AT THE OPERATIONAL LEVEL

"Competitor": If you see your department or organization as one in competition with others, whether it is a service provider, marketing company, or product provider then you are constantly assessing your results against those of your competition.

If you are striving to be an imitated competitor then your results will exceed those whom you consider to be your competition. This concept of looking at the competition in order to assess your own performance against that standard has the dual result of helping you assess what the current global performance standard is in your industry, with regard to those variables you consider important (such as price, quality, service, availability, profitability, etc.). It will also ensure that your organization is striving to be the model in each of those areas.

Striving to be an imitated global competitor at the operational level sets before the organization the challenge of being world-class in everything done, with world-class results.

This objective serves to effectively align the organization, and drive out complacency.

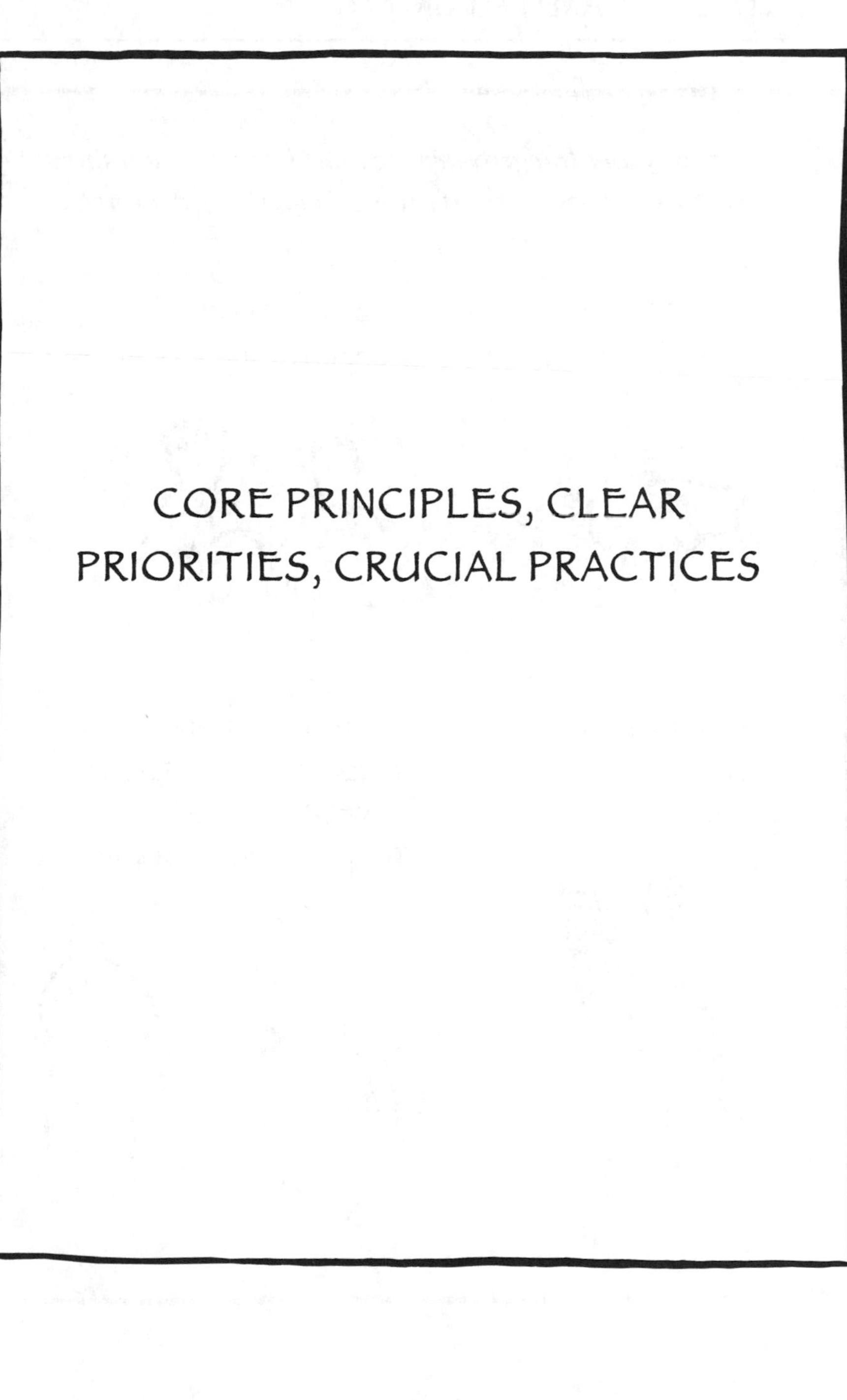

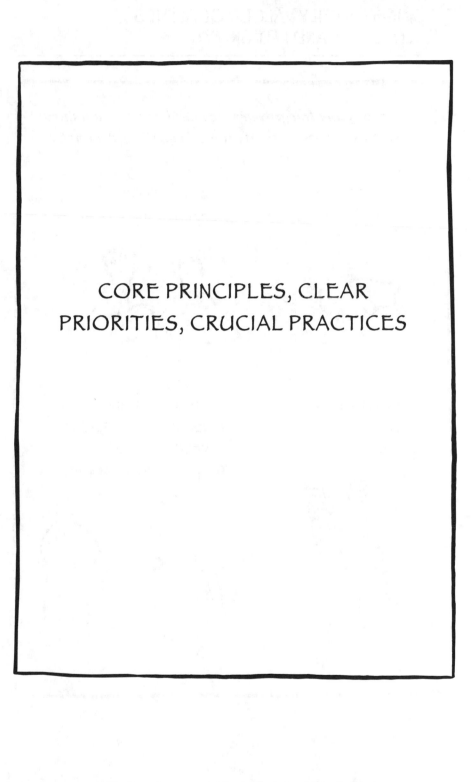

CORE PRINCIPLES, CLEAR PRIORITIES, CRUCIAL PRACTICES

TWO MOST HIGHLY VALUED QUALITIES: TEACHABILITY AND INTEGRITY

Teachability and Integrity are the most important qualities. Always assess first to see if these two qualities dominate.

WHEN RECRUITING
Get it from the start

WHEN MENTORING
To optimize the time spent

WHEN PROMOTING
To ensure quality leadership

WHEN COMMITTING TO AN INVESTMENT IN PERSONAL DEVELOPMENT
To optimize the investment

TWO MOST HIGHLY VALUED QUALITIES: TEACHABILITY AND INTEGRITY

Integrity and teachability are the two most important qualities to have in others, and so considerable effort should be made to build an organization where they are in evidence.

Recruitment: The first step is to recruit people who demonstrate a teachable spirit and have proven integrity. Since recruitment is the first door into the organization, and the first step to building a world-class organization, these two qualities should be uppermost on the recruitment list by looking for instances where the candidate has developed and demonstrated them.

Mentoring: One of the most effective tools within an organization for developing talent is through mentoring. This is the process whereby an individual learns the skills and strengths of another over a defined time period, through dedicated one-on-one coaching time. By selecting those who have a proven track record in integrity and teachability as mentors in the mentoring program, and placing with them those most likely to succeed, you will increase the opportunity for teachability and integrity to take root within the organization.

Promotion: When decisions are made on who should be promoted, and publicly recognized with additional responsibility, select those who have demonstrated both teachability and integrity. This will again serve as a model for the rest of the company, and also place individuals with those qualities in positions of leadership. Since like begets like, it will reinforce the value placed on those qualities and increase the likelihood of their being reproduced throughout the organization.

"When decisions are
made on who should
be promoted,
select those who have
demonstrated both
teachability and integrity."

TWO MOST HIGHLY VALUED QUALITIES: TEACHABILITY AND INTEGRITY

Development: Organizations must make decisions on where to place their development dollars as training and development costs are high – both in terms of opportunity cost and real expenses. Ensure that those who receive significant development are those who demonstrate both teachability and integrity. This will maximize the return on investment dollars, and continue to harness the potential of those individuals with these two crucial qualities.

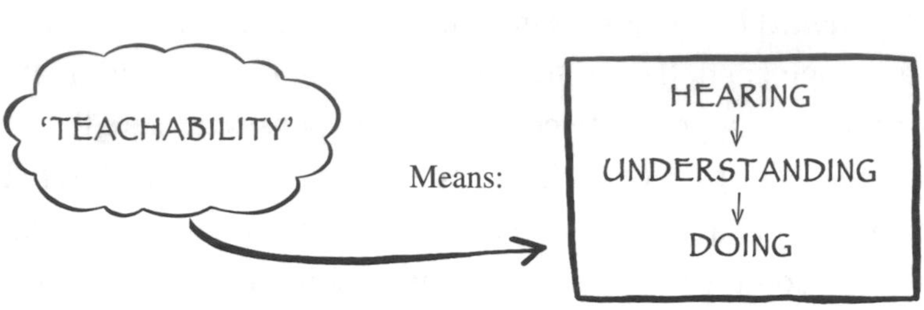
'TEACHABILITY'
Means:
HEARING
UNDERSTANDING
DOING

It is NOT:
- Listening politely
- Committing to personal development
- Acquiring diplomas, degrees, education
- Attending seminars, classes, conferences
- Being open to personal growth

Rather it IS: A teachable person is one who does things differently, who demonstrates a change in behavior, as a result of input received.

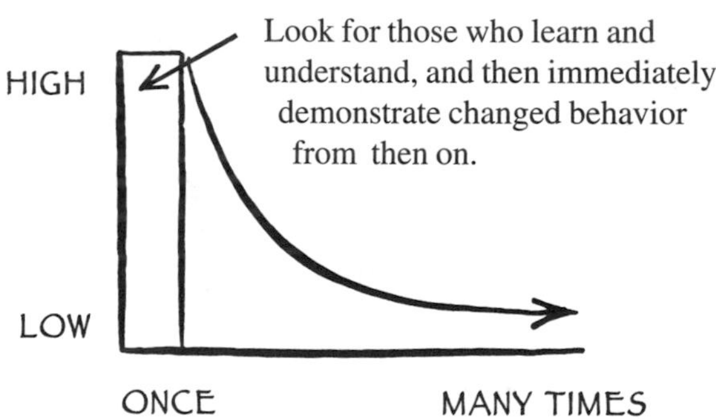
Look for those who learn and understand, and then immediately demonstrate changed behavior from then on.
HIGH
LOW
ONCE
MANY TIMES

Number of times you hear something before you actually behave differently, consistently.

TEACHABILITY: HAVING A LEARNER'S HEART

To be teachable is to have a learner's heart. This is evidenced by an individual who hears what is said, understands what is meant, and then does what is appropriate.

Teachability is not a description of someone who simply sits quietly and listens patiently while you talk. Rather it describes an individual who hears what is said, probes, questions, and asks until they have a clear understanding of what is meant, and *then* takes action. It is the "taking action" step which truly sets apart the teachable person.

It's relatively easy to be a good listener, it's difficult to be a good learner. A teachable person is one who makes implementing what was heard and understood a priority. Teachability in an individual then means they can be relied upon to do what they understood. They don't have to be told many times over, they don't take a long time to learn.

A teachable individual is a joy to coach in that they "get it" the first time, every time. They walk away with a clear understanding and then apply whatever discipline is necessary to ensure that their behavior changes to reflect what they have learned. Actions follow understanding, and changed behavior follows learning.

We sometimes confuse apparent teachability with real teachability. For example, an individual who has several degrees, awards, or certificates, or who speaks enthusiastically about personal learning, is not necessarily a teachable person. Individuals who attend seminars, classes, conferences, who read books, and who to all outward appearances seem to be "sponges for knowledge" are not necessarily teachable. They are clearly *learners*, and are very definitely willing to expose themselves to the ideas and opinions of others; they may well be *students*, in every sense of the word. But they are not necessarily teachable. To be teachable they must demonstrate a changed behavior as a result of this input which they have received.

"Teachability describes
an individual
who hears what is said,
probes, questions,
and asks, and then
takes action."

TEACHABILITY: HAVING A LEARNER'S HEART

A good measure of the teachability of an individual is how many times they must be exhorted to action on something which they clearly understand and on which they agree.

Teachability is something we must value highly in others, and cultivate in ourselves if we wish to maximize our own productivity and the results of our organizations.

Integrity shows up in many places, and in many formats; but each time it has in common the fact that an individual with absolute integrity is one who can be fully relied on to always do as they said they would.

If I said I'll do it,
I'll do it as I said I would.

INTEGRITY: DOING WHAT YOU SAY YOU WILL DO

Personal integrity is often considered to be a characteristic of an individual; someone has integrity or they don't. By this we usually mean the person can be trusted or relied upon. Within the context of an organization integrity takes on a broader meaning to encompass not only the character of the individual, but also the outcome of an individual's actions.

Individuals with integrity in the organizational setting are those who can be "trusted" to *do* what they say they will do. This is quite evident in straightforward instances, like a promise made to an individual. If I say to somebody that I will meet them at four o'clock with the report finished, and I have integrity, then I will be there at four with the finished report. It is more elusive when the issues are more complex; for example, when I say, "This was a good course, and yes, I now understand the importance of setting clear goals for my employees and I will do it." Then, if I have integrity, that is exactly what I'll do. This concept of integrity takes it beyond the normal meaning to include commitments made to oneself, commitments to principles, and to the application of learning.

It is *this* kind of integrity which is so impactful within an organization. If an individual has great integrity then you have every confidence that what that individual says will in fact happen to the best of their ability. They can be relied upon to wholeheartedly execute principles, values, or visions to which they have indicated their agreement; they can be relied upon to throw their whole weight in support of a practice which they have affirmed as appropriate.

"If an individual has great integrity, they can be relied upon to throw their whole weight in support of a practice which they have affirmed as appropriate."

It's important to see integrity in this broader context. It's easy for someone to have integrity when they make a promise to another individual which can be satisfied with a simple action. It's much more difficult to have integrity when you make a commitment to see a vision through to reality, or to the fully executed implementation of a policy, procedures, strategy, or tactics.

Take for example an organization committed to empowerment where leaders are asked to allow employees to contribute to their full potential, by encouraging them to interact with their internal customers and suppliers. Once the skills of empowerment have been taught leaders must then choose whether or not to behave accordingly. If an individual says they will, and they have integrity, then they can be relied upon to do so and not fall back into the previous management style. Most managers will verbally indicate their support of this kind of initiative, especially when they realize it is the direction in which the company is now going. However, *only those with integrity will actually do all in their power to implement it as intended.*

TEACHABILITY + INTEGRITY = AN UNBEATABLE COMBINATION

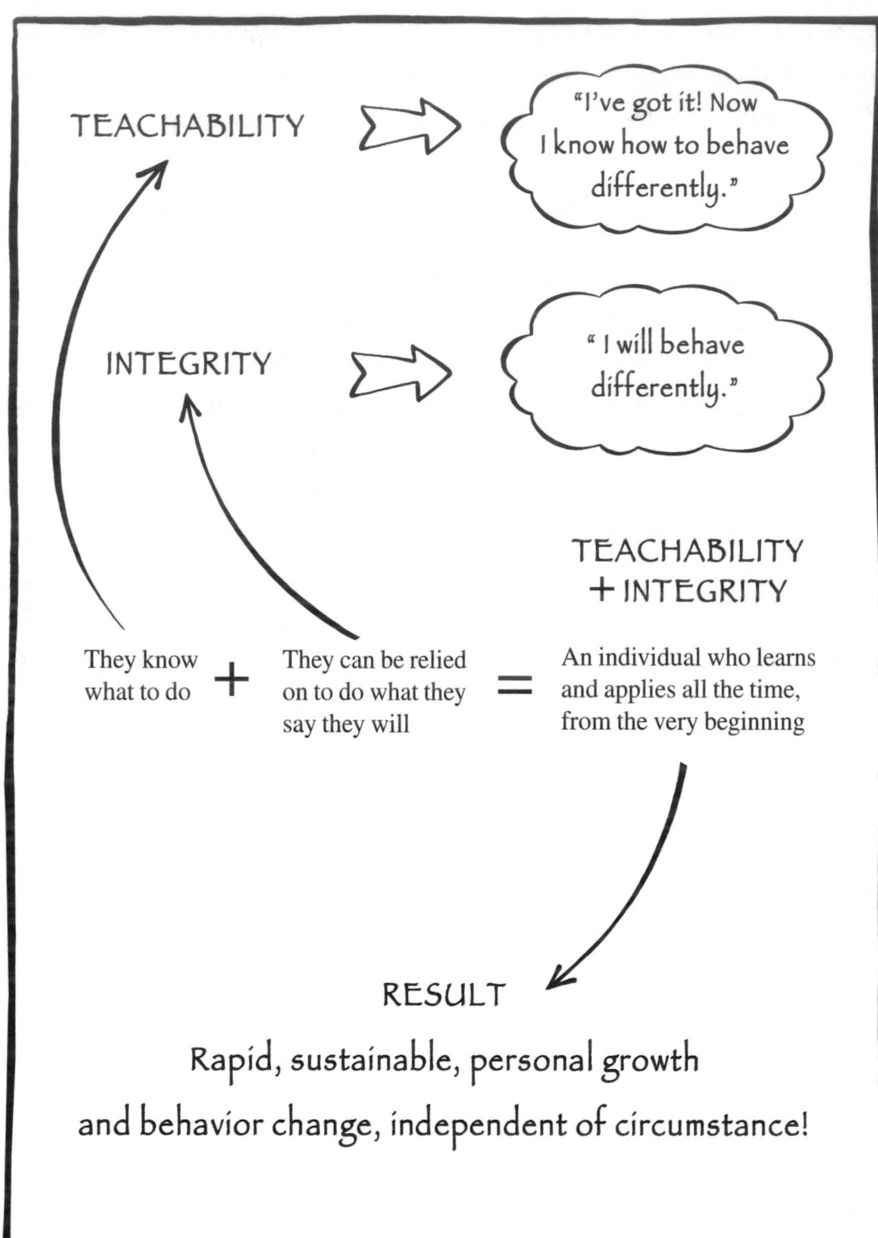

TEACHABILITY + INTEGRITY = AN UNBEATABLE COMBINATION

Teachability is that quality which an individual demonstrates when they show themselves willing to learn and then apply what has been learned. Integrity is that quality which gives confidence that they will do what they say they will do.

Put them together and you have an individual who learns new ways of behaving, commits to applying them, and then, because of their integrity, gives you every confidence that that commitment will actually translate into meaningful action.

When I recruit or make decisions on promotions, I place tremendous weight on the two qualities of teachability and integrity. If the individual is teachable then I know that they *can* grow. If they have integrity then I know that they *will* grow.

Over the years I have had occasion to observe many individuals who claim to be committed to learning, and who demonstrate varying degrees of integrity within this context. They do make every effort to apply the learning, and for the most part ultimately do so. However, in many cases it seems that individuals who have committed to applying the learning only do so intermittently, as inevitably other things surface which, they believe, block the application of the learning. They're "too busy," it was "easy to fall into the old way," they "didn't get support" from somebody, or other similar reasons. In most cases, ultimately they do persevere and acquire the learning.

However, I did come across one individual whose integrity and teachability were so high that learning and growth occurred at an astonishing rate. He would question or discuss the process of learning until he understood. If he then agreed, he said he would do it. And from that point on he did it!

TEACHABILITY + INTEGRITY = AN UNBEATABLE COMBINATION

"If the individual
is teachable
then they can grow.
If they have integrity then
they will grow."

TEACHABILITY + INTEGRITY = AN UNBEATABLE COMBINATION

In his case I never had to go back and repeat the teaching, he never gave an excuse for why the teaching wouldn't be applied, he never felt justified or personally vindicated for not applying the teaching for some particular reason which had surfaced. Rather, he heard it, agreed to it, committed to do it, and did it.

Because of this high degree of teachability and integrity his rate of growth and personal development was extraordinary, and he built quickly and effectively into his life. He did it independent of circumstances, and because of his integrity overcame many of the "reasons" which others would give for not being able to apply the learning "just now." To me he was the model of teachability and integrity.

Taken on their own, each of these qualities is important and powerful; taken together, they are tremendously so.

THE BENEFITS THAT COME FROM HAVING THOSE WHO DISPLAY BOTH TEACHABILITY AND INTEGRITY

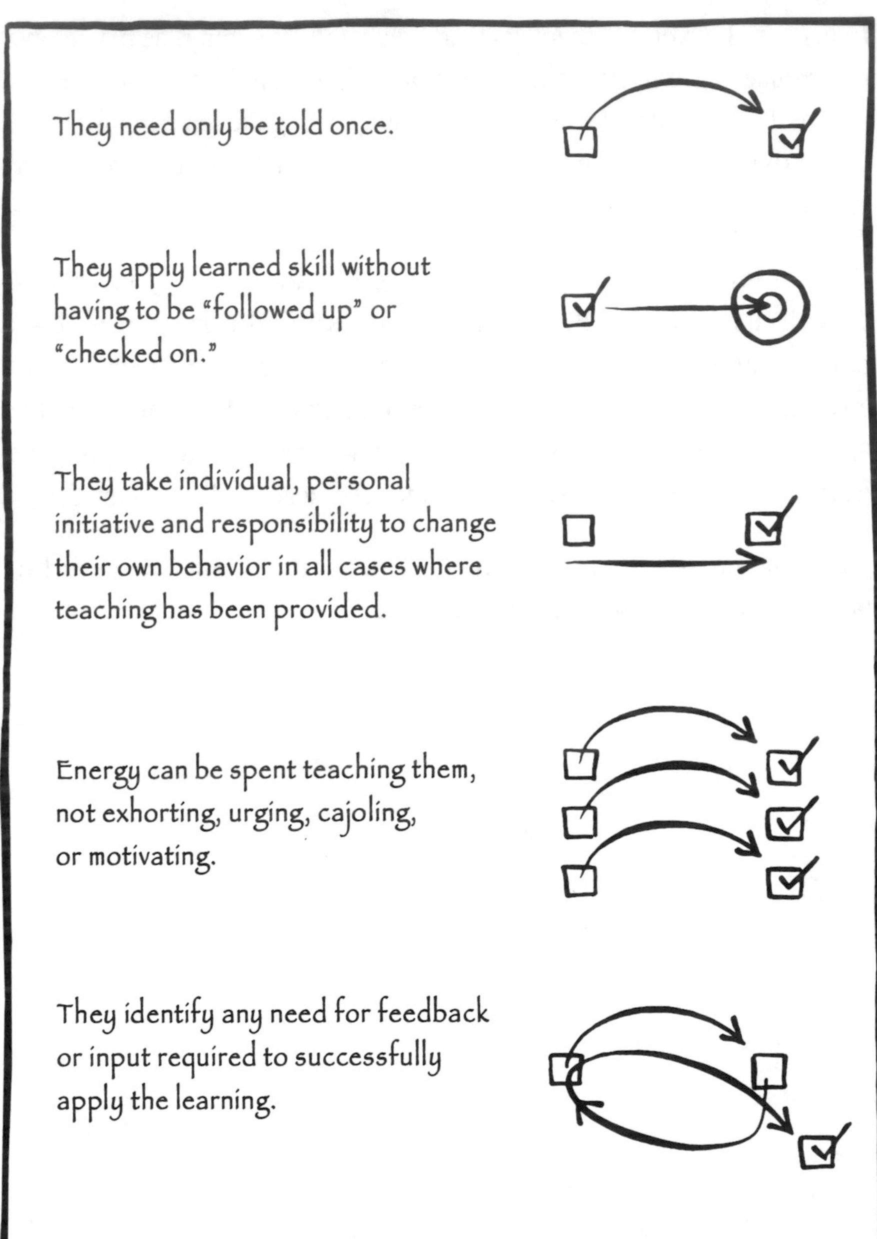

They need only be told once.
They apply learned skill without having to be "followed up" or "checked on."
They take individual, personal initiative and responsibility to change their own behavior in all cases where teaching has been provided.
Energy can be spent teaching them, not exhorting, urging, cajoling, or motivating.
They identify any need for feedback or input required to successfully apply the learning.

THE BENEFITS THAT COME FROM HAVING THOSE WHO DISPLAY BOTH TEACHABILITY AND INTEGRITY

Leaders have the responsibility of building teachability and integrity into the organization and its members.

Once we realize the importance of having people within our organization who display both teachability and integrity, then we can hire and promote based on each criteria. In addition, we can also aggressively seek to teach and encourage those qualities to flourish, and, in particular, seek to encourage and develop the behaviors that flow from the marriage of teachability and integrity. There are five specific *behaviors* that we as leaders should therefore be promoting.

1. Individuals should need to be told only once; and then should act accordingly.

Once an individual understands what it is that is required and commits to doing it, and you still find that constant repetition and frequent reminders are required in order for the appropriate action to occur, then that is an indication that either teachability or integrity are weaker than they should be.

It's lack of teachability if they understood, but did not learn.

It's lack of integrity if they had full understanding but seem constantly to have reasons or excuses for not applying the learning.

After you diagnose which it is, you will be better able to coach them through to the point where they demonstrate immediate application, on a sustained basis, right from the start.

"It's far more productive for us as leaders to spend time moving things forward, than it is to be having to constantly go back and urge that previous directions be maintained."

2. ***Once the skill has been acquired it will then be applied consistently,*** whether or not there is anyone there to follow-up, see it being put into practice, or measure it.

   This particular attribute frees up leaders to do other things, and so puts less emphasis on follow-up to ensure that the required procedure or action is occurring. The greater the checking up required, the greater the need to address either teachability or integrity.

3. ***They see the need to change as a personal obligation.***

   In this case, because they have learned what has been taught, and have committed to applying it, they now see it as a personal matter to be dealt with within themselves.

   This particular attitude is a powerful one in that the individuals do not see themselves as executing some corporate directive, some "new approach", or some externally imposed practice or behavior. Rather, they have decided to adopt it *for themselves* and have done so. They then provide their own internal motivation and implement it.

   This is one of the most powerful consequences of the combination of teachability and integrity. It takes tremendous pressure off the leader, as those on a team with these two qualities are truly committed, in every sense of the word.

"In the case of those
who have a high degree
of teachability and integrity
then they do the initiating:
they initiate the request
for feedback, reinforcement,
and input."

THE BENEFITS THAT COME FROM HAVING THOSE WHO DISPLAY BOTH TEACHABILITY AND INTEGRITY

4. Time is not spent in exhortation.

If you think of the amount of time which is spent following up, exhorting, encouraging, motivating, urging, and attempting to cajole others into doing what they said they would do, and in following up on the things they agreed were important, it's staggering. Conversely, in dealing with those who have a high degree of teachability and integrity, then all that time is spent inputting, and providing additional learning and opportunities for growth. If the individual learns the material and then commits to applying it, you as a leader can then focus on providing more learning or more opportunities for its application. This is positive, progressive, proactive and exciting. The need to constantly go back and refer to previously taught material, reminding others of their commitment, vanishes like vapor in the face of those who are extremely teachable and have great integrity.

It's far more productive for us as leaders to spend time moving things forward than it is to be having to constantly go back and urge that previous directions be maintained.

THE BENEFITS THAT COME FROM HAVING THOSE WHO DISPLAY BOTH TEACHABILITY AND INTEGRITY

"Leaders have the responsibility of building teachability and integrity into the organization and its members."

5. ***The feedback required to ensure success often originates with the learner, rather than with the leader.***

   In dealing with individuals who are low on either teachability or integrity, the leader must take the initiative to provide regular feedback, and constantly promote application of the learning.

   In the case of those who have a high degree of teachability and integrity, *they do the initiating*. They in fact are the ones who are so committed to applying the learning and delivering the desired behavior they promised that they initiate the request for feedback, reinforcement, and input.

The previous five characteristics can be used to help diagnose the degree of teachability and integrity presently in place. They can also serve as a guide for coaching and training as we seek to build in the *behaviors* that match teachability and integrity.

ALWAYS, SPEAK TRUTH

THE WHOLE TRUTH, EVERYTHING!
When presenting information, speak the full truth.

RESIST:
Saying the easy part, leaving unsaid the harder, but often more meaningful material.

RESIST:
Saying only something general with "a grain of truth," but almost too general to be recognized as the truth.

RESIST:
Saying almost all the truth, but leaving the real nugget, the essence, to only be guessed at.

ALWAYS:
Speak the full truth, in complete honesty, the full story.

This way the person knows where they stand, and having all the facts, are best able to take action, or respond.

ALWAYS, SPEAK TRUTH

As a leader one of the most crucial behaviors for you to adopt is to always speak the truth.

This may seem rather obvious until one pauses to consider what the "truth" really means. By "truth" I mean the whole truth, everything. Often we claim to speak the truth, but we leave out key pieces of information, because perhaps they are embarrassing, hard to say, or unwilling to be heard. This is not speaking the truth, this is speaking only a partial truth which does not generate a complete understanding, and so in fact is not really the "truth".

Consider the situation where you have to correct an individual for being excessively discourteous to one of their colleagues. This individual may otherwise be one of your best performers. The individual might be in high demand in the marketplace, with some very specialized skills. You greatly value their contribution, and recognize that the quality of their performance is consistently stellar and adding value to the organization. Further you sense that the link to your organization may be somewhat tenuous at present given the high demand for the kind of work which this person does.

Nonetheless you are dissatisfied with the level of inter-personal behavior which this individual shows to the colleagues with whom they must work. Perhaps this lack of courtesy is a by-product of their considerable functional skill, and that therefore their ego is large, and they feel they are in some fashion "superior." In this case you believe you should talk to the person. So you have, essentially, two choices.

"If you are not
speaking the whole truth,
then you are not
speaking the truth."

On the one hand you could be somewhat obscure, beating around the bush, hinting at the problem, but not too clearly for fear of offending the individual. You might say something like, "You know you provide exceptional value to the company, and we appreciate that. Periodically there are times when, I'm sure, you encounter others who do not provide the same level of service, or do not perform at the level of your own ability. I appreciate that this can be frustrating at times and I'm simply asking you to attempt to be tolerant should those occasions ever occur where you have to deal with someone with whom you may not be seeing eye to eye at that particular moment."

In my opinion this is the wrong approach. You arc in fact masking the truth in fear of offending the person. This is not being as effective a leader as you should. It is not the "truth" by my definition.

The second alternative is to speak the full truth, and it might go something like this: "I appreciate the tremendous value you bring to the organization, and the impact which you are making on the company. However, there are times when the level of interpersonal skill which you show is not up to the same standard as the rest of your performance.

"Since we are all mutually inter-dependent, it is important that we each show one another a high degree of mutual respect in all our dealings. I need you to be more sensitive to this, and develop the ability to deal with others that matches your ability to provide value in your other areas. Your current behavior in your dealing with your colleagues is not acceptable.

As an immediate first step, I would certainly be pleased to find an appropriate training course that might help you with this, or work closely with you in the coming weeks so that we can not only put this to rest, but bring you to a world-class level in this area as well."

"As leaders we may
shy away from speaking
the truth; but as
followers we want the full
truth in a simple
straightforward fashion."

In this latter case you have spoken the whole truth, but done so kindly and with an offer to help. You have not, however, spoken less than what you mean, nor minced your words.

There are many, many opportunities each day for individuals to provide one another with information, facts, direction, and feedback. In each case, and in every instance you should speak the whole truth. Anything that you feel is relevant should be included in your communication. If you are not speaking the whole truth, then you are not speaking the truth.

There are three specific pitfalls into which we all fall once we make this decision to speak the truth.

1. ***We speak the absolute truth, but we do not include the material which we personally find hard to address.*** For example, we may be willing to address the fact that the performance is inadequate, but less willing to indicate that if it does not improve the person might lose their job. When we fail in this regard, and the performance fails to improve, and we end up releasing the person from their employment, then it often comes as a shock to that individual. The reason for the shock is because we did a poor job much earlier of saying the whole truth. We left out the part that was hard to say. Resist this trap.

2. ***We speak the absolute truth, but we mask it so heavily that the small tiny tidbit of truth is lost in the great abundance of words.*** This often happens when we are afraid to raise the truth or we are afraid to actually deliver the message.

"Recognize that generally speaking people want and appreciate the truth so then they can take appropriate action."

A sure sign we have fallen into this trap is when the individual responds with something like "What did you just say?" or "Wait a minute, I'm not sure I heard right. Are you saying what I think you're saying?" These kinds of comments are definite indicators that we were too afraid to speak the truth clearly, and so we masked it heavily with a lot of other irrelevant and peripheral comments, until the truth was barely evident. Exercise discipline to avoid this trap.

3. ***We say everything except the absolute final bottom line, assuming that the other person will "get it" because we've been so clear with all the rest of the communication.*** This is often the case when an individual is being given a message that they will find surprising. Take for example the case where the individual fails to get a promotion and you're charged with telling them that another colleague received it. You might spend time in the meeting extolling the virtues of the individual who did receive the promotion as well as the virtues of the individual who did not. You might explain why the individual who did get it actually got it, and you might go so far as to talk at length about the future potential of the employee who failed to get the promotion. But you never quite come out and say, "Sally got it, and you didn't." Rather, you leave it to them to make that assumption as a result of all the other information which you provided. Don't leave these issues to chance, avoid falling into this trap, and speak the truth.

"Test your assumption that, as a result of your words, they have indeed fully understood the whole truth."

ALWAYS, SPEAK TRUTH

I've often found it surprising that as leaders we may shy away from speaking the truth, but as followers we want the full truth clearly, and in a simple straightforward fashion. We, as followers, believe that if we were simply given the truth in a kind and considerate but complete fashion we would then be able to understand it and take the appropriate action. I have seen that those who are looking to us for leadership feel the same way when they are the ones getting the message.

Recognize that generally speaking people really want to know the truth, and while it might be unpleasant at the moment, in the longer term it is kinder, fairer, and more courteous. As a leader your obligation is to recognize the other individual's needs to clearly understand the situation so they can act appropriately. They want the truth. They don't want it masked, hidden, clouded, hinted at, implied, or skirted around. They want and appreciate the truth so then they can take appropriate action.

It is our responsibility to give it to them.

Can be shattering, or devastating,
helpful and honest, but still very disturbing.

So always use tact -
demonstrated care, empathy, and consideration.

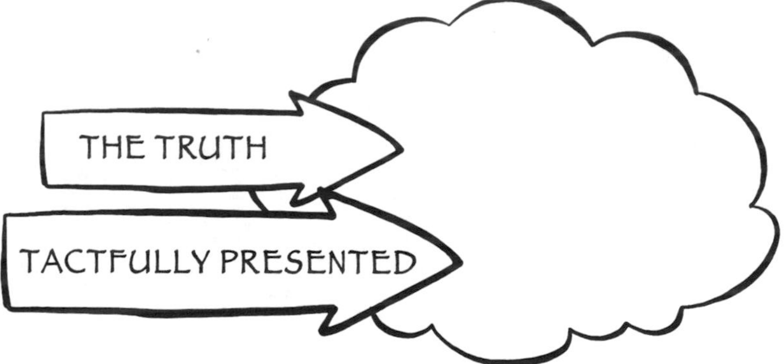

In this way the other person can focus on the content,
to the greatest possible degree,
minimally disrupted by jarred emotions.

NEVER NEGLECT TACT

As a leader, once you are committed to speaking the truth, you must also be committed to using tact.

There is the familiar caricature of a leader who has an unpleasant message to deliver, doesn't want to deliver it, and so simply blasts it out in a thoughtless, angry, barrage of words. In this caricature it's clear that the individual giving the message is more concerned about how *they* feel than how the person receiving the message feels! Remember – leaders carry the responsibility for considering the thoughts and feelings of others, often at the expense of their own.

Simply because we may not want to give a message is not a reason for us as leaders to be rude, overly quick, or unnecessarily insensitive. Because we want to get an unpleasant task over with quickly does not mean we should abuse our authority and do so in an insensitive manner.

Individuals receiving the truth will receive it much more effectively when the message is delivered kindly, or certainly with tact.

Tact is an interesting quality in that it allows you to show consideration for the other individual. Tact does *not* mean masking the message to the point where it cannot be understood. Quite the opposite. Tact means expressing the message clearly, but kindly and with sensitivity to the person receiving it.

The truth by itself, without tact, can be shattering and devastating. The truth is usually helpful and necessary but that does not take away from its often disturbing nature. However, when presented with tact, it allows the individual to focus their full attention on the message, with minimal disruption, because of the way in which you delivered the message.

"Tact does not mean masking
the message to the point where
it cannot be understood.
Quite the opposite.
Tact means expressing the
message clearly, but kindly
and with sensitivity to the
person receiving it."

NEVER NEGLECT TACT

If, for example, you have to be the bearer of the news that your neighbor's dog was just hit on the street, you certainly speak the truth by saying "Your dog is dead. It was run over by a truck." But this does nothing to help the individual truly absorb the message. It is the truth, but it is not tactfully presented.

A more tactful approach might be to say "Jim, I'm sorry to be the bearer of bad news, but there's been an accident at the foot of your driveway, and your dog was hit and killed by a passing truck. I know how much he meant to you and am deeply sorry."

In this second instance the individual giving the message demonstrates real compassion for the situation; and the delivery of the unpleasant message is not adding further emotional stress.

The ability to think in these terms, and present your message with tact, is a vitally important aspect of speaking the truth. It allows you to speak the truth with greater freedom because you've learned how to present the truth in a kind fashion. It also sets the stage for the next step, as you have presented yourself as someone who cares for the other individual, in spite of the message you have to deliver. This is an excellent foundation for any future help, coaching, assistance, or action required.

Speak the truth, but do so tactfully.

HOW TO SHOW TACT

1. Put yourself in the other's place, mentally, before speaking. Speak as you would like to be spoken to.

2. Pause periodically, to allow time for your words to be absorbed, and digested.

3. Recognize the intrinsic value, the worth, of every human being, and speak from that perspective.

4. Bear in mind the objective of honest communication is to enlighten another, not be an opportunity to feed one's own ego.

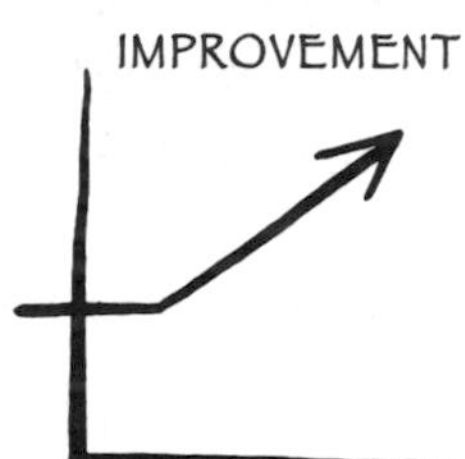

HOW TO SHOW TACT

Having a commitment to speak with tact when speaking truth is important. There are four ways in which you can demonstrate tact.

1. ***Picture to yourself what the other person is feeling, or will be feeling, and then speak from that perspective.*** "The Golden Rule" applies not only to actions but to words. If you speak to others as you yourself would like to be spoken to, then you will automatically demonstrate a caring and tactful approach.

   To most effectively employ this approach pause for a moment before speaking to consider the kinds of things the individual is going through, what they are feeling and what thoughts they might be having in anticipation of this discussion. Then adjust your own words accordingly – to show tact and consideration.

2. ***It's most effective if you measure your thoughts, pausing periodically to allow your words or phrases to sink in, and be considered.***

   Often in our haste to communicate the message we blast through it to "get it over with". Unfortunately this does not help the listener, because from their perspective they feel "bombarded" and overloaded.

   One of the ways to show consideration for another is to allow them time to absorb what you're saying, to mentally work through it for themselves, and then draw some quick conclusions. By pausing periodically you allow them a few moments to gather their own thoughts as a result of what you said. This shows consideration and tact.

"The tactful individual is one who does not allow their own emotions to interfere with the clarity and considered nature of the message."

3. ***As you speak truth to an individual and are attempting to be tactful, it helps to remind yourself that you are speaking to a human being who has great intrinsic worth.***

   Regardless of what an individual does, or perhaps says in a heated moment, their intrinsic worth is still extremely high. The value of a human being and all their thoughts, passions, hopes, and beliefs cannot be measured.

   Recognizing and having respect for each individual, and having respect for both the value and potential which each individual represents, will remind us to speak to one another with tact.

   We may often intensely dislike what someone has done, or the consequences of someone's action, or the way someone has spoken. But our dislike is directed towards the *outcome* of the person's behavior, not the worth of the individual. As we deal with those outcomes we need to remember that usually there was a cause for those actions, one which we may not fully understand. However, having a great dislike for a person's actions should not preclude us from having an appreciation for the worth of the individual. Speak from the perspective of their worth and you will be inclined to speak with tact and consideration.

4. ***The tactful individual is one who does not allow their own emotions to interfere with the clarity and considered nature of the message.***

   One of the greatest barriers to demonstrating tact is our desire to "win points at the other's expense." We may not be as blatant about it as that expression implies, but we do nonetheless fail to keep an adequate check on our own ego, feeling at times "morally justified" to speak without tact.

"Picture to yourself
what the other person
is feeling, or
will be feeling, and then
speak from
that perspective."

As we address this we need to master our own ego, and what may be a desire to release some of our own emotions or feelings in the discussion, seeing the other's behavior as a " legitimate" reason for doing so.

Successfully speaking with tact can be learned as we commit ourselves to mastering this important skill, and applying these guidelines.

The truth is often difficult to speak, in full, because of the anticipated interpersonal tension it might set up.

Smooth Connections

ANTICIPATED

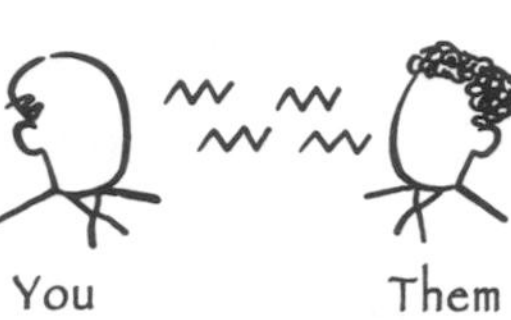

BEFORE

AFTER

THIS NEED NOT BE, IF YOU:

1. Use tact.
   Place a "blanket" around the message.

2. Recognize the receiver of your message can grow and improve as a result of your words – and so ultimately become grateful for your input.

3. Ensure your words are indeed the truth, not opinion, bias, hearsay, rumor, speculation, or gossip.

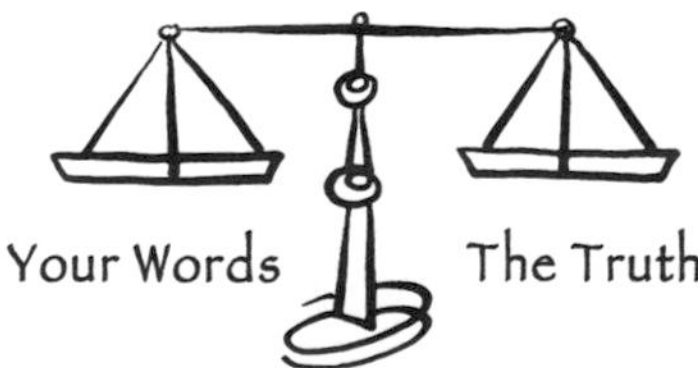

OVERCOMING THE "HARDNESS" OF SPEAKING TRUTH

When we choose to speak truth, experience may well have taught us that inter-personal tensions may develop, friction may occur, and the net result is a difficult situation, – one which is "hard" to be in.

This need not be so. There are three specific things you can do to avoid the creation of this tension, and to alleviate much of the discomfort which you anticipate.

1. ***Use tact:*** Speaking with tact does not dilute the message, rather it presents it in a way which places the message inside a "verbal blanket." Tact shows consideration and thoughtfulness for the point of view of the listener, and as a result the interaction is less stressful or jarring.

2. ***Growth:*** If you see your role of a leader as one of helping others to grow and improve, then you should see the opportunity to speak truth as simply another way in which to provide on-the-job coaching.

   By recognizing that as a result of your words the individual may perhaps be receiving some "pruning" to allow them to flourish even more, then you will approach the situation from the point of view of one who is seeking to help, and whose responsibility it is to promote growth. Clearly this thinking will have a significant impact on the way in which you tackle the issue, which will in turn create a different climate than might otherwise have been had it been seen simply as "a message of criticism".

   A true test of whether or not you have been successful at communicating this perspective is often the response of the person receiving the message. If they see it as you intended, then they will recognize it for what it is, personally benefit as a result, and so be grateful for your clarity and, essentially, kindness.

"We should not let the anticipated difficulty of speaking the truth keep us from doing so. Rather, we should work hard to ensure that we master the necessary skills required to speak the truth, and still maintain effective relationships."

3. ***Validate information:*** When speaking truth it is important for you to *ensure* that what you are about to say is indeed "the truth." We as leaders, and carriers of the message, have an obligation to validate it before we communicate it.

   We must be sure that what we heard is not gossip, hearsay, based on a superficial opinion or observation, or coming to us from someone with a biased perspective. Our job is not to be the conduit of communication, but rather to help others grow, by passing on what we have received and evaluated. Our own prior evaluation is crucial to the successful impact of the communication.

   If we do not validate what we hear before passing it on, then the interaction may well be as stormy as we are anticipating! We could be passing on what we believe to be the truth, but which, from the other person's perspective, is anything but. As we have not ensured that our message was irreproachably accurate, then we may find ourselves in the position where it will indeed be difficult to deliver the message. To avoid this we need to be sure our facts are correct before we speak.

We should not let the anticipated difficulty of speaking the truth keep us from doing so, as it is the correct thing to do. Rather, *we* should work hard to ensure that we master the necessary skills required to speak the truth and still maintain an effective relationship, conducive to ongoing personal growth and development.

The credibility of the leadership is crucial to making any organizational structure work.

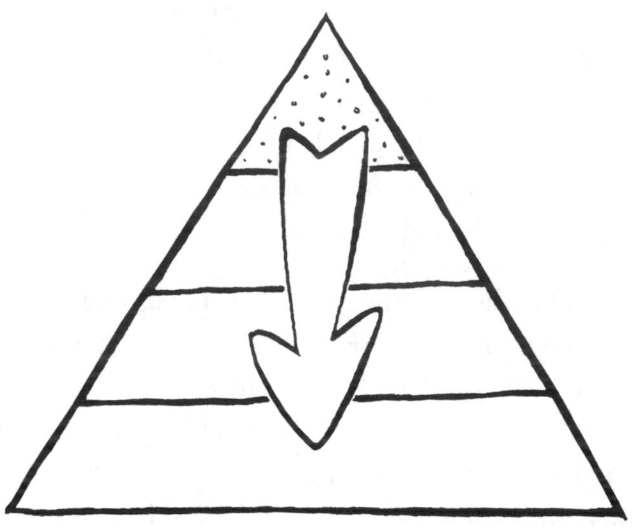

Do what you say you will do.

Demonstrate a track record.

Personally model the behavior wanted in others.

By virtue of their authority leaders can ensure action happens. Individuals have to do what they're told, but they will not do it with a will if the leadership is not credible. Leadership credibility is key to making any organization structure perform to truly world-class levels.

Often those in leadership positions, whether they be in the first line supervisory level or the CEO level, do not intend to have their credibility called into question, they are not seeking to be dishonest. Nonetheless a leader's credibility is at times questioned by those reporting to the leader, which undermines the ability of the organization to achieve its goals. This happens for one of three reasons and can be corrected as follows.

1. ***Inadequate Communication:*** Ensure that the communication between the supervisor and those being supervised is frequent, honest, and open.

   There must be frequent communication because every day things are happening, and happening quickly, and usually very efficiently, creating an ongoing need for understanding. There must be frequent communication in order for the manager or supervisor to provide the necessary clarity to the team or individuals at work. Often a group of empowered employees will not appreciate the full consequences to others of their contributions, suggestions or initiatives; and the manager also needs to ensure that the necessary links are made with the other affected groups.

"Individuals have to do
what they're told, but they
will not do it with a will
if the leadership is not credible.
Leadership credibility
is key to making any
organizational structure perform
to truly world-class levels."

2. ***Unintentional Failure to Deliver as Promised:*** Do what you say you will do. This should perhaps read; do what you say you will do, *when you say you will do it.* Those following the leader have a right to expect the leader to be true to their word. Credibility takes a long time to build, but is lost quickly when you fail to act as you have promised.

   This can come in a number of guises: "We'll tell you as soon as we know" means you have committed to pass on to the organization the information that they requested as soon as you have it. You must then do that. If that's not what you mean then say instead "We'll tell you after the information is available and when we feel that we are in a position to act upon it." This is a very different message, but perhaps the one which was meant when "we'll tell you as soon as we know" was said; and since creditability is always at stake, the second message is a far easier one to deliver on than the first.

   "We'll review the entire bonus structure before the end of January." It may happen that January is a month fraught with unexpected crises, problems and urgent requirements for the immediate attention of the whole organization. As a result, you may be unable to deliver the bonus plan as promised. This could call your credibility into question, so it would be ideal if you ensured that during that crisis-laden month you still had a team working on the bonus plan, in order to deliver what you said you would.

   In the above example, if it were physically impossible to put such a team together to deliver on your commitment, then *as soon as you are aware of that*, go to the organization with an update, indicating that your previous commitment will not be met, but for good reasons, and *provide the reasons.* This will go a long ways to retaining credibility.

"The more frequently you can
establish a track record
in as many areas as possible,
the greater will be your credibility.
This is extremely valuable
as the leader can then have
confidence that the team is acting,
now, on the basis of what the
leader has said; not waiting to test,
probe, and assess."

The critically important thing to realize is that you, as a leader, may choose not to do something which you said you would for a very good reason. The reason makes perfect sense, and is in fact the right decision from your perspective. What individuals often fail to realize is that for those who are not in the leadership position these reasons are not as clear, do not make as much sense, and appear to be, perhaps, an excuse for not delivering on previous commitments. In this manner the credibility of leadership can be undermined bit by bit and eroded over time. When told this, the leader's response is often: "But how can they think that? It was so obvious that I had to do this other more urgent task instead!" It was obvious – but to you, not to them, and so your credibility suffered. The first step to maintaining a high degree of credibility is doing what you say you will do when you say you'll will do it, or providing a detailed rationale why you did not.

3. ***Insufficient Track Record:*** Credibility can be gained over time as you demonstrate a "track record." This is a series of instances where you have consistently delivered on your promised intentions. If a sales manager says to the sales force that he will meet with each person once a week for half an hour for the next six months to review progress, and then does so, that is a track record. It builds immense credibility in the minds of the sales force. If the sales manager were then to say "The problems we are experiencing with getting sufficient product will be resolved within the next six weeks," this will result in the sales force acting and then communicating to their customers as if that were an absolute truth. The credibility of the sales manager has been established by his or her track record.

"Credibility is often seen
as a by-product of
good sound leadership;
in fact it should be a
focal point for leaders
who wish to be performing
at the world-class level."

The more frequently you can establish a track record in as many areas as possible, the greater will be your credibility. This is extremely valuable as the leader can then have confidence that the team is *acting*, now, on the basis of what the leader has said; not waiting to test, probe, and assess. This can significantly shorten the time from action to results, because the leader's team has such a high degree of confidence in the leader's ability to deliver as promised. The team quickly gets behind the leader in support of the objectives. There's nothing held back in reserve against the eventuality that the leader will not deliver their promise, or will change course in mid-stream.

4. ***Poor Personal Example:*** By modeling the behavior which is expected the leader establishes deep and immediate credibility in that area. If the organization requires bottom-up feedback to assess managerial effectiveness, and this is done for all but the most senior group, then the exercise is less than credible. In fact, the exercise is seen to be another tool or ploy of senior management, rather than a meaningful management tool that can significantly help to improve managerial excellence.

   If, on the other hand, the senior managers not only mandate bottom-up feedback, but delay its implementation until after each of them have gone through the process, been assessed, and begun to act on that feedback, then when it is rolled out to the organization it has high credibility. It has immediately become part of the culture, and an organizational norm.

"Leadership credibility
is key to making
any organization structure
perform to truly
world-class levels."

A PERFORMANCE IMPERATIVE: CREDIBILITY

> Leaders must constantly be on the alert to ensure that they model the behavior that they expect to see in others. If you as a leader wish to see effective communication, then you must model it; if you wish for your team to provide honest and straightforward feedback, then you must model the behavior yourself. This establishes credibility.

Credibility is an interesting attribute in that it is so intangible and yet so impactful. It is difficult for an individual to set out to obtain it, but easy for an individual to lose it. In the urgencies of the day-to-day it is often seen as a by-product of good sound leadership; in fact it should be a focal point for leaders who wish to be performing at the world-class level.

PERSONAL CREDIBILITY IS VITAL TO LONG TERM EFFECTIVENESS

Credibility is built on two things:

1. TRACK RECORD
History (recent and distant) shows that your input, judgements, actions, and commitments have been as you said they would be.

2. DEFENSIBILITY OF YOUR CURRENT POSITION
Your opinions, decisions, recommendations, and actions are clearly built on an observable, demonstrable, and rational basis.

These two will be in evidence in varying degrees depending on the issue at hand.
And they will be there in the future, so your present approach needs to build credibility against that future.

PERSONAL CREDIBILITY IS VITAL TO LONG TERM EFFECTIVENESS

Long term sustained relationships rely heavily on personal credibility.

While it's true that in the early dealings between two people there may be some polite wariness or uncertainty, generally speaking individuals take one another at face value. But each subsequent interaction in some way or another contributes to the development of personal credibility which will in turn influence all future dealings.

As an individual's credibility increases so does their effectiveness. People believe what you say; they feel they can trust you; and they are willing to place trust and confidence in you and your commitments.

Two things significantly influence personal credibility. The first is your track record. Track record is made up of many things: doing what you said you would do; seeing your visions materialize into reality; demonstrating that you can bring your promises to life; and consistently delivering results as promised and committed.

Clearly it takes time to build a track record and so personal credibility. This makes it all the more important to ensure that every single opportunity to lay a foundation relative to credibility is fully capitalized on, every time.

It's hard to argue with a successful track record when an individual commits to doing more of the same. On the other hand, it's difficult to place faith in an individual who wants to introduce an initiative when they have no track record, or at best a very poor one, in that area.

The second major contributor to personal credibility is a well-articulated rationale for your current position. If you have an idea, a suggested new initiative, a new point of view or a judgement to make, and these positions are rooted in an observable unbiased rationale, then your own credibility is significantly enhanced.

PERSONAL CREDIBILITY IS VITAL TO LONG TERM EFFECTIVENESS

"As an individual's
credibility increases
so does their
effectiveness."

PERSONAL CREDIBILITY IS VITAL TO LONG TERM EFFECTIVENESS

The more effective you are at gathering together supporting, complimentary experiences, or similar successes in support of your position the more effective will be the rationale you present. If this rationale is seen to be strong, your credibility is seen to be strong.

We often talk about being able to "shoot holes in their argument." This carries with it the implication that the point of view was not thought out, or did not have a sound basis on which it was built. It was not a defensible position.

Contrast this to a "rock solid argument" and there you have a point of view put forward which gets serious attention. Your own credibility is strengthened when you bring forth a rationale which is seen to be rock solid, and defensible.

As you seek to build personal credibility work hard to ensure that your arguments carry a clear and well thought out rationale, and that your track record demonstrates the ability to deliver as promised. As such, your personal credibility continually rises, and with it your effectiveness in the organization. The greater your credibility the easier it is for you to move quickly into action, spending less time on persuasion, or arguments in support of your position.

Credibility works like authority, it allows people to quickly fall in line with respect to an initiative or perspective, thereby allowing you to make change quickly and to make significant change – in short to be maximally effective.

A PERFORMANCE IMPERATIVE: REQUIRE ACCOUNTABILITY

Personal accountability must be rigorously demanded.

1. Up front - provide:
   - What's expected
   - By when
   - Using what methodology (ie. the "how")

2. Get agreement to the reasonableness, the "doability," of the assignment.

3. Then insist upon PERSONAL accountability for successful completion.

Individuals should be held accountable!

A PERFORMANCE IMPERATIVE: REQUIRE ACCOUNTABILITY

A truly world-class organization has as a performance imperative - a clear culture of individual accountability.

I find myself frequently amazed at the large number of people who are unfamiliar with this concept, or who are not committed to its mandate. An organization, whether it's large or small, corporate or volunteer, a single-family unit, or a large multi-dimensional team, cannot function to it fullest without the concept of personal accountability.

What is meant by this is essentially summed up in the statement "A commitment to do what has been agreed to." When an individual makes a commitment to do something, they should do what they said they would do. In cases where an individual has been employed to do something, and has indicated that they are able to do it, they must then do it! In those situations where an individual knows clearly what their responsibilities are, they must fulfill those responsibilities. These are illustrations of personal accountability.

I appreciate that a failure to fulfill one's accountabilities is rarely as a result of the individual waking up in the morning and saying, "I think that today I'll ignore my commitments. I will consciously choose not to do what I said I would do, and will in fact demonstrate great irresponsibility."

Instead I think people wake up in the morning with a very high degree of conviction that they should do what they know they should do, or said they would do, or have been contracted to do. They have a commitment that this activity should be uppermost in their minds, and be reflected in their day-to-day priorities.

"A truly
world-class organization
has a performance
imperative – a
clear culture of individual
accountability."

A PERFORMANCE IMPERATIVE: REQUIRE ACCOUNTABILITY

Why then is there a dichotomy between results and intention? Generally it's because other things "get in the way," other pressures enter, the person doesn't want to do what needs to be done "right now," people get tired, other pressures force a shift in attention, circumstances don't seem to favor desired outcomes, etc.

These all may be valid but they still do not take away from the fact that the individual has made a commitment to deliver an accountability, and that commitment must be upheld. From that light, all these other "valid" reasons are simply excuses. This may sound harsh and insensitive, but the individual making the commitment, or contracting to deliver the service, must learn to anticipate all possible eventualities which may hinder them in delivering on their commitments, and then modify their commitment if necessary, and accept the consequences of that modification. Once a commitment is made, then it should be fulfilled.

Personal accountability is another way of saying "I made a commitment that I would provide this product or service. I thought carefully through that commitment, I anticipated what hurdles might stand in my way, and adjusted my commitment accordingly. Therefore you can now rely on me to deliver what I said I would deliver." And then they deliver.

Very often many of the "legitimate" reasons for failing to deliver are only "legitimate" until someone else steps in with another idea, additional skill, or a greater determination to get the desired result. It is remarkable how frequently "legitimate" reasons for failing to deliver on a commitment vaporize before a more determined individual, or a more skilled individual, or a more creative individual, or someone more determined to press ahead and succeed.

"Leaders must be rigorous
in their expectation
that individual accountability
will be delivered.
If this is the absolute imperative
of a leader, then it naturally
follows that care must be taken
that the accountabilities
that are assigned, or assumed,
are reasonable."

A PERFORMANCE IMPERATIVE: REQUIRE ACCOUNTABILITY

This is really the crux of the issue; how determined are we to deliver on our accountabilities? Bear in mind – we should not take on accountabilities that we feel we are not able to deliver against. That would be unwise and irresponsible. But once taken on, then we need to be absolutely committed to letting nothing stand in the way of delivering on that accountability as promised.

As a consequence, leaders must be rigorous in their expectation that individual accountabilities will be delivered. Leaders must be immovable in their demand for personal accountability.

If this is the absolute imperative of a leader, then it follows naturally that care must be taken to ensure that the accountabilities that are assigned, or assumed, are reasonable. There are three steps necessary to ensure that this happens.

1. ***Prior to action being taking against an accountability, it must be clear what's expected.*** There must be enough detail so the individual receiving the assignment has the same expectation as the leader who gives it.

   In addition to clarifying the expectation there must also be clarity about timing, as inevitably deadlines, and due dates, play a large part in the overall delivery. The methodology to be followed also needs to be spelled out. By methodology is meant "how" the task will be accomplished.

   Clearly a more senior and more experienced person requires less discussion on the "how" than a more junior person.

   Methodology is important in that it is possible, for example, for an individual to deliver on an accountability but by doing so antagonize everyone around them.

"Once a commitment is made, then it should be fulfilled."

If this is accepted behavior, then fine; but if not, then part of the methodology must include indicating that it is not acceptable for the individual to fulfill their accountabilities and in the process leave chaos and carnage in their wake!

2. ***A very important step is to get agreement up front from the individual who is making the commitment*** that what is being asked for is in fact doable. This occurs when the individual personally commits to the outcome because they too believe that it is obtainable. It is this step which subsequently allows the leader to rigorously demand personal accountability.

3. ***The leader must then insist on the commitment being upheld as promised.*** It is not good leadership to go through the process of providing clarity around expectation, and then not including an equally strong insistence on the accountability being assumed as well.

   Measurement of some kind is a useful tool at this point, as are previously agreed upon checkpoints along the path to completion. Both measurement and checkpoints are ways in which the individual can be made aware that the leader is expecting the outcome as promised; but the leader need not wait until the deadline, or close to it, before reinforcing that personal accountability requires delivery as promised. If it's left too late, it may indeed be too late!

There are several other leadership behaviors which should be brought to bear during this process, such as providing help and coaching to the individual along the way if you see the possibility that the commitment may not be delivered as promised. These other behaviors are discussed throughout this book and can greatly assist those leaders who are committed to requiring personal accountability.

THREE MAJOR COMPONENTS OF ORGANIZATIONAL SUCCESS

Each of the three components must be fully developed and in place.

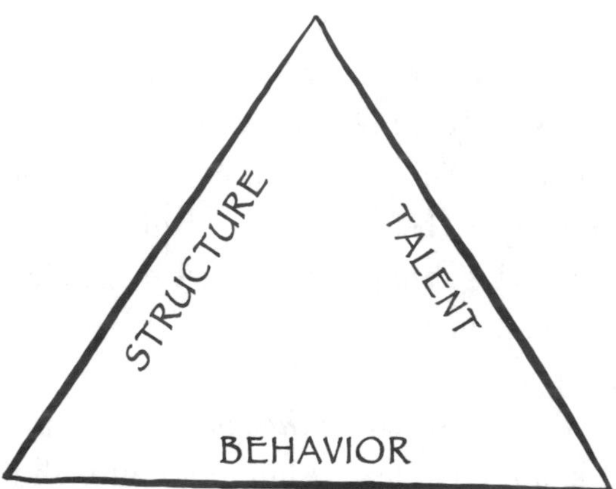

STRUCTURE
Ensuring the solid and dotted lines are in the right places – things are organizationally appropriate

TALENT
The individual abilities of the people of the organization are at the right, and highest possible, level

BEHAVIOR
Ensuring groups and individuals interact effectively among themselves, with team members, and team leaders, is vitally important

THREE MAJOR COMPONENTS OF ORGANIZATIONAL SUCCESS

From the human resource perspective of an organization, success is dependent on three specific criteria: structure, talent, and behavior. When these three have been developed to their optimum level, and are working effectively in harmony, then the potential for organizational success is at its greatest.

The interplay among these three elements is crucial. None can stand on their own and each is dependent on the other. To strengthen one at the cost of the other two will not give the same degree of effectiveness as strengthening all three equally, and concurrently.

1. ***Structure:*** This refers to the organizational structure which defines both the official and unofficial hierarchies of the organization.

   Structure includes the solid line reporting relationships, which are crucial to clear direction and feedback occurring on an ongoing basis. It is through these solid line relationships that organizational goals, objectives, and strategies are communicated throughout the organization. The solid line structure is also the official voice of the organization, and the one by which each individual should be kept advised of their performance level, and the degree to which they are impacting the organizational vision.

   Also included in structure are the unofficial, or dotted, lines which often represent the day-to-day working relationships, links with other areas of expertise, or the spontaneous relationships which form in order to accomplish things most effectively.

"The more clearly the structure is defined for everyone, the more effective everyone will be at operating within it, and pushing towards the common goal."

In a matrix organization these dotted lines are identified and considered to be as important as the solid lines. In other organizations the dotted lines form almost an unofficial infrastructure, not publicly acknowledged but none the less important to the organization's success. In a number of organizations the official structures are by no means linear, nor do they reflect the traditional "decision tree" formats. Organizational structure can be defined in any fashion, in two or three dimensions, linear or parallel, as circles, clouds, inverted pyramids, or whatever the organization uses to represent its structure and potential for maximizing its results.

Regardless of how the structure is defined, there must be a structure, and the structure must be clear to those who have to operate within it, so that they are able to function as effectively as possible. Structure allows individuals to know who to go to on each topic, and allows organizational mandates to flow freely throughout the company. Structure is crucial, even if the structure itself is constantly evolving, to provide the necessary context and framework for the individuals working within the organization. The more clearly the structure is defined for everyone the more effective everyone will be operating within it and pushing towards the common goal.

2. ***Talent:*** This refers to the capabilities of each individual employee. Talent is the skills and knowledge which people are able to bring to each of their responsibilities in order to ensure the responsibilities are carried out as intended in the most efficient manner.

   Talent can be grown, improved, developed, shaped, enhanced, and learned. It is an extremely important aspect of any organization as current talent is immediately felt, and potential talent has yet to be experienced. Potential talent can give an organization a significant competitive advantage and the ability to achieve its objectives over the long term.

"Talent walks in the door every day at the disposal of the organization. Using it, growing it, and effectively leading it are keys to organizational success."

Investment needs to be made in the talent pool of every organization in order to ensure that each individual is continuing to learn and grow. Investment also needs to be made in the leadership to ensure that leaders know how to properly harness existing talent. The investment in training, development, education, knowledge, and skill acquisition pays back many times over if the proper environment and leadership is there to harness that ever-growing talent capability.

Talent walks in the door every day at the disposal of the organization. Using it, growing it, and effectively leading it are keys to organizational success.

3. ***Behavior:*** Within any organization individuals and groups must interact. This behavior among them will either promote success, or discourage it. Issues such as innovation, team skills, continuous process improvement, and cooperation are all dependent on the individuals within the organization.

   "Behavior" shows up in many forms: the way in which a team member responds to a leader; the way in which individuals respond to one another; the way in which leaders respond to those they are leading; the way in which colleagues in different areas interact; and the way in which individuals several layers apart interact.

   If these behaviors can be aligned with corporate culture, and desired outcomes, then each interaction among individuals (i.e. their behavior) will contribute to the overall success of the organization.

   Ensuring that each individual understands clearly how they should act, and what's expected, is crucial to the success of the organization.

THE STRUCTURE MUST SATISFY TWO CRITERIA

1. BE ALIGNED TO THE STRATEGY
   Organize the lines of authority (i.e. who reports to whom) to directly support the priorities of the organization.

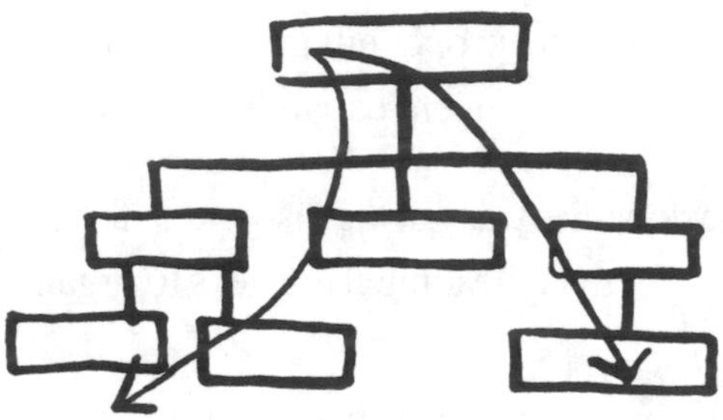

2. PROVIDE THE APPROPRIATE AUTHORITY REQUIRED TO EXECUTE THE STRATEGIES
   Ensure the organizational lines of authority give adequate control throughout the organization, to allow each group to support all goals and objectives to the greatest possible degree.

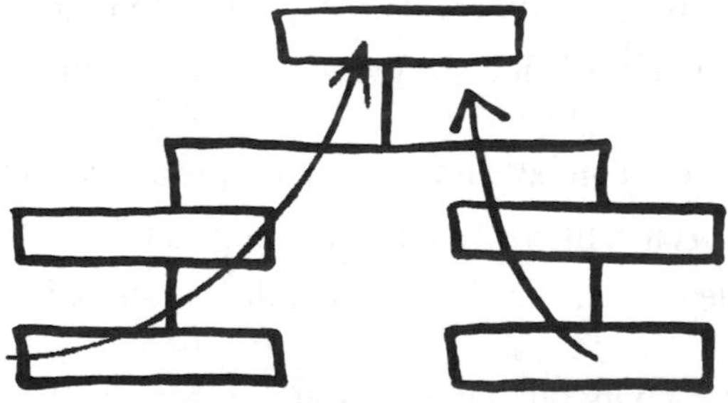

THE STRUCTURE MUST SATISFY TWO CRITERIA

In the crafting of an organizational structure two specific criteria need to be borne in mind.

1. Alignment to the Overall Strategy.

Organizational structures often reflect history, folklore and management theory, and are the results of constant changes in thinking. While the result of these influences may serve to move the organization ahead, it is not the most effective way to organize structure.

Structure must be aligned to strategy.

As the organization articulates clearly what it wishes to achieve, and more importantly, *how* it wishes to do this, then the structure should follow accordingly. This may result in "unheard of" ways of doing things; departments which never existed may be formed; or emphasis may be placed where none was before. If these events occur they should not dissuade you from pursuing the commitment to having the structure follow the strategy.

If, for example, an organization wishes to move heavily into innovation and believes that the current structure does not support that, they may create the addition of an "Innovation Department" and an "Innovation Champion" reporting to each division head. If they believe this is the way to address innovation then they should do so.

If many people who now report to several different individuals should work more cooperatively under a single banner, then restructure to accomplish this. If one segment of the organization should be closer to a customer in order to serve them better, which results in realigning the traditional reporting relationships, and physically moving a group into a customer's location, then do so.

"Aligning structure
to strategy is more than simply
deciding who reports
to whom; it includes identifying
what relationships must be
intact, at what level, and with
what degree of authority."

Once the strategy is defined, then this approach supports each individual being clearly focused on the strategy. This is far preferable to trying to force the strategy on an existing structure, which does not align well with the current corporate strategy.

Aligning structure to strategy is the kind of objective which makes a great deal of sense in theory, but when it comes to implementation it is harder to do as barriers, track record, and fear of the unknown loom. The *execution* is much more difficult to achieve than it is to acquire the conviction of the need for the execution. Nonetheless the structure must follow the strategy.

In this new structure it will be inevitable that the concept of individuals in pigeon holes reporting to neatly defined units will be a thing of the past; most strategies require many cross-functional teams and interactions. The strategies will require greater quality at less cost in a shorter period of time. In achieving this it will become apparent that the interaction among groups, teams, departments, and individuals must now be very different.

All this must be reflected in the structure by both the solid and dotted lines and the final illustration which captures the organizational structure. This then must be made clear to everyone so each knows how they are intended to operate, and with whom, and within what context. Aligning structure to strategy is more than simply deciding who reports to whom; it includes identifying what relationships must be intact, at what level, and with what degree of authority. The final structure must spell out both the official and unofficial lines of authority.

"The careful allocation of authority is crucial to ensuring the success of the structure's ability to deliver the strategy."

2. *Structure without authority can only lead to frustration and waste.*

Once the structure has been put in place then authority to execute must be provided. The challenge is to provide the *appropriate* amount of authority. Too much will jar the structure and cause decisions to be taken which are inappropriate when looked at from the perspective of the whole, while insufficient authority will block progress and impede the organization from moving forward at the greatest possible rate.

In order to determine the most appropriate authority, clear goals and objectives from any given segment of the structure must be well defined, and clearly aligned with those at a higher level. Once it is clear what needs to be accomplished, it's easier to determine how much authority is required to accomplish it.

Giving authority too soon would be rash, and consequently an assessment needs to be made as to whether the department, team or individual who requires a certain degree of authority is as yet competent enough to handle it. If not, then training is required prior to granting the authority.

Similarly, an individual may be ready for authority but the organization is slow in providing it. In this case there is wasted talent and potential that the organization is not using to the fullest degree possible. The careful allocation of authority is crucial to ensuring the success of the structure's ability to deliver the strategy.

"Authority
properly distributed
frees those at the
senior level to concentrate
more fully on the
larger corporate visions
and strategies."

One caution: Traditionally, individuals who have risen to significant positions of authority within an organization are reluctant to give away much of their authority, having spent a large part of their lives getting it in the first place! However they are not "giving authority away," rather they are *redistributing* it. If the individual receiving the authority is capable of executing it wisely then the authority has been appropriately redistributed to allow for the greatest possible success of the organization. This frees those at the senior level to concentrate more fully on the larger corporate visions and strategies; and to ensure that the organization is harnessing all of its potential to the fullest at all levels, in all areas.

A personal training plan for each individual, designed to train them to be fully competent in every key skill area, is essential.

This measurement and focus on individual talent is crucial to ensure ongoing competitive success.

FOR EACH INDIVIDUAL

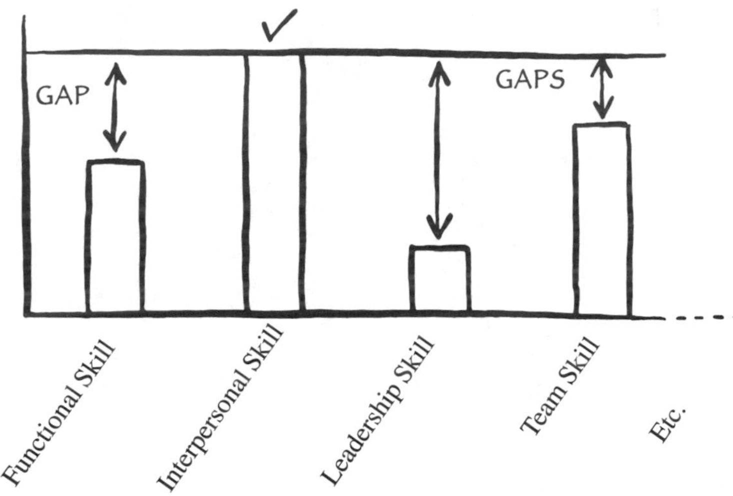

How well individual people do what they do, makes all the difference to the outcome – the overall effectiveness of the whole.

Strive for the highest possible talent levels!

INDIVIDUAL TALENT LEVELS ARE CRUCIAL

Wishing that an individual's talent would improve has little impact on final results. Similarly, merely providing development opportunities for individuals does not ensure that levels of talent will increase. Rather, clear and precise steps need to be followed to ensure that individual talent will be developed to its fullest possible degree.

The first step is a clear definition of those areas where there must be a focus on development. This begins with a general statement of the area, such as functional skill, interpersonal skill, leadership skill, etc.; it is then followed by a detailed description of what's required in each general area. For example, under "functional skill" one might wish to include: time management, project management, making effective presentations, etc.

Once these areas have been identified, standards need to be set for each area and individuals assessed against those standards. If they fall short, then the appropriate development should be provided, and the individual re-evaluated using a competency test until they achieve the expected standard. This is no different from what's frequently done for individuals acquiring competence in technical fields such as an airplane pilot, engineer, fireman, or doctor. This "competency" test which each must pass in order to demonstrate competence will allow the organization to focus on individual talent levels, and where required, bring them up to acceptable standards.

In considering what should be the standard, bear in mind other organizations around you. To grow competent talent at a world-class level will provide a world-class competitive advantage. However, if individuals who have successfully passed your project management competency test are still inadequate compared to those working in another organization, then your standard needs to be raised and the competency test adjusted to reflect this higher standard.

"The incremental cost of
training your staff
is relatively insignificant
if you can double the
productivity of that fixed cost,
by more effectively
harnessing their talent
or their potential."

INDIVIDUAL TALENT LEVELS ARE CRUCIAL

How individuals do things and how well they do them (with regard to cost, time, quality, waste, rework, effectiveness, and interpersonal effectiveness) is an opportunity for huge competitive advantage. Invest in your talent. They are a fixed cost; the incremental cost of training your staff is relatively insignificant if you can double the productivity of that fixed cost by more effectively harnessing their talent or their potential.

HOW PEOPLE BEHAVE CAN RADICALLY ACCELERATE, OR IMPEDE, AN ORGANIZATION'S PROGRESS

Each organization must decide where on this spectrum to settle. This will then define the expected behavior of the members of the organization.

BEHAVIOR SPECTRUM

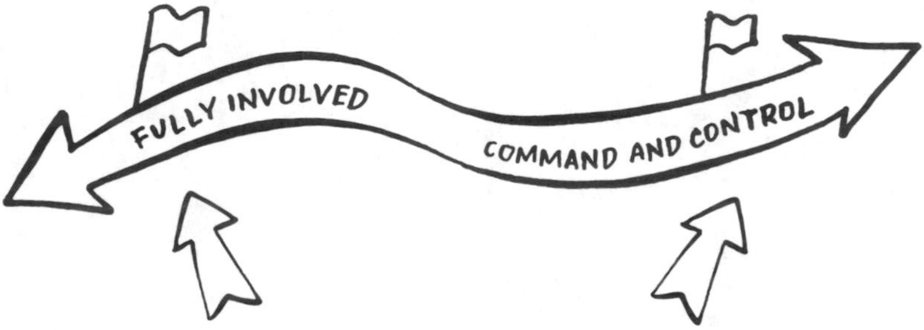

FULLY INVOLVED

COMMAND AND CONTROL

PARTICIPATORY
Freedom to Question
Talent (vs. Authority) Driven
"Empowered"

TOP DOWN
"Orders Only"
Extremely Hierarchal
"Don't Question, Just Do"

HOW PEOPLE BEHAVE CAN RADICALLY ACCELERATE, OR IMPEDE, AN ORGANIZATION'S PROGRESS

The behavior spectrum can move from fully empowered (where individuals have a great deal of autonomy in their decision making, commensurate with their talent) through to absolutely autocratic (where decisions and the methodology for the execution of tasks are handed down and are to be followed without question). As you move along this spectrum many factors within an organization influence where you'll choose to settle: the way in which leaders behave, the way in which employees respond, the degree to which innovation is encouraged, the opportunities for continuous process improvement, the role for teams, compensation schemes, and so forth. Each organization must decide for itself where to settle along the spectrum.

In order to maximize the outcome of the organization the appropriate position must be determined, clearly communicated, and supported by the organization in terms of its rewards and recognition systems. To move blindly to empowerment without an appreciation of the consequences, or without an organization properly trained to manage in that environment, would result in chaos. On the other hand, the fully autocratic control approach may provide less than full utilization of your human asset base.

In some specific cases it might be easy to decide where to locate: in a brain storming session full empowerment is usually desirable; and in the case of a crisis – for example a bomb scare – then fully autocratic behavior is probably preferable. However, for the day-to-day operations of the organization as a whole it may be more difficult. Nonetheless the employees must know what is expected, how to behave, and how to respond to the environment in which they find themselves.

"Full empowerment may not be
the ideal in every location,
anymore than absolute autocracy.
Settle where on the behavioral
spectrum the organization
will benefit most, and then ensure
that each individual is clear on
what is the expected behavior."

HOW PEOPLE BEHAVE CAN RADICALLY ACCELERATE, OR IMPEDE, AN ORGANIZATION'S PROGRESS

Generally speaking it would appear logical that the more opportunity individuals have to contribute, the more effective the organization; but this is only true when they have the ability to contribute wisely.

Picture yourself in a situation where a factory worker questions you regarding your organization's empowerment initiatives. They say, "If I'm empowered, does that mean I can shut down the line when I see product just falling off the belt and piling up as waste on the floor?" This is a challenging question, as you do not want to discourage their initiative, nor do you want to create anarchy in the factory. Your response should be, "Yes you may shut down the line, but *only* when you appreciate the *consequences* of doing so. You may eliminate the waste at your station, but cause such confusion and waste upstream that the overall impact on the company would be far worse than the waste you see at your feet."

In this case there would be an obligation to train this individual, so that they can truly appreciate what is going on upstream and downstream from them. They can then use their best judgement in any given situation, but that judgement will be based on skill, knowledge, and specific training.

Plus, there are other ways to eliminate the waste than simply shutting down the line; and with specific process improvement skills they can also be trained to look at these alternative approaches.

In addition to the training individuals require to operate in a more empowered environment, an even greater priority is that managers learn to manage and lead in an empowered environment. Empowerment has a way of growing individuals, and over time they'll grow from cats to lions.

"If the leaders are trained
as the cat matures
into a lion, then the leaders
can learn to handle lions
as effectively as they
currently handle cats."

From one perspective this is desirable, as it is far preferable to have that calibre of talent working on your behalf. On the other hand it is dangerous, as it is far more difficult to manage a lion than a cat. However, if the leaders are trained as the cat matures into a lion, then the leaders can learn to handle lions as effectively as they currently handle cats, and then you've been able to maximize the full potential of your work force.

However, full empowerment may not be the ideal in every location, anymore than absolute autocracy. You need to settle where on this behavioral spectrum the organization will benefit most, and then ensure that each individual is clear on what that behavior is, and how they should respond.

If, for example, you require behavior that depends heavily on trust between individuals then that needs to be spelled out, (i.e. what "trust" means in your context), measured within the organization, monitored, and individuals educated correspondingly. It is not sufficient to simply say, "Trust is important." Since this is a behavior which you value it needs to have significant time and attention given to it on an ongoing basis, to ensure that the desired behavior becomes the norm within your organization or department. With this clarity individuals will have the greatest possible likelihood of being able to deliver to that expectation.

As you decide where on the spectrum to settle, do not underestimate the talent, and ability within each individual, and the benefit which can be gained by fully harnessing it.

PROVIDING A CLEAR AND SIMPLE FRAMEWORK IS ESSENTIAL TO FULLY REALIZING INDIVIDUAL CAPACITY

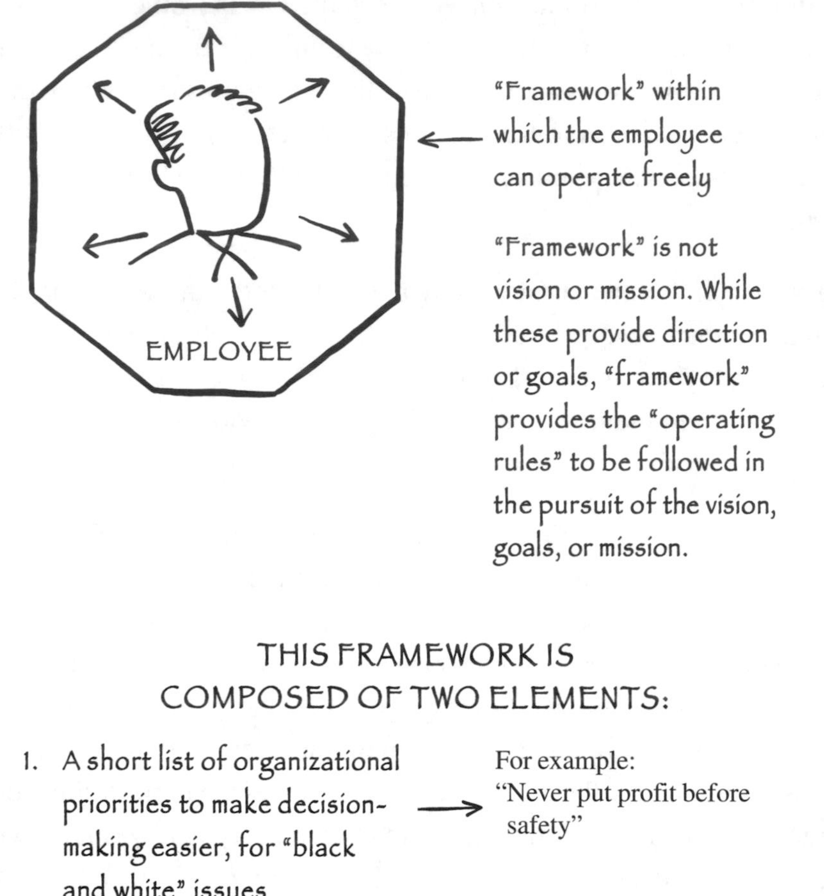

"Framework" within which the employee can operate freely

"Framework" is not vision or mission. While these provide direction or goals, "framework" provides the "operating rules" to be followed in the pursuit of the vision, goals, or mission.

THIS FRAMEWORK IS COMPOSED OF TWO ELEMENTS:

1. A short list of organizational priorities to make decision-making easier, for "black and white" issues → For example: "Never put profit before safety"

2. A well articulated value system to provide direction for those decisions in the grey areas – that is – those less tangible → For example: "Customers are best served when their expectations are exceeded while still making a profit for the organization"

PROVIDING A CLEAR AND SIMPLE FRAMEWORK IS ESSENTIAL TO FULLY REALIZING INDIVIDUAL CAPACITY

Individuals operate best when they are provided with a framework for operating.

For example, a child who "understands the rules" is then able to operate freely within these boundaries, that is: what is considered polite behavior, and what is not tolerated; what is considered a "neat" room, and hence acceptable, versus a "messy" room and hence unacceptable; and which television shows are suitable and which are not. These organizational frameworks, or guidelines, allow the child to see clearly when the boundaries are being overstepped.

Soldiers in battle require a similar operational framework: when you can fire and when you cannot, when to request clarification and when not, when to take the initiative and when to follow blindly. Athletes need to know the frameworks within which they must operate: for example the rules of the game, the authority of the referee, and the boundaries of the playing field.

When clarity is provided concerning "framework," the individual can then be most effective. It is only when the framework is fuzzy or not well defined that individuals inadvertently move outside those boundaries and experience consequences which were not anticipated.

To maximize the contribution of any individual the boundaries must be clearly set. The framework must be well established. This is not to say that each individual needs a set of rules. Quite the contrary. Each individual needs to be provided with a *framework*, as outlined on the following pages.

PROVIDING A CLEAR AND SIMPLE FRAMEWORK IS ESSENTIAL TO FULLY REALIZING INDIVIDUAL CAPACITY

"To maximize the contribution of any individual the boundaries must be clearly set. The framework must be well established."

PROVIDING A CLEAR AND SIMPLE FRAMEWORK IS ESSENTIAL TO FULLY REALIZING INDIVIDUAL CAPACITY

A brief note here: The framework I'm referring to is not the organization's vision, nor is it the goals of the moment. Although vision is, in a sense, a very large framework – e.g. "we're in the bicycle business not the lawnmower business," that is not the kind of framework I'm referring to here.

Similarly, personal goals are not this kind of framework; although they too provide a framework of sorts: e.g. "Complete the report by Monday not Tuesday." Vision is really intended to provide motivation, commitment and rationale. Goals are intended to provide clarity of direction and purpose for the individual as they act. When they actually come to act *then* they are moving into the kind of framework I'm referring to.

The two elements which make up the kind of framework necessary to fully realize individual capacity are:

1. ***A short list of organizational priorities. This list allows the individual to understand clearly what is and is not important to the organization, and so recognize that however they choose to tackle the tasks at hand it must be done within this framework.***

   Some examples of framework would be: "Place the team, and the team's benefit, before yourself and your own personal benefit." Another example might be: "Make responding to customer's input your highest priority at any given point in time." In a manufacturing setting a framework might be: "Place safety above all other considerations."

"Organizational values
are extremely important,
and need to be
crafted with care.
They set the course and
character of
the organization."

Clearly each of these statements will require clarification. They are open to interpretation, misunderstanding, and misapplication. However, for whatever statements are used the organization can provide the necessary clarity so that the individuals understand what is meant and can act accordingly.

A brief note of caution: avoid having too strict a framework. Sometimes in the effort to allow freedom through clarity of framework individuals or companies err by essentially handcuffing the person, by bogging them down with a whole series of regulations. This is not the intent. These framework statements are a short list articulating key organizational priorities and should be no more than three or four at most.

2. ***A well articulated value system:*** If the above list provides clear black and white direction, as it should, this second area provides direction to employees when operating in the gray area. For example, "How important are ethics to the organization?" "Is integrity a crucial component?" Organizations in the service industry will place less emphasis on profit than those who are listed on Wall Street, and as a consequence will generate a different set of values for the employees. What about the expected work ethic and the care of the individuals serving the organization? What are the values there, if any?

"If the framework
is understood, then each
individual can
operate knowing what
is expected,
and what is not."

Each of these questions highlight the kind of topics which need to be identified and spelled out for employees in order to provide a value system allowing them to make decisions. For example, Eagle's Flight provides value around the commitment to being profitable by stating that we will seek "ethical profit." This immediately provides employees with a context for decision making: they know that their decisions must generate a profit, but they must do so ethically. If they are then faced with an issue for which there is no immediate directive at hand, or individual to go to for counsel, they have an organizational framework that spells out the values allowing them to act.

Organizational values are extremely important, and need to be crafted with care. They set the course and character of the organization.

If the framework is clear – that is if the language used is simple and the phrases are short and concise; and the framework is readily understood, that is – simple, then each individual is able to operate freely within the framework that has been established. They can operate to their capacity knowing what is expected, and what is not.

CREATING A LIST OF ORGANIZATIONAL PRIORITIES TO SERVE AS AN OPERATING GUIDE

1. Identify corporate operational priorities →
2. Clearly define what is meant so all can understand
3. Place the priorities in order of importance →

SOME EXAMPLES MIGHT BE		
For a factory	For a sales unit	For a retail store
Safety Speed Improvements No Waste Quality	Service Sales Courtesy Knowledge	Friendly Knowledgeable Helpful Upsell Decor
eg. "**Safety**" Means: •No Injuries •No Accidents •No Close Calls	eg. "**Service**" Means: •Product deliveries are complete and on time	eg. "**Friendly**" Means: •Making the customer feel welcome in the store
1. Safety 2. Quality 3. No Waste 4. Speed 5. Improvements	1. Courtesy 2. Knowledgeable 3. Service 4. Sales	1. Friendly 2. Helpful 3. Decor 4. Upsell 5. Knowledgeable

4. For each of the priorities determine the "expected actions", the "upper and lower limits", the "things you should do"
eg. for "friendly": "Smile, listen without interrupting; be polite."

5 Communicate this to the whole organization making clear this is a priority list
eg. for a "factory": "Put safety first. Nothing comes before that. Then focus on quality, but we don't want quality at the cost of an injured worker. Next, eliminate waste, but not at the expense of quality – we'd rather throw it away than ship less than a top quality product. Next is speed ..." etc.

The objective is to get the list of priorities, and related understanding, into the minds of all employees!

CREATING A LIST OF ORGANIZATIONAL PRIORITIES TO SERVE AS AN OPERATING GUIDE

Having agreed on the need to define "organizational priorities" as part of the framework, it can then be difficult to identify what those organizational priorities are, and so coming up with a list, or defining them, may seem somewhat daunting. In order to help with this, outlined below are the five specific steps which are necessary in order to create this list of organizational priorities. You'll see on the left-hand side some examples for three different categories: factories, sales units, and retail stores. I'll use the factory example as I work through the steps, but clearly these principles will apply to any form of unit or operation.

1. ***Identify Corporate Operational Priorities:*** This refers to the day-to-day expectations which must be met to satisfy the organization.

   In the factory environment some of these might be: safety of the employees, the speed at which the line is moving, the need for continuous improvement to reduce fixed costs and improve efficiency, the elimination of waste, and the adherence to certain quality standards.

   I've just selected these five as those which typically appear, but each organization may have its own that differ from this list.

   In the creation of the corporate operational priorities it's important to ensure that relevant decision-makers and unit heads are brought into the process. Bear in mind this organizational priority list is one of the two major criteria that will be used to establish a framework to allow each employee to realize their capacity within the company (the other is the value system). Consequently this list is very important. Therefore, get input to ensure that nothing is missed; as a by-product, commitment to these priorities is also achieved through the process of involving those impacted.

"In the creation of the corporate operational priorities, it is important to ensure that relevant decision-makers and unit heads are brought into the process."

2. ***Establish Clear Definitions:*** Once the corporate operational priorities have been identified then each must be very clearly defined. In an earlicr example we talked about a child's "clean" room: "clean" must be defined. Does this mean no clothes on the floor, does it mean all surfaces clear, or does it simply mean no dirty dishes in the room? It's extremely important to provide great clarity of definition for each of the operational priorities.

   In the factory example, if we choose the operational priority of "safety" then this could be defined as "no injuries, no accidents, and no close calls". It is now clear what "safety" means, and therefore everyone in the factory will have the same understanding. If safety becomes an element of the organizational framework of the factory then people truly know what is meant: that there are to be no injuries, no accidents and no close calls. Any deviation from that will be considered unsafe practice. Clearly in your own environment you would have to define safety in whatever fashion you feel is appropriate (for example, safety might be defined in another factory as "absolute adherence to all posted lock-out procedures"). The important thing is to define it in your own terms in a way that provides clarity for everyone.

   Other examples of definitions for the sales unit and the retail store are also shown.

"Leadership should create an established framework which is universal for the whole organization."

3. ***Create a Priority order:*** Once the organizational priorities have been established and clearly defined they need to be placed in a priority order so that individuals understand what must be adhered to, even if it means having to compromise on something lower down on the priority list. For example, a factory which places safety above quality is saying to its employees that the quality of the finished product is less important than the health of the employees creating it. If an employee is about to be injured and the decision has to be made whether to keep the line running to maintain product quality, or shut it down to avoid an injury then the framework which has been provided makes it abundantly clear the line should be shut down, because safety overrides quality.

   Similarly quality might be placed above "no waste". In this example the individual operating the factory understands through the organizational framework that quality must not be placed at risk in the effort to reduce waste. In short the company will tolerate waste before it will tolerate poor quality.

   In a similar fashion individuals can work their way down the list of corporate priorities which make up the operational framework. You'll note in the factory example that "make improvements" is on the list. I personally think this is important as it creates the mental mindset that says, (using my above example) "Even though we will place quality above waste, we do operate within the framework of constant improvement and so it is a priority to identify a way of eliminating that waste without putting quality at risk."

"Established organization
priorities provide
clarity to all employees
which, if understood,
will allow them to operate
to their capacity."

Understand that the setting of the priority order is to provide the employees the ability to understand how to operate within the framework which you've provided for them. Once the priorities are in place from step one, defined in step two, and placed in order of priority in step three, you've gone a long way towards creating an effective framework.

4. ***Establish Expected Actions:*** Having placed the operational priorities in the appropriate sequence, time needs to be spent helping everyone understand what the expected actions should be, the upper and lower limits, the things to be done. It's at this step that you help individuals understand what specific actions they are to take, and very often it is at this step that training is necessary.

   For example, if in the area of safety, employees need to understand how to do CPR, then first aid training may be required. Similarly, the factory will inevitably have certain safety procedures which are standard; and each individual needs to understand what they are, and how they must apply them. If they're not clear on this then the appropriate training should be provided.

   In the area of improvement, individuals need to understand what "continuous improvement" really entails; that is, they need to operate in teams to identify existing processes and then review how that process can be improved to reduce cost and improve safety and quality.

   So for each of the items that make up the framework the specific steps or behaviors which are expected should be spelled out, and relevant training provided.

"Do not underestimate
the importance of effective
communication.
The message will be lost
if the only people
who understand it are the
people who wrote it!"

It's interesting just to look for a moment at the retail store example where they've identified "friendly" as one of the expected operational priorities.

At first glance this would seem straightforward, but only on reflection does it become apparent that the expected behavior here must also be defined. "Friendly" could, for example, be defined as "smile, listen without interrupting, and be polite". This provides clarity to the retail clerk who understands that friendliness is one of the items of the framework. They can now approach a customer with a smile, listen politely to the customer's requests without interrupting, and then courteously move to the next step in the process. This is a very different definition for being "friendly" than simply calling "Hi! I'll be with you in a moment," from across the store.

5. ***Provide Effective Communication:*** Once the process of identifying what would make up the framework is completed, with the necessary detail and clarity, then it must be communicated to the entire organization affected by that framework. The factory framework may not affect the whole organization, but rather only a given factory, and in that case only they need to know about it.

   However, the leadership should provide an established framework which is universal for everyone (for example "ethical profit") which is then understood by the whole organization.

   The communication must be done in a way that is simple, clear, and very motivating. You are, in fact, providing clarity to all employees which, once understood, will allow them to operate to their maximum capacity.

"Organizational priorities must be repeated, reiterated, and referred to constantly."

Do not underestimate the importance of effective communication after you've gone through all the work of getting this far. The whole exercise will be lost if the only people who understand it are the people who wrote it!

As an aside: These things need constant refreshing, so communicating the organizational priorities effectively, once, does not fully do the job. They must become something which is repeated, reiterated, and referred to constantly. They must be ingrained well enough to serve as an ongoing operating guide for all employees.

Follow the steps outlined in 'Creating a List of Organizational Priorities to Serve as an Operating Guide' on page 542, except that, since this is a values list, not a priority list, skip step 3 since all values must be taken into consideration when making a decision.

WHICH WAY TO GO?

VALUES SHOULD BE A SIGNPOST TO POINT THE WAY.

CREATING A WELL ARTICULATED VALUE SYSTEM

The second component of creating a framework for fully realizing individual capacity, as outlined in Section VII, Providing a Clear and Simple Framework is Essential to fully Realizing Individual Capacity on page 534, is to create a well articulated value system.

To do this the steps outlined in Section VII, Creating a List of Organizational Priorities to Serve as an Operating Guide on page 542 can be followed in exactly the same way.

If the *operational* guide provides clarity for specific *actions*, the *value system* provides clarity for *decisions*. True, a decision is an action, but the distinction is that the organizational priorities are intended to provide assistance with the "hands-on" kinds of activity involved in the day-to-day work. The values system is intended to provide clarity when individuals have to first make decisions which then affect action.

The values provide signposts, or directional assistance to help employees. They are perhaps not as "black and white" a framework as the organizational priorities; but on the other hand, they can be even more powerful because they reach deeper into the heart of the individual to provide the "moral compass" which individuals need if they are to function in a changing world, with many crossroads each day.

An example of a value system is one which was created for Eagle's Flight at the birth of the company, and remains ingrained to this day. New employees are given a framed copy of the company values, and are talked through the meaning of each phrase. It is a touchstone, a reference point for decisions, and referred to for clarity when guidance is required on a particular topic for which there is no obvious course of action. I've outlined this value system on the following pages as an example to help you with the crafting of your own. In order to make it more memorable we have used the first five letters of the word "Eagle" to create the following acronym.

For example, at Eagle's Flight

- **E** xceptional Service
- **A** bsolute Quality
- **G** enuine Friendliness
- **L** eadership Excellence
- **E** thical Profit

Exceptional Service: This refers to our desire to provide all customers (both internal and external) with exceptional service. We feel the concept of service is clear, but adding the word exceptional creates the value. We're not referring, therefore, to service to some pre-determined standard, but rather to service which will be deemed *by the customer* to be exceptional. If the world around us continues to raise their service standards, then ours must naturally follow if we are to remain exceptional. Employees are aware that they are expected at all times to provide all customers with service which that customer would consider to be exceptional.

Absolute Quality: We will not tolerate anything other than the highest quality work, product and output. In fact, this value states that we expect absolute quality. No exceptions. No excuses. No deviations.

It then follows that within any given environment (accounts receivable, production, sales, marketing, etc.) there must be a discussion between the manager and the employees as to what defines absolute quality in terms of the other company values.

Since one of our values is to make a profit, then clearly absolute quality cannot be "at any cost," because then one of the other values would be violated – that of making a profit.

Nonetheless, the value of absolute quality stands firm as individuals understand that within the day-to-day context in which they must operate the quality of their work must be such that it will be deemed to be of absolute quality – the very best possible.

"When providing values
within an organization, it is
important to realize
that all the values define
the framework.
The framework is not defined
by only one value."

Genuine Friendliness: In our organization we place a high value on the human being and the worth of each individual. This leads naturally to paying a lot of attention to ensuring that the individual is well cared for, content, and, to as large a degree as possible, prospering within the organization. We see creating this environment as management's responsibility, and includes the requirement to hire employees who are "friendly." However, the value system requires genuine friendliness, which means that individuals are to "be themselves" – hence the genuine – and focus on being friendly.

Each person has an obligation to reach deep inside themselves to overcome whatever current issues might be affecting their morale or emotions, in order to be friendly with one another and with those with whom we deal. Yet this friendliness is to be a genuine friendliness, which again provides the value that says we are not after an artificial friendliness that is superficial, but the real genuine friendliness which comes from caring. This does not necessarily mean that each person is happy all the time, or living a life devoid of worry, but it does mean that in the dealing with one another and with customers they should be friendly.

Leadership Excellence: This value is interesting in that applies to the leaders, as we have committed to provide the organization with excellence of leadership. Again this is a value in that the world around us changes and as leadership qualities improve so ours must continually improve if they are to be considered excellent.

"The operational guide
provides clarity
for specific actions,
and the value system
provides clarity for
decisions."

From the point of view of the employees who are not leaders, this value is still important to them in that it defines an expectation: they have a right to expect excellence of leadership. This particular value causes a great deal of behavior which other organizations might not experience, as we believe that it is our responsibility to act in such a way that the organization sees excellence of leadership demonstrated ("walking the talk"). Similarly customers who visit us should feel that the organization is unique in the way in which we manage our people, and the corresponding productivity we enjoy; this uniqueness is defined as excellence of leadership.

Ethical Profit: We are clearly in business to make money, and although we have a high degree of care for our employees, and a huge commitment to treating them in a way that depicts our values, we are still in the business of being profitable. Consequently there is a necessary focus on profit, and the corresponding initiatives relative to cost, waste, improvement, etc. The corporate value here is that the profit will be ethical. It is not our intent to make money in an unethical fashion. This provides very clear direction and very clear guidance for each individual within the organization as they evaluate both their profit generating activities, and their cost reduction initiatives.

When providing values within an organization, such as the five outlined above, it is important to realize that *all the values define the framework.* The framework is not defined by only one value.

"Values are in a
'web of tension' and each
plays a part in influencing
the other.
None can be treated
as if they were independent
of the others."

In other words, the organization is not committed to one value or one value above another (which could, in the example shown, be "exceptional service" or any one of the other five). Rather, the organization is committed to *all five* and *they* provide the framework. They all must act in concert and with one another. The sum total of the five values outlined make up Eagle's Flight. They are each in a "web of tension." Each is linked to the other, and each plays a part in influencing the other. None can be treated on a stand-alone basis.

USING THE FRAMEWORK DEFINED BY ORGANIZATIONAL PRIORITIES AND VALUES SYSTEM

This allows for maximum involvement, but within a pre-defined framework – which thereby allows each individual to personally contribute to their fullest.

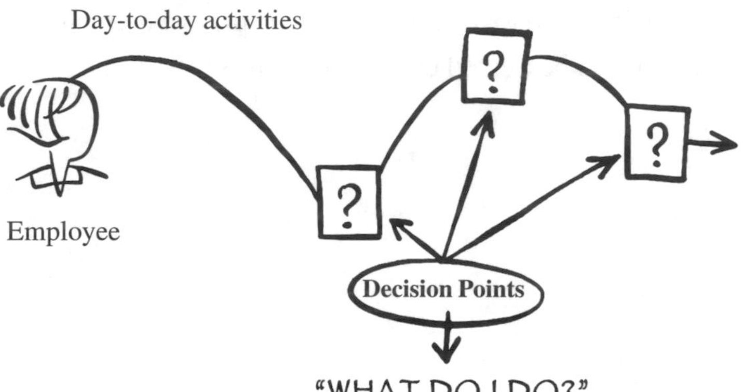

"WHAT DO I DO?"

If a: Black and White Issue

↓

Mentally review the priority list
(from page 542)

eg. Safety First,
Then Quality,
Then No Waste,
Then Speed,
Then Improvements.

If a: Grey Issue

↓

Consider the values
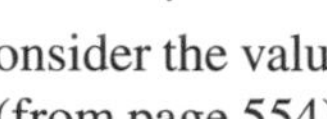
(from page 554)

eg. Exceptional Service,
Absolute Quality,
Genuine Friendliness,
Leadership Excellence,
Ethical Profit.

↘ 

Use your judgement to decide what's best and then take appropriate action.

Don't know? Ask your supervisor.

USING THE FRAMEWORK DEFINED BY ORGANIZATIONAL PRIORITIES AND VALUES SYSTEM

Once each employee is clear on the framework which has been provided, with the corresponding detail about both the organizational priorities and company values, then they are equipped to operate as independently as possible on a day-to-day basis.

Over the course of their activities each employee will be faced with a number of decisions as the day progresses. Many of these decisions will relate to issues which are part of their day-to-day responsibilities; but many will be new and require judgement as the specific course of action is unclear. At that point they'll ask themselves, "What do I do?"

Think for example of the situation where you bring a disabled friend out for a day's drive, and decide to incorporate a boat tour you see advertised. This tour will allow you to view the beautiful mountains from the water.

As you arrive at the dock with your friend in the wheelchair, you encounter the individual taking tickets at the gangplank. Now that individual is clear on their day-to-day responsibilities: ensure everybody who boards the boat has a ticket, and answer any questions they might ask, such as how long does the tour take, etc. However, when you arrive with your friend in the wheelchair you ask if you can be allowed to stay on deck at the bow of the ship, in an area which you can clearly see is roped off and not intended to be used by passengers.

The ticket attendant now has to make one of those many decisions outside of their job description. In a normal circumstance they would know the answer – "No". However this is a distinct situation, where someone in a wheelchair might not have as good a view in the areas normally reserved for passengers, and therefore a decision must be made.

"It is very important to understand that the fallback is always the individual's supervisor. No employee should be expected to use a framework when they are uncertain how best to do so. It should always be possible to refer to the supervisor for insight, direction, or instruction."

USING THE FRAMEWORK DEFINED BY ORGANIZATIONAL PRIORITIES AND VALUES SYSTEM

It's at this point that an organizational framework comes into play for the ticket taker. If the framework has been spelled out such that the greatest priority is customer service, then the ticket attendant might, under these circumstances, agree. If on the other hand the greatest priority is safety, and in the opinion of the ticket attendant there is a risk that the wheelchair will be unstable on the bow of the boat, then based on that criteria the attendant would say "No," and give the reason "That safety is our first concern and there could be a risk."

However, if customer service follows as a second priority after safety, and there is some way in which the wheels could be blocked to ensure a safe situation, then the attendant could move to the second priority (customer service) and be willing to try and make it happen, while bearing the first (safety) in mind.

The benefit of this kind of framework is that a customer is able to have an issue dealt with "on the spot," by someone normally considered to be a junior, unempowered employee with no authority. By providing this ticket attendant with a clear organizational framework, then the decisions that can be made at the front line are made, customer satisfaction significantly improves, the ticket collector's immediate supervisor is not interrupted, and the overall operation is seen to be efficient. Multiply this kind of behavior many times over for all employees within any organization and the power of the organizational framework is seen.

Coming back to the employee faced with the decision, "What do I do?" they must first decide whether or not it is a black and white issue, or a gray issue. If it's black and white, they can refer to the organizational priorities of the company. If it's a gray issue, they can refer to the values.

"Once each employee is clear on the framework, they are equipped to operate as independently as possible."

USING THE FRAMEWORK DEFINED BY ORGANIZATIONAL PRIORITIES AND VALUES SYSTEM

Once they've identified in which area their particular issue falls, then they use their best judgement to apply the principles they have been taught, and take the appropriate action. In this way clear organizational priorities can direct the employee on black and white issues, and the values can direct the employee when a gray issue surfaces that is not particularly clear.

It's very important to understand that the fallback is always the individual's supervisor. No employee should be expected to use a framework when they are uncomfortable, or uncertain how best to do so. It should always be possible to refer to the supervisor for insight, direction, or instruction. New employees may be less comfortable in applying a framework than more seasoned employees, and so fall back on the supervisor more frequently. Over time as these employees see the framework in action, and have coaching from the supervisor, they are better and better able to apply it for themselves.

The result of a clear framework of this nature is that each employee is able to contribute to the organization to the greatest possible extent.

PREDICTABILITY IS A MARK OF EXCELLENCE

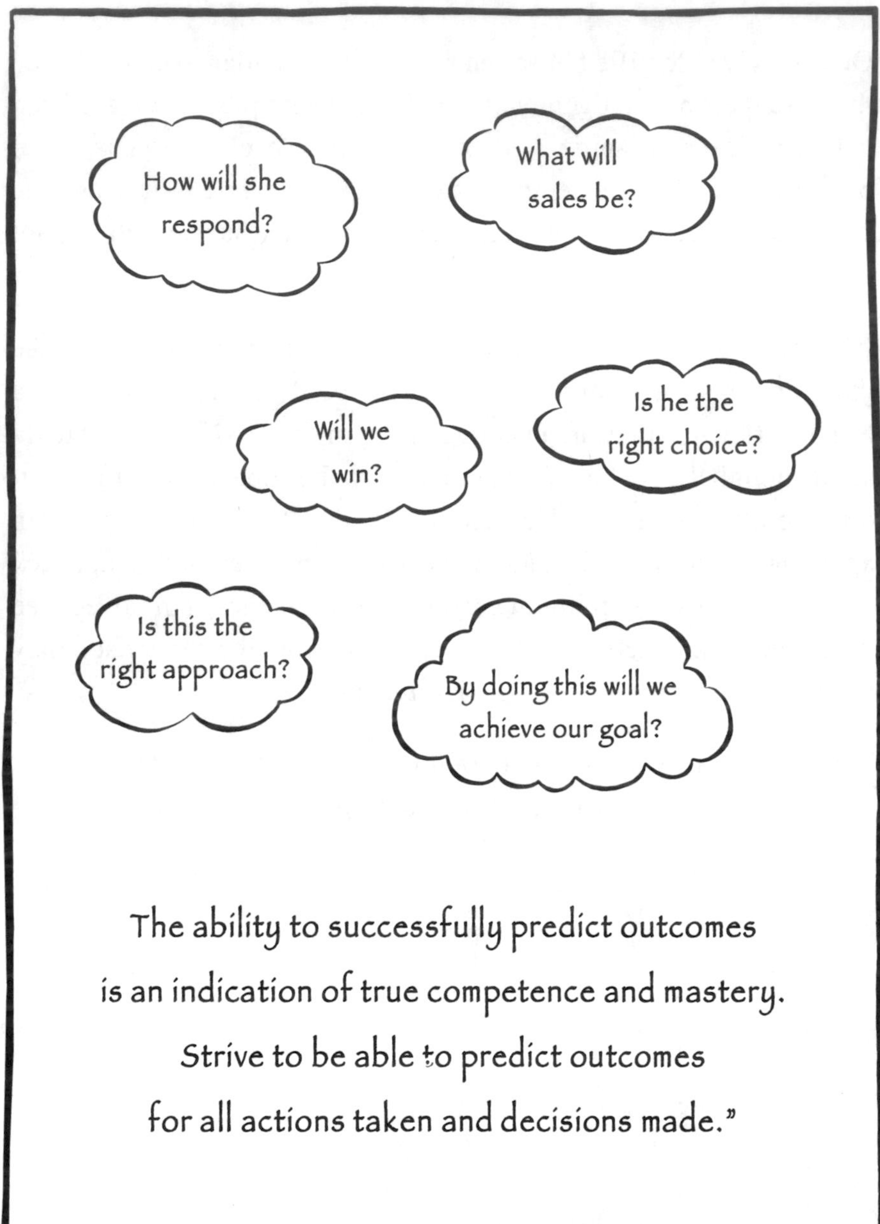
How will she respond?
What will sales be?
Will we win?
Is he the right choice?
Is this the right approach?
By doing this will we achieve our goal?
The ability to successfully predict outcomes is an indication of true competence and mastery. Strive to be able to predict outcomes for all actions taken and decisions made."

PREDICTABILITY IS A MARK OF EXCELLENCE

The ability to predict the outcome of organizational efforts is a mark of excellence. Clearly we're not talking about predicting the future with reference to cosmic events or some kind of mysticism. Rather, within the context that we control or influence as leaders, our ability to predict the results of our present initiatives is key to developing world-class results.

If we are able to accurately predict the outcome of our initiatives we are then able to determine whether or not those outcomes are acceptable, and if not take action to change them. Therein lies the importance of prediction.

Consequently, in discussing predictability it is within the context of attempting to ensure that the results to come are the ones sought after. It is not an attempt to sit down and look, crystal ball style, into the future in order to attempt to foresee what might happen. In the next section four steps are given to enhance predictability as it relates to our current activities.

There are many times when an organization clearly needs to extrapolate, or predict, from the present into the future, and leaders must master this ability. For example, in the recruiting process when a potential candidate is about to be hired, the better you are able to predict the performance of the various candidates the better will be the recruiting decision.

As another example, in the event you have to discuss an individual's poor performance with them, it's valuable to be able to predict the outcome of their response, given your intended approach. If you are able to determine which one of three possible responses you will receive based on three possible approaches, you're then able to select the best approach. In the area of sales, management needs to be able to predict whether or not sales revenue will be there as promised. In goal setting, it is a tremendous advantage when we can predict that the goal we have set will in fact take us to our desired destination, with the intended outcomes.

"If we are able to accurately predict the outcome of our initiatives we are then able to determine whether or not those outcomes are acceptable, and if not take action to change them."

PREDICTABILITY IS A MARK OF EXCELLENCE

Each of these examples illustrates the importance of the concept of predictability as a key to an organization's success, and a mark of excellence. As leaders we need to continually strive to enhance our ability to predict the outcome of our actions and decisions.

As we improve in this area we are better able to ensure that those outcomes are the ones we indeed want.

HOW TO INCREASE PREDICTABILITY

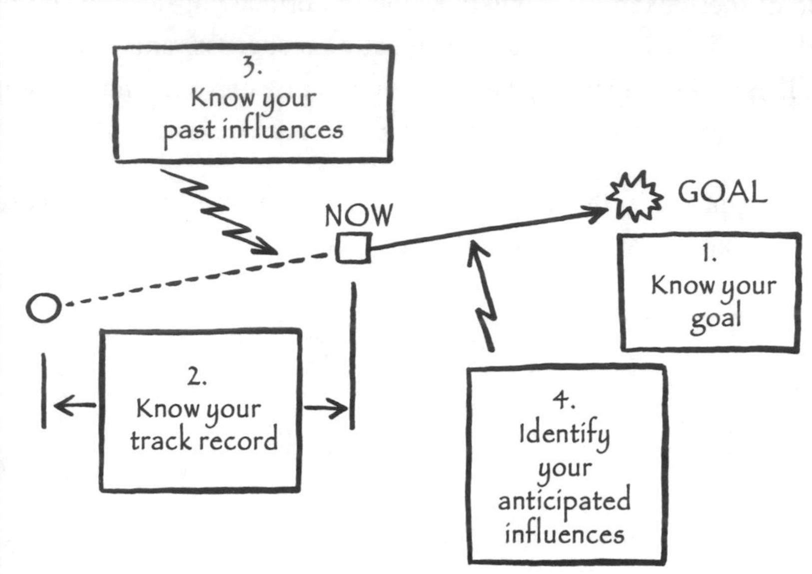

1.	GOAL:	Allows you to set a specific course, with a defined endpoint – which increases the possibility of arriving there.
2.	TRACK RECORD:	The past can be an indicator of the future as things tend not to change direction when left to run as they have in the past.
3.	PAST INFLUENCES:	It's important to know what things produced the past track record – both desirable (to maintain them) and undesirable (to eliminate them).
4.	ANTICIPATED INFLUENCERS:	Knowing what will likely influence outcomes can allow for preemptive action—either to capitalize on favorable forces, or avoid unfavorable ones.

HOW TO INCREASE PREDICTABILITY

Given the importance of mastering predictability there are four specific steps which can be taken to increase the level of predictability in the organization, and therefore the corresponding benefits.

1. ***Goal:*** The more precisely the goal is stated, the better the chance of arriving there. If our family all sits around the kitchen table and agrees that this year we will have a "great vacation" then we have a goal. However it is difficult to predict that once the vacation is over, it will really have been "great." The goal is too fuzzy.

   On the other hand, if the family sits down and decides that this year we will spend five days whitewater kayaking down the Wild Indian River, camping along the way, and documenting the trip on video, then we have a more precise goal. If on further discussion it turns out that each member of the family is excited about that, can visualize it, and each states definitely that that would be a spectacular vacation, then once we've completed it, we have a much higher likelihood of it being considered a "great", if not "spectacular", vacation. The predictability has just gone way up, simply because we have defined the goal in such a clear fashion that everyone has been able to understand it, visualize it, and then assess whether, on attainment, it satisfies the criteria of "great." Since they all agree, it's much easier to predict a successful outcome.

2. ***Track Record:*** When attempting to predict outcomes with some degree of certainty, looking at the past can often be a very reliable guidepost.

   By looking at the past and seeing what the outcomes have been, one can then determine if any activity or behavior has changed in such a way that the future outcome will be different.

"An analysis of what
influenced the
current results can go
a long way towards
predicting future results."

If the answer is "No," then, all things being equal, there is a high likelihood that neither will the outcome change from what it has been. For example, if a car has trouble starting every morning, perhaps because its owner failed to take it in for a tune-up, then it is relatively easy to predict that it will continue to have trouble starting in the future, if the owner does not change their behavior. Similarly from observing a change in behavior (for example, taking the car in for a tune-up) then it is relatively straightforward to predict a change in outcome (the car will now start more easily).

While the above example may appear trivial, it applies in the much more complicated situations of organizational behavior. For example, if a line manager verbally commits to supporting an empowered organization and even goes so far as to set up process improvement teams, but consistently refuses to listen to the ideas of that improvement team, or provide them with adequate opportunities to meet, or adequate training, then there is a strong likelihood that the team will continue to underperform, continue to be effectively disempowered, and fail to initiate any significant process improvements.

Knowing this, the leader is then able to intervene and either remove the manager, place the manager under the guidance of a mentor or coach, or provide additional training to allow that manager to change their behavior, and so change the outcome. In this example the situation is much more complicated, but the principle of track record predicting outcome is as relevant.

"By anticipating influences
we are more effectively
able to predict outcomes,
and so prepare,
and as a result maximize
the possibility for success."

3. ***Past Influences:*** When examining the current results an analysis of what influenced the current results can go a long way towards predicting future results.

   For example, if the marketing department has consistently brought in sales leads which have been converted to sales, then as long as the marketing department continues to bring in a comparable number of leads, of comparable quality, then it is more than likely that the sales force will continue to generate a comparable level of sales.

   When factors influencing outcomes remain the same it is usually safe to assume that the outcomes will continue as they have in the past. If these outcomes are unacceptable then changing the influences will change the outcomes. On the other hand if the influences change (e.g. in the illustration above marketing ceases to generate adequate leads) then the outcomes will change.

   To master prediction requires an analysis of the influences to determine which ones are supporting desired outcomes, and which ones are hindering it. By reinforcing the desirable, and eliminating the undesirable, one can predict the outcome with considerable certainty.

4. ***Anticipated Influences:*** Frequently it is possible to do an analysis of the current situation in which the organization is operating and identify *anticipated* influences. For example, the entrance of a new competitor into the marketplace, or the introduction of new technology making your current technology cost prohibitive, may both have a major, and predictable, impact on the overall performance of the organization.

"By looking at the past and
seeing what the outcomes
have been, one can
then determine if any activity
or behavior has changed
in such a way that the future
outcome will be different."

As these anticipated influences are identified, the consequence of the outcome can be determined. If they are significant, then preventative action can be taken in order to make provision that your desired outcome remain unchanged, once that anticipated influence comes into play, (if it does at all).

Often we are too busy dealing with the present, or correcting mistakes of the past (!), to think about the future and what might possibly surface to influence our outcomes. When we then encounter those influences and are not adequately prepared, we find ourselves moving off-track from our anticipated achievements; something unforeseen and unanticipated has influcnced our activities for which we had not prepared counter measures.

By anticipating influences we are more effectively able to predict outcomes, and so prepare for them, and as a result maximize the possibility for success.

By examining all four of the above factors we can increase our ability to predict outcomes and so deliver world-class results.

SUSTAINABILITY IS A MARK OF EXCELLENCE

A commitment to repeated effort or achievement (e.g. monthly sales numbers, daily personal exercise program, etc.) requires sustainability if it is to succeed.

Ideally:

Sustained Success, Every Time

Often:

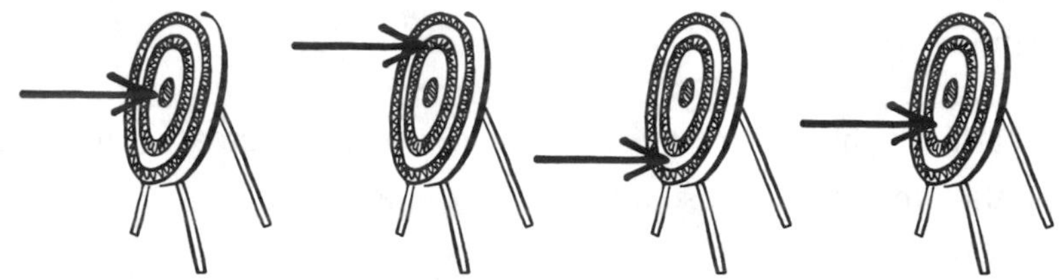

Early Success, Followed By Frequent Off-Target Results

Erratic, inconsistent results come from an inability, or unwillingness, to make the effort required to sustain the initial impetus, and success.

Yet ultimate success requires consistent regular success – and so there must be a focus on sustaining successful achievement.

SUSTAINABILITY IS A MARK OF EXCELLENCE

Sustainability as it relates to desired outcomes is a mark of excellence. This occurs when the organization or individual can continue to produce the desired outcome repeatedly, regardless of circumstance.

Very often success is not the result of a single brilliant action, but rather the cumulation of several actions each performed as intended, repeatedly over time. An Olympic athlete may demonstrate a sustained and repeated commitment to training which ultimately peaks at the Olympic competition; but without that sustained repeated exercise and training there would be little hope of success. However, with practice, repetition, and improvement day after day, often for years, the chances of success continue to rise. The commitment to train has been sustained.

A salesperson who has one brilliant month cannot simply stop. Rather, they must sustain that performance from month to month to month if they are to be truly excellent at their profession. They must sustain their ability to achieve their sales commitments on an ongoing basis if they are to add the value for which they're being paid.

At the more senior levels, sustainability is often measured in years, where one good year does not ensure success. Rather, that performance must be repeated year after year on a sustained basis in order to generate ongoing and continued success and value in the marketplace.

As human beings we are often inclined to do something a few times and then grow tired of it. We wish to change and move on to something else. But within an organization the situation is often quite the contrary: a sustained repeated behavior done consistently several times over is what's required, whether it is greeting somebody at the door, administering appropriate medication, perusing the accounts receivable, or making the sales numbers.

"Very often
success is not the result of
a single brilliant action,
but rather the
cumulation of several actions
each performed as intended,
repeatedly over time."

SUSTAINABILITY IS A MARK OF EXCELLENCE

The mark of a professional is someone who can do the job the fiftieth, or hundredth time with the same degree of enthusiasm and excellence as they did it when they first began. This is often a particular challenge for those who are in a profession where each event has a beginning and an ending, such as providing training to a class of participants.

In this case the participants come into the class rather uncertain about what they will be learning, and if the training is good, they'll leave with excitement and enthusiasm to use their new learning. The trainer's job is done. However the next day the trainer must start again with a new group of uncertain participants and exactly the same material, and bring them to the same degree of enthusiasm for application.

The trainer must do that day after day after day with the same material. If they are successful at that, if they have sustained the quality of their delivery, then they have demonstrated a mark of excellence.

People often stray from delivering the results as expected. They are close to the target but not "dead on." They are there, they are working, they are applying themselves, but they have grown weary, and are unable to sustain the level of excellence with which they began. They miss the mark slightly, hitting it perfectly only occasionally.

These erratic and inconsistent results come from an inability or unwillingness to make the effort required to sustain the original excellence and success.

"The mark of a professional
is someone who can do
the job the hundredth time
with the same degree of
enthusiasm and excellence
as they did it when they
first began."

The leader must identify this and take action to correct it. Very often early feedback is a great tool to allow people to reassess the fact that they have in fact missed the target, or been off-centre; and to allow them to re-focus, to allow the original level of excellence to resurface.

Without *sustained* commitment to excellence the individual or organization will meander, with an unpredictable outcome as a result. It is the leader's responsibility to insist upon a sustained level of performance, and provide the necessary support, motivation and clarity of direction required to deliver it.

HOW TO INCREASE SUSTAINABILITY

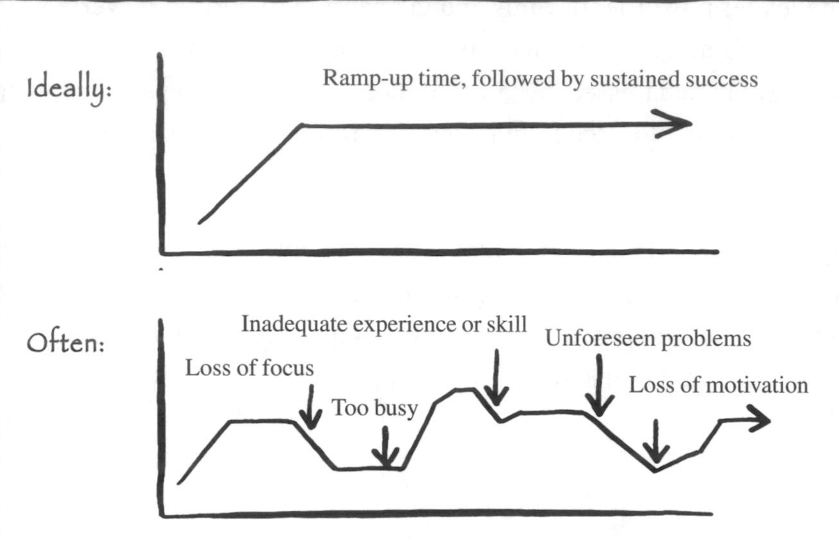

ADDRESSING THESE: THE ROLE OF THE LEADER!

1. LOSS OF FOCUS:
   Address by: Frequent follow up, recognizing success, and reinforcing the importance (the "why") of continued success

2. TOO BUSY:
   Address by: Regular, proactive, review of priorities; regular review of resources assigned versus outcomes expected, are they properly aligned?

3. UNFORESEEN PROBLEMS:
   Address by: Up front time spent identifying possible hurdles and devising solutions in advance; adequate contingency plans

4. INADEQUATE EXPERIENCE:
   Address by: Foreseen skill or experience required and or skill address in advance, or with just-in-time training

5. LOSS OF MOTIVATION:
   Address by: Reinforce rationale for the activity; identify source(s) of loss of innovation (root causes) and address

HOW TO INCREASE SUSTAINABILITY

Sustainability is of key importance where, after a short ramp-up time when individuals learn the function required or what is expected, they deliver sustained success over the long term. The ramp-up time is important as people do require time to understand what's expected before being able to focus on delivering it; but after this short period, a level of performance excellence should be sustained.

Often, however, one of five events occur which result in erratic performance and inability to sustain success. It is the leader's role to address each of these five cases when they occur.

1. ***Loss of Focus:*** Here the individual pressing toward the objective has lost sight, hopefully temporarily, of what it is that needs to be achieved. The focus has become blurred. This could happen for a number of reasons, such as failing to keep a line of sight on the big picture; or in discussion with one another there have been so many points of view expressed over time that the end product has become blurred.

   To address this, the leader must provide frequent follow-up, acknowledging and providing recognition for those who have succeeded, or are succeeding, in delivering results in support of the goal. It is the leader's responsibility to maintain focus so that each individual has a clear line of sight between what they are doing and what it is that needs to be achieved. By providing this, and reinforcing the importance of continued success, there is a greater chance that the focus will remain crisp, clear, and sharp. With that, individuals are more able to sustain their initiative towards the objective.

"Providing solutions in advance
and creating
adequate contingency plans
can go a long way towards
dealing with the unforeseen,
and maintaining the
sustained level of excellence
that is required."

2. ***Too Busy:*** Sustained success requires sustained concentration. When the number of priorities mounts an individual is distracted from the most important task at hand, the total effort is dissipated among many tasks, and performance of the key priorities suffers. The individual may be able to sustain the total energy expended, or the commitment to hard work, but they are unable to sustain the ongoing level of excellence for each task that they were originally able to deliver when they had fewer priorities.

   It's the leader's responsibility to regularly review priorities in light of the resources required, including time. There must be balance between what is expected in the way of results and what is available in the way of energy. When the balance is in place the individual can consistently deliver what's required.

3. ***The Unforeseen:*** One of the greatest hindrances to sustained excellence is the unforeseen. With all the will in the world it is virtually impossible to avoid being sidetracked when unforeseen problems or hurdles surface. In order to avoid this more time and effort needs to be spent identifying *possible* hurdles, unforeseen issues, or problems. As these are identified then solutions can be designed and put in place, ready at hand, in the event that these potential hurdles do materialize.

   Providing solutions in advance and creating adequate contingency plans can go a long way toward dealing with the unforeseen, and maintaining the sustained level of excellence that is required.

"Sustainability can be
the difference between the
life or death of the
organization, and so must be
managed with
care and commitment."

4. ***Inadequate Experience or Skill:*** Inevitably an individual will start with adequate skill or experience, otherwise they would not be in the role. However, over time the job may expand, the responsibilities may increase, or circumstances may require a higher level of knowledge and skill than what the individual now possesses.

   This also needs to be foreseen and provided for. It can be addressed by providing the training either in advance, or in a "just in time" manner. In either case, the early recognition that lack of skill or experience may surface as a significant detriment to sustained excellence must be identified and dealt with.

   Like some of the other issues which can block sustained performance, the issues that surface as a result of skill deficiencies are real, valid, and will in fact inhibit sustainability. But they are not insurmountable, and with foresight and planning they can be dealt with, allowing sustained success to be the hallmark of the organization.

5. ***Loss of Motivation:*** Because people are human they will lose their drive or motivation periodically, and as that falls off so their sustained commitment to excellence, or achieving the objective, will drop off as well. This is an understandable human failing, but it can be corrected.

   If this is recognized as a natural aspect of human behavior then the leader can provide continuous ongoing motivation, providing clarity about the rationale for the activity, and the necessary reinforcement of the importance of the role or the task.

   As a leader recognizes the importance of keeping the team or individual fully informed, abreast of current situations, and aware of the impact they are making, then motivation remains high and does not need to falter.

"Sustained success
requires
sustained concentration."

Other techniques are also available to maintain an atmosphere of fun and recognition with respect to achievement. The efforts the leader makes to maintain morale and motivation are also key to maintaining sustainability.

Like predictability, sustainability is a crucial quality in achieving a world-class organization. It is the leader's responsibility to do everything possible to sustain performance and success. This is particularly crucial when one realizes that in the current marketplace the success of yesterday is inadequate for today and so the *sustained* commitment to continuous improvement and world-class excellence is crucial. At this level the sustainability can be the difference between the life or death of the organization, and so must be managed with care and commitment.

Eliminate Waste

WASTE COMES IN MANY FORMS	Examples of PROACTIVE STEPS WHICH CAN BE TAKEN
Time	• Training, Education, Development
Talent	• Priorities Clearly Spelled Out
Product	• Strong Leadership
Money	• Explicit Goals
Effort	• Defined Values
Results	• A Commitment to Quality
	• Continuous Process Improvement
	• Widespread Measurement

But the focal point in each case is waste

- Identify it
- Identify its cause
- Source a solution
- Implement and measure results

A PERFORMANCE IMPERATIVE: FOCUS ON WASTE

Organizations must aggressively seek to eliminate waste.

In the early days of a change initiative that I was charged with managing I met with the training team to outline what we were trying to accomplish, in order to get their input on how best to accomplish it. As I spoke about the need for culture change, harnessing every individual's talent and potential to the fullest, reducing unnecessary costs, enhancing the value of each step in the process etc., one of the more senior trainers spoke up after listening intently. His comment was, "As I see it, what we're about to do is eliminate waste."

This seemed a somewhat simplistic response to me so I questioned him for more clarification as to how he arrived at that conclusion. His response was, to me, profound and something I've noted and borne in mind many times since. He said, "Waste comes in many forms. We can waste time, or we can waste money, or we can waste effort, or we can waste the commitment to our colleagues; we can waste the talent which each person brings, we can waste product when we let material fall on the ground. Waste produces errors, we can waste money on activities that are not productive; and we can waste results which may be good in themselves but have no value in the marketplace. By driving a culture within the company that capitalizes on the abilities of every individual, with a measurable focus on waste reduction, we will have achieved what you are setting out to accomplish."

He was right.

The object in any organization is to eliminate waste, especially when waste is seen in the broader context of my friend above, and defined accordingly.

"Develop a
personal commitment
to eliminate waste
in all its forms."

A PERFORMANCE IMPERATIVE: FOCUS ON WASTE

There are many steps which can be proactively taken which address this waste reduction. They include training, education, and development, which are intended to enhance the knowledge and skill of those who touch each area of the company, and correspondingly are directly or indirectly responsible for the waste. With knowledge and skill comes competency and the subsequent ability to make the changes necessary to eliminate the waste.

Setting clear priorities, providing strong leadership, and explicit goals can also serve to drive out waste. As leaders make clear what the priorities should be energy is not spent on things of lesser importance. As explicit goals are stated, *with the accompanying measurements*, then progress can be made in a single direction with everyone supporting that direction. In this way resources – both concrete, like money and equipment, and abstract, like talent and time – are all harnessed to a single focus.

Corporate commitment to things such as quality and continuous improvement can go a long way towards eliminating waste. A commitment to quality brings with it a commitment to ensuring that the product or services are provided as intended, each and every time. The cost of going back and eliminating errors, or redoing work, is eliminated. A focus on continuous process improvement allows teams to work towards newer and better ways of accomplishing the same objective, but doing so in a cheaper or more productive fashion, thereby taking waste out of the system.

An interesting concept is the "standard" against which work or products are measured. If the standard has a built in component for "waste", such as a ten percent error tolerance, then through continuous improvement that standard can be raised higher and the "built in" waste eliminated. This can pay back hugely to organizations who adopt this approach.

"With knowledge and skill
comes competency,
and the subsequent ability
to make the
changes necessary to
eliminate waste."

A PERFORMANCE IMPERATIVE: FOCUS ON WASTE

There are other ways in which waste can be eliminated, but the crucial message is to develop a commitment to eliminate waste in all its forms. Four clear steps need to be followed in this process:

1. Identify the waste to be eliminated.

2. Identify the cause of the waste.

3. Identify the solution.

4. Implement the solution and measure the results.

Clearly in support of the four steps above there needs to be a large infrastructure that comes with it, including elements of culture, communication, training, leadership skills, and so forth. However the very first step is to acquire a commitment to waste elimination. The other steps will follow.

Have a passion for eliminating waste in all its forms.

UNDERSTANDING CONTINUOUS PROCESS IMPROVEMENT

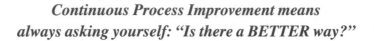

Continuous Process Improvement means always asking yourself: "Is there a BETTER way?"

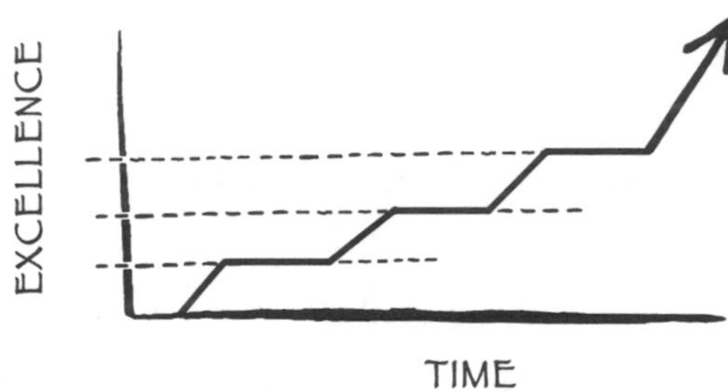

"BETTER" can mean:

Faster

Cheaper

Higher Quality

Less Waste

Improved Customer Service

UNDERSTANDING CONTINUOUS PROCESS IMPROVEMENT

A "process" is a series of actions with a defined beginning and end. The "process" of getting ready for work requires several steps: waking up, turning off the alarm clock, getting out of bed, showering, getting dressed, having breakfast, locking the door, driving to work. Those steps can be said to comprise the process of getting to work.

Within any process there are other sub-processes imbedded. For example in the situation above the step of "eating breakfast" could be broken down into a number of steps: enter kitchen, make coffee, make toast, pour cereal, etc. This could be further broken down, for example, "make coffee" could be broken down into the constituent steps required to make a cup of coffee, and so forth. When defining a process it's important to define the beginning and the end, and then the steps in-between. Judgement has to be made about how detailed each step will be and where the beginning and end will be. Once those two parameters (beginning and end, and size of step) are established, and the steps linked together, then the process has been defined.

In an organization most processes of any significance touch many people and many functions. Each process also has a cost: the cost could be money, time, energy, or other similar variables. The object of process improvement is to reduce the overall cost of the process as defined by one or more of those variables.

For example, in a labor intensive process such as hand packing boxes one might seek to improve the process so that fewer people are involved. A process involving a great deal of energy, such as the burning of gasoline to drive a motor, might be improved by reducing the amount of gasoline consumed, thereby saving costly energy.

"The quality of the finished product must not suffer as the process is improved."

UNDERSTANDING CONTINUOUS PROCESS IMPROVEMENT

In the manufacturing sector the overall financial cost of producing an automobile might be reduced by looking at the process involved and seeking to remove manufacturing steps, or determining how any given step could be done in a more cost effective manner.

Once we understand the concept of a process, and the fact that each process has a cost that can be influenced by changing steps in the process, then the concept of continuous process improvement is born.

Continuous process improvement is always asking yourself "Is there a better way? Can the process in which I am involved be done differently so as to reduce the overall cost (however "cost" is measured, i.e. people, dollars, time, material, energy, etc.)?"

The quality of the finished product must not suffer as the process is improved. In fact in many instances the objective of the process improvement is not only to reduce the cost but also to improve the quality. An organization can be committed to continuous process improvement by understanding the processes which make up that organization, at both the micro and macro level, and then seeking to continuously improve each process. There are two observations that follow:

1. This is clearly a mammoth task, and one which is virtually impossible for a small handful of individuals to accomplish. On the other hand if you enlist the assistance of every individual in the organization, the task then becomes much more manageable.

   Furthermore, each individual knows clearly their own part in those processes which involve them and so they are the ones most qualified to assist with the overall process improvement.

"Having everyone in the organization ask themselves if there is a measurably better way will drive continuous process improvement."

This often leads to an organization where each individual has a key role in improving the way things are done. In this case the role of the leader or manager is to be the catalyst for the process improvement to occur, and support those involved in it.

2. It is extremely rare that an organization does something that no one else in the world does. Production, distribution, purchasing, finance, manufacturing, human resources, marketing, etc. are all elements of organizations worldwide. Even activities at the more micro level such as invoicing, tracking pallets, training delivery, customer service, patient care, and administration are done by many organizations around the world.

   If you as leader undertake to improve processes within your organization it is wise to look at how other organizations do the same thing. These need not be competitive companies, but merely companies who have a reputation for doing these things extraordinarily well. You can visit them, or study them to understand more clearly how they do that particular process. There may then be learning that you can bring back and apply in your organization in your commitment to continuously improving processes. You may also be able to share some learning from your organization with them. This two way sharing is called "benchmarking" and is a valuable and effective way to make significant jumps in process improvement.

Having everyone in the organization ask themselves if there is a *measurably* better way, will drive continuous process improvement. As each person in the organization comes to understand what "better" means then each is able to effectively focus on contributing.

"Each process has a cost that can be influenced by changing steps in the process."

UNDERSTANDING CONTINUOUS PROCESS IMPROVEMENT

Each individual should be looking at the processes of which they are a part to determine if there is a better way to do it:

1. ***Faster:*** Reducing steps and time.

2. ***Cheaper:*** Reducing cost of: labor, materials, or resources.

3. ***With higher quality:*** Producing something of higher quality with no incremental cost and thereby providing a significant competitive advantage in the marketplace.

4. ***With less waste:*** Eliminating any by-product which does not contribute to the organization. This could be wasted material, wasted time, wasted money, or wasted human potential.

5. ***With improved customer service:*** Those who are willing to pay money for the service which you offer – your customers – place a high value on service, i. e. meeting their need in the manner which they expect it to be met. If this can be improved with no increase in cost then you increase your value in the marketplace.

As an organizational leader you need to understand and promote continuous process improvement.

MASTERING ORGANIZATIONAL
COMMUNICATION

PERSONAL CONVICTION: A PREREQUISITE FOR STUNNING ACHIEVEMENT

Drives an individual to take action until results happen...

AND IS INITIALLY ROOTED IN KNOWLEDGE.

1.	CIRCUMSTANCES	The surroundings
2.	EVENTS	What has gone on before, is happening now, and is likely to occur
3.	FACTS	Observed truths
4.	HISTORY	An extensive review or understanding of past events, their causes and effects
5.	CONSEQUENCE	An understanding and appreciation of "What will happen if ..."
6.	PERSONAL EXPERIENCE	That which has been learned through personal involvement

PERSONAL CONVICTION: A PREREQUISITE FOR STUNNING ACHIEVEMENT

It is essential that the leader have a strong personal conviction regarding the feasibility or benefit of a chosen course of action.

Strong convictions of this magnitude enable the leader to persevere until the desired outcome has been achieved, as well as motivate the team to follow the leader when this degree of personal conviction is projected.

It is often the leader's responsibility to initiate change, promote a new approach, generate enthusiasm for a given course of action, solve a problem, or seize an opportunity. Inevitably this requires a foray into the unknown in some fashion, which in turn can be overwhelming or apparently "impossible" to the team. Nonetheless if the leader demonstrates conviction that it can be done, and has perseverance, then those whom they are leading will support their initiative and do their best to make it a reality.

This is why personal conviction is so important. If you don't believe in the direction, and the success to follow, then it's difficult to maintain the drive and to persevere until the objective is met regardless of circumstance.

Conviction must initially be rooted in knowledge. There are times when faith is a strong motivator, but even that is based on knowledge of some sort, which has subsequently been translated into faith. Knowledge in six distinct areas can be used to generate conviction.

"It is essential that
the leader have a strong
personal conviction
regarding the feasibility
or benefit of a
chosen course of action."

PERSONAL CONVICTION: A PREREQUISITE FOR STUNNING ACHIEVEMENT

1. ***Circumstances:*** Knowing the environment in which one must operate, (i. e. the surroundings), can provide a strong degree of confidence, and so conviction, that an objective is doable. If for example a product is being launched that draws heavily on personal computing technology, then the present circumstances (universal acceptance of PC's) may well build conviction in the mind of the leader that the product is right for the times, and will be successful.

   Similarly, a change initiative within an organization that follows a series of focus groups which have indicated that the organization is ripe for change, may build a level of confidence in the leader that circumstances are right to initiate the change now; and so the leader has conviction that the change will be successful.

   Fully understanding the circumstances, the surroundings, in which the action is going to occur, is a powerful builder of conviction.

2. ***Events:*** A series of events can easily lead one to some specific conclusions, which in turn build conviction that a course of action is appropriate. To take a dramatic example, if a series of hikers are faced with the choice of going forward or backwards, but believe that the recent rainfalls have washed out the bridges behind them, then those events build a certain degree of conviction that forward is the best approach!

   Past, present, and future events can all serve to breed conviction. If sales results are running behind target, and marketing dollars have been cut back concurrently, then the leader might draw the conclusion that there is a link between these two events and decide that increasing marketing dollars will accelerate sales, which may in turn generate a personal conviction that the way to drive sales is to increase marketing.

PERSONAL CONVICTION: A PREREQUISITE FOR STUNNING ACHIEVEMENT

"Personal conviction

is a

prerequisite for

stunning achievement."

Examine events carefully, and as you draw conclusions from them allow them to feed your convictions, until a course of action becomes apparent and one to which you can lend your full support.

3. ***Facts:*** Certain truths are readily observed and they can serve to build conviction. For example , from my own experience I believe there is tremendous potential within every human being, which can be harnessed when that individual has the proper leadership and professional environment in which to operate. Because I see this as a fundamental truth it has developed within me a strong conviction to invest heavily in training – both for the leaders and for those on the teams.

   In this example my strong personal conviction is born out of an observed truth. Because of that conviction I can speak with passion and clarity in attempting to persuade others to support an in-depth and ongoing training and development initiative.

4. ***History:*** When history demonstrates predictable consequences as a result of a certain chain of events, then individuals can develop a strong conviction that as those chain of events begin to unfold again, the consequences will most likely be the same as they have been in the past. For example, unresolved conflict between employees over time generates bitterness and dissension and is ultimately disruptive to the team. History would indicate that if conflict between two members of a team goes unresolved, then ultimately the overall productivity and performance of the entire team will suffer.

"Conviction must be rooted in knowledge."

As a result of having seen this many times, then the leader will develop a strong conviction that, based on this kind of history, conflict between two individuals must be addressed immediately and resolved completely. This is necessary if the team is to flourish and continue to pursue their objectives optimally.

In the more macro sense, history is also a great guide to developing convictions. For example, civilizations that lose their moral fiber, their sense of values and respect for authority, have degenerated into anarchy and ultimate destruction. Seeing this historical truth easily supports the development of personal conviction that we should focus on values crucial to sustaining our culture and society, and that we should maintain those values which we feel were instrumental in bringing us to our current level of greatness. In this way personal convictions are again established on the basis of history.

5. ***Consequence:*** If you have a clear picture of what will happen as a consequence of something else happening, then this facilitates the development of personal conviction.

   If shop lifting and petty thievery is tolerated in an individual's youth, and it is felt that this leads to a greater level of theft in later years, it leads one to the conviction that the consequence of allowing this kind of thievery in youth is unwise.

   On the other hand, the consequence of individuals committing themselves to delivering on their commitments as promised, and supporting wholeheartedly the direction of the team, leads to overall success.

"If you have a clear picture
of what will happen,
then this facilitates
the development
of personal conviction."

Having observed the consequence of this level of commitment and team skill the leader may well develop a personal conviction that individual accountability and mastery of effective teamwork behavior is crucial to succeeding at the world-class level. As a consequence emphasis will be placed on these two qualities when selecting and training staff.

Again, personal conviction has grown from an observation of circumstance. As we recognize what will be the outcome of certain behaviors we then develop a strong conviction which behaviors to support and which to discourage.

6. ***Personal Experience:*** I suspect for most of us personal experience is the strongest force in developing conviction. Very often you hear the expressions, "Experience has taught me that...," "I know from experience that ..." Expressions of this nature are merely other ways of saying the individual has developed some very strong personal convictions on an issue or topic based on their own personal experience. This is a healthy thing, provided the individual remains open, teachable and objective.

   Personal experience is a way in which we integrate all the five elements of knowledge discussed above. It is our personal experience which allows us to evaluate circumstances, assess events, look at facts, judge history, and examine consequence. *We* are the individuals doing this, for ourselves, in the context within which we are accustomed to operate. As we integrate all these things into our personal experience it allows us to develop conviction, which then drives us to action.

"Conviction allows
you to
persevere when
others might quit."

PERSONAL CONVICTION: A PREREQUISITE FOR STUNNING ACHIEVEMENT

It is important though that the right interpretation be placed on these factors so that our experience can be used to further our progress; and not serve as a brake to forward momentum when our experience has taught us that something may not have worked. Often our experience has taught us not only that something may not have worked, but *why* it didn't work. By altering "the why" there would be a different outcome. In this fashion we must use our personal experiences wisely, judiciously, and with caution when using them as a basis for developing further action plans.

Personal conviction is a prerequisite for stunning achievement. It allows you to persevere when others might quit, and it allows you to provide the leadership which others require in the midst of challenging times. Our own convictions develop as a result of several types of knowledge. As we seek to strengthen convictions we must become more knowledgeable in each of those areas.

Passion is an inner fire...

...a personal excitement!

PASSION IS AN EMOTION

And it carries conviction...

From the heart of one person...

To the inner self of others.

ONLY FIRE KINDLES FIRE!

CONVICTION MUST INCLUDE PASSION

Conviction is a deep-rooted, heartfelt thing. It is something which is located in the very core of our being and which drives us to action. It is a good thing when it positively affects the well-being of others. And it is a good thing in that it provides clear visible guideposts for our actions in life.

In a leader, conviction must be shared, and coupled with passion if it is to ignite conviction in others.

Passion is the visible outworking of conviction or emotion. When we are passionate about something this is readily seen and observed by others. It is an excitement which excites others. It is a force which can be used to drive others to action, and if it is driven by our convictions then the actions that follow will be in support of those convictions.

Fundamentally passion is an emotion, with a weaker link to the intellect than to conviction. Emotion in leaders is a strong and powerful force, and a good thing. We are emotional beings, and harnessing the emotions as well as the intellect is crucial as we seek to lead others. Passion serves as the vehicle for carrying our conviction from our heart to the hearts of others; and in the same way that fire kindles fire so our passion will generate passion in others.

Do not allow your convictions to motivate only yourself, but through the magic of passion, your visible excitement, allow them to be passed on to those looking to you for leadership.

THE THOUGHTS, BELIEFS, CONVICTIONS
AND PASSIONS OF THE LEADER

IS THE SPARK...

...THAT
IGNITES THE SAME
IN OTHERS

FIRE KINDLES FIRE

One of the most exciting things about working with people is seeing that fire kindles fire.

When I'm excited about something others get excited. When I'm in contact with someone who is enthusiastic about a sport, then it's easy for me to want to try it, certainly at least when I'm with them!

Those who are "on fire" with an idea or concept, or a plan, or an execution can more easily persuade others to participate.

Those who are bland, unenthusiastic, and tediously slogging through from one point to another have a great deal of difficulty enlisting others to join them in working towards that objective.

As we seek to work with others, to provide leadership, and to harness the emotions of those who look to us for guidance, we must first demonstrate a raging enthusiasm to such a degree that others with whom we come in contact are swept up in our own enthusiasm, until they too are excited about the prospect, or journey, or goal for which we are striving.

The leader has thoughts, beliefs, convictions, and passions. As these are brought alive, they become the spark that ignites thoughts, beliefs, convictions, and passions in others.

To truly harness the inner drive of other individuals, their inner motivations, their own personal convictions, we as leaders must allow their inner drive to draw strength, to be kindled from, and be ignited by, our own.

Leaders with passion and enthusiasm engender passion and enthusiasm in others. Only fire kindles fire. Leaders without fire will have followers without fire, and so be without those inner forces which are so vital to sustained success.

CONVICTION MUST INCLUDE PURPOSE

THE REASONS

1. wwwwwww
2. wwwwwww
3. wwwwwww

THE RATIONALE

THE BENEFITS

A) wwwwwww
B) wwwwwww
C) wwwwwww

The logical basis for any initiative, the IMPORTANCE of taking action based on the conviction

Purpose describes the expected outcome once the conviction is acted upon.

CONVICTION MUST INCLUDE PURPOSE

While passion is crucial to the successful communication of conviction, by itself it is not sustainable. By its very nature passion is transitory, being an emotion; and emotions are significantly influenced by many factors and can be fleeting. For conviction to be sustained it must include purpose.

Purpose is the rationale, the intellectual reason, the satisfying of our desire for intelligent, logical, and reasonable arguments for a point of view. As we develop convictions which we seek to build into others we must couple them not only with passion but also with purpose. We must acquire the ability to communicate that purpose clearly and in a way that is memorable, so that it can be seized and remembered when we're not present.

There are three specific aspects which must be covered when communicating purpose.

1. ***The Reasons:*** This represents *why* we are doing something, the specific statement of reasons for adopting a course of action or approach.

   Reasons are the specifics, the details, as to why steps are being taken. Any conviction will be brought to life and implemented through a series of steps, and the reasons tell us why these steps were chosen and what they hope to accomplish.

2. ***The Rationale:*** The rationale takes one step backwards to explain the *motivation* for the conviction. When you provide clarity regarding rationale you allow individuals to understand why you adopted this particular course of action in the first place, and what led you to these conclusions and steps which you are outlining for them.

   In effect it gives them a window into your thinking to allow them to draw conclusions similar to your own, as you provide them with the rationale which led you to your own personal convictions.

"While passion is crucial
to the successful
communication of conviction,
by itself it is not sustainable.
For conviction to be sustained
it must include purpose."

3. ***The Benefits:*** Individuals seeking to build convictions must clearly understand the nature and the consequences of the benefits. In many ways this helps people appreciate the *value* of any particular course of action, approach, or thinking. The benefits are very important. They need not be self-serving, but they must be clear.

   Providing individuals with the benefits, and indicating who will be the recipient of those benefits, will allow them to develop a conviction for this particular course of action, that it is not only appropriate but also worthwhile.

In essence, by describing the *purpose* you are providing the intellectual basis people require to commit to something which, if you handle passion properly, they will also *want* to commit to.

Purpose describes the outcome once the conviction has been acted upon, and so creates within the minds of others a clear and logical framework on which conviction can be built.

CONVICTION MUST INCLUDE BELIEF

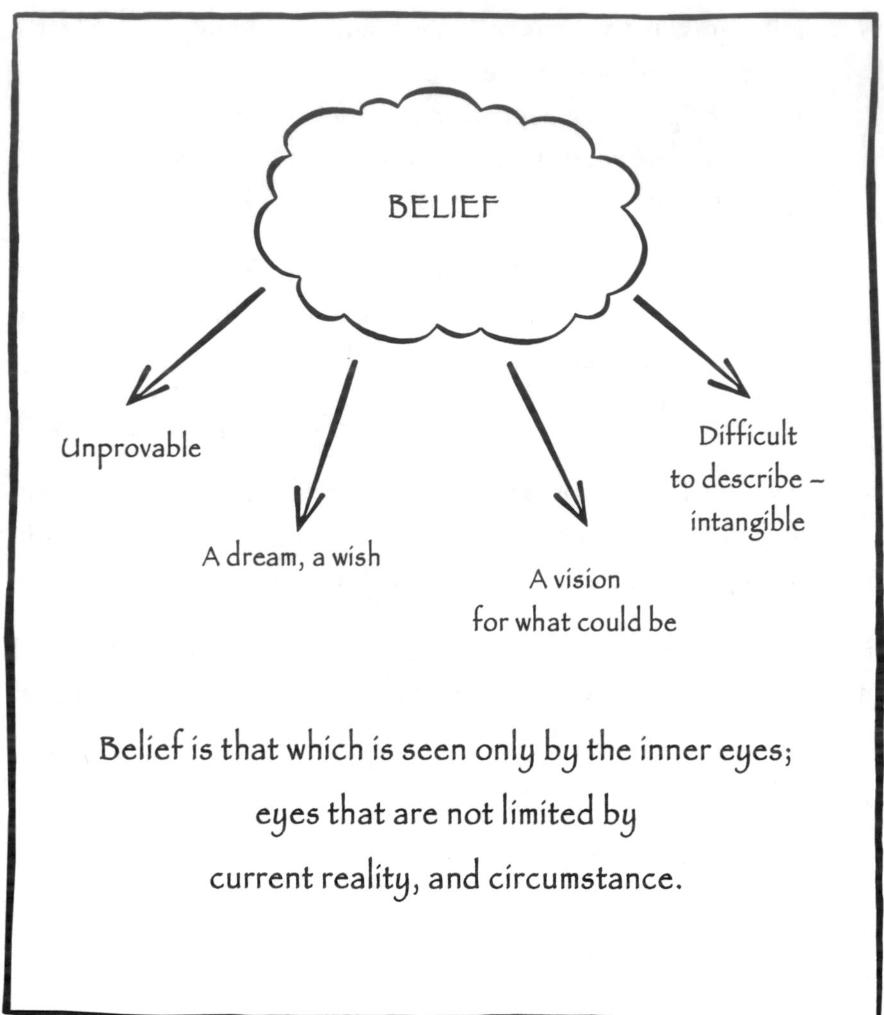

BELIEF
Unprovable
A dream, a wish
A vision
for what could be
Difficult
to describe –
intangible
Belief is that which is seen only by the inner eyes;
eyes that are not limited by
current reality, and circumstance.

CONVICTION MUST INCLUDE BELIEF

Belief is an interesting concept in that it borders on faith. Belief is something which is often unproven, untested, untried, yet nonetheless felt to be real, tangible and solid.

If we believe in something we often do so without hard, observable evidence. This is what makes it belief.

Our own convictions must carry a component of belief. True, they are based on knowledge to some degree, they carry passion with them, and they have purpose. But convictions that strike at the very innermost core also carry with them a certain component of belief. We believe that what we are doing, saying, or planning is the right approach and we believe that time will prove us right.

Conviction based only on belief may be unfounded; but conviction based only on purpose or knowledge may not be strong enough to stay the course until completion.

Belief is not only good, it is essential to establishing conviction, and is not something which we should avoid. You must be careful to ensure that belief is only a *part* of the *total* mix, but not shy away from recognizing its value and relying upon it appropriately.

By its very nature belief is something which cannot be proved, a dream or a wish, a vision for what could be. Our beliefs are our dreams for what we could achieve, or what might be possible, or what could happen; and as such they are powerful motivators and drivers of action.

"Beliefs are those things
which are seen
by the inner eye,
and as such are not limited
by the current realities
or circumstances."

CONVICTION MUST INCLUDE BELIEF

Beliefs are usually very difficult to describe, given their intangible nature. This too is okay because in the area of belief we are free to dream, to understand and create a sense of wonder as we imagine the future and what could be our impact upon it.

Beliefs are those things that are seen by the inner eye, and as such are not limited by the current realities or circumstances. Beliefs are an integral part of conviction and with them you are far more effective at building conviction into others.

CONVICTION COMES ONLY FROM AN INTEGRATED BLEND OF KNOWLEDGE, PASSION, PURPOSE AND BELIEF

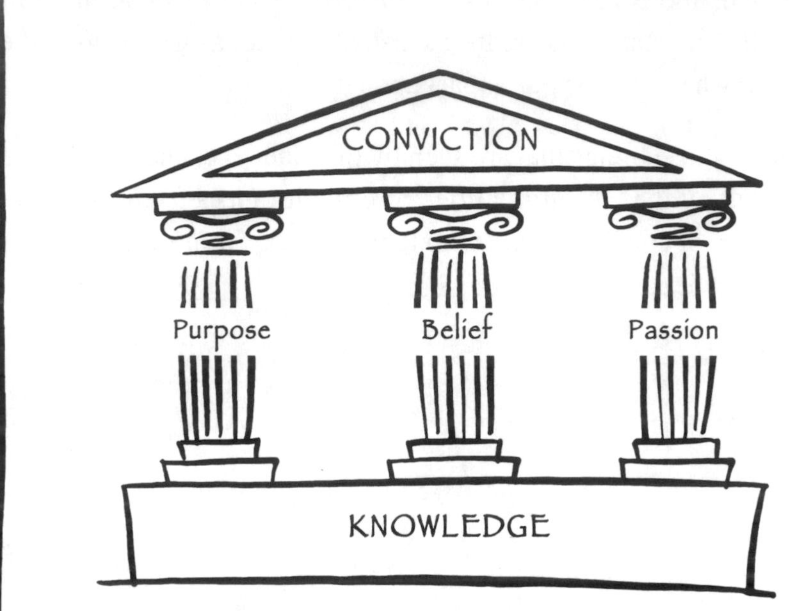

Knowledge is the base.

Purpose, Belief and Passion are the Pillars.

Together they support Conviction.

CONVICTION COMES ONLY FROM AN INTEGRATED BLEND OF KNOWLEDGE, PASSION, PURPOSE AND BELIEF

It is crucial to recognize that conviction is the final product, the end result of the proper blending of knowledge, passion, belief, and purpose.

Knowledge is the base, the foundation on which our convictions should be built. This knowledge must be sound, regardless of its source; and it then provides a good foundation from which we can draw our convictions, and on which we can build. We need to understand, and have a clear knowledge of, the basis for those things to which we will be giving ourselves, and towards which we will be leading others.

This knowledge can be rooted in many sources, such as our observations, our experiences, and our judgement; but whatever its source, it must be there. Convictions that are not rooted in knowledge are truly built upon unsteady and unstable foundations. However, once this base has been established, the pillars of passion, belief, and purpose can then rest upon it. Taken together these three support conviction.

Given what you know, and the convictions that begin to flow from that, you're able to explain clearly what has led to that conviction, the rationale for its development, the reasons for the actions to be taken, and the benefits that will accrue.

You're able to communicate your convictions with passion so that others see that there is an excitement around them and something of which they would like to be a part.

You're able to communicate your belief that you have every confidence that the outcomes are attainable.

"Convictions that are not rooted in knowledge are truly built upon unsteady and unstable foundations."

CONVICTION COMES ONLY FROM AN INTEGRATED BLEND OF KNOWLEDGE, PASSION, PURPOSE AND BELIEF

It is the *integration* of passion, purpose and belief which allows you to effectively create conviction in the minds of others. Not only are your own convictions strengthened, but others who rely upon you for leadership and direction are willing to follow, and develop within themselves convictions that mirror your own.

The conviction which leads to concrete action, and can sustain the hurdles and setbacks which inevitably occur, is one which is built on this foundation of clear and defensible knowledge, and shares a well-integrated blend of purpose, passion, and belief.

PERSONAL CONVICTION BREEDS RESULTS

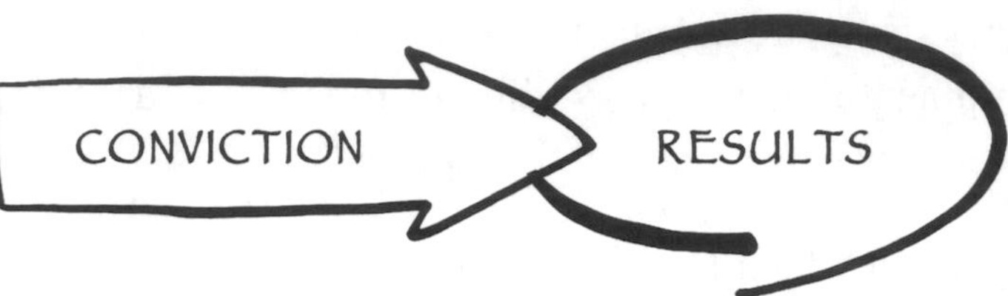

Conviction is a huge force!

It believes hurdles can be overcome.

It produces passion.

It energizes when times are tough.

It overcomes resistance.

HAVE CONVICTION!

PERSONAL CONVICTION BREEDS RESULTS

An individual with a strong personal conviction is far more likely to bear fruit from that conviction than an individual with limited conviction regarding a topic or course of action.

Personal convictions become the foundations of granite on which we build. The deeper and stronger our convictions, the more solidly and quickly we will be able to build, as we are not constantly having to double back, check, shore up and reassess.

Convictions which are rooted in fact, and which are seen to be valid, are respected and not considered to be idiosyncratic. Even those convictions that arise from innovation are respected when they are presented in a way that is considerate of the opinions of others, rather than in an egocentric way.

While your own convictions may not always be embraced by others, what matters is that you have the conviction, rooted deeply within you. If you can express it in a way that respects the right of others to disagree then they will respect you for it, and give you the room to pursue it.

As convictions are established they will become a powerful energy source within you that will enable you to drive for increasingly visible and meaningful results. Personal conviction allows you to persevere where others would stop because a hurdle or obstacle has surfaced. If you believe something can be done, then you will continue until it is done, and only see obstacles as things to be overcome. Others without such a great conviction may see the obstacles as a permanent impediment and back down. Your results will be far greater than theirs if you have a deep conviction that your objective can be achieved; for you'll then constantly seek, push, prod, pry, and work until you have overcome all obstacles that surface.

"An individual with a
strong personal conviction
regarding a course of action
is far more likely to
bear fruit from that conviction
than an individual
with limited conviction."

There are several examples similar to this, but imagine an individual deemed to be incapable of performing their job. In your judgement that individual may have significant ability and great potential, but you are unable to persuade their manager to that effect. Because of your own strong conviction you agree to take them into your department, assume the cost related to that move, and the responsibility if they fail to perform as anticipated. Because of your conviction that their weaknesses could be overcome, you are able to provide them with the opportunity to grow. As a result, they do grow, to the point that they are recognized within the organization as skilled in their field, whose opinion is frequently sought. The talent was there, it only needed another's conviction – yours – to allow it to develop.

Conviction also produces passion. Passion is one of the great energizers of life and with conviction comes passion. It's difficult to be passionate about things we do not believe in. The greater our beliefs, the greater our passion. We all know individuals who have a tremendous love for a sport or an activity, to such a degree that they are personally convinced that this activity is so rich and rewarding that they want all their friends to also be involved in it. They become passionate in their enthusiastic urging that we take up this activity for ourselves. Their passion is driven by their own conviction as to its value and worth. And in fact, in many instances we actually go out and try the activity for ourselves as a result of their passionate promotion of involvement in it.

When things are difficult, and not going according to plan, then we are forced to reassess our inner motivations and opinions. If that reassessment finds its way down to our deep felt convictions then we are re-energized to persevere despite the toughness of the moment.

"As you strive to
lead others, establish
your own convictions,
and let them become
foundations for your life,
and leadership."

PERSONAL CONVICTION BREEDS RESULTS

Things will not always go smoothly, but if our convictions are deep enough they will provide the internal motivation which we require to persevere and ultimately enjoy success. In this fashion conviction allows us to overcome resistance.

We experience resistance in many forms, some intentional and some unintentional. At times individuals might call us "crazy" or "silly." At times people will ridicule our approach, or our objective. At other times individuals may support our direction but believe that the pathway to success is simply too difficult, and the obstacles too great to be overcome. They wish us well but believe that success is impossible.

In other cases individuals are with us as we move forward, but they simply grow weary and stop out of exhaustion. Having stopped they then often find it difficult to get up and continue. In each of these three cases: ridicule, insurmountable hurdles, or fatigue – our own personal conviction can allow us to overcome and persevere when others might falter.

When we are in a leadership role this personal conviction draws us forward and those whom we are responsible for leading will follow. Individuals will often follow a leader if they are convinced of the depths of the leader's own convictions, whereas by themselves they would be hesitant to continue.

As you strive to lead others establish your own convictions, understand them, and evaluate them, thus ensuring that they are rooted in what you believe to be truth, and then let them become foundations for your life, and leadership.

OUTSTANDING COMMUNICATION: A LEADER'S SNAPSHOT

A. COMMUNICATION'S ONGOING NATURE

1. Why they (those you are leading) are involved with this task

2. How the task is progressing relative to why it's being done

3. What was the result relative to why it was done

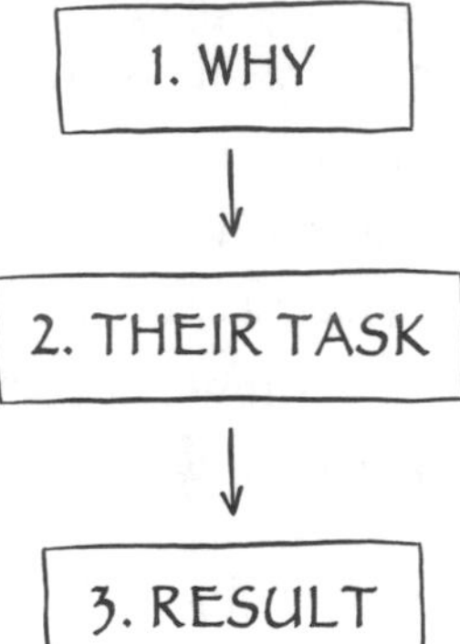

B. THE NEED FOR RELEVANCE

The task is defined by the process of which it is a part. The task is measured by its impact on the direct results or on those processes that in turn affect the results.

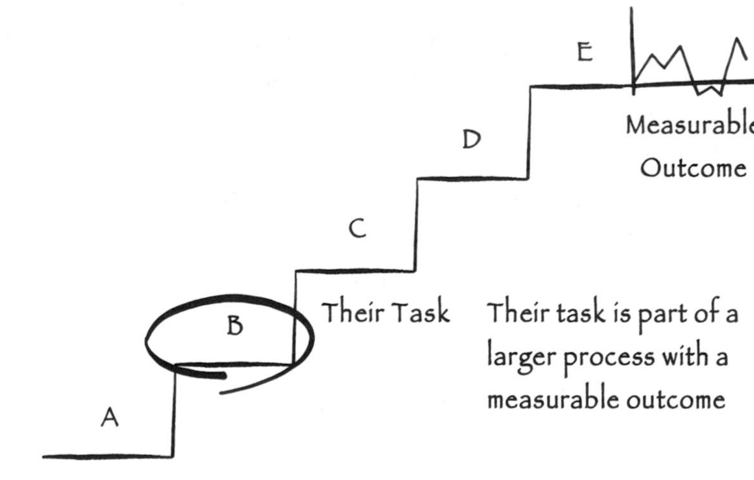

OUTSTANDING COMMUNICATION: A LEADER'S SNAPSHOT

Leaders need to understand from a macro perspective the ongoing nature of communication, and the importance of relevance.

A. ***Communication's ongoing nature:*** One of the great illusions about communication is that the objective has been accomplished when the communication has been delivered. This is far from the case. Rather, communication is an ongoing event, much like breathing – it ends when the subject is dead.

   There are three steps related to the ongoing nature of communication:

   1. ***Providing individuals with clarity regarding their role "in the scheme of things."*** Before becoming too heavily involved in any activity individuals appreciate understanding, from the leader's perspective, why they are involved, the importance of their role and the essential nature of their contribution. They also need to understand why the task is important, and what will be achieved by its completion.

   2. ***As the task progresses individuals need to understand not only how their portion is progressing, but how their portion is progressing with respect to the larger objective.*** They are interested in their task, but they are also interested in the overall, and need to be kept informed of this.

   3. ***At the task's conclusion they need to understand what was the result, and how it impacted what was intended to be accomplished.*** This then sets the stage for the next task and establishes an atmosphere of clear, ongoing, and effective communication.

OUTSTANDING COMMUNICATION: A LEADER'S SNAPSHOT

"Communication
is an ongoing event,
much like breathing –
it ends when the
subject is dead."

B. The need for relevance: Each individual has a task which will be part of some other larger task. We are all links in a larger chain. Understanding the links on either side of us gives us a greater appreciation of the importance of our task and, often more crucially, how we can improve our task in order to better support those on either side of us.

The overall process of which my task is a piece will have a measured result, an outcome that can be quantified. Each individual needs to understand this, appreciate the outcome, and ideally understand how their contribution influences the final outcome.

This provides relevance for the individual.

Communicate understanding, not facts.

ENSURE

T WO-WAY	=	Interactive among participants
L EADING EDGE	=	Let them know from you first, not by the grapevine
C IRCULAR	=	Discuss the past, present and future for any issue

USE

T OOLS:	Provide a talk sheet they can take away with them
L EADERSHIP:	Explain why things are occurring, from your perspective
C ONSIDERATION:	Always face-to-face whenever possible

TLC^2 COMMUNICATION

Communication is frequently recognized as one of the most critical elements in the success of any venture. The larger the venture, the more complicated the communication, and the more important that misunderstanding not occur.

Those charged with communicating effectively are sometimes at a loss to know what "effectively" really means. They're willing to speak, and they're often willing to set aside whatever time is required, but they are unsure whether or not that is adequate.

One approach to ensuring communication is truly effective is to use the "TLC^2 Approach." "TLC" usually stands for Tender Loving Care, which is appropriate given that communication requires the same attention to detail, compassion, and consideration that one requires when one is actually providing another with tender loving care. The "squared" usually refers to an extra multiple of whatever it is that's being squared. TLC^2 could mean a *really strong dose* of tender loving care. Similarly, outstanding communication is so important that it could be said to require a really heavy dose of tender loving care!

While this play on words is a good way to remember the "TLC^2" model, it also serves to reinforce the fact that communication requires a great deal of personal attention. I've used the "TLC^2" as a anagram to help remember the six elements of communication.

"Communication that is
effective must include some
feedback mechanism to
allow the sender to assess
the degree to which the
message has been
heard and understood."

Taking the first "TLC" (that is, before we square it) gives us the following:

"T" refers to ***"Two Way"***: Communication that is effective must include both the sender and the receiver. There must be some feedback mechanism to allow the sender to assess the degree to which the message has been heard and understood. Ideally there should be some form of question and answer session or opportunity for dialogue. People tend to understand better the things which they have a chance to participate in, discuss among themselves, or generally "mull over" together. So for maximum effectiveness, provide communication which allows for two-way interaction.

"L" stands for ***"Leading Edge"***: Leading edge indicates that the communication which individuals need to hear should be heard first from the original source. Often information comes from the grapevine. In many instances people hear things from their colleagues, or even outside sources such as suppliers or the media, before they hear from their own organization. This is definitely not leading edge communication! People want to hear from the source, and want to be "in the know." You demonstrate respect for those on your team if you ensure that the messages which are important are delivered by someone in authority within the organization, and not by the grapevine, the rumor mill, or some other source with a personal bias. For communication to be really outstanding it must be provided in leading edge fashion; that is, they hear first from you.

"People want
to hear from the source,
and want to be
'in the know'."

"C" stands for ***"Circular"***: Good communication should review what was communicated in the past, and include a brief history leading up to the present circumstances. Communication then moves to the present – the situation at hand under discussion; and finally to the future, that is, the anticipated outcome or result.

The next time a communication opportunity occurs, applying this "circular" approach will ensure that the current message references earlier information (the past), the present situation is discussed (what in the past was the future) and the future (from here forward) is presented. This ensures that those receiving the message are always in sync with what is being communicated: they have been provided with context, the situation, and some guidance on the anticipated outcomes which they can expect to be referenced at a later date.

The second set of TLC's refers to the approach taken. The first set is "what the communication should contain," or "what the messages should look like." The second TLC is more along the lines of "how," in that it provides guidance for the approach.

"T" here stands for ***"Tools"***: Whenever a message is being given, individuals need some way of referring back to that message. Over time the memory tends to lose bits and pieces, or begins to place personal bias or interpretation on what was heard. As individuals discuss messages among themselves opinions form, and in a few days it's difficult to remember what was originally said by the speaker, and what was said by those discussing the message.

"When communicating in person, provide a talk sheet which includes the key points, and which can serve as a reference in subsequent days."

To address these issues and ensure clarity, provide a talk sheet whenever any message is provided to others. This talk sheet does not have to be long and extensive, but should include the key points and key messages in simple and memorable ways. If possible, use pictures, or illustrations. This then provides the listener with something which can serve as a reference in subsequent days and a "marker" along the path to which you can refer at the next set of communications, and on which you can build.

"L" stands for ***"Leadership"***: Leaders are often set apart from those whom they are charged with leading by virtue of the fact that they understand more about why things are occurring then the rest of their team. This is usually because they have a broader perspective, and a larger context. As leaders it's important to recognize the need to communicate why things are occurring, that is, to pass on the perspective that you have as a leader. This is an important element of leadership as it allows those who are trusting in you to understand why it is that you are doing or saying the things which you are.

"Most communication that is
new requires interpretation, and
consequently you show
consideration for your listeners
when you deliver the message
face-to-face,
thereby allowing for dialog."

"C" stand for ***"Consideration"***: There are times when impersonal communication is valid – for example when issuing written material that reinforces what others already know or expect. However, most communication that is new requires interpretation, and consequently you show consideration for your listeners when you deliver the message face-to-face, thereby allowing for dialog.

Even simple messages between colleagues working in an office are often more effective when you take a moment to deliver a message face to face, rather then via voice mail, e-mail, memo, or through some third party. Face-to-face communication shows consideration for the other individual and allows you to be more effective in the first TLC's – that is, it provides for interaction, lets them know from you first, and best covers the past, present and future.

This format, the TLC^2 methodology, will go a long way to enhancing your communication. This is because it is intended to allow you to pass on *understanding* to your listener, and not just facts. With understanding comes clarity of communication.

COMMUNICATION INCREASES SIGNIFICANTLY WHEN THE RATIONALE IS INCLUDED

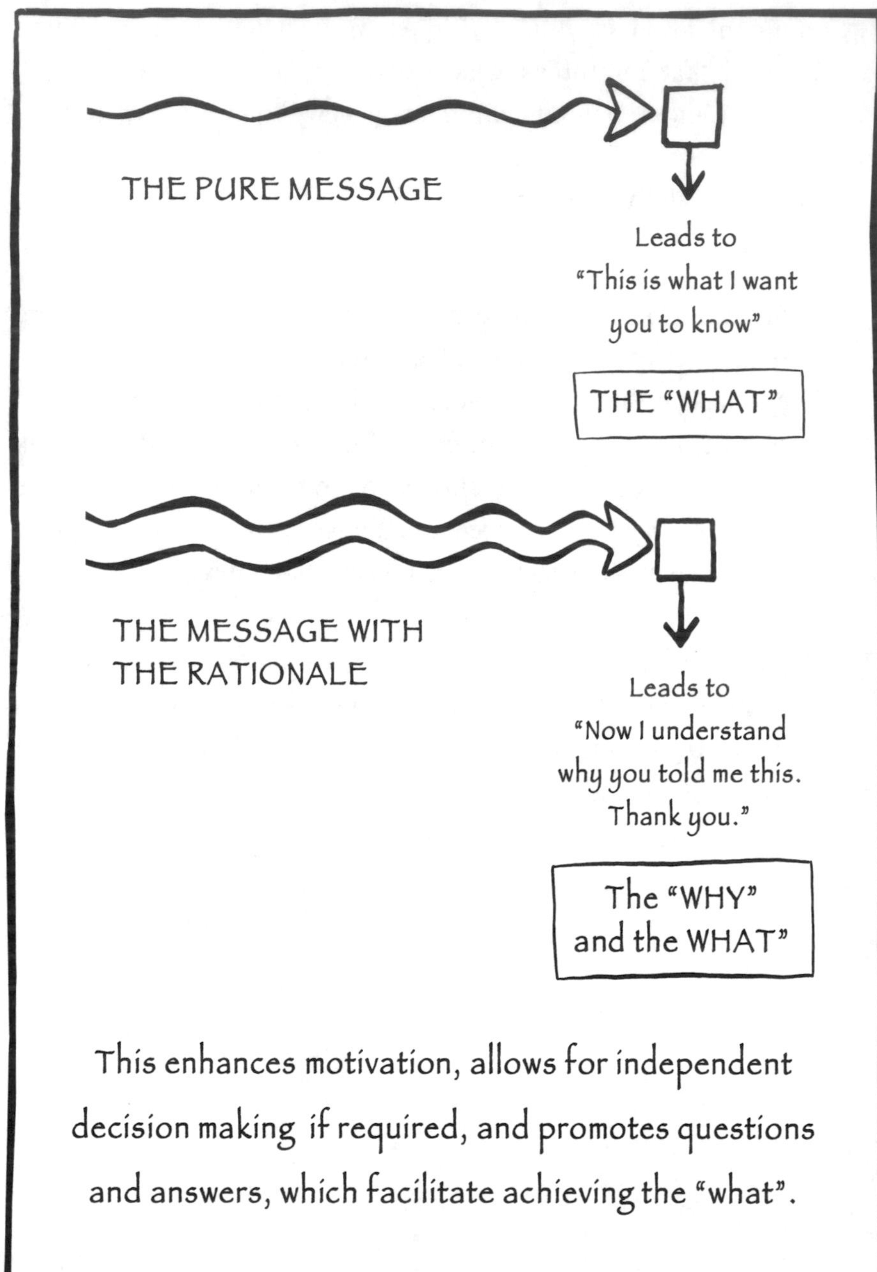

THE PURE MESSAGE
Leads to
"This is what I want you to know"
THE "WHAT"
THE MESSAGE WITH THE RATIONALE
Leads to
"Now I understand why you told me this. Thank you."
The "WHY" and the WHAT"
This enhances motivation, allows for independent decision making if required, and promotes questions and answers, which facilitate achieving the "what".

COMMUNICATION INCREASES SIGNIFICANTLY WHEN THE RATIONALE IS INCLUDED

"Do your homework now" is a less effective communication strategy than "Do your homework now because your cousins are coming over later this afternoon and there will be no opportunity then."

The reason why the second statement is more effective is because the rationale is provided. This is equally true in other forms of communication. A head of training seeking more money for training activities can put together a detailed plan as to how the money will be spent, how it will be monitored, and the number of people who will be trained as a result. This is "information," and it is valuable, but it would be far more effective when, for example, the request for training funds is accompanied by the rationale that explains how corporate profitability will increase as a direct result. In this case the reason for requesting the funds is provided in addition to stating the desired outcome.

When individuals understand *why*, it is much easier to harness their conviction, and their enthusiasm, for a project, an activity, or a topic.

Often to the speaker the "why" is so obvious that only a small percentage of the total communication time is spent on it because it is "obvious". The majority of time is spent explaining the "what." In fact, the communication will be much more effective if more time were spent explaining why the topic was initiated in the first place, and then followed with the what.

Helping people understand the reason for something enables them to respond more intelligently, ask better questions, and ultimately add greater value and participate more effectively in the outcome.

COMMUNICATION INCREASES SIGNIFICANTLY WHEN THE RATIONALE IS INCLUDED

"When individuals
understand 'why',
it is much easier to
harness their enthusiasm
for an activity."

COMMUNICATION INCREASES SIGNIFICANTLY WHEN THE RATIONALE IS INCLUDED

If as a result of the communication the listener is intended to take action and do something, they will be better able to act independently if they understand *why* it is they are being asked to achieve a specific outcome, instead of simply *what* the outcome is. Being given the rationale allows the individual to make decisions "on the spot" should they encounter a hurdle or roadblock, because they understand why the task was assigned. If they are only given the specific "whats" – do this, do that – then if for some reason they encounter a roadblock and are unable to "do" something, they'll simply stop.

Communication increases significantly when the rationale is included.

KNOWING WHEN TO WRITE AND WHEN TO SPEAK PROMOTES EFFECTIVENESS

Consider the desired outcome in advance of initiating the approach.

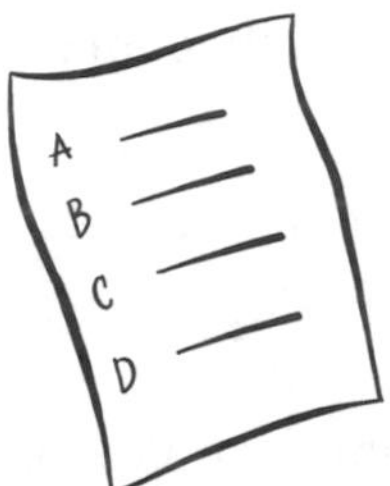

WRITING

A permanent record and for operational clarity.

SPEAKING

To foster motivation and to provide for discussion.

KNOWING WHEN TO WRITE AND WHEN TO SPEAK PROMOTES EFFECTIVENESS

The two major forms of communication available to us are writing and speaking. Clearly other more visual mediums such as video are also available, but they are simply a more effective form of speaking.

Writing has its strengths when there is no need to bring people together, when feedback is not immediately required, and when discussion is not necessary.

Writing is a very powerful communication vehicle when a permanent record is required, and clear "marching orders" are needed in order to ensure that things happen as intended.

The written word need not be complicated, but rather can be simple and straightforward, providing a touchstone to which the readers can frequently refer to check that they are "on track". The price that is paid for this form of clarity is that it is not interactive, and as such should not be used until you are confident that the message is clear and will not require additional interaction.

Speaking, on the other hand, allows for two-way discussion. It promotes dialogue, and can be used as a powerful motivational tool, given that passion can usually be introduced more effectively by the spoken word than the written word.

On the other hand, its down side is that unless notes are taken the message can be misunderstood and become fuzzy, or blurred over time. Inevitably the spoken form of communication takes longer than the written form as people are engaged, involved and responding.

Understanding the pros and cons of these two mediums is important, but the real key lies in considering the desired outcome *in advance*. Simply using the most convenient medium does not ensure that your communication is as effective as possible. Give thought to what outcome you wish and then select the most effective way to achieve that outcome.

EFFECTIVE COMMUNICATION: NEVER UNDERESTIMATE THE NEED FOR REPETITION

The message needs to come often, and clearly, and it must be consistently the same from all sources!

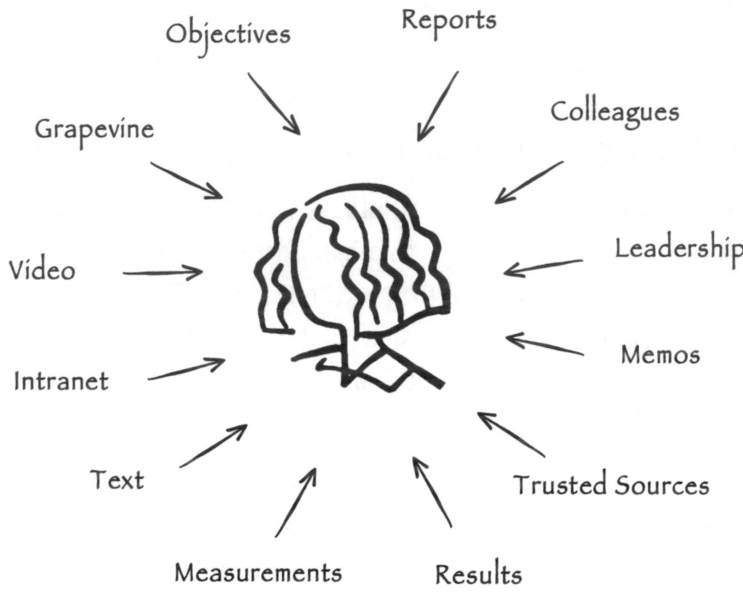

REPETITION means:

The same content (eg. a company vision) or the same focus (eg. productivity per shift).

EFFECTIVE COMMUNICATION: NEVER UNDERESTIMATE THE NEED FOR REPETITION

Communication events inherently carry with them the potential for their own failure, in that once done we believe it has happened. In fact communication has only really occurred when the person receiving the message has *internalized* it, not just heard it.

In order to facilitate this, and so drive effective communication, the messages need to be repeated several times, and preferably in many different ways and formats. Any company promoting its products through advertising demonstrates this truth brilliantly.

There are many vehicles available for communicating a message and they should all be employed. The message itself remains constant but each different medium allows for a different emphasis. In a written piece, detail can be provided; in a video piece, a visual image provided; in word of mouth, personal testimonials, etc.

As you strive for truly effective communication think of the many different vehicles available, but also think of the unique properties of each and harness those properties in order to link to a specific aspect of the message you are giving.

Every communication message can be approached in the above fashion, not just those which are seen as major, or important. This principle of frequent repetition of the message using many different media is equally valid for departments, focusing attention on issues on the factory floor, communicating vision, tracking performance results, and so forth.

In short, any situation that requires a clear understanding of a message by others will benefit from this thinking.

EFFECTIVE COMMUNICATION: ENSURE EVERYONE WHO NEEDS TO KNOW REALLY DOES KNOW

1. This is a LONG way for information to flow.

CEO
Sr. VP's
VP's
Directors
Managers
Supervisors
Staff

2. Made difficult by:
   (a) Each level feeling that once they know, knowing it "is really not that crucial"!

   If I don't know – I want to; but if I now know then I don't think anyone else really needs to know.

   (b) The normal corruption which occurs as information is passed on.

   (c) Each level losing the passion of personal conviction!!

Therefore each level must ensure, and verify, that the desired information is in fact being passed on as intended.

EFFECTIVE COMMUNICATION: ENSURE EVERYONE WHO NEEDS TO KNOW REALLY DOES KNOW

The nature of communication is such that key messages often carry the seeds of their own destruction within them. An individual who really feels the need to know about some topic or issue is deeply satisfied once they have that knowledge. This deep satisfaction works against their taking responsibility to pass the message on to others in the organization with equal clarity and conviction. Being human, their desire to know, once satisfied, fades in favor of the need to do other things.

However, those at a lower level who are relying on their supervisor for clear communication, with passion, have an equally great thirst to know, and as such are looking to their immediate supervisor for this communication. The supervisor no longer has any burning desires relative to this message, and so treats it as less valuable; consequently the chances of those next in line hearing and effectively understanding it greatly diminish!

This is a very dangerous reality and one must consciously work to overcome its influence. We intellectually realize the importance of each communication message, the importance of communicating it clearly, and the importance of communicating it with passion and conviction. From this should come the *discipline* to set aside the time to make communication a priority on an ongoing basis, to keep those who rely on us for information, well informed.

"The nature of communication
is such that key messages
often carry the seeds of their
own destruction within them.
The desire to know,
once satisfied, fades in favor
of the need to do other things,
then pass the message on."

EFFECTIVE COMMUNICATION: ENSURE EVERYONE WHO NEEDS TO KNOW REALLY DOES KNOW

If you have ever played the telephone game around the room where your aunt whispers a sentence into your cousin's ear who then whispers into an uncle's ear and so on until you, the twentieth person in the circle hears it, you realize how easy it is to have a message corrupted as it passes from person to person. Your aunt begins by saying, "My neighbor, Sally, has just bought a new cat." By the time you hear it the message is, "Sally sat on my neighbor to keep her from getting fat." Interestingly in that game, no one questions the message they just heard even though it becomes increasingly ludicrous as it moves from person to person. Each believes that they repeated exactly what they just heard, and trusts that somebody, somewhere, knows what is meant.

In order to address this concern, frequent checking should be done along the communication chain. Additionally, checking should occur *at the end* of the chain to ensure that in fact the message was received as intended.

It's relatively easy for a senior member of management to communicate a message clearly and to "require" that the message itself be communicated "throughout the organization." The senior executive then goes on to the next task believing that the communication flow will go right to the extremities of the organization. In fact this may well not be the case as the message is filtered, edited, shortened, deleted, or just plain forgotten as it passes through many hands (or mouths!). There needs to be ongoing and regular checking at various milestones between the senior manager and the extremities of the organization to ensure that the message is in fact flowing, and that it is flowing as intended.

We should never just *believe* that communication is occurring as intended with the intended results. We must *check* to ensure that this is in fact happening.

EFFECTIVE COMMUNICATION: GETTING FEEDBACK IS ESSENTIAL

INITIAL FLOW

1. Important information effectively cascaded

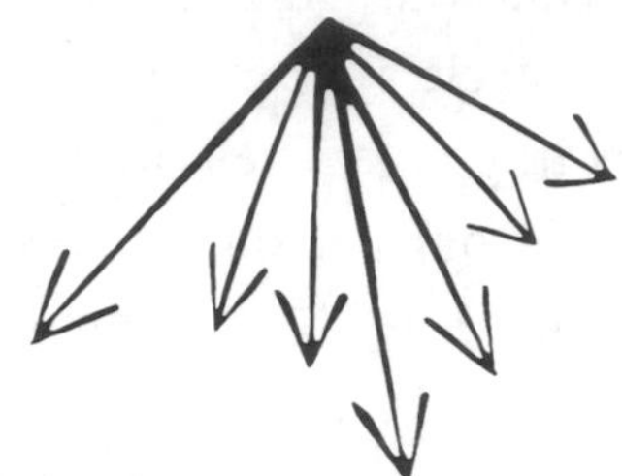

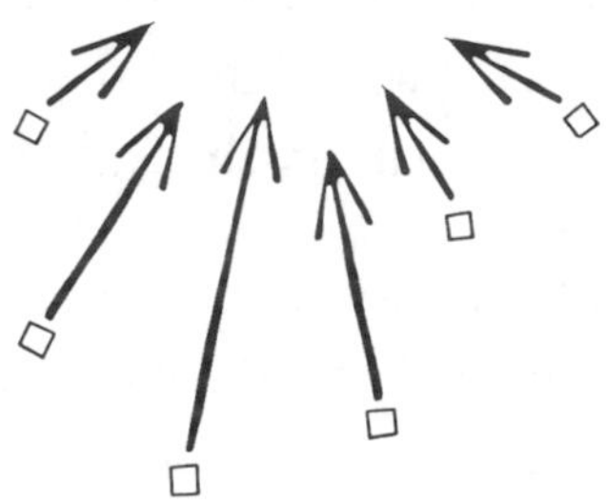

BUT WHAT IS CRUCIAL IS:

2. Responses: to ensure the information was heard and understood

This lets the initial sender know if the intention of the communication was achieved.

EFFECTIVE COMMUNICATION: GETTING FEEDBACK IS ESSENTIAL

Once the initial communication has been effectively moved out into the organization the next challenge is to ensure that that message was understood *as intended*. Knowing that the message was received does not ensure that the intention of the message was understood.

In order to check this, feedback must be part of the communication plan. How to get feedback is outlined on the following pages, but first a *conviction* of the importance of feedback is required.

The entire organization needs to appreciate that feedback is the mechanism for determining what was heard, what was understood, what actions are happening as a result, whether or not these actions are the intended actions, and the degree of acceptance the message has received. Shooting an arrow at a target may be a worthwhile exercise, but if the archer never checks to see where the arrow landed then there's little confidence in the effectiveness of the shot. The archer must make the effort to go to the target, examine how close the arrow was to the mark, determine why the shot landed where it did, and then identify the appropriate next steps.

Similarly, firing off communication requires a (usually greater!) effort to track down the target and determine whether or not the communication did in fact hit the mark as intended, with the desired result, and if not, what next steps are appropriate.

Equally important is knowing if in fact the communication did hit anything at all!

Never underestimate the importance or value of getting feedback. This allows you to move on in confidence knowing that that particular issue has been dealt with.

EFFECTIVE COMMUNICATION: HOW TO GET FEEDBACK

1. One on one: casually, during the day as opportunities arise

2. Up through the organizational levels

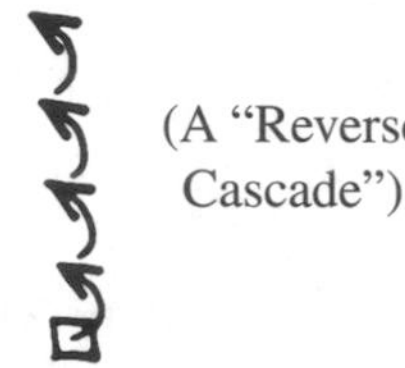

(A "Reverse Cascade")

3. Focus Groups

4. Surveys – instant on the intranet

5. Spot calls by phone to random recipients

6. Organized "Muffins & Musings" for a 1/2 hr first thing in the morning with a few invited recipients (or at lunch — etc.)

EFFECTIVE COMMUNICATION: HOW TO GET FEEDBACK

Recognizing the importance of feedback, there are six clear ways by which you can get it.

1. ***Take casual opportunities during the day to probe and ask about the communication message.*** At a training session I'll often ask participants during break "So what do you feel you're learning?", "Has the morning been worthwhile so far? Why?", "Is the course meeting your expectation to date?", etc. These questions are short, allow for short answers, and allow me to get the pulse of how that program is going.

   Similarly, when a key communication message has gone out to the organization there are many opportunities during the normal course of the day to ask simple probing questions on a one-on-one basis: e.g. at the end of a meeting, or before a meeting begins, in the halls or elevators, etc, as a way of getting some feedback as to the effectiveness of the communication.

2. ***Organizationally mandate that feedback flow bottom up.*** This is a method whereby department managers are asked for feedback as to how a given message was heard, whether it was understood, what action has been taken, and so forth. As the information is aggregated as it moves up it remains anonymous, and so accurate. Mandating this kind of feedback back to the senior levels is a very effective way of keeping a pulse on the organization. It does require, however, that the time be set aside at the senior management level to report on the feedback.

"Organizationally mandate that feedback flow bottom up."

3. ***Focus groups can be a very effective way to determine if a communication message has been truly understood and internalized.*** The focus group is a small group of people, perhaps six to eight, selected at random from a representative sample of the population who received the communication message.

   This group is joined by a moderator or facilitator, or trainer, who simply acts as a leader to facilitate interaction. The group is then asked questions regarding the communication such as; "What did you understand by the message?", "What actions have you taken as a result?", "How do you feel the message will influence your job on a day-to-day basis?", etc. The power of this approach is that it generates dialogue and discussion among the participants, which in turn gives a much deeper level of feedback than does simple summary statements passed on.

   The facilitator can then summarize information and feed it back into the organization, or the focus group itself can be observed in action by the initiator of the message at the time of the focus group, or by video or audio taping for later replay.

"The points of view employees present will be more than their own, they will also include their own sense for what their colleagues believe."

4. ***Written surveys provide an excellent source of feedback.*** They allow questions to be targeted and the responses to be very concrete. If intranet technology is available then this form of feedback mechanism can be done with little bureaucracy.

   "Written" surveys should not be underestimated in their ability to provide accurate feedback from large numbers.

   Instant feedback can be obtained in a similar fashion when the large groups are in one place and group response technologies are used. In this case the group is asked a question and they enter a response on a keypad right at their table. These responses are immediately aggregated and projected onto the screen in front of the group. This provides both the group and the leaders with immediate feedback on key issues.

5. ***Using a quick phone call to random recipients through the organization can give an immediate snapshot as to the effectiveness of the message's dissemination.*** If these calls are made to all levels of the organization at all geographical locations, then they provide an immediate sense for whether or not the message did get out as intended, and what in fact was heard. If the results of this are encouraging then further probing is probably not required. If on the other hand the results are disturbing, then more detailed feedback tools could be utilized to find out where the communication broke down.

"Instant feedback can be obtained when large groups are in one place and group response technologies are used."

6. ***Senior managers could meet randomly selected employees on a regular basis (say, once a week) for a short period of time (eg. half an hour) for "muffins and musings."*** This is best used in those cases where feedback on larger issues is required, such as how the culture change initiative is progressing; or whether or not training programs are having a significant effect; or whether the corporate values are being effectively implemented.

   This is an opportunity for senior managers to meet three or four employees selected from within the organization to talk over these topics and understand more clearly how those employees are feeling about them. If this occurred on a regular basis, then over time the executive involved in these sessions would stay closely in touch with the points of view of the organization on these various initiatives.

   These meetings provide value in that the employees can talk openly, and in depth, responding to more probing questions given the fact that it is a small intimate meeting with opportunity to chat, instead of being a managed discussion.

   Also, the points of view that the employees present will be more than their own, they will also include their own sense of what their colleagues believe. As such, there is much greater input received than simply that from the three or four people present.

The above methods for gathering feedback each have their own strengths and weaknesses, and need to be used as appropriate, depending on the level of feedback required, the nature of the message being sent, and the degree to which an immediate response is required.

EFFECTIVE COMMUNICATION: CONTROLLING WHAT IS REPEATED

Your words originally	Someone else	How you often end up being quoted!

TO ENSURE WHAT THEY SAY YOU SAID IS REALLY WHAT YOU DID SAY ...

1. BE PROACTIVE	Say what you think is important. This may not be what you were asked about!
2. KEEP IT VERY SHORT	A series of 10 second "sound bytes," each with one message
3. SAY IT WITHOUT USING NEGATIVES	This takes a lot of practice (hint: avoid "NO", "NEVER", NOT")
4. MAKE IT INTERESTING	Use simple, clear language
5. ADD A SHORT "STORY"	A personal or observed example, but keep it short. People repeat stories

EFFECTIVE COMMUNICATION: CONTROLLING WHAT IS REPEATED

There are often instances when we know that something we say is going to be repeated. This is clearly the case when granting a media interview, but it is also the case when your point of view is asked for by a member of the organization, and you know that your answer is going to be repeated to others.

Frequently circumstances occur when your comments or response provide the basis for subsequent direction, discussion, or action. Consequently it's very important to be able to influence what others say about what you said, after they walk away. In order to do this there are five specific things which you can do to ensure that what you say has the best possible chance of being passed on as you said it!

1. ***Look at the intent of the question or request and respond with your, and only your, message.***

   It's not always necessary to specifically answer the question, or respond exactly to what was asked. Sometimes it's important to be very precise with a specific answer to a specific question. However, often the question you are asked is phrased in a way that reflects the learner's lack of knowledge as they are seeking information, clarification or direction. In these cases respond to the message by stating what you want to leave them with, even if it is different from what was asked.

   For example, if you are asked, "Why did you cancel the Christmas party?" and you respond: "To save money" then that is the message that will be repeated. An alternate answer could be "Our job security depends on our ability to be the lowest cost producer in our business.

"Say only what
you want repeated,
without all
the accompanying
description, elaboration,
and background."

Competition is fierce at present and so we have to reduce costs everywhere we possibly can. We've done this in twelve different areas which I'd be happy to share with you, the Christmas party being one of those twelve."

In this example the message you are sending is the one which you want to be repeated, one which provides context and rationale, and enhances understanding. It's not, however, the specific answer to the specific question, but it does ensure that what's repeated is what you want communicated.

2. ***Long messages will inevitably be shortened.*** People cannot remember everything you said; and they will take out what they think is important and repeat only that.

   In order to manage this proactively from your point of view you need to keep what you say short, and present only one message at a time. In essence, say only what you want repeated without all the accompanying description, elaboration, and background thinking.

3. ***People seem to remember negatives much more than positives!*** When you use negatives in your language and your messages these are strong, and often repeated. "I will not go" and "I will go tomorrow" are often both repeated as "He's not going," despite the fact that in the second case you did not use a negative and gave more information. It just seems that human nature is biased towards shrinking the message down and putting it into a negative context. This trait is seen when individuals are asked to list both the things that could go wrong and the things that could go right in a given circumstance. Inevitably the list of things that could go wrong is significantly longer!

"Stories get repeated;
facts often
get forgotten."

In order to proactively address this, present your messages without negatives wherever possible. It's often very difficult and takes practice, but it does make the message more effective and it influences what's repeated. "Did you like the red car?" is better answered by saying "I much prefer the blue car" than by saying "No."

4. ***If what you say is interesting it is more likely to be repeated the way you presented it than if you said something that is boring, dull and uninteresting.*** In this latter case it's highly likely that your message will be distorted to make it more interesting, or embellished to add spice. It's much more effective if *you* add the interest so that is what's communicated. Very often an analogy, or an illustration can add the necessary interest to an otherwise dull topic.

   Referring to an earlier example, the speaker could say "The cost of last year's Christmas party was the same amount we pay to keep five people employed for a year. We felt it was more important to keep those people employed." This brings context to the message, adds interest and relevance to the listener, ensures greater understanding, and results in a more effective message being repeated in the company than simply "They're trying to cut costs again and so took away our Christmas party." Adding interest is a powerful way to control what's repeated.

"'Did you like the red car?' is better answered by saying 'I much prefer the blue car' than by saying 'No.'"

5. ***Short stories, especially personal ones, also significantly enhance communication and influence what's repeated.*** Throughout history people have passed on stories about their families, personal histories, and traditions. Repeating folklore from generation to generation is one of the most important aspects of the family history. Stories get repeated; facts often get forgotten.

   Another response to the question about Christmas parties could include a story as follows, "Some weeks ago I was shopping at the local department store and noticed proudly that our product was displayed beside our competitor's product. I was especially pleased to see how many more features our product had compared to those of our competitor. Interestingly, a customer came to the counter while I was standing there with a competitor's product in her hand. She bought the competitor's product! As I stood there five other people did exactly the same thing. I found this particularly distressing since we have just launched our new product and it seems to be so much better than what all the others have.

   "When the seventh person did the same thing as I stood there watching, I had to ask her why she had made that choice. Her response was 'I like the other product better, but this one's cheaper.' I realized consumers are now placing a much greater value on price than they ever did before, and are willing to forgo some of the features which they like in order to get a better price."

"Often an analogy,
or an illustration, can
add interest to an
otherwise dull topic."

> "If we are to capture the hearts and pocketbooks of the consumer we have to provide a product with better features *and* a lower cost. Then we'll scoop the market. As a result of that Saturday shopping trip I came back and looked for every possible way we could reduce costs without sacrificing people's jobs. The Christmas party was one of twelve things which we can do immediately to reduce costs – so the *next* seven customers buy our product!"

Telling stories is a great way to make communication memorable, and so be repeated as intended.

Select the most appropriate from these possible approaches.

PAST

"Looking back – experience, or history, or results clearly show that..."

PRESENT

"An analysis of current facts and opinions leads to the conclusion that..."

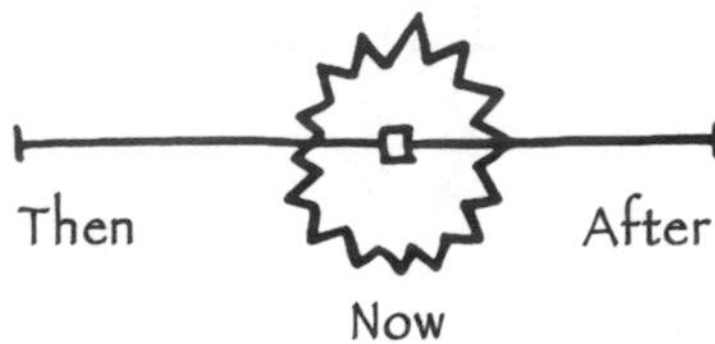

FUTURE

"Current projections show that..."

Be sure in all cases to make clear which conclusions come from observable facts and which come from considered opinion.

PERSUASION: THE IMPORTANCE OF APPROACH

When you are working hard to persuade someone else to accept what it is that you have to say, there are three very effective approaches from which you may choose – or even use a combination of all three.

The past: In order to make your point it's possible to reference what has gone before. This is a way of looking at history, bringing in what has been done before – perhaps in the form of an anecdote, statistics, or previous results.

The power of this approach is that we tend to get in the future what we got in the past if we follow the same path. Consequently as we look at the past it is likely that the future can be anticipated, and therefore the outcome foreseen.

As a result an individual wishing to persuade another can do so by referencing previous or historical data, and demonstrating how it can be projected to predict the desired outcome.

The present: In this case there is little historical data available, but there is a great deal of current fact or information at hand. This material can be analyzed, and an interpretation arrived at which leads to the conclusion. When persuading another a comprehensive and accurate analysis of current data can be a very effective way of bringing someone to your way of thinking.

In the present there is less predictability of results than from the past; but as circumstances are constantly changing, very often looking at the past might not lead to the right conclusion. Past information must be tempered with judgement drawn from the present realities.

"Your effectiveness
is often enhanced by
identifying clearly, upfront,
which of your thoughts
are rooted in fact, and which
are your
considered opinions."

The Future: Visionaries have the ability to anticipate what will come in the future as a result of looking at things in the present. If this future can be accurately predicted, it then provides a strong basis from which to make recommendations in the present. In some cases future predictions are quite straightforward (e. g. those based on demographics), in other cases they're much less clear (eg. those based on current opinion).

In those instances where you have a firm conviction of what the future will be, based on your present observations, and you believe you can present an accurate chain of events from the present to the future, and thereby accurately predict what will occur, then this is a powerful argument for galvanizing action in the present, with reference to what is foreseen in the future.

It is clear when looking at these three possible approaches to persuading others that in some cases fact provides the basis for the discussion and in other cases opinion provides the basis. Your effectiveness is often enhanced by identifying clearly, upfront, which of your thoughts are rooted in fact, and which are your considered opinions.

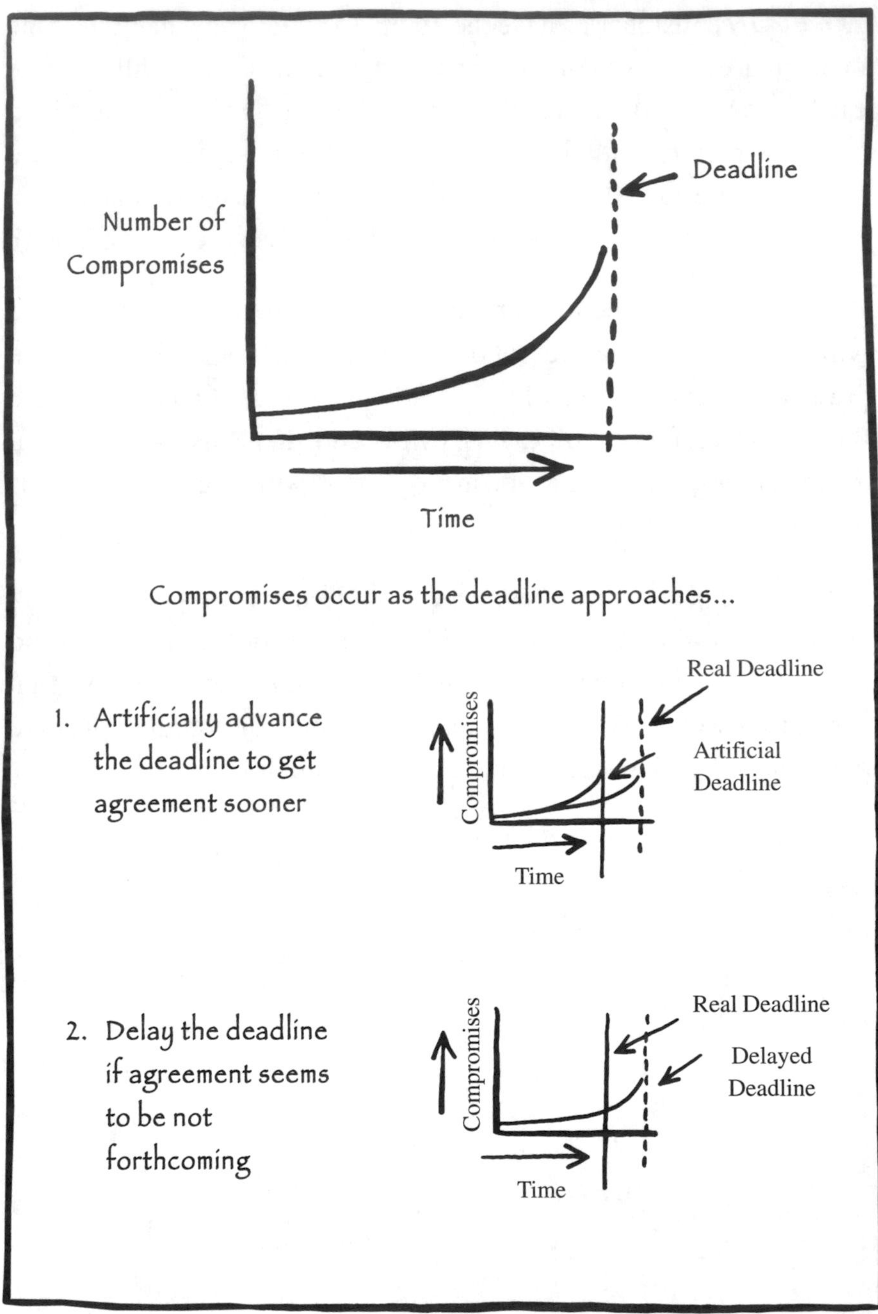
Number of Compromises
Deadline
Time
Compromises occur as the deadline approaches...
1. Artificially advance the deadline to get agreement sooner
Compromises
Real Deadline
Artificial Deadline
Time
2. Delay the deadline if agreement seems to be not forthcoming
Compromises
Real Deadline
Delayed Deadline
Time

PERSUASION: THE IMPORTANCE OF TIME

When attempting to persuade others time is a key variable that can work to your advantage or disadvantage.

If there is a deadline to which both parties have agreed, then human nature is such that significant give-and-take does not usually occur until you approach the deadline. In the early portion of the discussion, whether it's minutes, days, weeks, or even months, then somehow the parties feel that there is "lots of time," relatively speaking, and so use that time to present points of view, and clarify perspectives; not to compromise.

This early stage is an important time, because it is a period in which both parties can exchange information and seek to understand one another; but it is not usually a time when significant decisions are made. They are made as the deadline approaches. The closer the parties get to the deadline the more willing they are to make decisions, and, if necessary, attempt to work out compromises, provide concessions, or come to some resolution. They know that once the deadline arrives the opportunity for further agreement, discussion, or resolution will be past.

In light of this there are two ways in which you can be more persuasive.

1. ***Attempt to create an artificial deadline in advance of the real deadline.*** This will tend to get agreement sooner. For example, if a contract expires at the end of May and both parties agree that they will have a contract in place by the end of February, then this is an artificial deadline and one which both have agreed to. It becomes the new "deadline" and so people will often move forward sooner towards resolution and concession behavior, which would not normally have occurred until sometime later.

"If there is a deadline to which both parties have agreed then human nature is such that significant give-and-take does not usually occur until you approach that deadline."

Similarly one individual could move a deadline forward in an artificial fashion, for example by not being available just prior to the final deadline; they might have to leave the city early, or not be available on the weekend, or, in a shorter time frame, have to attend an unscheduled meeting which cuts short the amount of time that was thought to be available. Each of these kinds of actions move the deadline forward in an artificial fashion and so drive forward the concession behavior.

In most cases this artificial deadline is just that – artificial. Once the concession behavior has occurred at this new deadline then there is, in fact, time before the real deadline, if additional compromise would benefit the outcome.

2. ***If the concession behavior, or anticipated compromise, is not forthcoming then attempt to delay the deadline.*** Very often deadlines which are set are themselves a compromise and can in fact be changed.

   By delaying the deadline, some concession behavior or attempts at resolution or compromise may still occur after what was the original deadline.

   In order to persuade others be very conscious of the role of time as it relates to your ability to persuade, seek compromise, or resolution. By adjusting the deadline you increase your ability to affect the outcome, and so your ability to be successful in persuading the other party of your point of view.

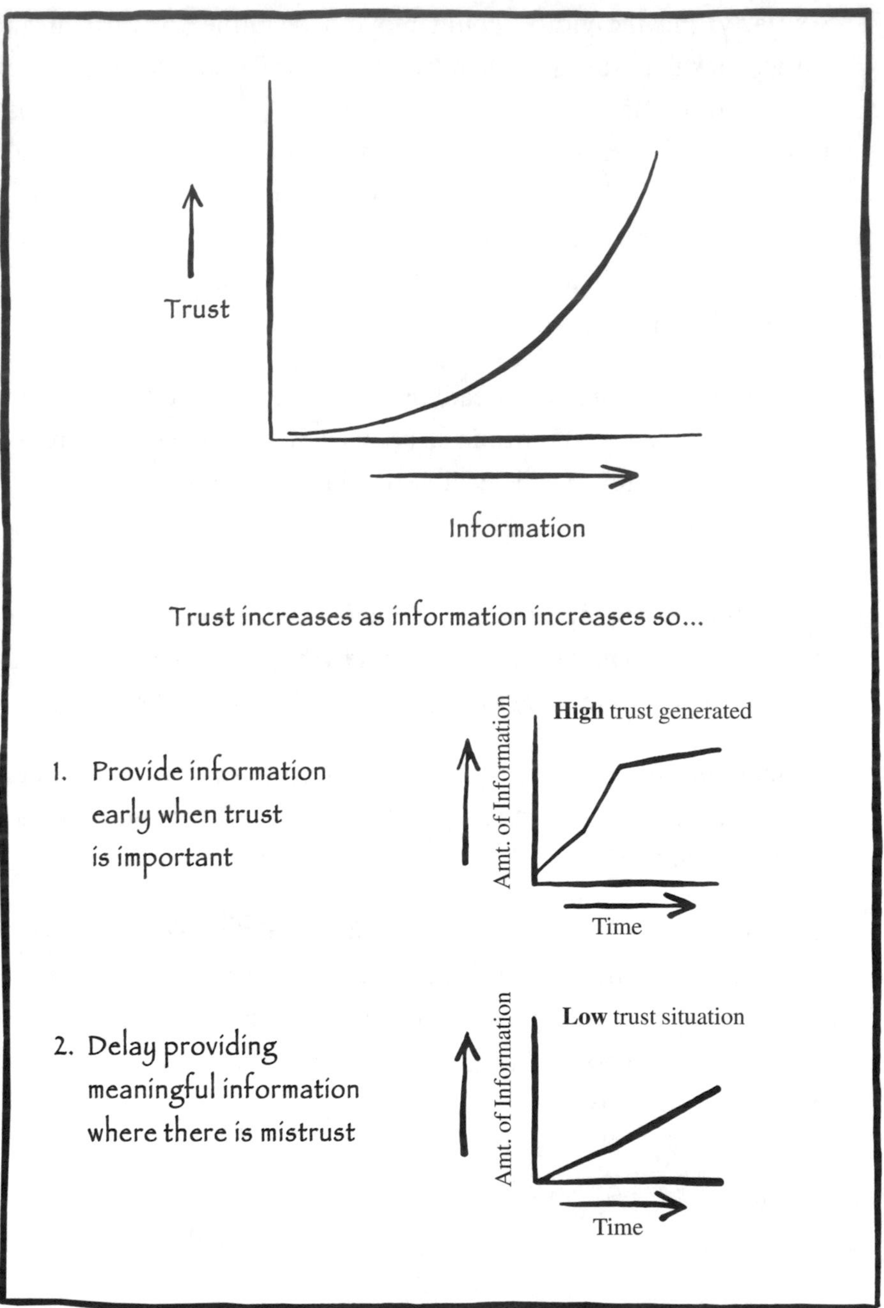
Trust
Information
Trust increases as information increases so...
1. Provide information early when trust is important
High trust generated
Amt. of Information
Time
2. Delay providing meaningful information where there is mistrust
Low trust situation
Amt. of Information
Time

Information is crucial to building trust, and so over time as information passes between the two parties, so does trust. As you seek to persuade others there is great value in managing the flow of information and so the degree of trust that occurs, and thereby your ultimate ability to be persuasive.

Given that trust increases as the information increases, there are two things which you need to focus on if you seek to be more persuasive.

1. ***When it is important to build trust, provide the information early.*** There are times when trust is not a crucial element in being persuasive so that providing information may in fact work against you. However, in those cases where in your judgement you would be more persuasive if there were greater trust between you and the other party, or parties, then there is a need for early information *flow*. I emphasize the word flow because the information must flow both ways. If all you do is provide information, and receive none in return, then there is no *mutual* trust established, which is a poor foundation for long-term trust and the persuasion that follows.

   When you are providing information it needs to be provided in "bite size" bits and not all at once. Trust is generated when information is exchanged and so there should be a constant flow of "packets" back and forth until ultimately all the packets are delivered. If this information flow happens early, well in advance of the deadline, then there is strong trust and clarity on both sides regarding the information relative to the issues at hand. This then allows you to be more effective, given that the other party will now have a greater degree of trust in your point of view and subsequent conclusions.

"Trust increases
as the amount of
information shared
increases."

2. ***In the case where there is mistrust initially, then adding additional information may only serve to fuel that, as it will also be mistrusted.*** In this case information should be delayed and not provided as early. Wait until the issue that generated the mistrust is addressed. Information relative to illuminating and eliminating the mistrust is good and should be provided to address the problem of mistrust.

   In low trust situations attempt to provide whatever information you can, and elicit whatever's possible from the other party, to move from a sense of mistrust to one of trust. Then you are in a position where you can provide additional information to now rebuild trust; which will in turn allow you to be persuasive.

Because information is indeed power, providing it to another gives them power, and receiving it gives you power. However, with this transfer of power is also a transfer of trust, and as individuals come to trust you increasingly, then it will be easier for you to persuade them to accept your point of view. Use this information flow judiciously and appropriately to achieve the objective.

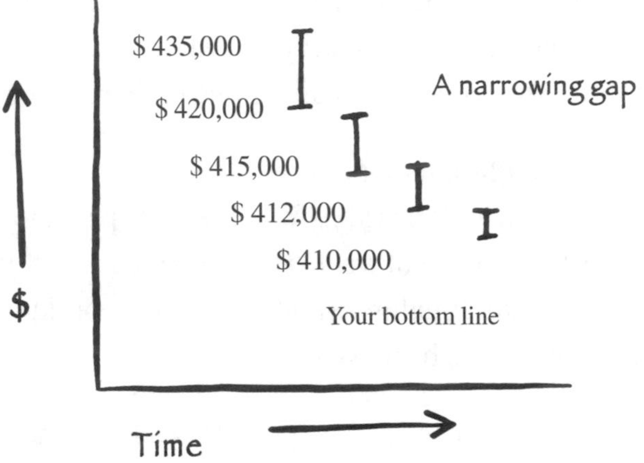

Your early indications should be consistent with your final desired outcome, so...

1. Control the content of your information, to signal your final intent early on

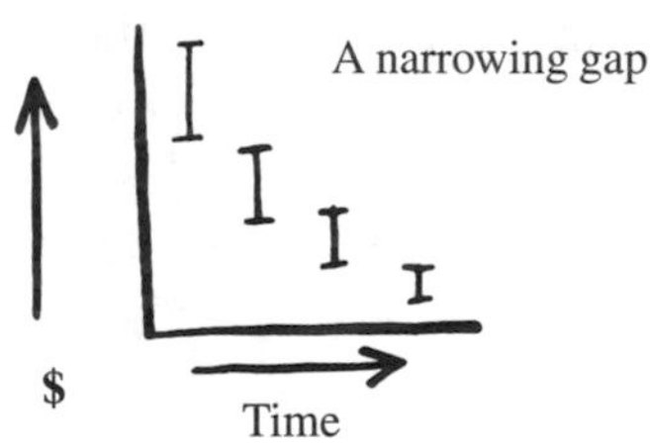

2. Allow adequate time for the final intent to be "predictable" (and so more acceptable)

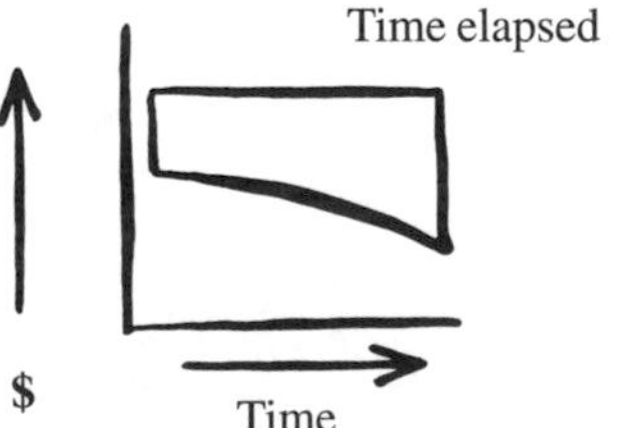

PERSUASION: THE IMPORTANCE OF PREDICTABILITY

When persuading others it is important to understand what their final position is likely to be, as well as to send signals regarding what your final position is likely to be. For example if you are negotiating the sale of a house, you would not start with a first price of $500,000 and then jump to a price of $100,000, because the buyer would feel as though you were either untrustworthy, trying to gouge them initially, or trying to unload something with which there is a serious problem!

Rather, you would start at a price which you hope to get, and then slowly move down to your bottom line, the lowest price which you could afford to take. This is a narrowing gap, and the rate at which the gap is narrowing is an indication of your final position. If you were to start at $500,000, narrow to $498,000, and then $497,500, it's pretty clear that you don't intend to move too far off the original $500,000, because the gap is not narrowing significantly over time.

"You need to ensure
that your early
indications are consistent
with your
final desired outcome."

Within the context of your communication with others, you need to ensure that your early indications are consistent with your final desired outcome as you seek to persuade them to adopt your point of view. There are two things on which to focus in attempting to achieve this.

1. ***Control the content of your information so that you signal your final intent early.*** If you are proposing something radical, but are willing to come off that position to something more conventional as long as you get agreement, then in your early efforts to persuade move from the radical to the conventional in reasonable and predictable steps.

   If on the other hand you are unwilling to move from the radical but are willing to make minor modifications or "tweak" it, then signal that early on in your discussions by holding to the more radical stance.

   The key objective is to ensure that early in your discussion, as you demonstrate movement from your original position to your final position, you signal your final intent appropriately. Don't jump quickly to the end; nor move so slowly that the individual believes that you are approaching the end, when in fact you are just making one more of your (too) many small steps! Place your position of compromise in an appropriately narrowing gap so that you move from your initial thought to your final thought within a time frame that is acceptable to both parties, and lead them, so to speak, down the path to your final conclusion.

"To be persuasive
you need to be sensitive
to the thinking and
positions of others."

2. ***Often individuals have difficulty moving quickly to a new position,*** a new point of view, a decision, or in response to some change. They need time. Consequently you need to give them this time.

   One of the ways of doing this is to begin with an initial position which is elevated, or more advanced then your final position. As you then move to your final position you allow time for them to come to grips with the new idea, concept, pricing, or whatever is the issue to be considered and assimilated by the other party. *You* are providing the time which *they* require to absorb this suggestion, idea, or position and become accustomed to it.

   If your timing is correct, by the time they have come to grips with the concept it has been presented in a way which they find acceptable. You have modified it over this time period, and so you will then be successful in persuading them of your position.

   Understand that to be persuasive you need to be sensitive to the thinking and positions of others. They are influenced by time, information, and also their own thought patterns. In order to help them, and give them time to align their thought patterns with your intent, ensure that you demonstrate the compromises you are willing to make in a predictable fashion, so that your final intended position is well received and "as predicted."

There must be mutual gain on the side of both parties, so:

1. Ensure there is gain for them

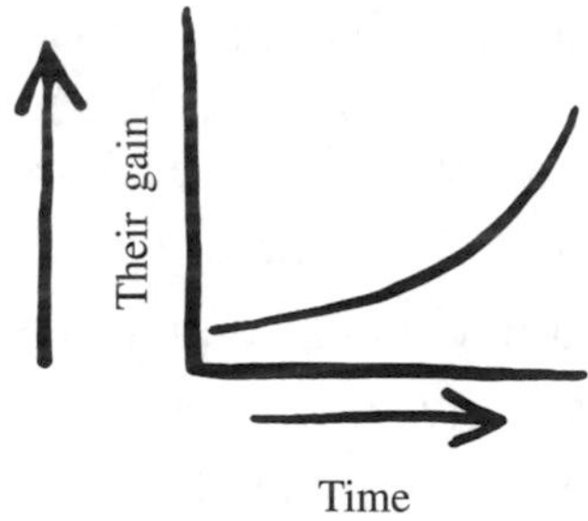

2. "Spell out" the value of this gain

PERSUASION: THE IMPORTANCE OF MUTUAL GAIN

As you seek to persuade others you need to be very mindful of the need for mutual gain. The parties with whom you are dealing will have their own interests, agenda, and desired outcomes. You must bear these in mind.

Mutual gain for both parties allows them, as well as you, to walk away feeling as though this was a successful encounter, and one which they can support and about which they can be enthusiastic. In order to accomplish this you must bear mutual gain in mind.

In order to accomplish this you need to focus on two issues.

1. ***You need to ensure that, over time, as you approach the deadline, that there is gain for them.*** They will naturally be seeking this for themselves, but if you make it a personal priority as well, then you may be in a better position to control the degree of gain, and ensure that it is consistent with your own objectives.

2. ***As they are making gains ensure that you courteously point these out,*** or keep track of them for them. This will serve to reinforce the fact that they are indeed making headway, and that they are achieving their own objectives.

   If, for example, you wish to introduce a certain policy within the organization, and they wish to retain a certain degree of control, then as you point out the various principles of your policy, indicate the way in which they are retaining control, or gaining as a result of the policy. Some of these may appear self-evident or trivial but they are nonetheless important, as they allow you to satisfy their concern about control, and show how your proposed policy addresses these concerns.

"To take your
initiative forward,
be sensitive
to their needs."

PERSUASION: THE IMPORTANCE OF MUTUAL GAIN

In seeking to be persuasive bear in mind the needs of the other side. Take your initiative forward, and attempt to enlist the necessary buy-in, but not in a fashion that forces it on others. Rather, be sensitive to their needs and seek to meet these while at the same time achieving your objective. If you do this you will be significantly more persuasive than with the sledge hammer method.

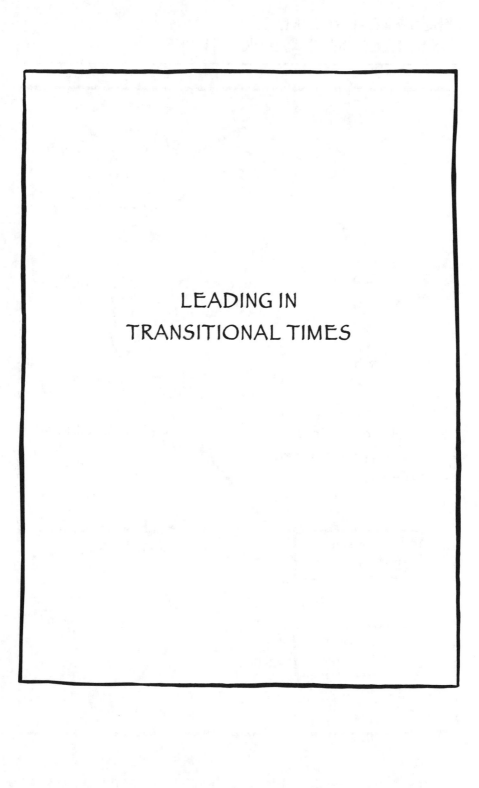

LEADING IN TRANSITIONAL TIMES

KNOW WHERE YOU'RE GOING OR WHERE YOU'RE TAKING OTHERS

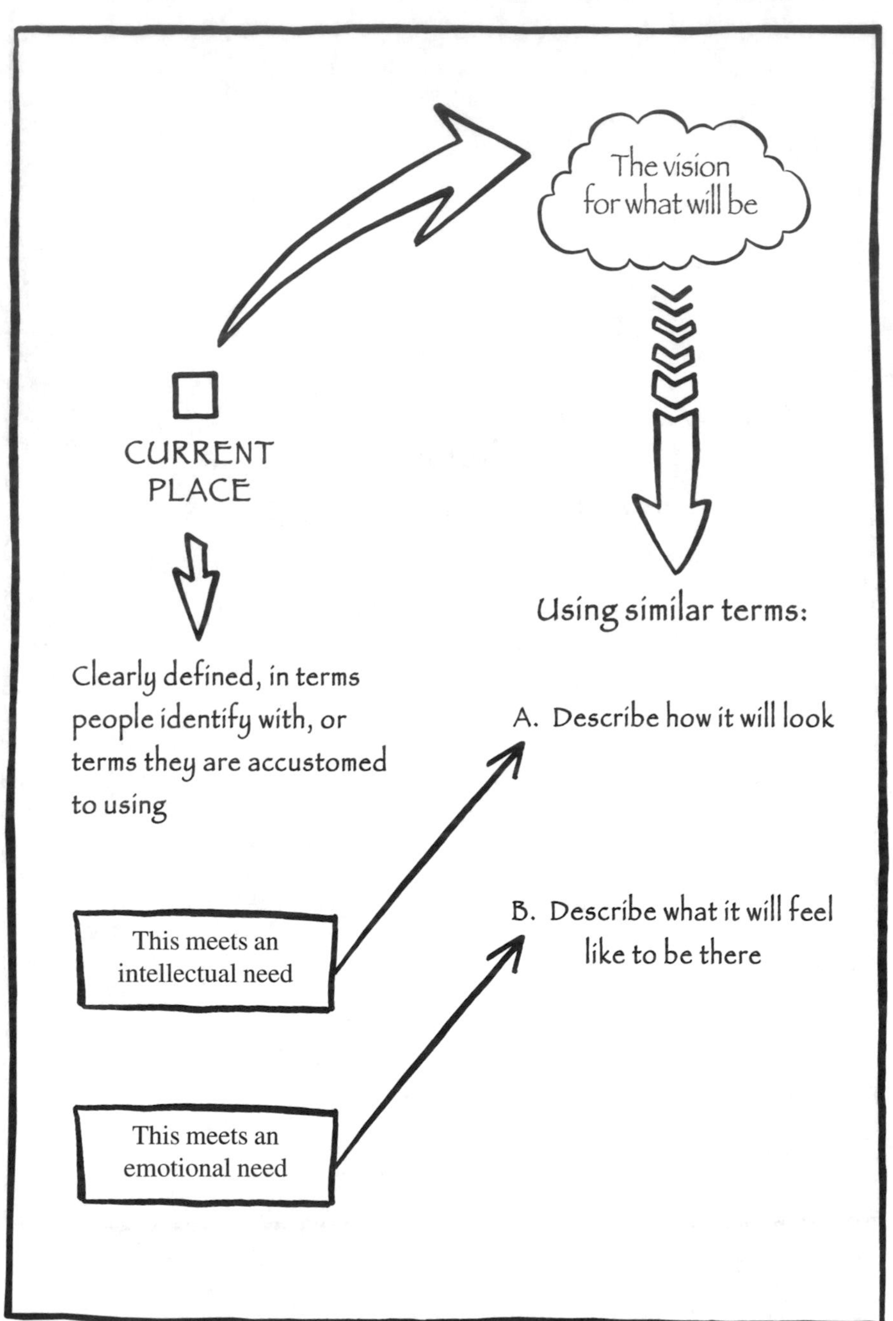

KNOW WHERE YOU'RE GOING OR WHERE YOU'RE TAKING OTHERS

It's important to explain to people exactly where they're going. This creates a comfort in them, as well as allowing them to get their thoughts and energy focused in the desired direction.

The first step to accomplishing this is a clear statement of where we are now. In the case of someone about to climb a mountain, it's obvious that "we're now at the bottom and we're going to the top." However, in the course of day-to-day activity it's often not so clear!

A clear statement should also include some form of measurement if at all possible. For example: in a competitive situation one might describe the current position as, "Market leader with a forty one percent share;" or in a non-profit service area, one might the describe the current position as, "Being not well known with donations coming in from six percent of the local community."

Sometimes the current position is extremely bad, but is not realized to be so. In that case it's insufficient to simply make clear the current position; you also must create *dissatisfaction* with the current position, otherwise people may be unwilling to move in a new direction.

Once the current position is clear, the statement of where you're going, and a description of what it will be like when you arrive there, becomes crucial. This excites people, and provides motivation for movement; it also provides clarity for people, which allows focus for individual activity and energy.

When making it clear where you're going, it's important to describe the finished product; for example, "We will have thirty-seven percent market share," preferably using the same terms and measurements that were used to describe the current position.

"The act of describing
what it will feel like when you
arrive at your destination
helps people to share
your vision, and understand
why it is so important
to move from
the current position."

This has the added benefit of allowing you to track progress using the same measures with which people are already familiar, until you ultimately achieve the desired objective. Measures don't have to be in numbers all the time, they can be qualitative such as "morale," "how we feel," and "satisfaction."

The act of describing what it will feel like when you arrive at your destination helps people to share your vision and understand why it is so important to move from the current position. When they understand that: "When we get there we will be able to celebrate our position as market leader, with enough revenue to begin to invest in the future and therefore not only create new products but also provide a greater measure of job security," then they can get really excited about the outcome. It is often not that easy to articulate what the final position will feel like, but the leader's responsibility is to spend enough time doing so that those who hear the message can identify with the outcome.

Describing how it will look in quantitative and measured terms, preferably the ones used to describe the current position, satisfies the intellectual need for clarity. Describing what it will feel like satisfies the emotional need, which is crucial to really harnessing enthusiasm.

This same principle applies when providing direction within a family. The present situation could be the need to clean the garage. The statement of the current position is one which outlines the difficulty of parking the car, and the mess caused by the bicycles, the skis and all the junk on the floor. A description of the finished product would describe racks for the skis, hooks for the bicycles, and a clean floor, etc. The greater the detail, the better. This helps everyone to share the vision for the finished product, and allows them to work towards achievement of that goal.

WHEN COMMUNICATING VISION, BRING BOTH INTELLECT AND PASSION (EMOTION) TO BEAR

Intellect and passion are two great forces which can be harnessed to influence outcomes.

They are very different, and so need to be handled differently. However, don't neglect one simply because the other is "your strength."

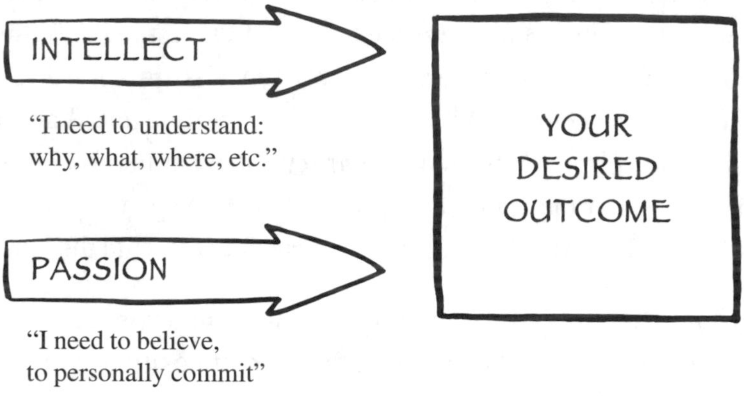

INTELLECT

"I need to understand: why, what, where, etc."

PASSION

"I need to believe, to personally commit"

YOUR DESIRED OUTCOME

WHEN COMMUNICATING VISION, BRING BOTH INTELLECT AND PASSION (EMOTION) TO BEAR

You're about to sit down to a beautifully prepared, piping hot dinner of your favorite meal when the phone rings. Just before that first bite is taken you replace the fork, rise and answer the phone. You hear an individual with an opening line something like this, "I apologize for calling you at dinner time but I wanted to be sure to get you in – would you care to buy some light bulbs?" Chances are at this point you are rather distressed, say, "NO!", hang up forcefully, and return to your now somewhat colder meal.

Replay the above scenario right up to the phone call when, instead of the description above, the voice says, "Hi son. Your father just fell and I think he's broken his arm. Could you come over and drive us to the hospital?" In this case chances are all thoughts of the meal vanish and you are immediately galvanized into action, with no distress at having your dinner interrupted.

The difference between the first and second scenario is the degree of personal emotion involved.

In the first case there was no emotional involvement with the light bulb seller, and in fact probably a greater emotional attachment to eating your dinner! In the second scenario, the strong emotional tie to your mother calling with an immediate and pressing need overrode any concern for the dinner.

Recognize the incredible power to direct and motivate action which is harnessed when one engages the emotions of others. When providing direction and focus for future activity be sure to do it in such a way that it involves the *emotions* of those whom you are asking to participate. This allows them to personally commit to the outcome.

WHEN COMMUNICATING VISION, BRING BOTH INTELLECT AND PASSION (EMOTION) TO BEAR

"Recognize the
incredible power to direct
and motivate action
which is harnessed when
one engages the
emotions of others."

WHEN COMMUNICATING VISION, BRING BOTH INTELLECT AND PASSION (EMOTION) TO BEAR

However, enthusiastic passion does not address the basic questions of what, where, when, and why. Doing that is also important, as without a clear statement of the outcome, the commitment roused by emotion can easily be lost.

This is often seen in volunteer organizations where the volunteers are highly committed to the task at hand, or the organization, or it's values, or it's impact on society. However, because the leaders are not skilled in clear communication or the establishment of readily understood objectives, much of the time of that volunteer army is wasted. People can often be seen standing around trying to decide what to do next; or they're involved in tasks which have relatively low pay-back compared to other pressing needs – of which they are often unaware. At times large numbers of people committed to a task are poorly organized and so can *impede* the overall progress by inadvertently "tripping over one another."

These problems can be readily eliminated by providing a very clear understanding of what is to be accomplished, by when, how, and where. The level of detail needed to provide this clarity depends upon the individual circumstances, but thought needs to be given to ensure the detail is appropriate if the emotional commitment is to be fully utilized.

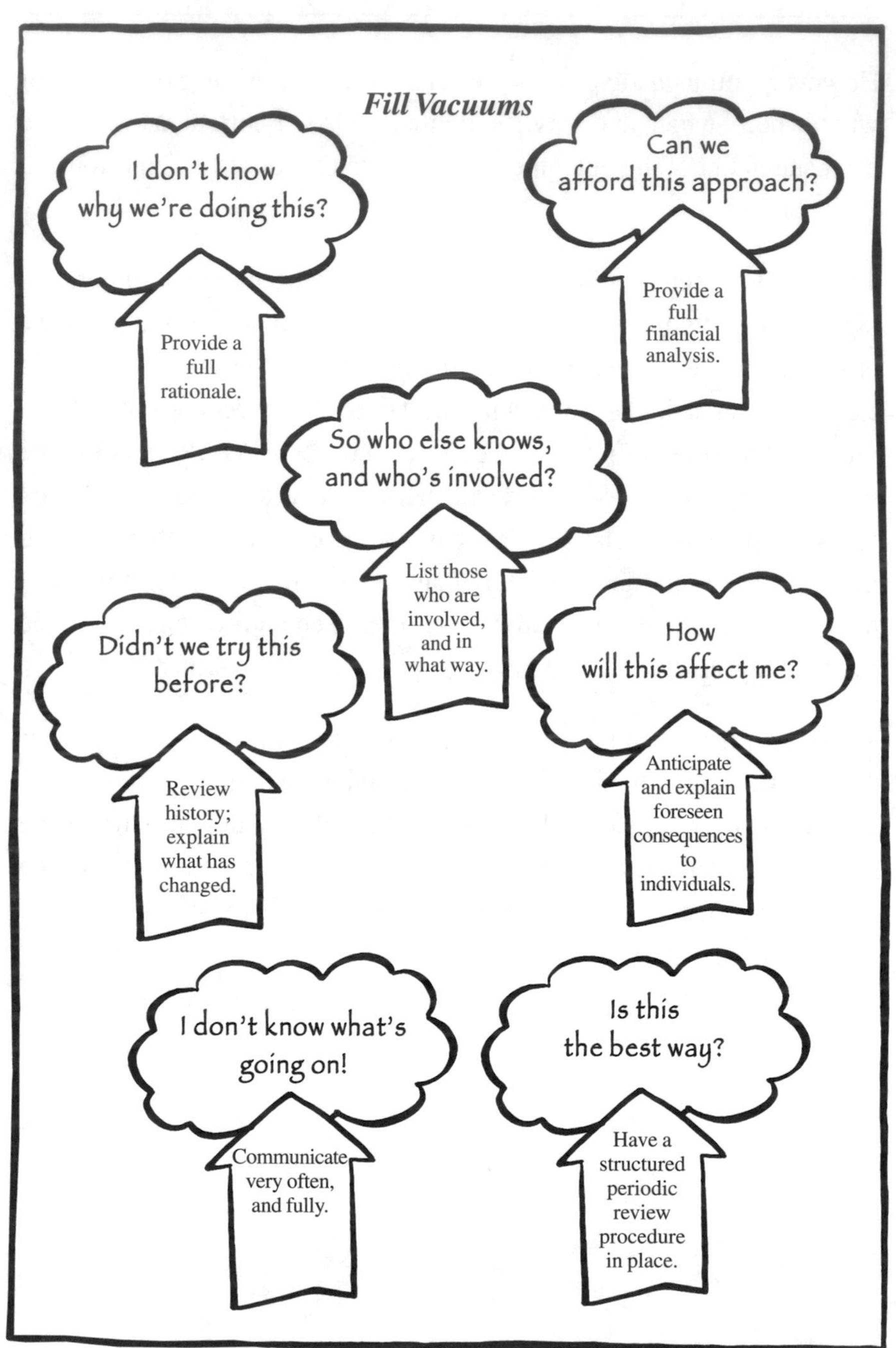
Fill Vacuums
I don't know why we're doing this?
Provide a full rationale.
Can we afford this approach?
Provide a full financial analysis.
So who else knows, and who's involved?
List those who are involved, and in what way.
Didn't we try this before?
Review history; explain what has changed.
How will this affect me?
Anticipate and explain foreseen consequences to individuals.
I don't know what's going on!
Communicate very often, and fully.
Is this the best way?
Have a structured periodic review procedure in place.

HOW TO GET THE INTELLECT ENGAGED

For an individual to be logically or intellectually committed to a direction which you are presenting requires that you proactively identify what answers they may require.

It's difficult to commit to something that is not well understood, or which leaves you with several unanswered questions. These questions and lack of understanding in key areas are "knowledge vacuums" which create uncertainty and tentativeness in the minds of those you are leading. As a result, the individual tends to fill these vacuums with supposition, diverting commitment away from the objective while attempting to deal with these vacuums.

The solution is to ensure that outstanding clarity and understanding exists, thereby eliminating the vacuum and allowing the people to focus their entire energy on the task at hand.

Seven examples of these knowledge vacuums, and how to fill them, follow:

1. ***"I don't know why we're doing this?"*** – The *rationale* for the activity needs to be provided *in full*, so that the person has a chance to really appreciate the significance of the goal or challenge that lies ahead.

2. ***"How will this affect me?"*** – Individuals are very concerned about the impact of activities and decisions upon them personally. If this is clarified up front it allows energy to be focused on the task, by providing calm, and an appreciation of how the outcome will affect the individual involved.

3. ***"Is this the best way?"*** – Often the approach initiated will undergo several alterations in the time that follows. The best way to capitalize on the ability of the people involved to make meaningful contributions is to have a structured process review procedure in place that allows them to present their ideas for improvement.

"For an individual to
be logically or intellectually
committed to a direction
which you are presenting
requires that you
proactively identify what
answers they may require."

4. ***"Can we afford this approach?"*** – As we move to more and more responsibility in the work place, people have a greater appreciation of the financial cost of activities and are more involved in questioning to ensure there is a sound financial basis for the activity. In order to nurture these questions, while at the same time providing confidence that the approach is fiscally responsible, a simple approach is to share with the entire group whatever financial analysis preceded the decision, to allow them the benefit of understanding the financial viability of an enterprise.

5. ***"So who else knows and who's involved?"*** – Often in the course of day-to-day urgencies we fail to make clear who else is involved, and what are their activities and responsibilities. This breeds misunderstanding, speculation, and promotes rumor. A more effective approach is to make clear to all involved who else is influencing the outcome and in what way. This has the added benefit of promoting cross-functional communication and idea sharing while building a common team with a common vision.

6. ***"Didn't we try this before?"*** – In cases where an activity or initiative has its roots in something similar which may have preceded it, individuals may feel that a previous failure will ensure future failure. At this point it's important to review the history and explain how the current approach differs from the initial efforts, and what specifically has changed – even if it's only the people involved – and so provide the rationale for why it is felt that this next effort has a greater chance of success.

7. ***"I don't know what's going on?"*** – As projects begin, the high quality communication with which they were begun can often deteriorate, and so an increasing sense of "being out of touch" develops. It's important throughout any initiative or process to communicate completely, frequently and openly.

Getting the emotion engaged requires:

1. Speaking with:
   Passion, Eloquence and Conviction

2. Painting a vivid mental picture

3. And thereby presenting the foreseen significance (both personal and organizational) of this achievement

HOW TO GET THE EMOTION ENGAGED

Emotion, unlike the intellect, is far less influenced by facts, and much more so by pictures.

For example, if the objective is to lose weight, the intellect can be harnessed by designing programs, counting calories, quoting statistics on life expectancy, taking measurements, etc. But these often have little impact by themselves in spurring motivation. The emotion can be harnessed by meeting for lunch once a week with a slim fit individual who is passionate about the joy of exercise, and excited about the personal benefits in terms of feeling good and having more energy. The emotion can also be harnessed by visualizing a new outfit, or going shopping for new clothes a size smaller, or looking back at photo albums before the additional weight was added, and so creating within the mind a desire for a certain look, and level of fitness.

If the emotion can be harnessed to *want* a certain state or objective, and be persuaded that the achievement of this state is possible, that powerful emotional component can then be brought to bear on the outcome. Leaders who are presenting an objective or vision must communicate emotion clearly. Explanations need to be passionate, eloquent, and spoken with conviction. A vivid mental picture needs to be painted of the final outcome. This "painting of a mental picture" requires digressing from facts, figures, and statements to attempting to paint in the listener's mind, in vivid colour, the image and power of the vision once achieved. If people can fully picture it for themselves, in considerable detail, with a personal appreciation of the power of that vision, then their emotion can be completely engaged.

"A vivid
mental picture needs
to be painted
of the final outcome."

HOW TO GET THE EMOTION ENGAGED

The third element (after passionate communication and creating a vivid mental image) is to make very clear the foreseen significance of success. For example, a team of social workers assisting the elderly need to understand the personal difference that can be made in the lives of those elderly people, the satisfaction which members of the team will personally derive, and the sense of worth which can be rekindled in the seniors as the result of the work of the team. Telling anecdotes from previous experiences with seniors, for example, will go a long way to helping people appreciate the significance of the activities in which they are about to embark.

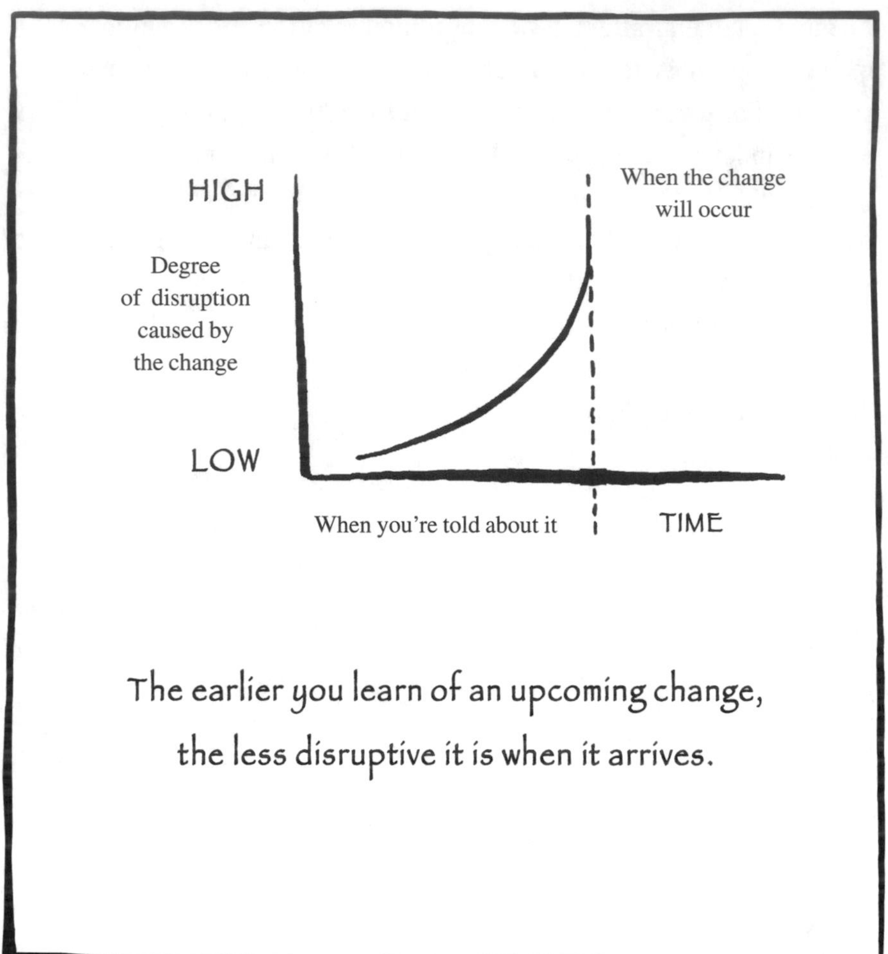
HIGH
Degree
of disruption
caused by
the change
LOW
When the change
will occur
When you're told about it
TIME
The earlier you learn of an upcoming change,
the less disruptive it is when it arrives.

In a world of change, especially today's world where the change is so fast paced, managing change seems always a challenge, a mystery, and something which is difficult to do.

Managing change can be made much, much simpler by understanding the importance of communication within the change process.

The reason change is so important to manage is that it affects people. But if it's not properly managed then the impact is often negative on those impacted, resulting in the corresponding loss of productivity or performance. When change is properly managed then people are excited about it, and can enthusiastically support it and the anticipated benefits to the organization.

One of the most powerful ways of managing change is understanding the role of communication. Usually leaders already have the information required to effectively manage change within the organization. And if they don't have the information, they are in a position to obtain it. *How* this information is used, and *when*, determines the degree to which change will be effectively managed in the eyes of those who follow the leader.

Change inevitably causes disruption – that is, change requires that people behave or respond differently from the way to which they have become accustomed. It is the anticipated change in behavior that often causes anxiety. They are not sure what is expected from them, what the impact will be on them, how they will then have to react, what new behavioral patterns they will have to set down, and what the consequences of the changes in the behavior of others will mean to them. Inevitably, once the change has occurred, over time these things are better understood and people adapt and a sense of normalcy returns.

"The earlier the information
is communicated, with
as much detail as possible,
the better the change
will be accommodated by
those affected.
The greater the detail the more
effective the communication."

MANAGING CHANGE – THE ROLE OF COMMUNICATION

Given that change will cause disruption, the degree of this disruption can be minimized with early communication. Individuals who are notified well in advance of a pending change, and preferably with a considerable amount of detail regarding the nature of the change and its impact, will have two responses:

1. Given the fact that the change is a long way away they will feel as though it has little impact on them at present, and so will neither be threatened nor disrupted. "It's out there in the future, it doesn't affect me now." But in fact, knowing that change is coming, they will begin almost subconsciously to take small steps in anticipation of the change.

   The earlier the information is communicated, with as much detail as possible, the better the change will be accommodated by those affected. The greater the detail the more effective the communication.

2. As the change comes nearer, their level of anxiety will continue to be low given that the unknown has become known. Rather than speculating, worrying about what will be, and imagining the worst, they will know what will be in place and begin to make mental shifts accordingly.

   Over time as the change event occurs, if constant and comprehensive communication is occurring on a regular basis, then the transition from the old to the new will be relatively seamless, rather than perceived as "change."

   Needless to say the fundamentals of good communication must be in place, such as getting and receiving feedback, and responding to individual needs and requests.

"The effective
management of change
is a two-way process with
both parties
carrying responsibility
for the outcome."

Imagine a supervisor coming to you and requesting that they attend a change management course. On asking why, they inform you that they just learned that in the next week two of the six people in their department will be moved to another location, and that many of the systems on which they had depended were going to be upgraded. Both they, and the people for whom they are responsible, need help responding to the degree of disruption that this change was going to create and they feel that a day at a course would be of help.

If you were to ask how long they had known that these events were going to occur, and they said they had just found out about the detail, but had "heard rumors" six months ago that "something was coming" (as is usually the case), then a "managing change" course is not the answer.

If the individual responsible for that department had met with this supervisor six months earlier and told them *at that time* that new systems were coming, and that two individuals were going to be moved to another department in six months, then they could have made the necessary provisions. They could have talked to the two individuals and helped them address the day-to-day impact on their lives (commuting, sense of job security, new duties, etc.); and they could have begun to prepare their staff for the new systems by initiating training for them in advance of their arrival. None of this happened. As a result they saw the change as disruptive.

"Managing change
can be made much, much
simpler by understanding
the importance of
communication within
the change process."

Had it happened as it should have, then the events would not have been seen as "change," they would not have needed a "change management course," and they would have effectively managed the transition of a growing and dynamic environment.

Clearly the manager who knew what was coming would be at fault for failing to communicate early enough. But the supervisor would also be at fault in that they should have pushed harder for more information, seeking to get clarity behind the "rumors" in order to proactively take the initiative and thereby avoid the disruption which they were now facing.

This is also illustrative of the truth that the effective management of change, and in fact all management, is a two-way process with both parties carrying responsibility for the outcome.

MANAGING CHANGE – RESPONDING TO INFORMATION

Use early notification and reap the benefits of minimizing the negative impact of change.

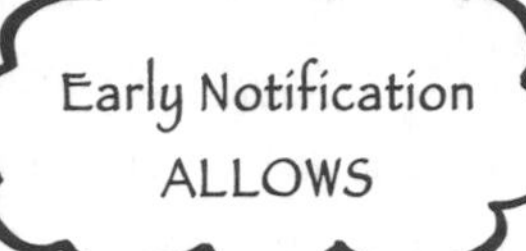

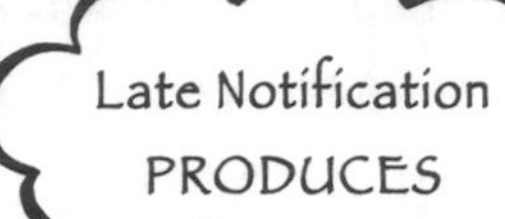

- Time for understanding the rationale
- Time to prepare
- Opportunity for Q & A
- Opportunity to adjust
- Time for personal buy-in to occur
- Proactive responses

- Panic
- Uncertainty
- Personal disengagement
- Rejection
- Rumor
- Reactive – and often expensive – responses

If communication is provided early, in advance of the change process, then there are considerable benefits.

Individuals have time to understand the rationale for change, to probe, to question, and ultimately to understand why that change will in fact occur. Concurrently with this understanding is the opportunity to contribute to the upcoming change, adding their bank of knowledge and experience, resulting perhaps in a smoother and more effective transition than would have been the case if it had simply "come down from the mountain."

Individuals need time to absorb new information. They also need time to question, ponder, and allow that information to germinate and bring its own fruit to the surface. Allowing people to "become accustomed" to a new idea, its rationale, and the anticipated consequences goes a long way towards minimizing the negative impact of change.

In addition, providing new information allows individuals to prepare. Often this preparation is physical: moving desks or furniture, acquiring some training, or establishing new relationships within the organization. However the preparation time can also be used mentally: to become accustomed to the idea, to probe and appreciate its value, and predict the positive impact the change will make on their own personal lives.

Advance notification provides opportunity for ongoing dialogue and debate. Questions and answers can flow freely. The debate is not about the decision, but rather about understanding why the decision was made and how best to implement it. Often this kind of question and answer discussion brings to light unanticipated consequences of the change which can then be dealt with in advance, thereby smoothing the transition.

"Allowing people
to 'become accustomed'
to a new idea and the
corresponding rationale
goes a long way
towards minimizing the
negative impact of change."

Picture yourself responsible for an office move and adopting this communication approach. As a result of the questions which would come you may uncover several unforeseen issues, such as, for example not having enough printers per square foot. Perhaps the previous office had a different floor plan from the new one and the intent was to simply bring the old printers to the new space without reference to the new floor plan. In the new office the number of printers would have been inadequate. True, you would have discovered that fact within three to four weeks of moving in, but by having a discussion in advance with the potential users you could avoid additional disruption during those three to four weeks, and so help to sustain the productivity.

When individuals are aware of what is coming they have the opportunity to mentally adjust, and to buy-in personally. Often new ideas are greeted with skepticism and disengagement by the hearers. Not everyone enthusiastically jumps into a new concept immediately. But when time is given to consider the new information, and the opportunity provided to see others excited about the change, and time allowed to personally understand it, then individual buy-in will grow until finally, at the time of the change, the majority of those affected are committed to its success.

If individuals do not find out about a change in advance then they can only react. If they find out in advance then they can proactively initiate, make suggestions, and take action. People much prefer to be involved in a process than to be passive recipients able only to respond to the outcome.

If these guidelines are not followed, and notification of upcoming change occurs at or near the time of the change itself, then a number of negative responses will be generated among those who are affected.

"If individuals are not told about a change in advance, then they can only react. If they find out in advance they can then proactively initiate, make suggestions, and take action."

Often a sense of panic sets in, which, although muted, is still there, and stems from people losing a sense of security and foundation. They no longer know how they or their behavior will fit into the new scheme. Their world around them is changing and they do not know how to change with it, and as a result have a sense of the "loss of one's moorings," which generates panic as individuals lose sight of their reference points.

When change is occurring without clarification of the rationale for the change, or the detail associated with it, uncertainty develops and grows. People can no longer predict the future with some certainty, and as a result grow apprehensive and nervous. They begin to spend time attempting to gain certainty in the changing world. Not only does this cause unnecessary anxiety but it is unproductive.

Individuals who have not been consulted tend to disengage. They tend to sit back and take the attitude of "Well, they made the decision; let's see if they can make it work." This does not mean that individuals will stop working, it just means that their commitment, their personal conviction that a given approach is vital and must work, is lost. To lose the engagement of a team, or even an individual, is to lose greatly in initiative, innovation, and productivity.

Very often late notification of change results in almost reflexive rejection. Inevitably they do not have the option of rejecting it corporately, but internally in their heart of hearts they have rejected the idea and therefore they are doing nothing to ensure its success. They've been ignored until the last minute and now are expected to respond enthusiastically. This is very difficult for most people to do, and as a result they reject the idea as poor, whether or not it is. They are really rejecting the fact that they have not been consulted and so believe they are deemed to be of little value.

"Individuals
need time to absorb
new information."

Rumor abounds in the absence of fact, and when notification is not provided early and clearly, then a natural consequence is that rumor will step in to fill the vacuum left by lack of information. Concurrently with this people will then respond to whatever rumors they hear, which will often have no relevance or reference to the truth. This can create expensive, and often totally unanticipated and unnecessary disruption to the organization.

In order to ensure that change occurs seamlessly, provide early notification!

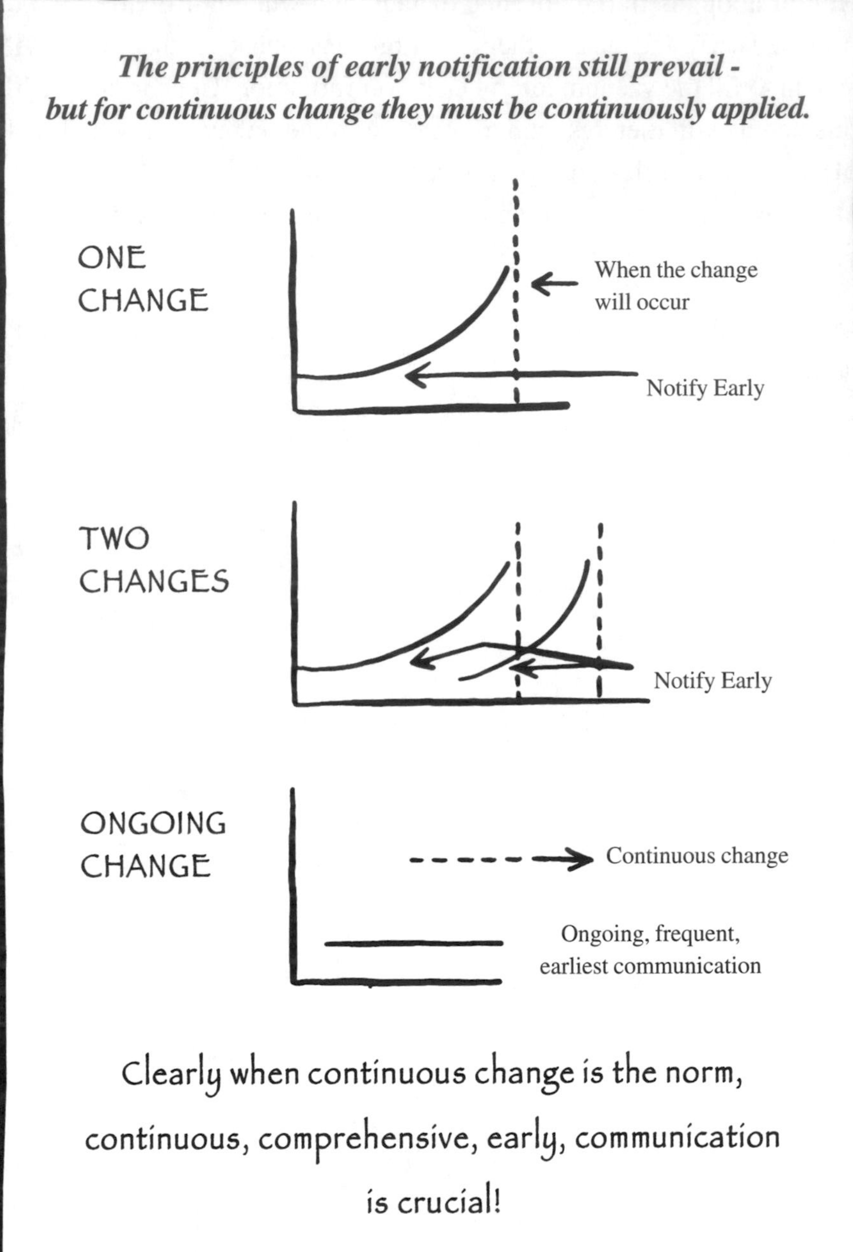
The principles of early notification still prevail -
but for continuous change they must be continuously applied.
ONE CHANGE
When the change will occur
Notify Early
TWO CHANGES
Notify Early
ONGOING CHANGE
Continuous change
Ongoing, frequent, earliest communication
Clearly when continuous change is the norm, continuous, comprehensive, early, communication is crucial!

MANAGING CHANGE – WHEN CHANGE IS CONTINUOUS

We previously discussed managing a change by early notification. However there are times when the organization is not faced with a single change event but rather with several events, or even sustained continuous change. In either of these cases the principles remain the same.

When there is more than one single event, say perhaps two or three, each needs to be treated as a separate event with the appropriate up-front early notification and communication occurring for each. Care must be taken not to confuse the people involved by running all the communications together; if we do so, people may then be unable to distinguish which communication applies to which event!

If there are two or more distinct change events occurring, then identify them, perhaps with a project name, or by location, or manager responsible. Provide each with a "key-word" so that individuals can immediately connect the communication with the change event being discussed. Colored paper can also serve to support this kind of clear communication.

Individuals need to understand what you are talking about. When there are several continuous events, each one representing a change to the norm, and all occurring simultaneously, the opportunity for confusion and misunderstanding is great.

Once clarity is established concerning which communication relates to which change initiative, then the same guidelines as in the previous pages apply.

"Comprehensive communication that is provided early is the key to gaining employee commitment."

At one time I was initiating half a dozen major changes to Human Resources policies and procedures, and failed to distinguish one from the other. Over the course of about eight months the organization received what they called a "blizzard" of memos from me regarding Human Resources. I felt they were responding poorly to my initiatives. In seeking to understand why, I realized that the initiatives were all blurred together in the minds of the recipients and so they were unable to separate one from the other.

Initially their comments seemed unfair to me, since the changes were all so clear in my own mind. I could not possibly understand how anybody could fail to see each change as clear and distinct. However I realized that each individual within the organization had their own priorities and urgencies, and as a result were not nearly as conversant with my area of responsibility as I was. I had failed to transmit the clarity which I saw out into the organization, as a result each additional piece of communication only served to muddy the waters still more, resulting in the sense that people were being "snowed under" with "stuff" from Human Resources.

Once I realized this it was easy to rectify. I provided the organization with a template that clearly outlined each of the initiatives in its own box. Then all subsequent communication carried a copy of that template with the appropriate box highlighted so they could immediately pigeon hole information around the change initiative into the appropriate compartment.

"If there are two or more distinct
change events occurring,
then identify them, distinctly
so that individuals can immediately
connect the communication
with the change
event being discussed."

Within a matter of weeks much of the confusion was cleared up and I had discovered a valuable tool for the following years, which allowed me to continually build on each separate initiative without loss of focus. The organization appreciated it, less disruptive response occurred, and the change initiatives succeeded.

Extrapolating this further to circumstances where there are not a series of change events but rather ongoing change, the principles of proactive communication still apply. The organization needs to be provided with continuous comprehensive and early communication. In effect an atmosphere of continuous change is simply one large change project and needs to be treated as such. If change is seen as sustained over a number of years then communication concerning this change must be focused, and a priority. Ongoing continuous sustained change requires ongoing, continuous and sustained communication, providing the organization with as much advance information and notification as possible.

If a large sustained change initiative can be broken into component parts, as I did with the HR initiative outlined above, then this might also help retain the necessary focus. In either case comprehensive communication that is provided early is the key to gaining employee commitment.

MANAGING CHANGE – THE ELEMENTS OF EARLY COMMUNICATION

If the manager, supervisor, or leader does not provide this content, those affected should proactively seek it out, and as early as possible.

PROVIDE:

1. DETAILS re: TIMING
   When will it occur?

2. SPECIFICS ON CONTENT
   What changes are expected?

3. IMPACT ON PEOPLE
   Who will be affected?

4. PERSONAL CONSEQUENCES FORESEEN
   How will I have to change?

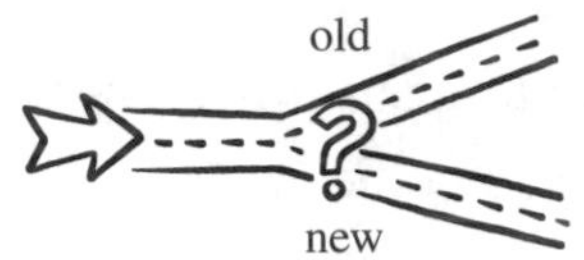

5. RATIONALE FOR THE CHANGE
   Why is this happening?

6. ACCESS TO RESOURCES
   Where do I go for help, tools, with questions, with suggestions, etc?

7. VISIBLE, AVAILABLE LEADERSHIP

MANAGING CHANGE – THE ELEMENTS OF EARLY COMMUNICATION

Once the commitment has been made to use proactive early communication as a primary vehicle to help the organization respond effectively to change, there are seven specific elements which then need to be included.

1. ***Timing:*** The organization needs to determine, in precise detail, the timing of any particular change event.

   Clearly this assumes that the change will take place at a given time; for example: "The old computers will be replaced with new computers next Monday," or "Harry will move to another department on May 3rd." Larger change initiatives that do not occur at a point in time but rather over a longer time frame need to have that information communicatcd as well.

2. ***Content:*** Exactly what is to happen, and how things will change, needs to be spelled out. This is an opportunity to provide the organization with the information they require regarding whether things will look differently, and if so in what way.

3. ***People:*** "Who will be affected?" "How will they be affected?" "What difference will it make to their present responsibilities, and even possibly to their future career?" Answering questions such as this as it relates to people is crucial. Again it's important to include everyone and not fall into the trap of including only those who are "senior." Everyone affected by the change has an equally valid interest in knowing how the change will affect them. Individuals also want to know how change will affect their colleagues, and to the degree that you can provide this information without violating confidentiality, or personal situations, this should also be included.

"When an individual understands why a certain initiative is occurring it is much easier for them to become personally committed to the outcome; consequently communication concerning change must include a solid and comprehensive rationale."

4. ***Consequences:*** In addition to knowing how the change will affect each individual they will also wish to know what the consequences will be. That is, once they are clear on what the change will mean to them, they will wish to know how they will have to respond to that, and change their own behaviors. They may, for example, need to operate out of a different geographical location, with a different computer system, under a different leader, with a different set of values, or with a different set of priorities. They will want to know what specific behavioral changes they should expect as a result of this change. This is particularly important as individuals recognize that assessment of their performance is dependent on their ability to meet the expectations that are placed on them, and so early notification of what the expectation will be allows them to prepare, and as a result maximize their level of performance.

5. ***Rationale:*** Many times people will be told what will occur, but not why it will occur. Being told what will happen is very important in allowing people to set clear goals and take the logical next steps. However, knowing why it happening allows people to go beyond goals to personal commitment. The 'why' is what provides the vision for the activity.

   When an individual understands why a certain initiative is occurring it is much easier for them to become personally committed to the outcome; consequently communication about change must include solid and comprehensive rationale.

"Throughout the process leading up to the change, or during the change if it is an ongoing one, leadership must be visible. People take confidence in seeing their leaders and observing how they themselves are responding to the coming changes."

6. ***Access:*** As a result of effective communication, inevitably additional questions will arise. People want to know where to go for help, further clarification, or even specific training in anticipation of the change. Clearly defined routes of access need to be made available to everyone.

   Sometimes the access point can be the individual's immediate supervisor, sometimes it is the new supervisor coming in as a result of the change. Often other support areas within the organization, such as Human Resources or Internal Communication, can be identified as key access points; if the change initiative is large enough then an individual or department can even be set up to coordinate change, and field questions and requests from employees.

7. ***Leadership:*** Leaders need to be visible and available throughout a change initiative. Ideally communication occurs first in face-to-face form and then in written form. Written text should only serve to supplement or augment earlier communication that has occurred at a personal level.

   Throughout the process leading up to the change, or during the change if it is an ongoing one, leadership must be visible. People take confidence in seeing their leaders and observing how they themselves are responding to the coming changes. Their accessibility allows individuals to question and feel confident in raising issues with the present visible leadership, rather than through some less personal and perhaps less credible vehicle. As in any initiative, strong leadership that is in touch with those affected generally maximizes the chance of a successful outcome.

"Effective implementation of change requires the involvement of all concerned, and any initiative from those receiving communication to seek clarity should be welcomed."

MANAGING CHANGE – THE ELEMENTS OF EARLY COMMUNICATION

These seven principles are valid whether they are initiated by those responsible for the change or not. If it's not forthcoming then those affected by the change should take the initiative to go and request this information, if the culture allows it.

Effective implementation of change requires the involvement of all concerned, and any initiative from those receiving this communication to seek clarity or additional detail should be welcomed. The leadership may have neglected some element that is required by the organization, usually not intentionally, but only because they were unaware that it was of value, or needed. The proactive requests by those affected provide a safeguard against such omissions.

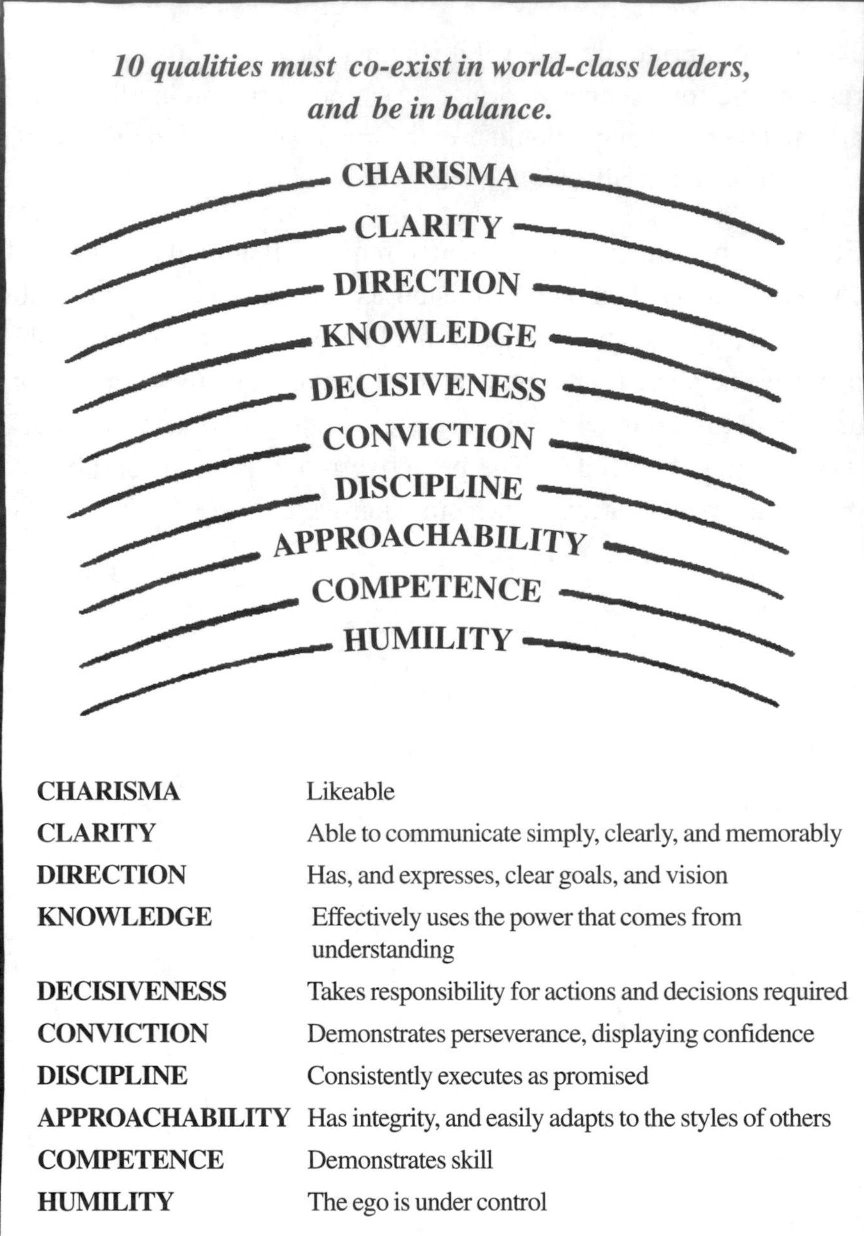

CHARISMA	Likeable
CLARITY	Able to communicate simply, clearly, and memorably
DIRECTION	Has, and expresses, clear goals, and vision
KNOWLEDGE	Effectively uses the power that comes from understanding
DECISIVENESS	Takes responsibility for actions and decisions required
CONVICTION	Demonstrates perseverance, displaying confidence
DISCIPLINE	Consistently executes as promised
APPROACHABILITY	Has integrity, and easily adapts to the styles of others
COMPETENCE	Demonstrates skill
HUMILITY	The ego is under control

Those who would strive to be exceptional leaders must also strive to acquire the following ten qualities. The important objective is the acquisition of all ten *in comparable measure*. Having one to the exclusion of the others can be far less beneficial than having all to a comparable but lesser degree. This integration of these qualities, "the having of them in balance," allows you as a leader to draw on each, and a combination of each, as required. Whether you lead many people as a senior executive, or few as a new junior supervisor, striving for skill and balance in each of these is a key element in becoming an exceptional leader.

1. ***Humility:*** This is the ability to *control* your ego, not permanently subdue it. Humility should not be confused with timidity. Humility is keeping one's ego in check.

2. ***Competence:*** This is the demonstration of knowledge and skill as it relates to your areas of responsibility.

3. ***Approachability:*** Individuals will approach those whom they trust, that is, those with integrity; and those whose personal style and manner is flexible rather than rigid. Learn to be adaptable to the various needs and personalities of others.

4. ***Discipline:*** Exercise the required self-disciple to deliver what you say you will deliver; and behave the way you know you should behave. Discipline puts feet to intent.

5. ***Conviction:*** People will follow those who believe in themselves, and display conviction regarding the course of action. Assess carefully how you will lead and then persevere, displaying confidence and conviction as you lead others towards your goal.

"Whether you lead many people
as a senior executive,
or few as a new junior supervisor,
striving for a
fully developed, well-rounded
and balanced skill set
is a key element in becoming
an exceptional leader."

6. ***Decisiveness:*** Assess and then act. Take responsibility for your actions, don't prepare a barricade or pass blame for your decisions in times of failure. When you must make a decision, make it. Make it decisively, and take responsibility for its outcome.

7. ***Knowledge:*** Use your knowledge wisely to promote effective action; and when in doubt gain the necessary knowledge.

8. ***Direction:*** Have clear goals and a clear vision for yourself which you then pass on to others. It is important that you have clarity of direction yourself, and the ability to clearly communicate this direction.

9. ***Clarity:*** Your communication needs to be simple and memorable. People must be able to understand it in your presence, and recall it in your absence.

10. ***Charisma:*** Charisma does not mean the ability to win a popularity contest, rather it means that you are likable. We all tend to gravitate to individuals we like, and so as a leader be friendly and likeable.

The integration of these ten qualities, taken together will provide you with the balanced set of competencies required in an effective leader and will keep you from over-playing one competency, at a cost to another. Strive for excellence and strive for balance.

NOTES

NOTES

NOTES

NOTES

NOTES

NOTES

NOTES